WORDSWORTH
AND THE WORTH OF WORDS

Sir George Beaumont's *The Thorn*, reproduced by kind permission of Richard and Sylvia Wordsworth

WORDSWORTH AND THE WORTH OF WORDS

HUGH SYKES DAVIES

Edited by
JOHN KERRIGAN
and
JONATHAN WORDSWORTH

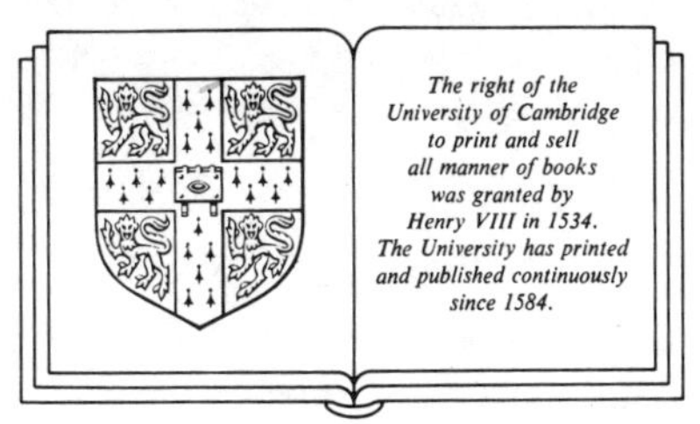
The right of the
University of Cambridge
to print and sell
all manner of books
was granted by
Henry VIII in 1534.
The University has printed
and published continuously
since 1584.

CAMBRIDGE UNIVERSITY PRESS
Cambridge
London New York New Rochelle
Melbourne Sydney

Published by the Press Syndicate of the University of Cambridge
The Pitt Building, Trumpington Street, Cambridge CB2 1RP
32 East 57th Street, New York, NY 10022, USA
10 Stamford Road, Oakleigh, Melbourne 3166, Australia

First published 1986

Printed in Great Britain at
the University Press, Cambridge

British Library cataloguing in publication data

Davies, Hugh Sykes
Wordsworth and the worth of words.
1. Wordsworth, William, 1770–1850 –
Criticism and interpretation
I. Title. II. Kerrigan, John.
III. Wordsworth, Jonathan.
821'.7 PR5881

Library of Congress cataloguing in publication data

Davies, Hugh Sykes, 1909–
Wordsworth and the worth of words.
Includes index.
1. Wordsworth, William, 1770–1850 – Language.
2. Wordsworth, William, 1770–1850 – Style.
3. Picturesque, The, in literature. I. Kerrigan, John.
II. Wordsworth, Jonathan. III. Title.
PR5894.D38 1986 821'.7 86–9536

ISBN 0 521 30909 3

Contents

A Note on Texts

Wordsworth's verse, his critical prefaces and the Fenwick Notes (*IF* Notes) are quoted from *Poetical Works*, ed. E. de Selincourt and Helen Darbishire (5 vols., Oxford, 1940–9) and the 1805 text, unless otherwise stated, of *The Prelude*, ed. E. de Selincourt, 2nd ed., revised by Helen Darbishire (Oxford, 1959), abbreviated as *PW* I-V and Oxford *Prelude*. *A Concordance to the Poems of William Wordsworth*, ed. Lane Cooper (London, 1911), is sometimes cited. Letters are quoted from E. de Selincourt's six volumes (Oxford, 1935–9), which divide into The Early Letters (*EL*), The Middle Years (*MY*) and The Later Years (*LY*). For ease of reference, however, letter numbers from de Selincourt's edition are followed by the equivalent numbering in the revised edition, prepared by Chester L. Shaver, Mary Moorman and Alan G. Hill (Oxford, 1967–). Coleridge's verse is quoted from John Beer's selection of *Poems* (London, 1963), and his *Biographia Literaria* from the edition by George Watson (London, rev. ed., 1965). For Shakespeare, the Alexander Text has been employed.

J.F.K.
J.W.

Editorial Preface

When Hugh Sykes Davies died in June 1984, he left among his papers the typescript of a book which drew on some of his deepest concerns. Wordsworth had always been, for him, a dominant creative presence. His father, a Wesleyan minister, lectured on the poet, and left Hugh 'his copy, marked with short-hand notes which are not now to be deciphered'. Childhood holidays were spent in the Lake District, 'on Wordsworthian pilgrimages of a kind familiar to late Victorian and Edwardian culture'. Coming up to Cambridge in 1928, Sykes Davies found himself in a milieu at odds with such traditional pieties. This was the Cambridge of Cockroft and Russell: scientific, mathematical and with aspirations to metaphysical wit. Eliot's campaign against romanticism was reaching its powerful climax. As a friend of Richards and Empson, and the protégé of Eliot – publishing, as an undergraduate, in *The Criterion* – Sykes Davies was fully aware of this anti-romantic tendency. Yet his admiration for Wordsworth persisted and, if anything, grew during his early years at the University. Indeed his first substantial critical essay, commissioned by Herbert Read for the classic collection *Surrealism* (1936), adulates Wordsworth as the precursor of everything vital in contemporary writing. A romantic materialist and mythologist of paranoia, Wordworth stands, for him, in the line that runs through Marx to Magritte. He is not 'eccentric' or 'idiosyncratic' but central to a romanticism which still pervades European culture. It would be wrong to imply that the same Wordsworth is sketched in *Wordsworth and the Worth of Words*, but Sykes Davies' advocacy of the poet was continuous,[1] and there are clear links between the Grasmere surrealist of 1936 and the haunted poet of the following pages, visited by images of a former self.

The mischievous title is also descriptive. Sykes Davies is genuinely concerned in this book with the *Worth of* Wordsworth's *Words*. Yet his argument leads him to attend at once to the texture and to the wider context and deeper implications of the verse. 'Linguistic studies', he writes, 'especially of texts of great literary quality, cannot afford to stop short of that deeper analysis of thought and feeling which the words themselves serve to convey. And literary critics cannot afford to be ignorant of all that linguistic study can tell them about the words themselves.' The criticism which flows from this is ample, humane and shifting in focus. Sykes Davies may in one section offer a history of the picturesque, yet he does so not for its own sake but to define the insights of Wordsworth's poetry against the more limited perceptions of his age. Elsewhere, he presents a minute statistical analysis of Wordsworthian vocabulary, in pages stiff with documentation, but he does this in order to bring back to the verse an enhancing awareness of the power conferred on words by 'repetition and apparent tautology'. 'One topic', he writes in a manuscript note about the book, 'has arisen from another, and from that another again, and so on, until the last leads back to the first. The form, if there is one, reminds me of people playing leap-frog, one over-leaping another until they have resumed their original order.'

Though the image is apt, it is unnecessarily self-deprecating. Order in this book, as in *The Prelude* itself, derives from a process of seeking out the universal in the particular. A single word, such as 'one' or 'naked', can expand to tell us something not just of the makings and workings of language, but of the nature of experience. A single experience – the Wordsworthian 'spot of time', enshrined in what Sykes Davies, following De Quincey, calls the 'involute' – tells us not only of a private individual, but of

> the very world which is the world
> Of all of us, the place in which, in the end,
> We find our happiness, or not at all. (*Prel.* x.726–8)

By means of these quests and forays, constantly deepening and expanding in significance, the book conducts its readers towards a fuller understanding of Wordsworth's creative vision. Yet, in one sense, it does end where it began: opening with the poet's wish 'either to be considered as a Teacher, or as nothing', it concludes – again, as does *The Prelude* – with a thought for the future of mankind. Wordsworth, we are told, remains in our rootless urban civilisation, riven by alienation and strife, 'a poet of potentially great use'.

The Wordsworthian analogy can be taken further. Just as the poet worked and reworked his experiences through a long sequence of manuscript and printed versions, so *Wordsworth and the Worth of Words* represents one recension from a whole series of lectures, drafts and articles. When Sykes Davies died, indeed, his material was taking on yet another form, as a critical anthology of significant passages. As it stands, the book dates from the late sixties, and it is, in some obvious respects, of its time. It quotes, for instance, from the five-volume Oxford Wordsworth, edited by de Selincourt and Darbishire. If the author had completed his typescript a few years later, there is no doubt that he would have keyed the early poetry to the edition he was using for his anthology – the Cornell Wordsworth, with its manuscript facsimiles and extensively recorded variants. Yet *Wordsworth and the Worth of*

Words is not constrained by the editorial choices of de Selincourt and Darbishire. It rests on a close familiarity with the Dove Cottage manuscripts, and quotes liberally from the variant passages printed by the Oxford editors. In important respects, indeed, it anticipates the interest in Wordsworthian revision which has marked so much recent work on the poet.

Equally prophetic is Sykes Davies' emphasis on landscape-painting and poetry. Here again the book has not been displaced by the work which it foreshadows. In its detailed consideration of the picturesque as it influences contemporary views of Cumbria, and thus Wordsworth's sense of his native environment, it explores what is still fresh territory. In its analysis of *The Vale of Esthwaite* as the germ of much later writing it is once more proleptic. And more remarkable still is Sykes Davies' insight into the poet's marriage. When composing his typescript, the author cannot have known about the correspondence between William and Mary Wordsworth. The intimate letters first published in *My Dearest Love* (Scolar Press, 1981) were not discovered until 1978, in a Carlisle stamp-dealer's garden shed. Yet from hints and traces in the poetry and elsewhere, and out of a deep empathy with the Wordsworthian menage, Hugh Sykes Davies arrived at a generous and – as it now appears – just assessment of a relationship which, though essential to the poet, had been ignored, and even slighted, by readers and critics.

Undoubtedly, however, the book makes its most original and far-reaching contribution to our understanding of Wordsworth's language. Sykes Davies' analysis of recurring words and phrases in *The Thorn*, initially so unpromising, ushers in a finely persuasive account of 'repetition and apparent tautology' as sources of greatness in the major poems. Similarly impressive is the semantic work, which demonstrates that, though Wordsworth did employ 'a selection of the language really used by men', he elicited a new expressiveness from ordinary speech by exploiting the rare meanings of common words. Important parts of the poet's vocabulary are thus idiolectal or 'ecolectal' in significance though commonplace in appearance, and it is to these private, cumulative and (as Sykes Davies shows) interconnected meanings that we must, as Wordsworthian readers, become 'sensitised'. Moreover, Sykes Davies argues, 'repetition and apparent tautology' lent the poet's distinctive vocabulary the density of material substance. Words became, as Wordsworth said they should, '*things*'. Through an extended analysis of the word-cluster surrounding 'gleam', Sykes Davies carries us from the flashing of chivalric shields, through key passages on art and the imagination, to the *Immortality Ode* and *Composed upon an Evening of Extraordinary Splendour and Beauty*. He shows the substantiality of words lending the *Ode* its peculiar weight and fulness, and points to a corresponding source of weakness in the later text. 'Perhaps the trouble with the poem, as with so much of [Wordsworth's] later verse', Sykes Davies suggests, 'was that words had turned too thoroughly into things, losing too much of their original pressure of thought and feeling, with little capacity for further growth and richness of association.' Computers may one day refine Sykes Davies' statistics, achieved so arduously with a card-index and old-fashioned concordances, but his analysis of the verbal hiding-places of Wordsworth's achievement and decline lies beyond statistical quibbling, in the realm of inspiration.

After some thought, we have left the typescript largely unrevised. It would merely obscure the author's percipience to amend, for instance, the pages on Mary Wordsworth. The Oxford edition is still readily available and widely read, and though we would, at a few points, prefer readings from alternative texts, our disagreements rest on personal taste and editorial principle and do not put us in conflict with Sykes Davies' argument. We have silently corrected a few mistakes, chiefly in dating (but see p. 312, n. 28), and are grateful to Richard Martin, Nicola Trott and Duncan Wu, for checking certain quotations. Peter Kerrigan word-processed the index and John Beer acutely read page proofs. At CUP, Michael Black, Sarah Stanton and Jane Hodgart were patient and supportive. Thanks are also due to Richard and Sylvia Wordsworth for permission to reproduce Sir George Beaumont's *The Thorn*, and to The Henry Fund for subsidising the plate's publication. The book carries no dedication, but one is implied by the author's acknowledgements. In a long and sometimes troubled life, a notable loyalty remained unwavering – to his, and Wordsworth's, Cambridge college. 'The Evangelist St. John my Patron was.'

John Kerrigan
Jonathan Wordsworth

Acknowledgements

In all Wordsworthian literalness, I have been helped by the memory of two thorn trees, each with a pond beside it, about three feet long and two feet wide. The first was on the Yorkshire moors, a familiar friend of many childhood walks. It was there, as a matter of course, that the note was left for the fairies, telling them of the gift earned by counting a hundred white horses. When, on the next anxious visit, neither the note nor the gift was lying under the bush, it was not blamed, nor the nurse who had told me about the horses. The mishap was explained by supposing that some of the horses so laboriously counted might have had black patches on the side away from me. The second thorn, with its pool in a small outcrop of chalk near the top of a Somerset down, was so near to my school that it could be visited even in the morning break. And these visits were both frequent and very necessary to me. From these experiences, I learned that the real problem in the study of Wordsworth is to account for his use of words like *thorn* and *pond*.

The broad directions of my approach to this, and similar problems in the reading of Wordsworth, are most easily indicated by acknowledging, in the customary way, the help which I have received from others. First, of course, and incomparably foremost, from Wordsworth himself. Very nearly all that his reader needs to know is inside knowledge to be gained from his own text. There is no occasion here for tracking down 'sources' and 'influences', or for much literary history. The best commentary on one passage of Wordsworth is always another passage of Wordsworth. And no one can understand him, or much respect him, until they have, by constant and careful reading, sensitised themselves to his own intensely personal use of words – or rather, of some words, and the force of their repetition. Where knowledge of his life is needed, as it sometimes is, it is best gained from himself, and from Mrs Moorman, whose work precludes all need for further biography for a long time to come. Some general aids have been gratefully used, above all the devoted editions of Professor de Selincourt and Helen Darbishire. More specially fortunate help came from my father, who lectured on Wordsworth, and left me his copy, marked with short-hand notes which are not now to be deciphered, but which are usually found against passages which arrest my own reading. It was because of his passion for Wordsworth, and for the Cumberland of his own boyhood, that most of our childhood holidays were spent in the Lakes, on Wordsworthian pilgrimages of a kind familiar to late Victorian and Edwardian culture. Their real nature was not wholly intelligible to me at the time, but they have since unfolded all kinds of significance.

To my later education, and to my College, I owe the pervading influence of the place where Wordsworth spent three years which did him remarkably little harm. Some of this book has been written in a room overlooking the brook beside which once grew that ancient ash which was the only really intimate friend he made at Cambridge. It was dead or felled long before my time, but its lineal descendants still swayed over the water until recent building brought them down in their turn. The history of this 'lovely Tree' – the only Cambridge sight piously visited by Dorothy Wordsworth when she first came to the place – was traced by the Rev. J. S. Boys-Smith, then Senior Bursar, and lately Master of the College, one of the few readers of Wordsworth I have known whose reading was never blunted by the world and its affairs, and to whom I owe a very large debt for advice and encouragement. It was the College, too, that put me in the way of Udny Yule, then a very senior Fellow, while he was working on that first classic of the new literary criticism, *The Statistical Study of Literary Vocabulary*. It was, on his part, an act of pure courtesy to a very junior Fellow; a pretence to consult me on the more literary side of the work. For me, it was by an otherwise improbable piece of luck that my education should have been directed and furthered in that particular direction. There was, of course, nothing that I could tell him, but there was everything for him to tell me. To him I owe the very little of statistical theory that I possess, and all the mathematics. Over his long drawers full of cards bearing the vocabularies of Thomas à Kempis, Chaucer, Bunyan and Macaulay, he taught me how to look for significant patterns in material of this kind. Had it lain in his power, he would even have taught me to find them. It is entirely owing to his skill, patience, and enlightened courtesy that I owe my initiation into a mode of study which happens, by what must be statistically a very long chance, to suggest solutions to the most forbidding problems of Wordsworth's style – solutions which, moreover, seem to be in line with Wordsworth's own sense of what he was doing.

H.S.D.

PART I

Introductory

1

Every great Poet is a Teacher: I wish either to be considered as a Teacher, or as nothing.
Wordsworth, Letter to Sir George Beaumont, February 1808 (*MY* 317/96)

Originality is not the same thing as greatness, but in some ways the two qualities are alike. And they are most alike when the originality comes not from being born original, or achieving originality, but from having it forced on a man by the pressure of what he sets out to do, and the obstacles to be overcome. Both greatness and originality were forced on Wordsworth because he wished to be both a Teacher and a Poet, and because of the inherent tensions between these two aims, between the kinds of teaching and the kinds of poetry established in the time upon which he fell. By their nature, these tensions could be resolved only by originality, and by their acuteness they ensured that this originality would bear the marks of greatness.

The problem which forced great originality on Wordsworth can be shortly defined in answers to one question. Why could he not rest content with Thomson's *Seasons?* The poem contained much real poetry – 'written from himself, and nobly from himself', as Wordsworth said in his *Essay, Supplementary to the Preface* of 1815 (*PW* II, 419). It was on the subject which was to be Wordsworth's own, the relation between Man and Nature; it was in a style not wholly dissimilar, at its best, from that which Wordsworth evolved. But there was this vital difference between their versions of the subject: that while Thomson's thoughts and feelings were deeply sincere, they owed almost as much to books as to life itself, to the *Georgics* and to the Deists, above all Shaftesbury; Wordsworth's thought and feelings, on the other hand, owed comparatively little to books, and nearly everything to his own special fate, as a boy born and bred in a particular place. The reader of Wordsworth cannot for long go ignorant of the part played by the Lakes in making him everything that he was. The reader of Thomson has to search in a dictionary of literary biography for the name of the place where he spent his childhood. What distinguishes Wordsworth's dealings with Nature and Man from Thomson's is an intensity of personal experience, localised, individualised. And his problems as a writer, as a poet, his enforced departure from the style of Thomson and his age, all rise from the need to render not merely the general theme, but also this personal intensity and individuality.

This special and highly personal situation is very precisely represented in *The Prelude*:

> Thirteen years
> Or haply less, I might have seen, when first
> My ears began to open to the charm
> Of words in tuneful order, found them sweet
> For *their own sakes*, a passion and a power;
> And phrases pleas'd me, chosen for delight,
> For pomp, or love. Oft in the public roads,
> Yet unfrequented, while the morning light
> Was yellowing the hill-tops, with that dear Friend . . .
> I went abroad, and for the better part
> Of two delightful hours we stroll'd along
> By the still borders of the misty Lake,
> Repeating favorite verses with one voice,
> Or conning more . . . (v.575–89)

The contrast, the tension, is between the scene and the verse that was being cherished in it. The Lake and the Vale of Esthwaite had already given to Wordsworth the most vivid and formative experiences of his life, and was still to give him more of them; they had created a thirst which only they could satisfy. But the verse was adding its own more complex gift. On the one hand, it was conferring on him the perception that words were *things* in their own right, that they had, when used in certain ways, the force of charms and incantations; on the other hand, the particular verses which they read by the Lake were, he later discovered, 'false, and in their splendour overwrought' (*Prel.* v.594). They were creating an appetite which they could not themselves satisfy. Worse, they were, so far as they were 'false' and 'overwrought', interposing a veil between the immediacy of the experience of the Lake and the Vale and the medium in which it could be thought of, felt, and remembered. And the singular good fortune of Wordsworth's early experience, upon which his later teaching rested, could be made effective and useful only insofar as he might be able to solve the poetic problem of tearing the veil apart, of finding a way of using words in which their full incantatory power and simplicity would replace the prevalent falseness and over-elaboration of the current fashions.

The problem was, of course, inevitable. The young are always at the mercy of fashion and conformity, and young writers can hardly do other than conform with the literary conventions contemporary with their youth. Whatever their merits, or demerits, they have a tang, an immediacy of communication, not to be found in older writings. Wordsworth's prospects of growing out of them were probably the better because it was a period without major poets, and of many minor ones. As one of the least of them rather pathetically wrote:

> Write what we will, our works bespeak us
> *Imitatores, servum Pecus.*
> Tale, Elegy, or lofty Ode,
> We travel in the beaten road.
> The proverb still sticks closely by us,
> *Nil dictum, quod non dictum prius.*[1]

It was a period, in fact, dominated less by writers than by a few pervading moods, and by the conventions which both expressed and fostered them. And of these, the most characteristic was the elegy, in content mildly moralistic, moderately melancholy, against a setting of evening in a graveyard. Poems of this kind had been written early in the century, and the best of them, for it had at least the freshness of novelty, is Parnell's *Night-Piece on Death*, published in 1721. In the 1740s, this mood for a time broadened beyond the limits of the elegy, spilling over into the larger meanderings of blank verse, such as Blair's *Grave* and Young's *Night Thoughts*, and even into the placid ponds of meditative prose, in Hervey's *Meditations among the Tombs*. But at the end of this graveyard decade, the tighter discipline of the elegiac convention was powerfully reasserted by Gray and Collins, and for Wordsworth their poems were what 'modern poetry' is to each generation in turn.

Their influence, however, was not exerted through some vague and impersonal force – the 'influence of A on B' which occupies so much room in histories of literatures. It came quite as much through people as through books, and above all through William Taylor, who came to Wordsworth's school as master in 1782, the year before those early-morning walks by the Lake. The Free School at Hawkshead has for so long now been replaced by superior educational arrangements that it is unfortunately necessary to explain that it was a place of excellence, distinguished even among the best of the northern grammar schools. It sent a steady stream of boys to Cambridge (and a trickle to Oxford), several of whom became Fellows of their Colleges. Taylor himself had been a Fellow of Emmanuel College, and when he arrived at Hawkshead he brought with him the characteristic literary tastes of a young man of his period. When he died, only four years later, he desired a verse from Gray's *Elegy* to be engraved on his tombstone. And it was at Taylor's suggestion that Wordsworth first wrote poetry.

The first rather dreadful result of this encouragement was a poem in the manner of Pope – so Wordsworth himself later described it – on the bicententary of the school's foundation. But it was followed by other poems, 'from the impulse of my own mind', and one of them, a *Dirge Sung by a Minstrel*, is quite comically what was to be expected from a gifted boy at just that time and place. It owes most to Collins' *Dirge from Cymbeline*, but three lines are nicely worked in from Chatterton's *Ælla*, in ye olde spellynge. The first version was written for a boy, and at the sound of the death-knell 'each worm stops his dreadful trade for joy'; it was then altered very economically to suit a 'maid', by making 'each worm stop for joy his dreadful trade'.

Taylor, however, was to infuse a bitter enough reality into the elegiac mode by one of those actions which speak louder than words. As he lay dying, only thirty-two years old, he summoned the older boys to his bedside and took his leave of them. For many years, Wordsworth's memory and imagination dwelt on the man, and on this parting scene, altering both to some extent, and with each alteration moving further away from the modishly elegiac transformation of it and nearer to what had been real in it. In 1798, in the midst of his most intense period of poetic discovery and composition, he made another version of the youthful *Dirge*, much less in the manner of Collins, and with four added stanzas headed 'By the side of the grave some years later'. He had, in 1794, made a pilgrimage to Taylor's grave at Cartmell, and had seen for himself the verse from Gray's *Elegy* on the tombstone. One of these stanzas, and only one, reflects the reality, rather than the mode:

> Oh true of heart, of spirit gay,
> Thy faults, where not already gone
> From memory, prolong their stay
> For charity's sweet sake alone. (65–8 [*PW* IV, 258])

Two more long elegies, never published, were written in a notebook of 1798–9, and, in them, Taylor begins to be called 'Matthew'. With the change of name from the real one goes a nearer approach to the real man. Amid elegiac trappings retained from the earlier versions – a mourning woodman, a milkmaid with her pail – there is a rough sketch of an individual being, in whom seriousness and mirth were oddly mingled:

> But Matthew had an idle art
> Of teaching love and happiness . . .
>
> And weep thou School of fair Glencarn,
> No more shalt thou in stormy weather
> Be like a play-house in a barn
> Where Punch and Hamlet play together.
> (*i*.23–4, *ii*.69–72 [*PW* IV, 452, 454])

In the 'Matthew' poems which Wordsworth published, two apparently opposite processes of change are found, and found in poetic harmony. On the one hand, the individual personality of Taylor is altered – he is turned into an old man – and mingled with traits from quite other people, Hazlitt among them. Yet the result is not to blur the realism of this partly composite character. On the contrary, he grows still more real. None of the poems would be ranked among Wordsworth's very best, but taken together with the earlier elegies, they show with singular clearness how deeply the elegiac mode had influenced his early sense of poetry, and how completely he had freed himself from it by 1800. The later poems are in a manner entirely his own, and above all different from the manners of Gray, Collins and Chatterton. The scenery has nothing to do with evening and not much with graveyards; is is morning in the open country. The dialogues – and dialogue is the basis of all the poems – are conducted in real terms, and all lead up to a kind of climax which was one of the most characteristic features of Wordsworth's most powerful writing: the scene, the 'moral', the persons involved, all focussed into a brief phrase of illuminating perception. Thus in *The Fountain*, Matthew describes his own ageing, his loneliness and his lack of kindred, until his young pupil protests:

> 'And, Matthew, for thy children dead
> I'll be a son to thee!'
> At this he grasped my hand, and said,
> 'Alas! that cannot be.' (61–4 [*PW* IV, 73])

This simple gesture, and the even simpler phrase that follows it, have a depth and intensity of implication quite comparable, in force of effect, with the best of the elegiac moralisings of Gray and the rest. But the quality of the effect is different, and differently attained. The most moving aphorisms in Gray are statements about human life of great generality, condensed into a very small space, yet suggestive of their broadness of reference by a complex use of language and by deliberate reference to the great classical tradition of commonplaces. Wordsworth's effect is the very opposite of the condensation of aphorism, for it is essentially dramatic, and drama needs time and space for the development of its exposition and its final climax. These poems have their own scenes – an April morning, a spreading oak – and the two dialoguists are particularised into individuality. It is only against this setting that the climactic gestures and phrases of their dialogues, like the last speeches of a tragedy, suddenly force the auditor to make for himself the awareness that these particular persons and sayings bear more generalised application and significance.

Such potentially dramatic and significant particulars must not, of course, be confused with literal facts. On the contrary, they demand of their user the most carefully selective and imaginative activity. Most of the particular detail of real life has no such potentiality; much of it stands in need of transformation, as well as selection. And Wordsworth, in his own comment on the later 'Matthew' poems, shows himself to have been fully conscious of this difference between literal fact and fact imaginatively transformed and selected:

> This and other poems connected with Matthew would not gain by a literal detail of facts. Like the Wanderer in 'The Excursion', this Schoolmaster was made up of several both of his class and men of other occupations. I do not ask pardon for what there is of untruth in such verses, considered strictly as matters of fact. It is enough if, being true and consistent in spirit, they move and teach in a manner not unworthy of a Poet's calling. (*IF* Note [*PW* IV, 415])

This firm declaration of the independence of literal fact should be set beside the many passages in which Wordsworth speaks of the role of memory in poetic composition. There is, for example, the almost too well known definition in the *Preface* to *Lyrical Ballads*: 'poetry is the spontaneous overflow of powerful feelings: it takes its origin from emotion recollected in tranquillity' (*PW* II, 400). And in the same *Preface* is the twice-repeated phrase defining a Poet partly – indeed chiefly – as 'distinguished from other men by a greater promptness to think and feel without immediate external excitement' (*ibid.* 393 and 397). And there is the light-hearted and so the more revealing description of his own habits of composition in *The Waggoner*:

> Nor is it I who play the part,
> But a shy spirit in my heart,
> That comes and goes – will sometimes leap
> From hiding-places ten years deep;
> Or haunts me with familiar face,
> Returning, like a ghost unlaid,
> Until the debt I owe be paid. (209–15 [*PW* II, 204])

The memories on which his poetry was built – and he is pre-eminently the poet of memory – were never literal records, printed on the mind once and for all in their original lineaments. In their deep hiding-places, and on their successive revivals in tranquillity, they underwent a continuous process of transformation, matching his own growth in maturity and understanding. There is no more foolish branch of Wordsworthian scholarship (at least I think not) than that which laboriously proves the literal fact of some poem of his to have been inaccurate, as to time, places or persons, and then accuses him of inaccuracy. What is significant in such cases is precisely the gap between the literal history and his free transformation of it in this active memory, which is so nearly allied to imagination.

This imaginative freedom is nowhere more active than in his later dealings with the elegiac memories of his earliest writings, where it is the chief agent in freeing him from the mode of Gray and the rest of those who had been modern for 'Matthew'. But they, and 'Matthew', remained among his memories too, and at times the elegiac mood reasserted itself in his later writings, sometimes as a way of getting himself out of a tight spot – a troublesome but minor conflict between his own conception of poetry and that still in high fashion with most of his readers. And when the great impulse of his main creative period was on the wane, when his imagination was all but swept and garnished, the spirit of the elegy returned, with seven other spirits duller than himself, and the last state was worse than the first. Much of *The Excursion* – but fortunately not all – is too much like Gray's *Elegy*, but with none of Gray's power of aphorism and of language resonant with wit and learning; long, too, in Wordsworth's dramatic mode of presentation, but without his earlier rigour of selection from the literal events of life.

2

I must *decline* even *looking over* the MSS of yourself or your Friends. I am sure that I should find some thing which I should attempt to change, and probably after a good deal of pains make the passage no better, perhaps worse – This is my infirmity, I have employed scores of hours during the course of my life in retouching favorite passages of favorite Authors, of which labour not a trace remains nor ought to remain. (*LY* 1320)

So Wordsworth wrote in January 1840 to Thomas Powell, who was making up a volume of modernisations of Chaucer, including Wordsworth's own. And no writer has ever reported of himself a more singular infirmity. To retouch, to amend for the better, the worser passages of one's favourite authors would be an exercise ambitious enough for most of us. To make the same attempt upon their best passages seems almost perverse. It is perhaps fortunate that Keats never had a sight of this letter, for had he done so, he would almost certainly have regarded it as a damning new piece of evidence of the famous Wordsworthian 'egotism'. He would, however, have been wrong. It is evidence of a remarkable humility, in all that concerned the minor, the more or less disputable, points of literary technique. For these, Wordsworth always showed an almost niggling care, and a very un-egotistical readiness to be corrected by those whose judgment he respected, rightly or wrongly, or by his own apprehensions of what was liable to offend or puzzle his readers. And as he was, of course, his own favourite author – as is every author, for why else should he write at all? – it was upon his own work that this humble and hesitant care was most fully bestowed. The most massive demonstration was the constant revision of *The Prelude*, and the most dramatic the alteration of *The Leech Gatherer* to meet the criticisms made by Sara and Mary Hutchinson a few months before his marriage to Mary (see below, pp. 161–5). But many of the shorter poems underwent similar periods of correction, and there is much to be learned both from the corrections, and from the reasons for which they were made.

Outside his own family, Coleridge was the critic whose judgment Wordsworth most deferentially respected, and more often wrongly than rightly. For Coleridge's sake he struck out some entirely effective lines of the *Immortality Ode*, and the exact description of the pond in *The Thorn*:

> I've measured it from side to side;
> 'Tis three feet long, and two feet wide.
>
> (32–3, variants [*PW* II, 241])

Yet this information was neither funny nor otiose. It was needed to show that the pond was big enough – and only just big enough – for the woman to have drowned her infant in it, and that if she had done so, it must have been a terribly deliberate act; just as the thorn itself was 'Not higher than a two years' child', so that if she had indeed hanged her infant on the tree, it was a gallows of dreadfully fitting height. Perhaps Wordsworth felt that if Coleridge could not see the point of the description, no one else was likely to. If this was the case, neither of them was in the right. At least once, however, Coleridge's view did happen to be right, and Wordsworth rather shamefacedly tried to scrub round it. He mentioned his attempt in a letter written in 1828:

> After having succeeded in the second *Skylark* and in the conclusion of the poem entitled *A Morning Exercise*, in my notice of this bird, I became indifferent to this poem [*To a Skylark*], which Coleridge used severely to condemn and to treat contemptuously. I like, however, the beginning of it so well that, for the sake of that, I tacked to it the respectably-tame conclusion.
>
> (*PW* II, 491)

In this case, we may as well be grateful to Coleridge for having provoked Wordsworth into so clear a confession that he was not above tacking onto a valuable piece of poetry (in his own view) a practically worthless conclusion, so as to round the thing off for the ordinary reader. The addition bears him out. At first it read:

> Hearing thee, or else some other,
> As merry as a Brother
> I on the earth will go plodding on,
> By myself chearfully, till the day is done.
>
> (26–31, variants [*PW* II, 142])

So it stood from 1807 to 1820, but by 1827 the rounding-off had itself been rounded out into a still more respectable rotundity:

> Alas! my journey, rugged and uneven,
> Through prickly moors or dusty ways must wind:
> But hearing thee, or others of thy kind,
> As full of gladness and as free of heaven,
> I, with my fate contented, will plod on,
> And hope for higher raptures, when life's day is done.[2] (*loc. cit.*)

So, like a ploughman and with watered-down antitheses like diluted Gray, Wordsworth figures himself plodding on through the parting day, until the time came to cast one longing, lingering look behind, and another upward. Into the swept and garnished vacuum, so abhorrent to Nature, have crept all eight of the elegiac devils.

It did not matter very much here, for there was little to be bedevilled. On other occasions it mattered more, and might lead to something not much less than falsification of the original experience. Of this there are at least two notable examples. The first is *There was a boy*, written in that fearful cold in Germany at the end of 1798, when Wordsworth, cooped up in a rather drab little German town, without any society but that of his sister (and that, of course, was much to him), without books, was writing, as he said, in 'self-protection', and by a superbly fortunate accident, discovering exactly what he had to write. This was its first version:

> There was a boy ye knew him well, ye rocks
> And islands of Winander & ye green
> Peninsulas of Esthwaite many a time
>   when the stars began
> To move along the edges of the hills
> Rising or setting would he stand alone
> Beneath the trees or by the glimmering lake
> And through his fingers woven in one close knot
> Blow mimic hootings to the silent owls
> And bid them answer him. And they would shout
> Across the watery vale and shout again
> Responsive to my call with tremulous sobs
> And long halloes & screams & echoes loud
> Redoubled & redoubled a wild scene
> Of mirth & jocund din. And when it chanced
> That pauses of deep silence mocked my skill
> Then often, in that silence, while I hung
> Listening a sudden shock of mild surprize
> Would carry far into my heart the voice
> Of mountain torrents: or the visible scene
> Would enter unawares into my mind

With all its solemn imagery its rocks
Its woods & that uncertain heaven received
Into the bosom of the steady lake.

(From MS JJ, Oxford *Prelude*, pp. 639–40)

There is no doubt whatever that these lines described an early experience of his own, and that he regarded them as recording a mental and imaginative process of great importance. They were given a place of honour in the 1815 edition, being placed first among *Poems of the Imagination*, with a special explanation in the *Preface*:

> . . . in the series of Poems placed under the head of Imagination, I have begun with one of the earliest processes of Nature in the development of this faculty. Guided by one of my own primary consciousnesses, I have presented a commutation and transfer of internal feelings, co-operating with external accidents, to plant, for immortality, images of sound and sight, in the celestial soil of the Imagination. The Boy, there introduced, is listening, with something of a feverish and restless anxiety, for the recurrence of those riotous sounds which he had previously excited; and, at the moment when the intenseness of his mind is beginning to remit, he is surprised into a perception of the solemn and tranquillizing images which the Poem describes. (*PW* II, 440)

That this was Wordsworth's settled and continuing view of the poem is shown by De Quincey's remarkable account of a conversation between them on Dunmail Raise, at about midnight, probably in 1810 or thereabouts.[3] But in that conversation, and in the previously published version of the poem, he had taken the trouble to pretend that the 'boy' was someone other than himself. The pronouns had been put into the third person in Germany, and not long after, the description had been turned into an independent poem, which might be published separately, by means of a pretty grim example of the respectably-tame and elegiac conclusion:

Fair are the woods, and beauteous is the spot,
The Vale where he was born; the Churchyard hangs
Upon a Slope above the Village School,
And there, along that bank, when I have pass'd
At evening, I believe that near his grave
A full half-hour together I have stood
Mute, – for he died when he was ten years old.

(*Prel.* V.416–22, variants)

Wordsworth's motive in introducing this pathetic lad cannot have been to conceal the fact that the experience was indeed his own – though on other occasions a similar motive produced similar disguisements. Here, there was nothing intensely private, nothing to be concealed from prying minds. Most likely he wanted to fill out a page or so of the 1800 *Lyrical Ballads*, and felt that the naked experience could hardly stand by itself, as a separate poem. And when it came to rounding it off, the devils of elegy were all too ready with their respectably-tame conclusion.

In this case, the elegiac immolation of a fictitious character does no great harm – indeed it has afforded a little innocent pleasure to 'scholars' who have thumbed through the parish registers at Hawkshead to find the name of the non-existent lad, and have found it. But there are other poems in which the distinction between the spare economy of the real poetry, and the rotundity of the tacked-on conclusion matters a great deal more. It is of the first importance in reading Wordsworth that this distinction should never be missed, and that the rotundity, even when good enough of its kind, should not be mistaken for the real thing. A minor example of such a mistake – and one of the very few mistakes made by Professor de Selincourt – was to give as one proof that his 'poetic inspiration was not so shortlived as is sometimes supposed' the lines added to the description of his bedroom in St John's in later versions of *The Prelude*. In 1805, it was mentioned that on moonlight nights he could see the Antechapel of Trinity

> where the Statue stood
> Of Newton, with his Prism and silent Face. (III.58–9)

The addition in 1850 was:

> The marble index of a mind for ever
> Voyaging through strange seas of Thought, alone. (*1850* III.62–3)

This is not bad stuff, of its own kind. The bust has been animated a little. But the added pomp has nothing to do with the real Wordsworth. It is the pomp of a poet whose brother has become Master of Trinity, and who has stayed at the Lodge.

Much the most important poem put in jeopardy of misconstruction by an elegiac addition is *Three years she grew*. Its importance is of many kinds, and in many rather different fields: in its use of the ballad form, in its content generally, in its more specific relation with central doctrines of Wordsworth's 'teaching', and in its biographical bearings. The last two of these will be discussed later (pp. 281–6), the first two here.

A prime aspect of *Lyrical Ballads* not directly explained in either of its two *Prefaces*, the very short one of 1798, before the visit of Germany, and the very long one of 1800, is the title itself. In both it is suggested that most of the poems are experiments in the use of a simpler language than had been usual in verse, but neither establishes a direct relation between the choice of words and the ballad-form itself. In a very general sense, perhaps it needed no great explanation. For the ballad, recently revived as a fashionable form by Bishop Percy, was evidently the popular kind of poetry, as opposed to the more sophisticated and cultivated forms of blank verse and couplets. In his German period, Wordsworth was still hesitating between the two forms, and examples of both had been given in the first edition of *Lyrical Ballads*. Coleridge, however, had already made up his mind that Wordsworth's true poetic future lay with the more sophisticated blank verse, like *Tintern Abbey* – partly, perhaps, because he seems to have moved more rapidly than Wordsworth away from those actively democratic ideas which had a year or two earlier seemed to fit so well with the conception of a democratisation of poetry as well as politics, by poetry for nearly all, just as by votes for rather more. But whatever the reason may have been, while Wordsworth was still writing ballad-like poems as well as blank verse, Coleridge was urging him to concentrate on the latter, and to let nothing stand in the way of *The Recluse*, which they had planned together at Alfoxden. When, therefore, Wordsworth and his sister wrote to Coleridge sending specimens of verse, they were apt to be a little apologetic about the poems in ballad form. In the most remarkable of their letters to him from Goslar, they wrote:

> Dorothy has written on the other side of this sheet while I have been out – she has transcribed a few descriptions. You will read them at your leisure. She will copy out two or three little Rhyme poems which I hope will amuse you. As I have had no books, I have been obliged to write in self-defence. (*EL* 89/105)

The 'descriptions' were all in blank verse, the passages on skating and on the stolen boat, which later went into *The Prelude*, and an early version of *Nutting*, which did not. The 'little Rhyme poems' were *She dwelt among the untrodden ways* and the first version of *Strange fits of passion*. At least one other similar letter was sent – it is now lost – containing the same mixture, *There was a boy* in blank verse, *A slumber did my spirit seal* in rhyme. It is likely enough that it introduced them with the same very significant difference: the blank verse was to be read 'at your leisure', as befitted serious things; the 'little Rhyme poems' were for amusement only.

But while Wordsworth might hesitate between the two verse-forms, and all that they implied in terms of choice of language and – what mattered still more – choice of readers, the subjects which concerned him in Goslar were not readily and clearly divisible into one kind or the other. On the contrary, many of them were equally ready for expression in either form, and several were indeed expressed in both. Broad themes, images, phrases link the two kinds of composition together, and open the way to mutual comment. Thus *A slumber* nearly shares its most striking phrase, 'earth's diurnal course', with the skating description, which has 'earth's diurnal round'. The 'violet by a mossy stone /

Half hidden from the eye', in *She dwelt* looks very like a condensation of some lines from *Nutting*: 'Perhaps it was a bower beneath whose leaves / The violets of five seasons re-appear / And fade, unseen by any human eye.' The only two references in Wordsworth to fawns are 'You yet may spy the fawn at play' in *Lucy Gray* and 'She shall be sportive as the fawn' in *Three years*.

But the main affinities, both of theme and phrase, are those which link *Three years* with the blank-verse descriptions, and also with the earliest drafts of parts of *The Prelude*, which were being written at the same time. It is these links that give the poem its special place among the 'Rhyme poems', and that demand careful study. The most obvious link with *Nutting* is this:

THREE YEARS

she shall lean her ear
In many a secret place
Where rivulets dance their wayward round,
And beauty born of murmuring sound
Shall pass into her face.

(26–30 [*PW* II, 215])

NUTTING

. . . it was a bower . . .
Where fairy water-breaks do murmur on
For ever; and I saw the sparkling foam,
And – with my cheek on one of those green
stones . . .
I heard the murmur and the murmuring
sound . . .

(30–8 [*PW* II, 212])

A less obvious, but still more significant, link with the *Nutting* group of drafts will be studied below (pp. 281–6).

With the early *Prelude* drafts these are the main parallels:

Nor shall she fail to see
Even in the motions of the Storm
Grace that shall mould the Maiden's form
By silent sympathy.

(21–4)

. . . a storm not terrible but strong
With lights and shades and with a rushing
(power?)
With loveliness and power.

(MS JJ.Z verso, Oxford *Prelude*, p. 642)

The floating clouds their state shall lend
To her . . .

(19–20)

. . . there are spirits which when they would
form
A favor'd being open out the clouds
As at the touch of lightning
Seeking him with gentle visitation.

(MS JJ. R recto, Oxford *Prelude*, p. 640)

Three years she grew in sun and shower,
Then Nature said ". . .
This Child I to myself will take;
She shall be mine, and I will make
A Lady of my own.

Myself will to my darling be
Both law and impulse . . ."

(1–8)

Ye powers of the earth
Ah not in vain ye spirits of the springs
And ye that have your voices in the clouds
And ye that are familiars of the lakes
And standing pools, ah not for trivial ends
Through snow & sunshine & through [rain
and storm] . . .
Did ye with such assiduous love pursue
Your favorite and your joy.
(MS JJ. W recto–verso, Oxford *Prelude*,
p. 635)

There can be no mistaking the general similarity of the theme: it was exactly the theme which made Palgrave entitle *Three years* 'The Education of Nature' in *The Golden Treasury*. But there is one very significant difference in the handling of it. Both the maiden and Wordsworth had been chosen by Nature or the 'powers of the earth' as their favourite or 'darling'; but upon him they had conferred only a heightened perception of the meaning of the universe. Upon her, they had conferred not only this, but also moral beauty and physical beauty. It is, in fact, a love-poem, but one so different from the general run of love-poems that this aspect of it is easily overlooked. And the more certainly because Wordsworth chose to add the most perplexing of his elegiac roundings-off, in a stanza which has no organic connection whatever with the theme of the rest of the poem:

> Thus Nature spake – The work was done –
> How soon my Lucy's race was run!
> She died, and left to me
> This heath, this calm, and quiet scene;
> The memory of what has been,
> And never more will be. (37–42)

Thus 'Nature's darling' was killed off as roundly as the boy who hooted to the owls, for poetic purposes, good or bad. But in fact, the boy lived on, and this favourite of Nature, this lovely maiden, also lived on. She is not particularly difficult to identify, and the identification will be made later. For the moment, it is enough to observe that the respectable tameness, the conventional conformity of that last stanza is quite sufficiently avouched by the sudden drop in poetic quality, the flatness of the language – 'race was run' – the routine catalogue of 'this heath, this calm and quiet scene', and most of all by the mournfully flaccid half-antithesis of the last two lines very like the weak antitheses of the 'respectably-tame conclusion' to the lines on the skylark. It is, taking all things together, the worst single piece of elegiac bedevilment in Wordsworth.

3

> The Poem [*The Vale of Esthwaite*] . . . was of many hundred lines, and contained thoughts and images most of which have been dispersed through my other writings.
>
> IF Note to *Extract*, etc. (*PW* I, 317–18)

The clearest demonstrations of Wordsworth's eventual emergence into originality, and of his astonishing power of transmuting his early experience by the action of memory, imagination, and a powerful yet simple poetic technique, are most easily found by tracing the influence of his earliest long poem, *The Vale of Esthwaite*, on his later writings. It was written in the spring and summer of 1787, as he prepared to leave his own country for the first time in his life; he came up to Cambridge in the autumn. It is both a salute and a farewell: a salute to the memories of his childhood and boyhood, to the influences of his family, of Taylor, who had died the year before, and a farewell to all that he was about to lose, as he then thought, for ever. The surviving manuscripts give only a part of the poem, perhaps about half of the original 1000 lines or so. In its surviving and mutilated form, it is a rather shapeless meander in rhymed octosyllabics, but it reads as if, even unmutilated, coherence and shape had never been remarkable in it. Professor de Selincourt, who has reduced it to something like order, believed that the missing part was pillaged mainly to provide material for *An Evening Walk*, and that it was chiefly descriptive of scenes and places. What is left, he points out, is preponderantly 'romantic', that is to say, Gothic and elegiac. This is particularly fortunate, for the importance of the descriptive element in Wordsworth's mature writing stands in little need of emphasis, while the 'Gothic' element has generally been much under-rated, no doubt because it has been so remarkably transformed. Without the evidence of *The Vale of Esthwaite* we should know little of this transformation, and should hardly dare to guess at its raw materials. As things are, the poem deserves to be studied with sympathetic care, and in its mutilated entirety, not dismissing the more bizarre elements lightly, for they are undoubtedly part of Wordsworth's thoughts and feelings at that time, and for long afterwards.

To the well-known and obvious literary influences of Gray, Collins, Chatterton and the rest, *The Vale* adds the almost forgotten name of James Beattie, whose long poem *The Minstrel; or, The Progress of Genius*, published in two parts in 1771 and 1774, has few modern readers, but ranked high in Wordsworth's boyhood. A single quotation is enough to indicate its mood and quality:

> When the long-sounding curfew from afar
> Loaded with loud lament the lonely gale,
> Young Edwin, lighted by the evening star,
> Lingering and listening, wander'd down the vale.
> There would he dream of graves, and corses pale;
> And ghosts, that to the charnel-dungeon throng,
> And drag a length of clanking chain, and wail,
> Till silenced by the owl's terrific song,
> Or blast that shrieks by fits the shuddering isles along. (I.xxxiv)

Yet even this strange stuff for a time chimed in with the sensibility, not only of Wordsworth himself, but also of his sister Dorothy. In a letter to an intimate friend written in 1793, she went so far as to admit that in some matters of conduct William had been 'somewhat to blame', but she went on:

> . . . yet I think I shall prove to you that the excuse might have been found in his natural disposition. 'In truth he was a strange and wayward wight fond of each gentle etc., etc.' That verse of Beattie's *Minstrel* always reminds me of him, and indeed the whole character of Edwin resembles much what William was when I first knew him – after my leaving Halifax – 'and oft he traced the uplands etc., etc. etc.' (*EL* 31/31)

As for Wordsworth himself, there can be no doubt that at school he had relished Beattie, and imitated him close to the point of plagiarism, as here:

> Then musing onward would I stray
> Till every rude sound died away,
> And nought was heard but at my feet
> The faint rill tinkling softly sweet.
> [ ] Gothic mansion stood
> In the black centre of a wood . . .
> And oft as ceased the owl his song
> That screamed the roofless walls among,
> Spirits yelling from their pains
> And lashes loud, and clanking chains,
> Were heard by minstrel led astray
> Cold wandering thro' the swampy way . . .
>
> (*The Vale* 43–56 [*PW* I, 271])

After a longish interval of many hundred lines, concerned, if Professor de Selincourt is right, mainly with natural description, this high Gothic strain resumes, and *The Vale* rises to a climax which liquidises the blood, to such a pitch of horror that it provokes a very significant reaction:

> Now did I love the dismal gloom
> Of haunted Castle's pannel'd room
> Listening the wild wind's wailing song
> Whistling the rattling doors among;
> When as I heard a rustling sound
> My haggard eyes would turn around,
> Which strait a female form survey'd
> Tall, and in silken vest array'd.
> Her face of wan and ashy hue
> And in one hand a taper blue;
> Fix'd at the door she seem'd to stand
> And beckoning slowly wav'd her hand.
> I rose, above my head a bell
> The mansion shook with solemn knell.
> Through aisles that shuddered as we pass'd
> By doors flapping [ ] the blast

And green damp windings dark and steep,
She brought me to a dungeon deep,
Then stopp'd, and thrice her head she shook,
More pale and ghastly seem'd her look.
[   ] shew'd
An iron coffer mark'd with blood.
The taper turn'd from blue to red
Flash'd out – and with a shriek she fled.
With arms in horror spread around
I mov'd – a form unseen I found
Twist round my hand an icy chain
And drag me to the spot again.
  But these were poor and puny joys
Fond sickly Fancy's idle toys. (240–69 [*PW* I, 275–6])

This sudden *volte-face*, this revolt against the skimble-skamble stuff, comes not a moment too soon. But the really striking thing is that it comes at all. That he was capable of it, at seventeen, was by itself enough to mark him off from the scores or hundreds of boys who were, at the same time, gibbering away with the same horrific gestures. And still more striking was the fact that his revolt from artificial horrors arose, not from a mere superiority of aesthetic taste or of literary perception, but from real experience of natural fear. The passage goes on:

I lov'd to haunt the giddy steep
That hung loose trembling o'er the deep,
While [G]hosts of Murtherers mounted fast
And grimly glar'd upon the blast.
While the dark whirlwind rob'd, unseen,
With black arm rear'd the clouds between. (270–5)

He was saved, in fact, from continued indulgence in Gothic toy terrors by the thrill of a terror none the less real for being deliberately sought, and natural because it was part of the scenes and superstitions of the place in which he had lived.

There is, indeed, even with this passage, just a possibility that the 'giddy steep' and the '[G]hosts of Murtherers' may refer, not to these scenes and superstitions in general, but to a particular scene and experience. Eleven years before he wrote *The Vale*, he had been riding on the fells with a servant of his father's, and was somehow parted from him, so that he found himself lost – a quite specific experience for any child, in town or country:

. . . and, through fear
Dismounting, down the rough and stony Moor
I led my Horse, and stumbling on, at length
Came to a bottom, where in former times

A Murderer had been hung in iron chains.
The Gibbet-mast was moulder'd down, the bones
And iron case were gone; but on the turf,
Hard by, soon after that fell deed was wrought
Some unknown hand had carved the Murderer's name.
The monumental writing was engraven
In times long past, and still, from year to year,
By superstition of the neighbourhood,
The grass is clear'd away; and to this hour
The letters are all fresh and visible. (*Prel.* XI.286–99)

It matters very little whether or not this was the chief experience of 'steeps' and the '[G]hosts of Murtherers' which Wordsworth had in mind when he wrote the lines in *The Vale*. The point is that he had passed through at least one such experience, with its real terrors, by comparison with which the Gothic machinery of ruined castles and ghosts, shrieks and owls, blue ladies and iron chains, seemed thin and fanciful. As indeed they were. What was real and effective in the Gothic poetry of the time and its matching novels was not the architectural apparatus of turrets and dungeons, nor their baronial and bandit tenants, but the dressing-up into this exotic costume of the actual fears, the partly pleasing terrors, of anyone's childhood: of the dark, of supernatural visitations, of noises in the night. And though Wordsworth shed, after his juvenile poems, the outward trappings of Gothic, this inner basis for its eerie terrors was as strong in him as in any normal child, and it lingered among his memories more strongly than with most. The weird lineaments of these early Gothic ghosts are distinctly seen in one, at least, of those half-ghostly figures in *The Prelude* which are often taken too literally, because they are presented with all the illusory appearances of realism – perhaps, too, because *The Vale* had not been read quite as carefully as Wordsworth's own comment on it demanded.

Though most of the poem, in its truncated form, is in the Gothic manner, there are also some veins of elegy which furnished significant raw material for transmutation into mature Wordsworth. A minor, but curious, example is this rambling and sketchy episode, which deals – somewhat obscurely – with the connection between a 'tender tale' and the death of a charcoal-burner:[4]

How sweet in life's tear-glistering morn
While fancy's rays the hills adorn,
To rove as through an Eden vale
The sad maze of some tender tale,
Pluck the wild flowers and fondly place
The treasure in the bosom's face.
Yet ah! full oft the enchanting while

We croud the heart with pile on pile.
[ ] rising high
Well from the heart, they droop, and all is dry.
To mark the white smoke rising slow
From the wood-built pile below,
Hang like a Spirit on its way,
Hang lingering round with fond delay
Round the dear Spot where late it fell,
And it had lov'd so long and well.
Methinks my rising soul would smile
With joy, to linger here awhile. (176–93 [*PW* I, 274])

In the eighth book of *The Prelude* this early fancy – or experience – for it might have been either, is used to conclude a discussion of the mingling of two elements in experience, the first based on the 'solid world / Of images' provided by the region of the Lakes, the second derived from 'notions and the images of books', not least those in the Gothic mode, which provided a specially 'dismal look' for the elder that grew beside the 'Charnel-house', and a 'Ghost' for the yew-tree, 'That took its station there for ornament.' This artificial need for the 'tragic' to be 'super-tragic, else left short' was less harmful, Wordsworth argued, when it was controlled by a wealth of significant natural images:

Where the harm,
If, when the Woodman languish'd with disease
From sleeping night by night among the woods
Within his sod-built Cabin, Indian-wise,
I call'd the pangs of disappointed love
And all the long Etcetera of such thought
To help him to his grave? Meanwhile the Man,
If not already from the woods retir'd
To die at home, was haply, as I knew,
Pining alone among the gentle airs,
Birds, running Streams, and Hills so beautiful
On golden evenings, while the charcoal Pile
Breath'd up its smoke, an image of his ghost
Or spirit that was soon to take its flight. (*Prel.* VIII. 610–23)

Even in this quite minor instance, the characteristic processes of the mature transmutation are at work. The feelings of childhood, 'recollected in tranquillity', are revived and sharpened as they are re-enacted in the richer memory of maturity. What had been real in them is now distinguished from what had been merely conventional and sentimental with a care critical yet loving, so that this gentle disentanglement ends, not in the mere rejection of the elegiac element, the 'tender tale', but in a perception of the underlying harmony between it and the more solid constituents of the original experience.

These processes are most significantly and comprehensively exhibited in the relation between the lines of *The Vale* on the death of his father and their transformation into the climactic 'spots of time' passage in *The Prelude*. Here they are:

No spot but claims the tender tear
By joy or grief to memory dear.
One Evening when the wintry blast
Through the sharp Hawthorn whistling pass'd
And the poor flocks, all pinch'd with cold
Sad-drooping sought the mountain fold
Long, long, upon yon naked rock
Alone, I bore the bitter shock;
Long, long, my swimming eyes did roam
For little Horse to bear me home,
To bear me – what avails my tear?
To sorrow o'er a Father's bier.
Flow on, in vain thou hast not flow'd,
But eas'd me of a heavy load;
For much it gives my heart relief
To pay the mighty debt of grief,
With sighs repeated o'er and o'er,
I mourn because I mourned no more. (416–33 [*PW* I, 279–80])

So far, the passage has merits, and touches of real concern with the event. And the last line, though with curiously enigmatic reference, seems to hint at a complication of feeling far beyond the smooth conventions of elegy. It goes on, however, with an unwavering decline into the shallow depths of the true elegiac mood:

Nor did my little heart foresee
She lost a home in losing thee.
Nor did it know, of thee bereft,
That little more than Heaven was left.
Thanks to the voice in whisper sweet
That says we soon again shall meet;
For oft when fades the leaden day
To joy-consuming pain a prey,
Or from afar the midnight bell
Flings on mine ear its solemn knell,
A still Voice whispers to my breast
I soon shall be with them that rest.
Then may some kind and pious friend

Assiduous o'er my body bend,
Once might I see him turn aside
The kind unwilling tear to hide,

. . .

Ah! may my weary body sleep
In peace beneath a green grass heap,
In Churchyard, such at death of day
As heard the pensive sighs of Gray . . .

(437–49, 456–9 [*PW* I, 280])

What is really most moving about this sad stuff is the contrast between these elegiac sighs, straight from the original horse's mouth, and the realities of Wordsworth's position as he wrote this poem. The death of his father left him, with his brothers and sister, orphans in the care of grandparents who were neither affectionate nor understanding. At the very time when he was writing these lines, his sister Dorothy was giving a prose description of the reality that underlay these verses. It is, indeed, by a pleasant coincidence that the first letter of hers to have survived should do what so many of her later letters and journals were to do later, recording in plain prose what he transformed into poetry:

Many a time have W[illia]m, J[oh]n, C[hristopher], and myself shed tears together, tears of the bitterest sorrow, we all of us, each day, feel more sensibly the loss we sustained when we were deprived of our parents, and each day do we receive fresh insults. You will wonder of what sort; believe me of the most mortifying kind, the insults of servants . . . I was for a whole week kept in expectation of my Brothers, who staid at school all that time after the vacation began owing to the ill-nature of my Uncle who would not send horses for them because when they wrote they did not happen to mention them, and only said when they should break up which was always before sufficient. This was the beginning of my mortifications for I felt that if they had had another home to go to, they would have been behaved to in a very different manner, and received with more chearful countenances, indeed nobody but myself expressed one wish to see them. At last however they were sent for, but not till my Brother W[illia]m had hired a horse for himself and came over because he thought someone must be ill; the servants are every one of them so insolent to us as makes the kitchen as well as the parlour quite insupportable.

(*EL* I/I)

This vivid and concrete prose reveals the reality behind the pawky lamentations of the verse; the orphans had indeed 'lost a home', and much more besides. Above all Dorothy's letter makes it easy to understand how deeply wounded they all were by the failure to send the horses to bring the boys back from school. All the more reason why Wordsworth himself should, in his verse, have looked back with such intense regret and such a detailed memory of the occasion, to that last end of term when he had looked out for their own horses – his father's horses, to which they had unquestioned right, and which would be sent of course, whether anyone were ill or not, and never a week late. But with all the more reason too must the verse be dismissed as a very limping account of the event and of the feelings which gathered round it. The *Prelude* version of the same events and feelings, on the other hand, is at least as concrete as Dorothy's prose, gives as full an account of the mere facts, but also goes on to do much more. It is, of course, generally and rightly regarded as one of the most central passages of his poetry, and it is quoted in full here for convenience, for the commentary upon it will introduce the main topics to be studied, in relation not only to Wordsworth's exploration of the role of memories in the formation of a human personality, but also to the highly individual style which both grew from, and made possible, this exploration.

So feeling comes in aid
Of feeling, and diversity of strength
Attends us, if but once we have been strong.
Oh! mystery of Man, from what a depth
Proceed thy honours! I am lost, but see
In simple childhood something of the base
On which thy greatness stands, but this I feel,
That from thyself it is that thou must give,
Else never canst receive. The days gone by
Come back upon me from the dawn almost
Of life: the hiding-places of my power
Seem open; I approach, and then they close;
I see by glimpses now; when age comes on,
May scarcely see at all, and I would give,
While yet we may, as far as words can give,
A substance and a life to what I feel:
I would enshrine the spirit of the past
For future restoration. Yet another
Of these, to me, affecting incidents
With which we will conclude.
One Christmas-time,
The day before the Holidays began,
Feverish, and tired, and restless, I went forth
Into the fields, impatient for the sight
Of those two Horses which should bear us home;
My Brothers and myself. There was a crag,
An Eminence, which from the meeting-point
Of two highways ascending, overlook'd
At least a long half-mile of those two roads,
By each of which the expected Steeds might come,
The choice uncertain. Thither I repair'd
Up to the highest summit; 'twas a day
Stormy, and rough, and wild, and on the grass

I sate, half-shelter'd by a naked wall;
Upon my right hand was a single sheep,
A whistling hawthorn on my left, and there,
With those Companions at my side, I watch'd,
Straining my eyes intensely, as the mist
Gave intermitting prospect of the wood
And plain beneath. Ere I to School return'd
That dreary time, ere I had been ten days
A dweller in my Father's House, he died,
And I and my two Brothers, Orphans then,
Followed his Body to the Grave. The event
With all the sorrow which it brought appear'd
A chastisement; and when I call'd to mind
That day so lately pass'd, when from the crag
I look'd in such anxiety of hope,
With trite reflections of morality,
Yet in the deepest passion, I bow'd low
To God, who thus corrected my desires;
And afterwards, the wind and sleety rain
And all the business of the elements,
The single sheep, and the one blasted tree,
And the bleak music of that old stone wall,
The noise of wood and water, and the mist
Which on the line of each of those two Roads
Advanced in such indisputable shapes,
All these were spectacles and sounds to which
I often would repair and thence would drink,
As at a fountain . . . (*Prel.* XI.326–85)

The elegiac elements of the version in *The Vale* have been completely removed – or rather, driven out by memories and feelings of altogether greater weight. The reference to the death is minimal, and almost brutally factual. The only word associated with ordinary mourning is 'sorrow'. The whole emphasis has, in fact, been shifted away from the death itself, to that day ten days earlier, when the death was not even foreseen. The factual details of the earlier version, and they only, have been picked up again: the weather, the crag, the hawthorn, the sheep, waiting for the horse. But they have been made more impressive by an essentially isolating mode of description, in which the attention is focussed on the single objects one by one; no longer 'flocks', but most emphatically a 'single sheep', twice repeated, and 'the sharp Hawthorn', which might have been collectively applied to a hedge, has now become 'the one blasted tree', and again twice repeated. Additions have been made to the scene, with the same sharp concreteness. There is a 'naked wall', iterated as 'that old stone wall', and those two roads half-covered with a shifting mist –

these two twice repeated. This is, indeed, an entirely new mode of description, whose extreme originality is more than half-hidden by its extreme simplicity.

As for the feeling, reported and implied, the ready lush mourning of the elegiac mode, with its melting mood of piety and self-pity, has given way to a bare and truthful revelation of a conflict which Wordsworth himself reports fully, but without pretending to understand it fully. 'With trite reflections of morality' is fair comment on the lines in *The Vale*, and it is, of course, almost certain that Wordsworth had the whole passage pretty clearly in his mind while he was writing the version in *The Prelude*. He had, above all for his own poetry, which was mostly composed orally and memorised, a formidable capacity of recall, and if this had faltered, his manuscripts of *The Vale* could be consulted. But however clearly, or unclearly, he meant this comment to be applied to his own earlier record, it is significant that he adds at once a comment insisting on the force of the feelings which underlay the 'trite morality' – 'yet in the deepest passion'. It is a significant distinction, and very typical of him: to dismiss the conventions of feeling and the verse which depended on them, while at the same moment recognising the validity of the experience which had once generated them. His realism, to put the same thing in another way, was restorative rather than revolutionary; it worked, not by absolute novelty, but by the uncovering and recovery of thoughts and feelings long overgrown by custom and fashion, by stripping away the veil which an accumulation of formulaic words had interposed between the mind and reality.

At the same time, he is partly baffled by the nature of his own feelings, and with skilful honesty, having reported all that he could clearly perceive in himself, he went on to record its limits. That the death of his father had been a 'chastisement' he certainly felt, and that his desires had been 'corrected' by God. But how had they deserved punishment and correction? By any usual moral standards, the anxiety of a schoolboy to return to his home at the end of term would be no more laudable than sinful. Very likely he was not himself aware, with any fullness of consciousness, of the possible answer. But one speculation is perhaps justified by that one remarkable line from *The Vale* – the only one that strikes on the mind sharply – 'I mourn because I mourned no more.' Perhaps he had been a little lacking in duty and affection if, as he waited on the crag, his anxiety to return had been for the house at Cockermouth, with its memories of his dead mother, for the living Dorothy and the one brother not yet at school with him – for any or all of these, rather than for his father. And so it might have been an all too fitting 'chastisement' if the one thing he had not wanted as much as he should were the one thing taken from him – and should prove to have been the very one thing on which all else depended. It is, at any rate, noticeable that the reference to his father, both in *The Vale* and in *The Prelude*, is lacking in any expression of positive affection; and the more noticeable because it is the only reference to him throughout the verse, and because there is, in Book V of *The Prelude*, a long and affectionate description of his mother, who had died five years earlier. There is no need, of course, to imagine that he had been on bad terms with his father, still less that his father had been lacking in affection for his children. But he had been over-burdened with affairs, harried almost to distraction by a villainous employer, Sir James Lowther. And after the death of his wife, as Wordsworth said towards the end of his own life, in the *Autobiographical Memoranda*, he had 'never recovered his usual cheerfulness of mind'. But however this may have been, the outstanding fact about the *Prelude* passage, so far as it concerns his bereavement, is that it records a complexity of feeling which Wordsworth did not fully understand, yet with a fidelity and directness which is itself a total contradiction of the trite commonplaces of the elegiac conventions.

All this has been achieved, however, by a change which is more far-reaching than a mere improvement of technique – though it also produces a remarkable change in technique. What Wordsworth had discovered, in the twelve years or so between *The Vale* and *The Prelude*, was that embracing and transcending all particular memories was memory itself, in all the cumulative force and complexity of its recurrent life. Every new experience is, at the moment of its perception, more or less modified by previous experiences, and any memory may be changed, at every recurrence, by all that has been experienced and remembered since it was first recorded, or last brought back to life. So 'feeling comes in aid / Of feeling', or, as he puts it in the more philosophical-sounding prose of the *Preface* to *Lyrical Ballads*, 'our continued influxes of feeling are modified and directed by our thoughts, which are indeed the representatives of all our past feelings' (*PW* II, 388). In *The Vale*, then, he had been writing about himself and his own feelings, for his and for their own sake, with an 'egotism' and self-indulgence natural enough in a youth of seventeen, above all in one bred in the heyday of the elegy. But in *The Prelude* he is writing about the structure of the human personality, any human personality, and his concern with it is 'egotistical' only in so far as he is compelled to illustrate his discoveries from his own experience, exemplary because no other could lie so fully open to his scrutiny.

This discovery of the power of memory, however, had gone hand in hand –

each aiding the other – with a crucial change in literary technique: one which intimately and accurately reflects the role of recurrence in the life of feelings and thoughts, and of recurrence with constant variation as in memory itself. It has been noted already that the *Prelude* version is clearly distinguished from that in *The Vale* by the repetition of the main elements in the crucial experience. It remains to examine this more closely, and with as much attention to variation as to repetition, for it is the two together that make this technique both new and effective. A comparison will help to illustrate their combination, and it is not far to seek, for it comes in the preceding 'spot of time', that which follows immediately on the lines describing the sight of the murderer's gibbet quoted above:

forthwith I left the spot
And, reascending the bare Common, saw
A naked pool that lay beneath the hills,
The Beacon on the summit, and more near,
A Girl who bore a Pitcher on her head
And seem'd with difficult steps to force her way
Against the blowing wind. It was, in truth,
An ordinary sight; but I should need
Colours and words that are unknown to man
To paint the visionary dreariness
Which, while I look'd all round for my lost Guide,
Did at that time invest the naked Pool,
The Beacon on the lonely Eminence,
The Woman, and her garments vex'd and toss'd
By the strong wind. When, in a blessed season
With those two dear Ones, to my heart so dear,
When in the blessed time of early love,
Long afterwards, I roam'd about
In daily presence of this very scene,
Upon the naked pool and dreary crags,
And on the melancholy Beacon, fell
The spirit of pleasure and youth's golden gleam;
And think ye not with radiance more divine
From these remembrances, and from the power
They left behind? So feeling comes in aid
Of feeling . . . (*Prel.* XI.302–27)

Here the central description is given no less than thrice. First, in its literal appearance – 'An ordinary sight'; then with two successive variations, each adding vital elements to the first version. It may help to set them out in this skeletal form:

1	2	3
a naked Pool . . . the hills	the naked Pool	the naked pool and *dreary* crags
Beacon on the summit	Beacon on the *lonely* Eminence	And on the *melancholy* Beacon
Girl who bore a Pitcher	The Woman	
force her way	her garments *vex'd* and *toss'd*	
Against the blowing wind	By the strong wind	

When the three versions are set out in this way, the process of transformation reveals itself without the need for much detailed comment. But it needs to be said that it would have been enough, merely for the 'meaning' of the passage, to have observed that the scene had about it a 'visionary dreariness'. What is remarkable, and in the principle novel, is that the scene is repeated in full, with just such changes of words – they are italicised above – as will express more forcibly this emotional change in its colouring. And in the third version, the new words, also italicised, carry the same process further, while the 'dreariness' mentioned only by way of comment in the second version has now entered the description itself as the adjective 'dreary'. The third version, however, having gone to the extreme of negative feeling in its description of the scene itself, suddenly changes the girl with her wind-swept garments for the 'golden' contrast with Dorothy Wordsworth and his future wife, Mary Hutchinson.

With this example in mind, it will be enough to set out in the same way the varied repetitions of the passage from which we started. It is given only twice, but the variations are more extensive:

1	2
a crag, / An Eminence	*the wind and sleety rain*
overlook'd . . . half-mile of those two roads	*all the business of the elements*
choice uncertain	The single sheep
a day / Stormy, and rough, and wild	and the one *blasted* tree
half-shelter'd by a naked wall	the *bleak* music of that *old stone* wall
a single sheep	The noise of wood and water
A whistling hawthorn	the mist . . . on . . . those two Roads
the mist / Gave . . . prospect of the wood / And plain beneath	Advanced in such *indisputable* shapes

Again, it is perhaps necessary to make the very simple observation that the mere 'meaning' of the passage as a whole demanded no more than that there should have been some brief resumptive reference to the first description, such indeed as occurs in the two lines

That day so lately pass'd, when from the crag
I look'd in such anxiety of hope . . .

The passage could, for example, without any loss of mere meaning, have read something like this at the end:

And afterwards, these spectacles and sounds
To which I would repair, would yield me drink
As from a fountain.

Yet the repetition is far from being otiose, for it carries with it many alterations, some of considerable magnitude. The first description, as in the Beacon passage, is literal in vocabulary, however evocative in effect. But in the second, the 'visionary dreariness' has been strengthened in many ways; 'sleety rain' has been added to the weather, the 'business of the elements' is more vaguely and powerfully suggestive than 'Stormy, and rough, and wild', the hawthorn has been very emphatically singularised, as 'the one', and its whistling has been turned into 'the bleak music' of the naked wall, itself turned into 'old stone'. The mist, finally, has been partly personified, so that it now advances, in ambiguous shapes, on the two roads.

Here, then, in descriptive technique is exactly the kind of repetition with variations which Wordsworth regarded as the vital process of the memory in building up the human personality. Before the reader's very eyes, as it were, an experiment has been conducted to illustrate a general principle, and as usually happens with really significant experiments, its sheer simplicity tends to hide its enormous demonstrative force. It is one of the long-established procedures of Wordsworthian commentary to use his sister's *Journals* and letters for a rather similar purpose: to pick up some account in her vividly direct prose of an experience which they had enjoyed together, and then to show how it was transmuted into his verse. But instructive as such comparisons are, they are altogether less astonishing that what is transacted in these repetitions and variations, for in both of them we are shown the successive transformations within Wordsworth's own imagination, the shaping action of the memory in actual action. And what is more, the variation is deliberately presented: it is the very essence of the writing. What, in the comparisons with Dorothy's prose, comes about by lucky accident is done here by choice and design.

So far as these passages are typical – and they are widely regarded as being among Wordsworth's best and most characteristic – they suggest that repetition and variation are central features both of his content and of his style. And what is repeated and varied, on the page, is a set of words both small in number and apparently simple in meaning, depending for their large effect not on imagery, aphoristic compactness, or complexity of reference, but on mere iteration and significant variation. It is attained, whether the wall be 'naked' or 'old stone', whether the whistling music be made by the hawthorn or the wall, whether the pool lie beneath the 'hills' or the 'dreary crags'. It has, in fact, very little to do with scenic accuracy and consistency of description. It may well be, as Wordsworth himself said, that the eye of the Poet should be 'steadily fixed upon his object' (*PW* II, 420), but through the eye, as through all the senses, 'feeling comes in aid / Of feeling'. One glance can never see quite what is seen by another; for under the apparent steadiness of gaze, memory and repetition work their constant office of variation and growth.

One single exception may be noted: the pool remains always 'naked', and the wall too was 'naked'. The repetition, it would seem, need not always be varied. But it is also possible that, even when the word remains the same, its sense may insensibly shift from one occurrence to another – may, indeed, so shift for no other reason than that it is often repeated. 'So are they all, all honourable men.'

PART II

Wordsworthian words

4

Words are too awful an instrument for good and evil, to be trifled with; they hold above all other external powers a dominion over thoughts. *Upon Epitaphs* III[1]

Wordsworth's views on poetic diction, and Coleridge's strictures on them, have been so often discussed by critics and scholars that only two kinds of comment can now be added; one, of necessity very lengthy, would review previous discussions, resume their best points, judiciously arbitrate where they differ; the other would ignore all this accretion of learning, or at least omit to mention it, and deal with the matter as it were *de novo*, on just such a scale as happened to suit the writer's purpose. The second mode of treatment is needed here, and on a scale small enough not to defer for very long much weightier matters.

Wordsworth's argument had two sides: it was partly negative, engaged with the errors in existing theory and practice; and positive, so far as he described the manner in which the language of poetry ought to be managed. Broadly speaking, the negative side of his theory was sound – even Coleridge thought so. The positive side, however, was more tentative, patchy and ill-defined, so that it was always easy to discover apparent inconsistencies within it, and between it and his own practice as a poet. It is, on the other hand, more interesting, for it is an attempt at original thought, however imperfect, and, however imperfectly, it really does illuminate some aspects of his practice. It is not, in fact, wholly inconsistent with the more negative side of his theory, if minor details are disregarded, and the general drift is followed with a certain tolerance.

This broad overall consistency can be seen best in the *Appendix* on poetic diction added to the *Preface* to *Lyrical Ballads* in 1802:

The earliest poets of all nations generally wrote from passion excited by real events; they wrote naturally, and as men: feeling powerfully as they did, their language was daring, and figurative. In succeeding times, Poets, and Men ambitious of the fame of Poets, perceiving the influence of such language, and desirous of producing the same effect without being animated by the same passion, set themselves to a mechanical adoption of these figures of speech, and made use of them, sometimes with propriety, but much more frequently applied them to feelings and thoughts with which they had no natural connection whatsoever. A language was thus insensibly produced, differing materially from the real language of men in *any situation* . . . [T]his distorted language was received with admiration; and Poets, it is probable, who had before contented themselves for the most part with misapplying only expressions which at first had been dictated by real passion, carried the abuse still further, and introduced phrases composed apparently in the spirit of the original figurative language of passion, yet altogether of their own invention, and characterised by various degrees of wanton deviation from good sense and nature. (*PW* II, 405)

What is being condemned, of course, is that collection of tricks of diction which enables any reader of poetry to identify almost any passage written in the eighteenth century at sight: 'finny tribes', personifications, classical allusions, words found rarely if ever in prose.[2] But his description of it is perhaps less definite because he intended to define it by illustrations and comparisons – as he did. And what really concerned him was to make clear that this diction was not something wholly arbitrary and invented, but that it had arisen from the gradual corruption of a kind of writing once wholly justified. In rejecting this accretion of rubbish his object, as so often with him, was not merely to overturn an existing state of things, but to get back to the more natural state which had preceded it. His own view of poetic diction was, in fact, simply that poets ought once again to write 'naturally, and as men', and with real passion, making only those modifications of ordinary language which properly and naturally accompany real passion.

So far, Wordsworth was mainly in the right, and Coleridge handsomely granted that he had even been effective: 'the comparison of such poems of merit, as have been given to the public within the last ten or twelve years with the majority of those produced previously to the appearance of that preface leave no doubt on my mind, that Mr. Wordsworth is fully justified in believing his efforts to have been by no means ineffectual' (*Biog. Lit.* ch. XVII). It was only when Wordsworth tried to define more closely the kind of modification needed to adapt the ordinary language of men to poetic purposes that disagreement arose. 'A selection of the language really spoken by men', 'the language of humble and rustic life', these were descriptions very vulnerable to argument unless very carefully defined. How selected? Is it true that rustics speak a 'more permanent and far more philosophical language' than other men? Coleridge had little difficulty in running rings round these notorious half-way descriptions. But his arguments are now of no more interest than those which he was contradicting – or rather, both alike are of purely antiquarian interest. Both of the contestants were necessarily unaware that they were trying to make observations in a tricky field of linguistics, without even glimpsing its existence. Now, however, that such a field of study has been identified, however rudimentary its present state may be, it reduces the whole argument between them, and any argument in the terms they chose, to about the same level as that held in meteorology by old saws about red skies and shepherds, and new moons with old moons in their arms. They were a pair of weatherwise bards, and nothing more. They were as simpletons in the theory of 'registers' as were nearly all their contemporaries, and it is one portent of the abstract and remote character of their speculations that neither of them ever tumbled to the special importance, in the native language, of the contrasts and tensions between the Teutonic and Romance elements in the vocabulary, with all their implications for the social and literary status of words. It should not have been quite beyond their reach, for their young disciple, De Quincey, wrote brilliantly on exactly this subject only a generation later. But it needed a careful look at the simple facts, and this is what neither of them gave it, so long as they were talking about broad theories.

Wordsworth's really interesting and informative observations on poetic diction, on a selection of real language under the influence of passion, are to be found, not in his formal discussions in the *Prefaces*, but as *obiter dicta* in other places, where he had been brought fair and square up against one actual problem or another. On language in general, apart from the special problems of poetic diction, there are three passages which all touch on his perception of a fundamental property of words never so clearly described by anyone before him. The brain is not capable of 'thinking' or 'feeling' without the aid of some code or other: words are the most commonly used, but in specialised fields, the formulae of mathematics, physics, chemistry, the diagrams of engineers, the drawings of architects may serve approximately the same purpose. And this code, especially if it is the code of human language, is far from inert. It has its own properties, its own powers to exert; and they are especially powerful when their existence is ignored. Wordsworth's own dealings with words had taught him of this power, and the passages in which he describes it are the best clues we have to the ways in which he mastered it, submitted it to his own purposes. The earliest, and slightest, is in the *Preface* to *Lyrical Ballads* itself:

> For, to treat the subject (the theory upon which the Poems were written) with the clearness and coherence of which it is susceptible, it would be necessary to give a full account of the present state of the public taste in this country, and to determine how far this taste is healthy or depraved; which, again, could not be determined, without pointing out in what manner language and the human mind act and re-act on each another. (*PW* II, 385)

The second of these references is a little more precise, and it comes into his most penetrating analysis of the defects of the poetic style which he strove to displace, in the essays *Upon Epitaphs*. Having given, in the second essay, a remarkably perceptive, hostile analysis of that epitaph by Pope which Johnson thought the best, he goes on in the third essay to criticise generally

> . . . the artifices which have over-run our writings in metre since the days of Dryden and Pope. Energy, stillness, grandeur, tenderness, those feelings which are the pure emanations of

Nature, those thoughts which have the infinitude of truth, and those expressions which are not what the garb is to the body but what the body is to the soul, themselves a constituent part and power or function in the thought – all these are abandoned for their opposites . . . Words are too awful an instrument for good and evil, to be trifled with; they hold above all other external powers a dominion over thoughts. If words be not (recurring to a metaphor before used) an incarnation of the thought, but only a clothing for it, then surely will they prove an ill gift; such a one as those [poisoned] vestments, read of in the stories of superstitious times, which had power to consume and to alienate from his right mind the victim who put them on. Language, if it do not uphold, and feed, and leave in quiet, like the power of gravitation or the air we breathe, is a counter-spirit, unremittingly and noiselessly at work, to subvert, to lay waste, to vitiate, and to dissolve. From a deep conviction then that the excellence of writing, whether in prose or verse, consists in a conjunction of Reason and Passion, a conjunction which must be of necessity benign; and that it might be deduced from what has been said that the taste, intellectual power and morals of a country are inseparably linked in mutual dependence, I have dwelt thus long upon this argument. (*Literary Criticism*, pp. 129–30)

In the third of these passages, this solemn verdict on the function of language in the life of a culture is expressed from another point of view, more intimate and personal, as it affects the writer himself, in the very act of writing. It is in a letter conveying his advice to the sister of his friend, the mathematician Hamilton:

I assure you, I have never given way to my own feelings in personifying natural objects, or investing them with sensation, without bringing all that I have said to a rigorous after-test of good sense, as far as I was able to determine what good sense is . . . She will probably write less in proportion as she subjects her feelings to logical forms, but the range of her sensibilities, so far from being narrowed, will extend as she improves in looking at things through the steady light of words; and, to speak a little metaphysically, words are not a mere *vehicle*, but they are *powers* either to kill or to animate. (*LY* 898/488)

The really significant thing about all these descriptions of the active role of words is that Wordsworth had discovered it for himself, not deduced it from any theories of his own, or derived from other sources. And the discovery was made at the moment when he moved towards his great creative period, in the process of writing *The Thorn*.

5

. . . the interest which the mind attaches to words, not only as symbols of the passion, but as *things*, active and efficient, which are of themselves part of the passion.

Note to *The Thorn* (*PW* II, 513)

Among Wordsworth's earlier poems, *The Thorn* is noteworthy for two opposite reasons. By Wordsworth's critics, it was singled out for specially vicious attack. Southey, for example, reviewing the 1798 *Lyrical Ballads*, wrote:

> The other ballads of this kind are as bald in story, and are not so highly embellished in narration. With that which is entitled The Thorn, we were altogether displeased. The advertisement says, it is not told in the person of the author, but in that of some loquacious narrator. The author should have recollected that he who personates tiresome loquacity, becomes tiresome himself.[3]

And this, of course, was from a 'friend', brother-in-law of Coleridge, fellow-author in the book reviewed. Many years later, Coleridge faithfully repeated Southey's gibe in the *Biographia Literaria*: 'It is not possible to imitate truly a dull and garrulous discourser without repeating the effects of dullness and garrulity' (ch. XVII). From him, it passes into the main stream of critical orthodoxy, and one recent writer reports of another: 'Professor Hartman points out rather unkindly that the Captain's garrulity and "adhesive mind" do not really serve to differentiate him from his author' – this with reference to the retired captain by whom Wordsworth thought the tale might be told.[4]

Wordsworth himself, however, always attached the highest importance to the poem, and regarded an ability to appreciate it properly as the touchstone of the reader who could understand his poetry. A well-known letter of his to his sister-in-law, Sara, insists upon it: the letter is quoted fully on p. 164 below. A painting based upon it by his friend Sir George Beaumont – the frontispiece of this book – was of great concern to him, and in writing to inquire about it he said: 'the poem is a favourite with me' (*EL* 216/268). It was a 'favourite' for the best of all reasons, that in the course of writing it, he developed, almost for the first time, what was to become the basic characteristic of his whole handling of words for poetic purposes. It was a kind of language utterly different from that of the eighteenth century, indeed directly opposite to it, as he himself defined it in the essays *Upon Epitaphs*. Yet it was by no means novel, but a return to a much older – indeed a very ancient – form found in folk poems, and before them probably in charms and incantations. Finally, it was in writing about the poem – and he wrote a good deal about it, one way and another – that he gradually reveals his own conscious discovery of what he had done, and how.

The imaginative problem which he set himself in writing it was described in his note to Miss Fenwick:

> Alfoxden. 1798. Arose out of my observing, on the ridge of Quantock Hill, on a stormy day, a thorn which I had often passed in calm and bright weather without noticing it. I said to myself, 'Cannot I by some invention do as much to make this Thorn permanently an impressive object as the storm has made it to my eyes at this moment?' I began the poem accordingly, and composed it with great rapidity. (*PW* II, 511)

The imaginative ambition, nothing less than to enter into competition with a storm, was grandiose, and the technical problem correspondingly severe. But after all, it is only by involving himself with such ambitions and problems that a writer is forced to find remarkable solutions for them – or to fail altogether. Wordsworth's first step was to associate the thorn with the ballad-like theme of a maiden deserted by her lover, bearing alone an illegitimate child, and perhaps killing it. Several analogues and possible sources have been found by the annotators, and there is no need to emphasise the antiquity of the theme or its connection with the traditional ballads.[5] But though this association would clearly lend 'human' interest to the poem, it carried with it the obvious danger that it might unduly distract attention from the real subject, which was the thorn itself. This was avoided in the poem itself by giving the thorn rather more space than the maiden and her history, and by adopting a shape which served to emphasise it rather than her. It is, indeed, a remarkable piece of composition, once the reader has got past its apparent naiveté, its air of simplicity. It turns out to be both tightly controlled and highly original. The overall pattern is tripartite. It has the classical 'beginning, middle and end'. The beginning, 10 of the 22 stanzas, describes the thorn and its surroundings – the pond, the heap of moss, the woman, the mountains and the weather – storm, whirlwind, frost. The middle, stanzas 11 to 16, narrates the woman's unhappy love. The end, from stanza 17 onwards, returns to the thorn, telling how the narrator first found the woman there, and repeating much of the opening description of the thorn and its surroundings, but now, of course, in the light of the further knowledge of its history in relation to the woman. The obvious musical analogy (and music often offers useful analogies in discussions of pure form or shape) would be with two themes, stated separately and successively, then brought together in a contrapuntal relationship. Perhaps a more naturally Wordsworthian analysis would be to regard the beginning as dealing with the present appearance of things, the middle as giving their past, and the end as presenting the first appearances, now modified by knowledge of the past. But however the form of the poem as a whole may be regarded, it helps to secure the main purpose of giving more prominence to the thorn itself than to the woman, for it dominates the beginning and the end.

This purpose, however, is still more insistently served by repetition. And in his use of this, Wordsworth was reviving, and raising to a higher level of literary complexity, what seems to be one of the most ancient forms of imaginative writing, that which is often called by students of folk-lore the 'cumulative' form. It is found, and very often, in that mass of traditional material which has lived for so long on the lips and in the memories of children, and those who take pleasure in entertaining children – material which only began to find its way into print in the eighteenth and nineteenth centuries. The most widely known examples in England are *The House that Jack Built* and *The Old Woman and her Pig*. What they have obviously in common is a series of actions performed, or refused (it does not seem to matter which), by animals and objects. A dog or cat eats, or refuses to eat, some smaller animals, is beaten, or not beaten, by a stick, which is burnt, or not burnt, by fire which is quenched, or not quenched by some water, which is drunk, or not drunk by an ox, and so on. This narrative is always told in the same form. Indeed the form is the narrative, and with minor variations it has been found in every country of Europe, in Africa and in India. There can be no doubt that it is one of the oldest and most widespread of all traditional literary shapes.

Its earliest written version is in the Hebrew *Haggadah* printed at Prague in 1590. This is used now as a chant in the Passover service, and its religious variation can be seen from the last of the accumulated elements:

> Then came the Holy One, blessed be He and destroyed the Angel of Death who killed the butcher, who slaughtered the ox, which drank the water, which quenched the fire, which burnt the stick, which beat the dog, which bit the cat, which ate the kid that my father bought for two zuzim.[6]

But there is good evidence that chants of this kind existed earlier, and at least one form can be traced back to the Middle Ages, at Münster. Another form must have been well known in Spain, for there is a clear reference to it in *Don Quixote*, published in 1605 and 1615. In describing a fracas in an inn, Cervantes comments: 'As we say, *The cat to the rat*, *the rat to the rope*, *the rope to the staff*, so the carter was beating Sancho, Sancho the servant . . .' It is clear from the opening phrase that the story was so widely known as to be proverbial. There is no doubt either that variants of the form were widely known in England and in Scotland in the eighteenth century. Like so many nursery tales, few of them were written down until the nineteenth century. *The Old Woman and her Pig*, for example, was 'collected' by Halliwell in 1842. But *The House that Jack Built* was printed as a chap-book in about 1770, the year of Wordsworth's birth, and it is no great stretch of assumption to suppose that he was acquainted with it in his childhood. Certainly, he would have known it by 1797, when Coleridge parodied the text as Nehemiah Higginbottom.

It would indeed be a very wild stretch of assumption to suppose that in *The Thorn* and other repetitive poems, or parts of poems, he was in any sense imitating, consciously or unconsciously, the nursery rhymes of his youth.[7] He was, like any other writer deeply concerned with forms, well able to invent them for himself, and to this invention childhood memories may have contributed only in so far as they had once helped to determine his sense of form in general. The point is rather that, whatever the origin of his use of repetitive forms, when he did come to use them, some of the effects he attained were not unlike those of the more primitive materials, though applied to more varied and complex ends.

One of the simpler examples of this kind of repetition is in a poem probably written shortly after *The Thorn*. It is well-known, and perhaps a little under-rated, at any rate for its formal quality:

THE REVERIE OF POOR SUSAN

At the corner of Wood Street, when daylight appears,
Hangs a Thrush that sings loud, it has sung for three years:
Poor Susan has passed by the spot, and has heard
In the silence of morning the song of the Bird.

'Tis a note of enchantment; what ails her? She sees
A mountain ascending, a vision of trees;
Bright volumes of vapour through Lothbury glide,
And a river flows on through the vale of Cheapside.

Green pastures she views in the midst of the dale,
Down which she so often has tripped with her pail;
And a single small cottage, a nest like a dove's,
The one only dwelling on earth that she loves.

She looks, and her heart is in heaven: but they fade,
The mist and the river, the hill and the shade:
The stream will not flow, and the hill will not rise,
And the colours have all passed away from her eyes! (*PW* II, 217)

The form itself is adapted here in its more dramatic variant, that in which a series of items are built up cumulatively, and then taken away again in the same order. And it shows that Wordsworth was already beginning to feel the possibilities of repetition in the rendering of 'passion'.

It is the same dynamic variant of the form which, though more flexibly, controls the relation between the 'beginning' and the 'end' of *The Thorn*. Unfortunately, there seems to be no standard method of demonstrating the working of such formal patterns as these, still less of comparing them with one another. After making various experiments (some of them numerical), I have been driven, as a last resort, to a 'skeletal' presentation of tautologies in *The Thorn*, as in Table I.

The one advantage of this barbarous anatomy is that it needs no further comment. The reliance upon repetition, almost to the exclusion of all other and more elaborate devices of diction, is self-evident. And it was, of course,

Table 1

A	There is a Thorn – it looks so old so old and grey It stands erect It stands erect, and like a stone With lichens it is overgrown Like rock or stone, it is o'er grown, With lichens And hung with heavy tufts of moss Up from the earth these mosses creep This poor Thorn they clasp it round To bury this poor Thorn for ever
AB	This Thorn you on your left espy And to the left You see a little muddy pond
AC	And, close beside this aged Thorn A beauteous heap, a hill of moss Of olive green and scarlet bright, This heap of earth o'ergrown with moss Which close beside the Thorn you see
ABC	Now would you see this aged Thorn, This pond, and beauteous hill of moss.
CBD	You must take care For oft there sits between the heap And that same pond A Woman in a scarlet cloak
ADCB	And there, beside the Thorn, she sits And why sits she beside the Thorn? I cannot tell But would you gladly view the spot The hillock like an infant's grave The pond – and Thorn, so old and grey
	Stanzas 10–18 omitted.
ABCD	But what's the Thorn? and what the pond? And what the hill of moss to her?
DEA	She hanged her baby on the tree
DEB	She drowned it in the pond
EC	The little Babe was buried there Beneath the hill of moss so fair

Table I (*Cont.*)

	The moss is spotted red With drops of that poor infant's blood
BE	if to the pond you go The shadow of a babe you trace
CE	The hill of moss . . . began to stir The little Babe lies buried there Beneath that hill of moss so fair.
A	The Thorn is bound With heavy tufts of moss that strive To drag it to the ground . . .

A=Thorn
B =Pond
C=heap of moss
D=Woman
E =Babe

quite obvious to Wordsworth himself, at any rate when he had done it, when he had 'composed it with great rapidity'; that he had deliberately planned it so is much less likely.

His observation of its pervading presence presented him with something of a problem, for he felt – and events showed him to be right – that many readers would fail to react to this repetition in the appropriate way, that they would, for example, be merely irritated with it, dismiss it as mere tautology, pointless loquacity etc. He therefore made two separate explanations or defences of his new style of writing, hoping to ensure by one or the other that the poem might get its proper chance, and be read in the right way, however unfamiliar that might be.

The first explanation was outlined very briefly in the *Advertisement* prefaced to the first *Lyrical Ballads* in 1798: 'The poem of the Thorn, as the reader will soon discover, is not supposed to be spoken in the author's own person: the character of the loquacious narrator will sufficiently shew itself in the course of the story' (*PW* II, 384). In the second edition, however, Wordsworth pushed the idea of this loquacious stalking-horse much further, and in a very curious additional note he outlined the character who would be introduced as the narrator, carefully relating it to the special characteristics of the narration itself. It deserves very careful attention, for it is necessary throughout the description to disentangle the picture of the man, which is of no importance whatever, from the steadily growing perception of the qualities of the poem itself:

This Poem ought to have been preceded by an introductory Poem, which I have been prevented from writing by never having felt myself in a mood when it was probable that I should write it well. The character which I have here introduced speaking is sufficiently common. The Reader will perhaps have a general notion of it, if he has ever known a man, a Captain of a small trading vessel, for example, who being past the middle age of life, had retired upon an annuity or small independent income to some village or country town of which he was not a native, or in which he had not been accustomed to live. Such men, having little to do, become credulous and talkative from indolence; and from the same cause . . . they are prone to superstition. On which account it appeared to me proper to select a character like this to exhibit some of the general laws by which superstition acts upon the mind. Superstitious men are almost always men of slow faculties and deep feelings; their minds are not loose, but adhesive; they have a reasonable share of imagination, by which word I mean the faculty which produces impressive effects out of simple elements; but they are utterly destitute of fancy, the power by which pleasure and surprise are excited by sudden varieties of situation and an accumulated imagery.

It was my wish in this poem to show the manner in which such men cleave to the same ideas; and to follow the turns of passion, always different, yet not palpably different, by which their conversation is swayed. I had two objects to attain; first, to represent a picture which should not be unimpressive, yet consistent with the character that should describe it; secondly, while I adhered to the style in which such persons describe, to take care that words, which in their minds are impregnated with passion, should likewise convey passion to Readers who are not accustomed to sympathize with men feeling in that manner or using such language. It seemed to me that this might be done by calling in the assistance of Lyrical and rapid Metre. It was necessary that the Poem, to be natural, should in reality move slowly; yet I hoped that, by the aid of the metre, to those who should at all enter into the spirit of the Poem, it would appear to move quickly. (*PW* II, 512–13)

On the one side, a wooden ventriloquist's effigy, not very remotely modelled on the Ancient Mariner of three years before, of whom it can be said with certainty that Wordsworth could never have been 'in the mood' to write well. On the other side, phrases and definitions of growing value: 'imagination . . . the faculty which produces impressive effects out of simple elements', 'the turns of passion, always different, yet not palpably different', 'words . . . in their minds . . . impregnated with passion', and the last very precise distinction between the appearance of rapid movement in the poem, and its real quality of slow, eddying growth.

It was apparently while he meditated on this rather ludicrous lay figure, and on these perceptive definitions, that Wordsworth really tumbled to what he had done, not only in *The Thorn* itself, but also in many other poems. This is the real basis of his own realisation of the nature of his special diction, and also, therefore, the soundest basis for a study of it:

Upon this occasion I will request permission to add a few words closely connected with 'The Thorn' and many other Poems in these volumes. There is a numerous class of readers who imagine that the same words cannot be repeated without tautology: this is a great error: virtual tautology is much oftener produced by using different words when the meaning is exactly the

same. Words, a Poet's words more particularly, ought to be weighed in the balance of feeling, and not measured by the space which they occupy upon paper. For the Reader cannot be too often reminded that Poetry is passion: it is the history or science of feelings; now every man must know that an attempt is rarely made to communicate impassioned feelings without something of an accompanying consciousness of the inadequateness of our own powers, or the deficiencies of language. During such efforts there will be a craving in the mind, and as long as it is unsatisfied the speaker will cling to the same words, or words of the same character. There are also various other reasons why repetition and apparent tautology are frequently beauties of the highest kind. Among the chief of these reasons is the interest which the mind attaches to words, not only as symbols of the passion, but as *things*, active and efficient, which are themselves part of the passion. And further, from a spirit of fondness, exultation, and gratitude, the mind luxuriates in the repetition of words which appear successfully to communicate its feelings.
(*PW* II, 513)

In this passage, Wordsworth brings his own practical and immediate experience of a particular act of writing into line with his more general views on the active role of language in determining feeling and thought. The dictum, 'virtual tautology is much oftener produced by using different words when the meaning is the same', defines exactly the abuses of poetic diction against which he was striving – 'the finny tribe', 'the feathered kind', and all their non-variant variations. And, above all, in his statement that 'repetition and apparent tautology are frequently beauties of the highest kind', he is describing exactly his own practice, not only in poems where the form is one based on repetition, such as *The Thorn*, *Poor Susan*, and many other of the stanzaic poems, but also, as became evident in the analysis of the 'spots of time' descriptions above, in his most weighty blank verse.

There is only one important aspect of this poetic style which is not mentioned here – and it would have needed an almost preternatural gift of prophecy for him to have seen it at that moment, since it involved his whole future development as a writer. It was this: the effects of repetition and apparent tautology were not by any means necessarily confined to particular poems, or to short passages in the longer poems. On the contrary, they naturally tended to extend their influence from poem to poem, over the whole range of his writing – even to his prose. Once a word, together with its close associates, 'words of the same character' as he puts it, had effectively become a *thing*, or a group of things, in his mode of expressing feeling and thought, it was never quite the same again. And when it had been used repeatedly, by a kind of extended tautology, in poem after poem, in year after year, as his meditations eddied round in their circling progress, such word-things would acquire a power in *his* vocabulary, in *his* poetry, quite out of proportion to their usual force in the language really spoken by men, even though they might well be a very common part of it. The 'selection', in fact, was made by this completely personal, individual process, and not by any general or philosophic or political principles whatever. And it was upon words thus selected that his highly individual poetry was based.

It is this use of language, above all, that should determine the approach to his poetic style. Many of the methods so much and – on the whole – so effectively used in modern criticism are simply inapplicable to Wordsworth's best and most characteristic writing. It will yield very little to the deft analyser of imagery. For there is very little imagery, and most of what there is turns out to be almost commonplace. It will not fall readily under the scalpel of the 'New Critics', or conform to the coding of 'structuralism'. What is needed in the study of Wordsworth is not ingenuity or brilliance, but a dogged faithfulness to his own text, aided by the Concordance and a good memory for the many important variants and drafts not yet Concordanced. For the only way of determining the meaning of any word in his poetry is to take all its contexts together; and to ensure that the closest attention is indeed given to those words which, by the process of repetition and tautology, had come to bear in it a weight, a power, greater than they usually carry. It is for this reason that readers of Wordsworth are addicts or nothing. The casual or desultory reader never gives himself the chance of becoming sensitised to these words, and, taking them at their usual instead of their Wordsworthian weight, he is simply puzzled that anyone has ever taken the poetry very seriously. But once a certain point in this sensitisation is reached, there is a sudden, an almost inexplicable extension in understanding, as personal and intimate as the language through which it has been reached.

Wordsworth's tautologous words may in one respect be compared with those recurrent images which critics find so significant in Shakespeare, as expressions of the internal coherence of scenes and acts, and of the broader imaginative bearings of each play. The tautologies also link one passage with another, and bring out powerfully the dominant trains of thought and feeling throughout the poetry. The comparison, however, ends here, in certain resemblances of function. The tautology is in itself very different from the Shakespearean image. First, it is only rarely an image, and even more rarely a striking one; it may, as a word, have concrete origins or associations, but in its characteristic use in Wordsworth it is nearly abstract. Secondly, the tautologies do not, like the images, vary from one play to another; they remain constant throughout the whole body of the poetry. Thirdly, they do not, as the images often do, suggest broader, universal implications of a particular or limited action or saying; on the contrary, they derive much of their special power from their frequent use in association with universal processes. And finally, they are clearly marked off from images by an inherent numerical, even statistical characteristic; their force derives, not merely from their own meanings, but from the frequency of their use, and the manner of it.

6

> The purer elements of truth involved
> In lines and numbers . . .
>
> *The Excursion* 1.253–4 (*PW* v, 16)

The notion of repetition, of frequency of occurrence of words, even though Wordsworth himself introduced it into his own discussion of his manner of writing, is not to be welcomed with much enthusiasm. It might, indeed, be disposed of easily and quickly, if it were only a question of simple and local repetition in *The Thorn* and a few other poems. But it is quite a different matter to explore the uses of frequently repeated words where the repetition is not local and obvious, but pervasive, and unobtrusive at first sight. Two main issues are involved. First, what exactly is meant by such repetition, such heightened frequency? And second, if it is found, what are its effects upon the words so used?

Unfortunately, both of these problems can also be approached in one of two very different ways. The first method of approach is that of the literary critic, who depends upon his general impressions, based upon (let us hope) a careful reading of the text, and supported by a few illustrations and comparisons. The second method is that of the linguist, who is bound to investigate the facts of the matter more extensively and objectively, and to ask such questions as these: how far can a word be regarded as being frequent in the work of any writer in terms of that writer alone? Is it enough that he uses it very often in comparison with other words in his vocabulary? Or is it necessary to compare the frequency of its occurrences in him with its frequency in some other author, or a whole group of authors? Can any practical meaning be attached to the idea that each word may have a sort of average frequency of occurrence in any language? And if any word is found to exceed this by a large margin, what effect may this exceptional frequency of use have upon the meaning, or meanings attached to it? All these questions are so difficult to answer simply that it would be better if they had never been asked. But once they have been asked, it is almost more difficult merely to dismiss them.

And it is the more difficult because they are all more or less involved in the assumptions usually made by literary critics, above all when they come to deal with 'style'. In doing so, they are all loyal followers of the great French zoologist, Buffon, who announced in the course of his official discourse on election to the Académie that 'le style c'est l'homme même'. They assume that in some respects, every writer – at least every considerable writer – uses his native language in a manner of his own, distinguished from that of other users. He will have certain turns of phrase, patterns of syntax, and above all he will have some favourite words, which he uses more often than others, either because they are related to topics of special concern to him, or because they are embedded in linguistic habits imposed by his social and educational background. They are, in fact, what a linguist would probably call his *idiolect*, the special form of a natural language used by one individual, as a *dialect* is the special form used by those who live in one district, or who belong to one class or profession.

It may well be that in dealing with many other writers – perhaps most others – it is enough to follow the usual impressionistic method of literary criticism in discussing this aspect of style or idiolect. But since Wordsworth himself drew attention to it as a special aspect of his own writing, it is almost necessary, in this case at least, to take the problem seriously and as systematically as is possible at present. It must be added at once, by way of warning, that the supply of hard facts in this field is still very limited. We know very little about the frequencies of words, in particular authors, in groups of authors, or in large mixed samples of authors. And we know hardly any more about the implications of such figures as we have, and about the ways of eliciting them. There is, however, just enough information of both kinds to make possible a beginning of an answer to some of the questions asked above, and enough is now known of the methods of handling it to avoid some of the more obvious dangers. And even the very tentative answers that can now be given offer some new suggestions about Wordsworth's way of using his tautologous words.

It so happens, moreover, that an attempt was made to study Wordsworth's vocabulary numerically by Franklin Bliss Snyder as early at 1923.[8] It is still of the greatest interest, for it started from the usual assumptions about the problem of style, or idiolect, and tried to make them more precise, first by listing the most frequent words in Wordsworth, then by comparing the result with similar lists compiled from several other poets, and it went on to suggest – though much more vaguely – some questions about the relation between the frequency of words and their uses, or meanings. It was probably inevitable that any such attempt made at that time would meet with little success. The material available for comparative purposes was even more scant than it is today. The large accumulation of word-lists which were made in the thirties and forties still lay ahead. And worst of all, the theoretical and practical problems besetting this kind of study were almost entirely unexplored. Snyder was almost bound to fail. And fail he did, in all three phases of his inquiry, but in such a way as to make a study of his failure thoroughly profitable even now. There could be no better introduction to the problems themselves, and to the methods which are beginning to emerge for solving them.[9]

Snyder with proper caution acknowledged at once that words by themselves, taken as separate lexical units, are something very different from their actual uses in syntactical structures and in their larger contexts. But he went on to define his limited aim thus: 'Nevertheless there will probably be some interest in finding out what the poet's favorite words really were – favorite in the sense that he used them most often – and, once ascertained, the list may throw a little light on Wordsworth's mental habits and poetic practice' (p. 253). He proposed to gather his material from the Concordance, though this meant omitting such common words as *the*, *and*, *in*, since they were not included by the editor. Moreover, the listing of many other common words, such as *about*, *one*, *very*, was incomplete. He himself added to these omissions by leaving out of his list some words which, as he says, he 'arbitrarily' judged to be without significance, such as *long*. With these omissions, he presented this list, arranged approximately in order of frequency:

> Love, heart, man, mind, life, eye, nature, power, light, earth, heaven, hope, pleasure, soul, spirit, truth, joy, sun, shadow, death, mountain, time, hand, fear, night, happy, friend, flower, deep, child, rock, rest, vale, place, silent, sight, sound, fair, free, human, peace, wood, word, wind, cloud, field, bliss, beauty. (p. 254)

There are 48 words here, and Snyder noted that the first, *love*, had occurred over 1100 times, and the last, *beauty*, about 300 times. From this list he reached his first conclusion:

> Here is the vocabulary of a man who lived much in the open, and enjoyed the nature of which he wrote: *light*, *earth*, *sun*, *shadow*, *mountain*, *night*, *flower*, *rock*, *vale*, *wood*, *wind*, *cloud*, *field*. Here is the vocabulary of a lover of men: *heart*, *man*, *mind*, *soul*, *spirit*, *friend*, *child*, *happy*, *human*, *free*. Here is the vocabulary of one whose life among men and in the fields brought him the quiet happiness which others seek in his poetry: *love*, *power*, *hope*, *pleasure*, *truth*, *joy*, *rest*, *peace*, *bliss*, *beauty*, *silence*. Or to put the matter differently, here in these *disjecta membra* of Wordsworth's poetry is the material from which even a bungling artificer can construct the fundamental framework of the poet's philosophy. (pp. 254–5)

No doubt he could. But there are easier and more reliable ways of doing it. Yet the fact that this investigation revealed only what was already obvious would be no disadvantage, if this were to be regarded as a preliminary test of a new method of study. Its general correctness, its banality even, would go some way to prove its applicability, and it might be possible to go on next to more novel discoveries, once the method had been tried and perhaps improved by trial.

But is the method being used here a correct one, apt for handling the kind of material to which it has been applied? There can, of course, be no doubt that the first step in any study of this kind is to make a list of the word-frequencies in the writer with whom the student is chiefly concerned. And so far Snyder is following a proper method. But it is much less certain that he was right in supposing that any conclusions might be drawn from this list – even if the list itself were to be regarded as adequately made – without comparing it with any other list of the same kind. It would readily occur to any reader of English literature that words like *man*, *eye*, *heart* and *hand* are very frequently used in all our writers: that they are, so to speak, everyone's 'favorite words'. One would expect them to occur very frequently in Wordsworth too, but this would be without any special significance as evidence of his 'mental habits and poetic practice', unless it were clear that he used them even more frequently than most other writers. At first sight, it would seem that Snyder, while rightly making his starting-point a list of Wordsworth's word-frequencies, was wrong in supposing that useful conclusions might be drawn from this alone. Any frequency, including that of words, is relative, not absolute. It is either high or low, or somewhere between the two, only in relation to other frequencies of the same kind. And there appears not to be any real sense in which the comparison of word-frequencies within a single text could be made significant.

In making these premature conclusions, however, Snyder was probably misled to some extent by the kind of list he had compiled from the Concordance. He had wholly omitted from consideration the really common words, and also the many words for which only partial lists are given. He was left with only a part of the whole vocabulary in use, and what was worse, he was without any indication of the total number of word-occurrences to which this vocabulary gives rise in the text, or of the contribution to this total made by each word. This Concordance, in fact, does not give the whole of the text, nor is it an adequate substitute for the text. We shall perhaps be able to see more clearly how it is deficient, and why it misled Snyder, if we contemplate an actual sample of the text, though necessarily a small one. Table II gives the first 875 words of Book II of *The Prelude*, re-arranged so as to show clearly the relative frequencies of the words used. The numbers in the left-hand column show how many times each word has occurred: those in the right-hand column

Table II

61	the	1
45	and	1
30	of	1
27	be (*including inflected forms*)	1
21	a	1
19	to	1
16	in	1
13	we, with	2
10	I, our	2
9	from	1
8	who	1
7	or	1
6	have (*including inflected forms*), my, yet	3
5	by, for, might, now, old, on, so, than, there	9
4	its, one, more, though, when	5
3	come, day, friend, ground, hence, if, know, left, not, round, stone, thus, where, which, year	15
2	alike, birds, both, but, corporeal, daily, dame, desire, every, fields, green, grey, give, her, holiday, island, large, length, mind, month, much, nor, place, pride, race, river, sand, sate, small, soft, solitude, some, sports, spur, steed, still, strength, summer, supplied, sweetly, through, time, trees, walls, week, will, woods	47
1	(*a*) after, along, amid, among, asleep, beat, bed, befal, before, Being, beneath, best, between, birth, black, blessing, boisterous, bound, boyish, breezes, bright, brightly, built, cannot, childhood, church, clouds, cool, could, dark, deep, delight, do, doors, drew, dropped, drops, earth, edged, else, empty, ended, ever, fare, fast, fearless, feel, fiddle, first, flew, frame, games, giddy, gloom, gone, grazed, half-holidays, half-yearly, half-years, haply, happy, he, heart, hoard, holy, home, horses, how, huckster, hunger, inland, inn-keeper, ivy, knight, last, later, leaves, leaving, led, less, let, like, lingerer, little, long, loud, love, man, mankind, meals, mid-day, midway, mouldering, myself, named, needs, nights, no, none, O, oak, oars, often, once, other, Our Lady, overhead, penniless, perhaps, proud, purse, ran, rested, rock, roofless, scant, scream, seem, seen, shade, shady, shelter, shone, showers, shrine, shuddering, side, sister, sixty, skill, sly, smart, smooth, sobbings, sometimes, sown, span, stands, starry, stars, steps, stirring, stud, sun, sweep, sweeping, tame, taught, tell, temper, them, then, these, think, third, thither, three, threshold, till, too, truth, turf, twinkling, two, uncouth, unfelt, unsapped, unsought, uproar, walked, want, wares, warning, watched, ways, weary, weekly, weightier, went, west, whip, while, wide, wind, winning, wisest, wished, within, worshipped, wren, ye, you, yore, young (195)	
1	(*b*) abbey, absence, add, adventure, aim, air, antique, appear, approach, arch, assembly-room, assiduous, attached, belfry, bench, blame, bourne, calmer, ceased, centre, chair, chanted, chauntry, chiefly, collaterally, comfortless, conquered, conqueror, conscious, consciousness, continued, costly, course, courteous, covert, covets, cross-legged, curb, dedicate, delicate, diffidence, dinners, disappointment, distant, divisions, druids, duly, duty, eager, eagerness, employ, endeavoured, ensued, exclude, failed, faint, famed, feverish, forms, fountains, fractured, frugal, funds, furnish, future, galloping, grateful, honour, images, independence, infantine, intellect, internal, invisible, isle, jealousy, joints, joy, labourer, languidly, largely,	

Table II (*Cont.*)

market, mass, modesty, motion, motionless, musical, musing, native, Nature, nave, neglected, nourishment, ocean, pain, passion, pass-time, peace, pile, plain, pleased, pleasures, poverty, power, presses, produced, prolonged, pursued, quartered, quiet, quietness, recent, regular, remained, remounted, repaired, repose, respirations, retrace, revelry, rites, rival, rude, ruins, rustic, Sabine, safe-guard, scene, scheme, school, selected, self-esteem, self-presence, self-sufficing, sequestered, served, silent, simple, single, spirit, square, stipend, stone-abbot, subterfuge, sufficed, summons, superior, survived, sustained, table, temple, touched, towers, treats, tumult, tumultuous, umbrageous, uneasiness, union, unvisited, usurped, vacancy, vainglory, vale, viands, vigorous, village, virtue, voice (169)

Total (a) and (b):	364
Total of all words:	457

show how many words have occurred that number of times. Words occurring once have been divided into (*a*) those derived from Teutonic sources and (*b*) those wholly or partly Romance.

It is remarkable how many of the problems which beset the study of words may be deduced from this one table. For it is, after all, but a minute sample of *The Prelude* itself – under 1000 words out of about 60,000, a still minuter fraction of Wordsworth's verse, which amounts to about 400,000 words of text, and but an infinitesimal part of the vast wordage represented by the major authors who make up 'English literature' – let alone all the other writings in English, literary and otherwise. It is necessary, of course, to bear in mind its smallness, but its suggestions are so unequivocal that it is usually possible to predict with some certainty how these problems will be changed as the size of the sample examined increases.

The first difficulty in the way of listing 'favorite words' in F. B. Snyder's fashion is real enough, but comparatively trivial. It is suggested by the very obvious fact that in the upper part of the range of word-frequencies, the words making up the vocabulary (the total 'stock' of words used, irrespective of their number of uses) are clearly separated into an order of ranks (1st, 2nd, 3rd etc.), because each of them occurs a different number of times. Lower down in the list, however, they are grouped in larger and larger 'clusters' of many words all having the same frequency. Thus *we* and *with* each occur 13 times, *I* and *our* 10 times. It is possible to describe such pairs as 'equal eighth' or 'equal tenth', like candidates in a competitive examination, but this way of ranking them begins to look very artificial even when we go down to the 15 words which occur 3 times each, for they would have to be called 'equal 31st'. As for the largest single group, those which occur but once, they would have to be described as 'equal 94th', and this is not a very illuminating way of describing 364 words out of the 457 which make up the whole vocabulary.

Moreover, a little reflection shows that this difficulty will not decrease as the size of the sample grows. On the contrary, it will become more serious. As the sample is enlarged, more words at the top of the list will tend to become separated by occurring distinct numbers of times, but in the lower part of the list, the 'clustering' will also increase, and it seems all too probable that even in very large samples, we shall meet with a long list of words which occur once each, which cannot be ranked numerically at all. These abstract expectations are confirmed fully by comparing this minute sample with the whole text of *Ulysses* by James Joyce.[10] This consists of some 260,000 word-occurrences, and has a vocabulary of about 30,000 words. The most frequent 101 words each have distinct numbers of occurrence, but words 102 and 103 both occur 252 times – clustering has begun. The 1000th word is concealed somewhere in a cluster of 48 words, each of which occurs 26 times, and the 10,000th is hidden somewhere in among 4776 words, while the number of words which occur once each is a great haystack of 16,432 – more than half the total vocabulary. The large sample, in fact, makes the ranking of words even more difficult than does the small one.

The comparison between these two samples, however, suggests very much more than this. Indeed the implications of these figures are so many and so surprising that they are rather like a Jack-in-a-box. They reveal, in fact, the two main features of all word-distribution lists made in this way. The first of these is that words, when so listed, sort themselves out into two large classes, one of those very frequent, the other of those very infrequent, with but a small intermediate group between them. Of the many ways in which this could be illustrated, this is one:

In the small sample, the 364 words which occur once account for 37% of the word-occurrences. The most frequent tenth of the vocabulary (words occurring 3 or more times) accounts for 42.4% of occurrences. The middle group is therefore 20.6% of occurrences.

In the large sample, the 16,432 'oncers' account for 6.3% of occurrences. The most frequent tenth of the vocabulary (words found 8 or more times) accounts for 80% of occurrences. The middle group is 13.7% of the occurrences.

Both sets of figures, then, show how strongly words tend to be either very frequent or very infrequent, and it seems likely, even from this one comparison, that the middle group will tend to be smaller, the larger the sample taken.

The second characteristic of these two samples, however, is even more fraught with awkward consequences. It is that, while they agree in making the middle group of words relatively small, they do it in quite different ways. The smaller sample cuts it down, so to speak, both at the top and at the bottom, in nearly equal proportions; 42% of all occurrences are taken up by the 'top' tenth of the vocabulary, and 37% by the 'oncers'. In the *Ulysses* sample, on the other hand, the cutting-down is done almost entirely at the top. For 80% of the occurrences fall to the top tenth of the vocabulary, and only 6% to the oncers. It is clear that there has been a large change in the internal make-up of the distribution, as the size of the sample has grown.

This change is, however, one that can be predicted on general principles, if we contemplate the probable results of increasing the size of the sample or – what comes to the same thing – increasing the number of samples of the same size. With each addition, the 'score' of the very frequent words will increase, roughly in proportion to the size of the added samples. Lower down in the list, some words will both increase their 'score', and improve their position relative to their former neighbours; others, however, while increasing their scores, may well fall lower in the ranking order. Towards the bottom of the list, the number of words in each group, especially that of 'oncers', will certainly grow, but its growth will slow down eventually because it is subject to an ultimate limit: the number of words available for use. In the case of a very large mixed sample, from many different writers, this limit must be something like the half-million words which – so the editors claim – are to be found listed in the *OED*. In the case of a particular writer, it will be very much smaller, depending upon his age, educational status, range of interest, and so on. The actual figure here is difficult to fix, since account must be taken not only of words used by the writer, but also of those which he might have used – those words which he recognises or understands when he meets with them elsewhere, though he does not yet happen to have used them himself. The best available information suggests that, for a well-educated and wide-ranging writer, the total vocabulary will lie between 40,000 and 50,000 words.[11] When, therefore, James Joyce used 30,000 words in *Ulysses*, he was making use of much the greater part of his personal vocabulary, and, had the book been twice as long as it is, the addition of infrequent words to the whole vocabulary would have been comparatively small, and quite certainly not in proportion to the increase in the size of the sample.

This very important change in the proportions of word-frequency lists in response to increase in size of sample may be envisaged in a more concrete way by those not used to more abstract expositions in this field. Suppose the sample to be very small, so that each word in it occurs but once. We may represent this by imagining a small snake, lying horizontally along the ground at the foot of a wall, with its body at right angles to the wall. Now envisage the snake beginning to grow, and thus to represent an increase in the size of the samples in the word-list. A few of them will now occur more than once, and if they are taken to be the head of the serpent, it may be imagined to raise its head a little way up the wall, with an uncomfortably sharp bend in its neck. As its growth continues, the head and upper part of its body will rise higher and higher up the wall, but a large proportion of its body – at least half – will remain flat along the ground. Meanwhile the bend behind its head will have become slightly less uncomfortable, for it will have become a little more rounded, and will be somewhere in its body instead of in its neck. The general posture will not have changed very much, since the samples became fairly large, but – and it is this that matters – the proportions of the body occupying various positions in this posture will have changed considerably. And it is this internal change within the whole shape that makes the ranking of words in order of 'favoritism' difficult, if not impossible. For the place of any word will depend not only upon the choice of the author, his mental and linguistic habits, but also upon the size of the sample upon which the list is based.

There is, moreover, another less obvious but still more important difference between the two parts of the snake, horizontal and vertical. The frequent words have one kind of numerical behaviour, the infrequent ones another. This can best be illustrated by extending our samples from *The Prelude*. Let us now add the first 1000 words from Book I, and from Books III to X, thus giving altogether ten samples of roughly the same size. These are the figures for the occurrences of *the* in each of them:

48 61 42 36 48 29 36 45 59 53

These figures vary a good deal, and it so happens that the one for Book II, in the table above, is the highest of all, and proves to have been somewhat misleading. On the other hand, there is a *prima facie* air of consistency about this row of numbers. It is obvious that their average lies a little below 46, and that 7 of them lie no more than 10 away from this average. In such cases, the non-mathematical layman is inclined to have an intuition that if the sampling were to continue, the average would tend to settle down at some one figure, or within a very small range of values, while the number of eccentric figures would not be very large. It is the same kind of intuition which makes him feel that, were he to toss a coin for a few minutes, the proportions of heads and tails might not be nearly equal, at 50% each, but that if he were to persist in the experiment for a whole day, these proportions would be very near to 50%, while the number of times on which 10 heads or 10 tails had turned up in succession would be very small. And this intuition turns out to be movable on to more solid ground, for the statistician and the mathematician have been able to find good reasons why it should be so. It is often called, with unusual lucidity, 'the law of large numbers', and more precisely it states that if the proportion of occurrences of a particular event, p, is relatively high compared with the proportion of its non-occurrences, q, and if the total number of occurrences examined is large, then both p and q will approximate to their values according to the laws of probability. The word *the* fulfils the first of these conditions, for it is clearly the most frequent single word that can 'eventuate' in Wordsworth's text. If we were to fulfil the second condition, by taking more and larger samples of the text, we should discover with a fair degree of certainty the steady average rate of its occurrence. If the sample were to include the whole text, we should of course know this for a certainty. Fortunately there is no need to go so far, since an average based on much smaller samples is clearly reliable enough for all practical purposes.

The same intuition, and the same principle, hold good for words much less frequent than *the*. For example, in the table above the word *for* occurs only 5 times, at a little less than one-tenth of the rate of occurrence of *the*. But the same 10 samples from *The Prelude* give these figures for its occurrences:

2 5 5 1 2 3 2 3 3 3

These numbers are even steadier than those for *the*, and one would have the right to be surprised if larger samples showed a very different result.[12] But when we go to the lower part of the list, to the horizontal portions of the serpent, the position is very different. Take, for example, *love*, the most frequent of Snyder's 'favorite words'. This is found 1100 times in the whole text of 400,000 words, so that its average rate of occurrence is much lower than that of *the* and *for*. And it will be noticed that it occurs but once in the table. If the occurrences are counted in the 10 samples of 1000 words each from *The Prelude* they give these figures:

1 1 0 1 0 1 2 2 1 0

It is not so easy to have comforting intuitions about a row of figures like these – indeed it is not easy to have any at all. An average can, of course, be calculated (it is 0.9) but it does not feel as though further samples would be very likely to settle down around it. The figures look more erratic, and look like remaining so over many samples. Let us, however, compare it with the word which Snyder placed lowest in his list of 'favorite words', *beauty*. He remarks that this word occurs about 300 times in the whole text of Wordsworth. This is less than one-third of the occurrences of *love*. Yet in our 10 samples for *The Prelude* these are its occurrences:

0 0 1 1 1 0 0 3 1 2

Table III

	% of occurrences		
	Prelude	Ulysses	actual
the	6.1	5.7	(14,877)
and	4.5	2.8	(7170)
of	3	3	(7786)
a	2.1	2.5	(6396)
to	1.9	1.9	(4907)
in	1.6	1.9	(4884)

Their total is 9, exactly the same as the total for *love*. It is at once apparent that, in dealing with words of relatively low frequency, the variation of occurrences from one sample to another tends to be large. Or, to put the same thing in another way, the rate of their occurrence is not, and does not tend to be, consistent throughout the text. One piece of it will be very different from another. There is, indeed, at least one sample of 1000 words in *The Prelude*, lines 140–270 in Book XIII, which contains 15 occurrences of *love* – a figure which could not be predicted from the 10 samples already given.

Since words, as we have seen, tend to occur either very frequently or very infrequently, this distinction between large and small numbers of occurrence is central to the study of vocabularies and their behaviour. For these two main groups of words assume directly contrasting characteristics, in their numerical and in their more 'literary' aspects. One group, that of very frequent words, presents enough numerical regularity to make it amenable to quite reliable study. This is clearly illustrated by a comparison between the first 6 words in our very small sample from *The Prelude* and our large one from *Ulysses* (see Table III). They are in each case the same 6 words, at approximately the same rates of occurrence, and with but one change in their rank.[13] But as against this numerical regularity, these high-frequency words are of little interest from a literary point of view.[14] They do not result from choices on the part of the writer, from his selection of topics or his linguistic habits. They are imposed on him by the laws of chance, in the sense that they result from the simple fact that he has chosen to write in a language in which these words have these probabilities of occurrence. Most of them are articles, pronouns, prepositions, conjunctions and auxiliary verbs. Indeed in the top 100 words of *Ulysses* apart from words of these kinds there are only 7, the nouns *Bloom* (30th), *Stephen* (56th), *toe* (65th), *man* (70th), *eyes* (80th), *hand* (90th), and *street* (93rd).[15]

Table IV

	Wordsworth	Shakespeare	%+ or − difference
man	1400	2000	+43
love	1100	2200	+100
heart	1030	1040	0
time	670	740	+10
mind	650	360	−45
life	650	720	+11
eye	650	910	+40
soul	640	440	−31
nature	630	350	−45
power	630	370	−41
earth	630	350	−45
heaven	630	640	0
sun	600	200	−67
hope	560	380	−32
joy	470	320	−32
spirit	450	300	−33
light	450	200	−56
mountain	380	60	−158
fear	360	580	+61
hand	320	880	+175
truth	310	250	−19
death	230	820	+213
pleasure	230	170	−26
shadow	130	80	−38

The other main group of words, those of low frequency, are exactly opposite in their numerical and 'literary' characteristics. These are precisely the words with which the critic is concerned, for they represent choices on the writer's part, in topics and in language itself. But they represent choices only because they are exempt from the laws of chance, from the overall probabilities of word-occurrence. And because of this freedom from subjection to the laws of probability, they are the very words that are not amenable to simple numerical analysis. Little or no significance can be attached to their rank in a single list, derived from the work of one writer.[16]

F. B. Snyder, then, was unfortunate in his attempt to draw significant conclusions from the list of words which he obtained for Wordsworth alone. But this was, after all, only the first step in his investigation. The second step was more promising, because it recognised the fact that frequencies of words are necessarily relative, that the idiolect of one writer is determined by its differences from the idiolects of others. Having extracted what information he could from this first list, Snyder went on to ask the necessary question: '"But," one asks, "is the use of these words in any way really Wordsworthian? Will it not appear that most English poets make similar habitual use of them?"' (p. 255). He went on to complete similar lists from the Concordances of Spenser, Shakespeare, Gray, Cowper, Shelley, Keats and Tennyson. These lists (or parts of them) were then placed together, and some deductions were made about the relative frequencies of all the words in all the lists. They did not turn out to be, from a literary point of view, very interesting. What was worse, they were open to two objections, one very serious, the other crucial. First, no account was taken of the very different sizes of the samples on which the lists had been based and, as we have seen, size of sample is always of importance in determining the frequencies of words. In a sense, what Snyder was doing was simply to compare, by a very roundabout and unreliable method, all these poets in respect of the amount they happened to have written. Still worse, however, was the fact that each of these lists was open to the objections already raised to his list from Wordsworth: all of them dealt with those words which, because of their relative infrequency, cannot safely be numbered in this way. He was, in fact, comparing the one set of nearly random figures with several other sets of the same kind. The results of making this attempt can best be illustrated by taking an example. See Table IV, where the first 24 of Snyder's 'favorite words' from Wordsworth are compared with the same words in Shakespeare. Against each word is the approximate number of occurrences in each writer, with a column giving the % difference of Shakespeare's uses from Wordsworth's.[17] What is at once obvious is the very wide range of variation here, and the general air of independence of the two distributions. Only in two cases, those of *death* and *hand* does the ratio between the two writers approximate to that which might have been expected, if this ratio were simply determined by the size of sample. For the ratio of Shakespeare's word occurrences to Wordsworth's is about 2 to 1 (800,000 to 400,000). Quite clearly this is not a suitable method of adjusting our expectations of occurrences for differing sizes of sample. Indeed the table fails to suggest any such method. One can hardly say more of these comparisons than that the greatest caution should be used in drawing any conclusions from them, and that only when the differences between them are great should any conclusions be drawn at all. For example, they probably demonstrate that Wordsworth used *sun* and *mountain* much more frequently than Shakespeare. More tentatively they may indicate that the same is true of *mind*, *soul*, *nature*, *power*, *earth*, *hope*, *joy*, *spirit*, *light* and *shadow*. Of these 24 'favorite words', in fact, the comparison reinforces the view of Snyder in 10 cases. On the other hand, it also shows that *man*, *love*, *eye*, *fear* and *death* cannot reasonably be regarded as words specially favoured by Wordsworth, since they occur in Shakespeare many more times. And about the remaining 9 words it would be wrong to draw any conclusions at all, for the difference either way is too small.

Meagre as these results are, they are obviously liable to two serious objections, which must diminish their value even further. First, since about two centuries separate the two writers, there may well have been differences in the word-frequencies of English itself, quite apart from those of the two individuals. Certainly some words were in the language in 1800 which were not there in 1600. But this objection is perhaps less serious than it looks at first sight, because the proportion of words added to the language after 1600 is, in fact, relatively small, if we exclude technical and scientific terms, which neither Shakespeare nor Wordsworth would have been likely to use anyhow. Nevertheless, differences in the date of authors being compared should not be forgotten, for there may be cases in which they are crucial. The second objection goes much deeper. It is that we have no reason to suppose that Shakespeare offers a suitable measuring-rod for frequencies of word-use; on the contrary, there is every reason to suppose that he had his own 'favorite words', and that the list of frequencies drawn from his works represents these personal preferences and not any objective standard; and this will be true even though he offers a fairly large sample. The only way of overcoming this difficulty would be to make similar comparisons between word-frequencies in all the other authors named by Snyder – Spenser, Gray, Cowper, Shelley, Keats and Tennyson – adding to them all those writers for whose verse Concordances have been published more recently, such as Donne, Dryden, Pope, Arnold. But it is all too clear that the labour of making such lists would be far greater than the results are likely to justify. The mathematical technique, moreover, involved in comparing the large number of figures would be complex, and would pass far beyond the stage at which it could be followed and checked by the common-sense, or intuition, of the merely literary scholar.

Nevertheless, from all these negative conclusions, one or two helpfully positive ones may be rescued. In this comparison, there was good reason to believe that some words used by Wordsworth were indeed specially frequent in his work, and this is worth knowing. Similar conclusions may reasonably be made, in similar comparisons, whenever the margin of differences between the occurrences in the authors compared is very large, always having regard to the differences in the sizes of the texts on which their Concordances are based. We shall shortly make use of a few comparisons of this kind.

Since Snyder wrote his article on Wordsworth's vocabulary, another way of establishing comparisons between one writer and another has been tried, and it offers some attractive possibilities, as well as a few immediate uses. It rests upon the assumption that it should be possible to take a very large number of samples from many writers, by no means all of them 'literary' in the technical sense, and so to determine, for each word in a given language, a kind of average or standard frequency, against which the usages of particular writers might be measured. Theoretically, there is much to be said for this, since there is always an advantage in having very large samples. And the outstanding attempt to achieve such a list, that made by Professors Thorndike and Lorge and published in 1944, is a notable example of what can be, and even more of what might be achieved by this method. Their *Teacher's Word Book of 30,000 Words* was based upon a mixture of samples amounting in all to 18 million words of English of all kinds, from literature, journals, private letters, text-books, concordances and other word-lists, and collections of quotations. The work of listing the words and their frequencies was all done 'by hand', and was only possible with the aid of the Federal unemployment relief agency in the great economic depression of the 1930s. If, and when, another such list is made, it will certainly be done by computers, and very probably it will not be thought of until computers, and those who manage them, are in need of some kind of unemployment relief programme. For computers, like human beings, do not turn their attention to literature and linguistic problems associated with it until they have a good deal of leisure at their disposal.

In the meantime, the Thorndike–Lorge list deserves to be more widely used, though with the caution due to its inherent defects, which were many, and mostly inevitable in a pioneer enterprise. Its method of choosing samples, for example, was lacking in system, and it lumped together the linguistic usages of many different periods of history without distinction. The results of the listing, moreover, were presented in a way which makes the book difficult to use by students of language, however it may have suited the 'teachers' for whom it was intended. Homonyms are not distinguished, so that Hamlet is irretrievably confounded with *hamlet*, and the actual frequencies of occurrence in the main list can only be extracted with the utmost difficulty, though it is somewhat easier to see whether a particular word falls into the 1st, 2nd, 3rd thousand and so on, down to the 30th, and this is often well worth knowing. It is at its best and most reliable, as one would expect, in providing data for dealing with large groups of words, such as long and short, Teutonic and Romance, old and new. Used in this way, it not only yields meaningful results, but is capable of passing the far harder test of predicting accurately the results of further analyses. It is at its weakest in suggesting the relative frequencies of particular words, but even here it can give useful, if rather vague, information, and some examples of its use will be found in the following pages.

7

I am sensible that my associations must have sometimes been particular instead of general, and that, consequently . . . I may have sometimes written upon unworthy subjects; but I am less apprehensive on this account, than that my language may frequently have suffered from those arbitrary connections of feelings and ideas with particular words, and phrases, from which no man can altogether protect himself . . . [T]he critic ought never to forget that he is himself exposed to the same errors as the Poet, and, perhaps, in a much greater degree: for there can be no presumption in saying of most readers, that it is not probable they will be so well acquainted with the various stages of meaning through which words have passed, or with the fickleness or stability of the relation of particular ideas to each other.

Preface to *Lyrical Ballads* (*PW* II, 402)

It needs no effort of imagination on my part to suppose that the last few pages have been very painful to many readers. It is bad enough to plague them with lists of figures. But it is even worse to do so while admitting that they prove very little, and cannot be made to prove more than a very little. Worst of all must be the strong suspicion that what matters about words is not, after all, the number of times they occur, but what they mean, whenever they are used.

It must be made clear at once, then, that these prolegomena about the frequency of words have been an unfortunately necessary introduction to the much more positive study of the relation between their frequencies and their meanings. Here, at last, we begin to stand on firm ground, from which some further advances seem to be possible. And here again it happens that we rejoin Wordsworth's own sense of what he was doing, for we shall be concerned precisely with the possibility that his 'language may . . . have suffered from those arbitrary connections of feelings and ideas with particular words and phrases from which no man can altogether protect himself'. Indeed we shall find some reason for believing that the specific quality of his poetic style was that it developed an extensive network of just such connections, and that they were not so much 'arbitrary' as personal aspects of his idiolect.

The relation between frequency and meaning was briefly mentioned by F. B. Snyder in his discussion of the list of Wordsworth's 'favorite words':

I realize that this plan might result in some misrepresentations, if many of the words listed were capable of widely different meanings; but as it happens that most of the words involved have one outstanding meaning, I believe the practice which I have adopted, and which again is in keeping with that of the Concordance, will not materially distort the facts.

('Wordsworth's Favorite Words', p. 254)

It must be supposed that what Snyder meant by this was that in those cases where the possible meanings of the same word differ so widely as to make two homonyms, one always predominates: for example, that in Wordsworth *cheek* refers always to part of the face, and not to 'impertinence', that *chased* always means 'pursued', and not 'decorated with fine lines', and that *flat* always means 'level' and never one floor of a house. To a large extent this would have been right, though there would have been some awkward exceptions if his inquiry had taken him beyond a mere handful of words. *Grave*, for example, occurs most frequently for 'burial-place', but also often in the meaning of 'sober' and 'serious'.

What Snyder cannot possibly have meant is that frequent words have just one meaning, or even one 'outstanding' meaning. For it is one of the most firmly established laws of language – of all languages – that the more frequently a word is in use, the more meanings it will have: or, if the word 'meaning' is felt to be too vague, the more definitions it will carry in a good dictionary. It was first noticed, incidentally, in one of those *Forewords* to the earlier volumes of the *OED* which are among the most neglected of all the great contributions to the study of vocabulary. In the volume F the editors thus express it: 'The words that have come down from Old English are very numerous, and many of them have necessarily occupied an unusually large proportion of space, on account of the very great variety of senses and applications which they have acquired in the course of their long history.' This is a little oblique, since it appears to attribute the multiplicity of meanings not to the frequency of use, but to the age of these words. But since the older words in any language are also the most frequently used at any one time, the editors had rightly observed the fact itself.[18]

More direct attention was paid to this remarkable correlation in the 1940s, partly by G. K. Zipf, an indefatigable investigator of the numerical aspects of language. He showed that, within certain limits, the relation between the frequency of a word and the number of its definitions was a strict one, in the sense that if words were to be assigned a rank, r, in order of frequency, f, then the product r/f would be constant. An example of this can be drawn from the *Ulysses* word-list. There the word with rank 10 occurs 2653 times, making the product r/f 26,530; the word ranked 100 occurs 265 times, so that r/f is 265,000. This is indeed remarkable – so remarkable that Zipf was inclined to push what may only have been a coincidence too far, and transform it into a

Table v

Number of *OED* definitions	Occurrences *per mille* of the word so defined
5	146
5c	63
6	104
6c	104
8	417
9	167

general principle of language, with all kinds of other applications. For example, he also tried to prove that the meanings of a single word could be brought within the same pattern. That is to say, if they were assigned a rank, in order of their frequencies of occurrence, for them too *r/f* would be constant.[19]

At the same time, however, a much more detailed and empirical study of word-frequencies and frequencies of their meanings was going on, as a belated continuation of the work of Professors Thorndike and Lorge mentioned above. Their lists were carried on, again with the help of Federal unemployment relief agencies, into the frequencies of meanings, by a method almost incredibly laborious. Each word in each text, making up a sample of about 5 million words of text altogether, was examined, and its 'meanings' at each occurrence were classified under the various definitions given in the *OED*. The original intention was to exclude the commonest words, but before this first project was complete, it was realised that this exclusion was undesirable, for, as Professor Lorge explained, 'near the end of the work with the original sample, it was recognized that the most common words had the greatest variety of meanings'.[20] The large task of counting the frequency of the meanings of the most common words was therefore undertaken, and published in 1949. There can be no doubt that it is the most important collection of numerical data bearing on words and their meanings now available, and it is surprising that no use has yet been made of it by linguists. It is a great pity that this notable mass of material was not available to Zipf, who published his last work in the year of its publication, and died a year later. For it throws some light on his suggestion that the relation between the frequency of words and that of their meanings was the same, insofar as both might be regarded as falling under his suggested law that *r/f* is constant.

There is no doubt that some words can indeed by found which obey this 'law'. *Speculation* is one of them. The figures given for it in the Lorge List are

Table VI

r	f	r/f
1	417	417
2	167	334
3	146	438
4	104	416
5	104	416
6	63	378

Table VII

r	f	r/f
1	550	550
2	142	284
3	124	372
4	60	240
5	33	165
6	30	180
7	24	168
8	24	192
9	9	81
10	3	30

shown in Table V. These figures can be rearranged (see Table VI) to show the rank order, *r*, with the frequency, *f*, of meanings occurring for each rank and the product *r/f*. The figures in the last column may perhaps be regarded as constant, if that Atlas among words, 'approximate', is made here to carry its usual heavy burden.[21] But even here we run into that awkward problem of ranking meanings of the same frequency which we encountered in the ranking of words. If one of the frequencies 104 in this list is ranked as 5, the *r/f* product rises to 520, and rather spoils the look of the whole thing. If it is not so ranked, should not the last number be 5, rather than 6? But if only 5, the product is 315, and this too spoils the look of the thing.

But though some words can indeed be found whose meanings fall into a pattern of this kind, it is much easier to find others which show no sign of falling into Zipf's pattern. Table VII shows one of them, *speech*. The numbers of meanings for each *OED* definition are arranged in rank of frequency. There is no resemblance, even of the vaguest kind, to Zipf's pattern. Nor is there in the meanings of most of the less common words, which often show quite different patterns. Thus *spouse* has two meanings, each of which occur 500 times *per mille*: *spurious* has three meanings, each 333 *per mille*; and *spout* has four, each 250 *per mille*.[22]

So far, so bad. Until these lists have been much more fully examined, no clear judgment can be given either way, but it looks likely that the only hypothesis ever advanced to describe these frequencies is wrong. It remains to consider, however, whether the lists already quoted (together with the many more which have been examined, details of which the reader has been spared) suggest any other hypothesis. As it happens, very faint indications are to be found in the last two lists, and in the examples of rarer words with few meanings, *spouse*, *spurious* and *spout*. In both lists, and especially in the second, that for *speech*, the *r/f* constant shows a tendency to fall markedly for the less frequent meanings. And apparently it is not exhibited at all by the meanings of words which have few of them – that is to say, the less frequently used words. Is it possible, then, that the contrast between the laws of large and small numbers, which we found to be of such great significance in considering the relative frequencies of whole words, may also apply to the relative frequencies of meanings of single words? That is to say, are the most frequent meanings fairly regular in their rates of occurrence from one sample to another, while the less frequent ones are much more liable to vary from one sample to another, or one writer to another? The possibility is attractive from a purely numerical point of view, because it is rather more what would be expected from the general behaviour of items or events numbered in this way than Zipf's hypothesis: it harmonises a little more readily with the rest of what we know about language, and above all with the contrast between those uses of words determined by chance, by the general probabilities of a particular language, and those which are more at the choice of the user. And for the purposes of literary study, it presents the advantage that we can, as with whole words, distinguish between those meanings which are, as it were, compulsory, giving us no special information about the user, and those which are idiolectal, and in some sense peculiar to him.

To prove or disprove this hypothesis would take a much wider examination of the data than has yet been possible. All that can be said at present is that it seems to work rather better than Zipf's. As an illustration of its working, let us take (hoping it will be for the last time) the word which headed Snyder's list of 'favorite words' in Wordsworth, *love*. The Lorge list shows the distribution of the meanings under 38 headings from the *OED*.[23] In Table VIII these have been put in order of rank, save that groups of identical frequency have been shown together, and the table has been interrupted twice, at the 8th meaning

Table VIII

r	f per mille	r/f
1	206	206
2	164	328
3	108	324
4	79	316
5	61	305
6	52	312
7	49	343
8	42	336
Total	761	
9	34	306
10	32	320
11–12	30	330
13	24	312
Total	120	
14	18	252
15	9	135
16	7	112
17	6	102
18–19	5	90
20–22	4	80
23–27	3	69
28–31	2	56
32–38	1	32
Total	55	

and the 13th, to show the total number of occurrences reached at each point. In this way it is easy to see how they are distributed between the more frequent meanings, those of medium frequency, and those of low frequency.

The general likeness between Table VIII and the frequency-list from *The Prelude*, Table II, is obvious without much numerical analysis. The top 8 meanings account for more than 75% of all the occurrences of all meanings; the lowest-ranking 24 meanings accounts for less than 10%; and a middle group of 5 words accounts for roughly 15%. The list could, of course, be divided at somewhat different points, but however divided it will show that the meanings of *love* are either very common or very rare, with a relatively small group of medium frequency. They are, in fact, very like the frequency-distributions of whole words. So far as this one illustration goes, our hypothesis about large and small numbers seems to be reasonable.[24]

It needs, of course, to be much more extensively tested, and a few further examples will be given in what follows. For the moment, I shall permit myself to adopt it, simply as a working hypothesis, and until there is a reason to abandon or modify it. But before we turn – at last – to some actual applications of it to the study of Wordsworth's idiolectal vocabulary, the numerical hypothesis must be translated into a more linguistic and literary statement. Any word, it suggests, which is in itself relatively frequent, and which therefore has many meanings, will be found used in two different ways in actual texts. If the writer uses it at about its usual rate (judged by comparison with other writers, or with large mixed samples), then we should expect that the relative frequencies of its meanings in his text will be near to those suggested by the Lorge list – or, of course, by any better list of the same kind that may be produced. That is to say, most of the meanings will be those imposed by the large-number probabilities of the language itself, and by the chance of averages. They will be, in this strict sense, the 'usual' meanings of the word. On the other hand – and this is a much more important aspect of the same hypothesis – if any word, taken as a whole, occurs much more often than its usual frequency (judged by comparative figures) then an unusually large proportion of its uses will carry one or more of its less usual meanings. For while it is not in the power of the individual writer to modify widely the proportion of the 'usual' meanings, it is entirely within his power to increase his rate of use of the 'unusual' ones, for in reference to these, and to these only, he can make personal choices. It is not open to him to increase his rate of using the whole word in any other way than by increasing the rate of occurrence of its less usual meanings. It is under these circumstances, and under these alone, that, to use Wordsworth's own phrase, there can be 'arbitrary connections of feelings and ideas with particular words'.

It follows that there is a possibility that a writer may indeed use common words, a 'selection of the language really used by men', but that he may use them in uncommon ways, imposing upon them his own idiolectal meanings. It remains to look at some of the words in which Wordsworth may have developed this possibility in practice.

8

And saw a woman in the naked room . . .

Guilt and Sorrow 165 (*PW* I, 103)

The context shows that this line is not, as most modern readers would suppose, an example of the transferred epithet. The woman was clothed, if but ill, and it was indeed the room that was naked. And it has already been noted that Wordsworth used the word of pools, walls, in the 'spots of time' passage. There seems to be a *prima facie* case for supposing that he used the word often – that it was one of his 'favorite words', and also that he used it in senses rather different from those which occur commonly in other authors. Both suppositions must now be tested by the methods (however defective) at present available, making use of the Thorndike–Lorge frequency lists based on large mixed samples of text, and of the Concordances of those poets with whom it is sensible to compare Wordsworth. It may make these procedures clearer if they are set out in something like a tabular form: they have, in any case, little in common with the kind of literary criticism which is conveyed in elegant continuous prose.

RELATIVE FREQUENCY OF 'NAKED'

(a) *As against mixed samples (Thorndike–Lorge; referred to as T–L)*

Naked appears to be a relatively common word. In the main T–L List it is given as occurring fairly low in the 3rd thousand (counting the commonest thousand as the 1st). The significance of this placing can be very roughly indicated by noting that the List itself contains 30,000 words, and that any well-educated English-speaker would find, in the 30th thousand, a substantial proportion of words which he would not know. In the succeeding thousands, if lists were available, the proportion of these would grow, so that by about the 40th thousand, most of the words would be strange to him. The total 'vocabulary', in fact, of a well-educated person of not less than thirty years of age (since there is a constant, if slow, increase in 'vocabulary' until senility sets in), probably lies between 30,000 and 40,000 words.[25] The rate of occurrence of *naked*, in the main List, is 31 times per million words of sample-texts. Since the total length of Wordsworth's verse is about 400,000 words, *naked* would be found 12 times, if it were being used there at the same rate. It is in fact used 78 times.

The main T–L List gives separate information about the words of an early count by Thorndike, based on about 4½ million words of mixed samples, taken mainly from 'readers, textbooks, the Bible, and the English classics' (*Teachers' Word Book*, p. x). It is therefore specially suitable for testing the use of words in an 'English classic': indeed the sample included all of Wordsworth.[26] In this List (T), *naked* scores 220. Since Wordsworth's text is about one-tenth as long as the total sample, about 22 occurrences would be expected in him, and the actual 78 is markedly in surplus.

A further check was made by taking all the words in three letters of the alphabet (A, N and S) found to occur about as often as *naked* in the Lorge Semantic Count. (*Naked* there scores 64; the other words chosen scored 60–69.) This yielded 43 words, of which only 29 are found in Wordsworth. Since the sample-texts for this Count ran to about 4½ million words, the scores to be expected for these 29 words in Wordsworth, if he had used them with about the same relative frequency, would have been about 6 each. Nine of the 29 were used less frequently than this, and the mean of the deficiency was 3.4. The scores for the other 20 were in excess, with a mean of 30. The most notable excess occurrences were these:

naked (78), *nest* (60), *abode* (77), *aspire* (43), *awe* (54), *splendour* (42), *steep* (104), *sustain* (66).

The texts on which this Count were based included pages from the *Encyclopedia Britannica*, the magazine *Literary Digest*, text-books, novels, biographies, books of science and manuals of information (*Introduction* to the Count, p. 2). It was, therefore, much less 'literary' than the Thorndike Count (T), and seems to have included no verse, save that which might be quoted in sources such as the *Literary Digest* and text-books. It is much more a measure of the relative frequencies in modern English prose, and one would expect that it would differ much more widely than T from Wordsworth's usage. It does so very clearly, and *naked* scores about 12 times as often against the frequency shown in this Count, compared with the 3 times as often against the T Count.

By all these tests, however, it appears that Wordsworth used *naked* much more often than most writers of English, even writers of verse, who seem to use it more than writers of prose.

(b) *As against other poets, as shown in concordances*

These are the figures:

Shakespeare 48, Spenser 39, Milton 17, Keats 11

By themselves, most of these mean very little, for the reasons given above. But one at least, that for Shakespeare, is valid, for it shows a much smaller number of occurrences of the word in a much larger text, 48 as against 78, in a text of about 800,000 words against about 400,000. The other figures are no more than suggestive but, like the evidence drawn from the mixed-sample lists, they suggest strongly that *naked* was indeed one of Wordsworth's 'favorite' words.

Table IX

	% in L	% in Wordsworth
I Unclothed, bare-backed, bare parts of body; *of qualities or actions personified*, destitute, unarmed, defenceless.	63	17
III Bare, clean, clear, devoid of trees or vegetation, barren, waste, leafless, devoid of cover, exposed (*of ground*), destitute of sails or tackle, unfurnished, uncovered by ceiling, devoid of ornament, plain.	16	74
IV Left without any addition, bare, mere, absolute (*as in* naked faith); *of the eye*, unassisted.	20	9

RELATIVE FREQUENCY OF THE MEANINGS OF 'NAKED'

(a) *Compared with the Semantic Count, called* L

It is unfortunate that L, as explained above, tends to differ very widely in relative frequency of words themselves from Wordsworth's usage, because it is likely, for the same reasons, to exaggerate somewhat any differences which may exist in the relative frequencies of meanings, as defined by the *OED*. But there is no way of overcoming this difficulty, and there is no other count of the same kind. We must make the best of it, with due caution in interpreting the results of the comparison.

The *OED* article divides the 50 or so definitions of *naked* into 4 main sections. One of these, II, can be omitted at once, for none of Wordsworth's uses fall under this heading, and it represents only 0.02% of the occurrences in L. The three which concern us are those numbered I, III and IV. These are exemplified in Table IX with the meanings actually found in L or in Wordsworth. The two figures on the right give the percentages of meanings in each section found in L and in Wordsworth.

The last figures, for heading IV, are probably without significance. The difference in the number of occurrences is not great, and it happens that 11% of all the occurrences in L are accounted for by the phrase 'naked eye', which Wordsworth never used. If allowance is made for this, the figures come even closer. It is, however, a very different matter with the other two headings. There the proportions are almost exactly reversed, and even when all allowances have been made for the possible errors in the definitions and in the count of meanings in L, it seems most unlikely that this reversal might have come about by pure accident. This set of figures, in fact, fully bears out the hypothesis advanced above, that if any writer uses a word at much above its usual rate of occurrence, he will also be found to be using it with an unusual distribution of its meanings, and that one or more of its less usual meanings must occur in his text with a relatively high frequency.

It is also worth noticing that had Wordsworth used the word with about the same proportion of meanings for headings I and III as in the L list, the total number of its occurrences in his text would have been much reduced. It would not then have occurred at an exceptionally high frequency, as whole word. There remains, however, one last comparison to be made.

(b) *Distribution of meanings, compared with other poets*

The distinctive feature of the *OED* definitions under heading III is that they apply *naked* to features of landscape, vegetable objects, or buildings. Of Shakespeare's total of 48 uses of *naked*, only 2 fall under this heading: 'forlorn and naked hermitage' in *Love's Labour's Lost*, and 'Upon the naked shore at Ravenspurgh' in *I Henry IV*. Of Milton's 17 uses, none falls under this heading, and of Keats' 11, only 1: 'naked sky'. In Spenser, it accounts for 7 out of 39 uses, higher than the rest, but at 18% still far below Wordsworth's figure of 74%.[27]

This completes the information needed to establish the relation between the frequencies of *naked*, as a word, and the relative frequencies of its meanings. And it points clearly enough, and consistently enough, in the one direction. The word itself is used by Wordsworth with unusual frequency, judged either by other poets or by mixed samples; and his most frequent uses of it are in one of its less usual meanings, again judged by other poets and by the L mixed samples.

It must be emphasised once again that in dealing with a whole vocabulary of several thousand words, the evidence derived from but one of them cannot be held to prove anything. Much wider search is needed for that. But in this particular case, we are able to make a useful cross-check by looking at the same data for a near-synonym of *naked*, the word *bare*. One would expect that it would show the same kind of departures from the normal frequencies as *naked*, both as a whole word, and among its meanings. And it does so. It occurs 107 times, against an expected 40 from its rate of occurrence in the T List. It is found 54 times in Shakespeare, and 11 in Milton, and 32 in Spenser. By the standard of both these comparisons it is therefore relatively very frequent in Wordsworth. When we turn to the distribution of its meanings, we find the same kind of eccentricity as in the case of *naked*. One of the *OED* headings for *bare* which is relatively unusual in the Thorndike–Lorge Semantic Count is found very often in Wordsworth. It is that headed IV in the *OED*, and thus described: 'Of natural objects, as earth, heavens, trees: Without such covering as they have at other times, *e.g.* without vegetation, clouds, bark, foliage'. In the Semantic Count 24% of all occurrences of *bare* are placed under this definition. In Wordsworth the proportion is 65%. The same difference is found in comparison with the other poets just mentioned. Of Shakespeare's 54 uses, only 3 fall under this heading (including his 'bare ruin'd choirs'); of Milton's 11, 3 again have this meaning, once each of *strand*, *oaks and pines*, and *mountains*. And of Spenser's 37 uses, 12 are of the same kind, including no less than 4 of *boughs* or *branches*, 2 of *paths* and of *ground*, with 1 of *mountains*. Again there is no doubt that, judged by the same tests, the frequencies of *bare* as a word are linked with the relative frequencies of its meanings, as our hypothesis suggests they might be.

So far, so good; and we shall have occasion to look at at least one more example of the same relation later. For the moment, two other and rather different aspects of the same hypothesis deserve mention. The first concerns the more general theoretical problems which are suggested by the possibility that a characteristic of Wordsworth's idiolect may be his use of uncommon meanings of relatively common words. If this is indeed characteristic of his diction, it might be said that we had merely expressed rather more technically his own definition of 'imagination' in the note to *The Thorn*: 'the faculty which produces impressive effects out of simple elements'. But it also happens that we have established a very close connection between this characteristic diction and the modern theory of Information. For it is one of the basic theorems of this theory that in any code (including the 'natural' languages) the amount of information carried by any element is inversely proportional to its frequency of occurrence. Applied to whole words, this means that *animal*, a very common word in English, carries much less 'information' than *kangaroo*, which is a very uncommon word in the same language. It is less specific, as it were; and it provides the answer to many fewer questions – though it does answer some. Many writers of literature, perhaps most, rely for this sharply focussed and concentrated communication upon relatively rare words. Wordsworth, on the other hand, may perhaps have achieved the same end, the same concentration of much information into a small amount of code, by using the uncommon meanings of relatively common words.

The second aspect of this hypothesis about Wordsworth's use of words is one which arises naturally from his own comments upon 'repetition and apparent tautology'. It would seem that not only may they become 'frequently beauties of the highest kind', but that their effect may depend precisely upon the kind of relationship between word-frequencies and meaning-frequencies which we are examining. The tautology is effective in a literary sense, is something other than mere repetition, because the comparative novelty of the meaning of the repeated words gives them unusual force and clarity: they behave much more as rare words do. On the other hand, this effect can be achieved in no other way than by frequent repetition; only so can the reader become sensitised to what is essentially personal and novel in this unusual selection among their meanings. For this selection always depends upon the broader context, and it is only when the reader has encountered the word in several contexts enforcing this unusual meaning that he is 'sensitised' to it by repetition.

Finally, it must be remembered that this process of repetition may well affect not only one word but also other words closely related to it in meaning and frequency of use. As Wordsworth himself put it, in the *Thorn* note, so long as the writer is conscious of the inadequateness of his own powers or of the deficiencies of language, he will 'cling to the same words, or words of the same character'. In the example just studied, it is clear that the special uses of *naked* are closely related with the equally special uses of *bare*. It is therefore probable that we shall encounter in his poetry groups or 'clusters' of near-synonyms, frequently repeated, both singly and in connection with each other, so that they form larger wholes, in which the 'meanings' of a group of such near-synonyms may all together be influenced in a common direction, reinforcing and elucidating one another. There will be, of course, some slight shift of emphasis among them, a continuous play of light, as it were. And of the delicately shimmering word-cluster of which *naked* is a part, this far from exhaustive list will give some indication:

naked waste of scattered stone
rocks rise naked as a wall
. . . up Castrigg's naked steep
. . . stript naked as a rock
Tower like a wall the naked crags
Shouldering the naked crag
In silent beauty on the naked ridge
The naked summit of a far-off hill
'mid the hollow depths of naked crags
Girt round with a bare ring of mossy wall
Look round her when the heavens are bare
Forc'd from my native mountains bleak and bare

... reascending the bare common saw

A naked pool that lay beneath the hills

Invested moorland waste, and naked pool

I sate half-sheltered by a naked wall

Beside a pool bare to the eye of heaven

Upon the naked pool and dreary crags

You see a little muddy pond
Of water – never dry,
Though but of compass small, and bare
To thirsty suns and parching air.

It is by repetition of this kind, and on this scale, that the tautologies become apparent. By this process, not the words only, but also the separate meanings of words, acquire the power of *things*. And by this process too words pass through 'various stages of meaning' and acquire 'stability of the relations of particular ideas to each other' (*PW* II, 402). It is usually enough for the reader to feel the effects of this stability, but it is sometimes possible for him, if he wishes, to see something of the stages by which it has been reached. To do this is to trace, in very small part, not merely the special nature, but the development, of Wordsworth's 'apparent tautologies'.

9

... there can be no presumption in saying of most readers, that it is not probable they will be so well acquainted with the various stages of meaning through which words have passed, or with the fickleness or stability of the relations of particular ideas to each other.

Preface to *Lyrical Ballads* (*PW* II, 402)

In discussing Wordsworth's uses of *naked*, no account was taken of the date at which they occurred. The Concordance does not lend itself easily to a chronological survey of the uses of any word, since it is based on Hutchinson's Oxford edition, which follows the non-chronological classification of the shorter poems adopted by Wordsworth from 1815 onwards. For many purposes, it is probably unnecessary to attempt a full chronological study of the use of words, and not much harm will result from treating the whole body of a writer's text as a single specimen of his linguistic usage. But it should not be too easily assumed that this is so, and the assumption should at least be checked on a small scale. Wordsworth, in particular, was writing actively for more than half a century, and it is very likely that substantial changes occurred in his linguistic usage over so long a period. Indeed it is impossible to read much of the later verse without becoming conscious of such changes, in a general way – and without concluding, with some regret, that they were on the whole for the worse. Altogether more interesting and important, however, are the changes which occurred in the great creative period from 1798 onwards, and in the preparations for it in *The Vale of Esthwaite* and the early poems. Here his special way of using words was taking shape, and the process will be studied in two examples, one of central significance in his vocabulary, the other more marginal. Both will serve to illustrate the force of tautology and repetition in transforming what might at first have been 'arbitrary connections of feelings and ideas with particular words and phrases' into natural and forceful parts of his poetic vocabulary.

This passage from Book I of *The Prelude* contains a simile which is at once striking and slightly puzzling:

> Thus, often in those fits of vulgar joy
> Which, through all seasons, on a child's pursuits
> Are prompt attendants, 'mid that giddy bliss
> Which, like a tempest, works along the blood
> And is forgotten; even then I felt
> *Gleams like the flashing of a shield*; the earth
> And common face of Nature spake to me
> Rememberable things . . . (*Prel.* I.609–16)

It does not seem very likely that Wordsworth, any more than his modern reader, had ever seen the gleams flashing from a distant shield. It is this that makes the simile puzzling, for the relation between the tenor and the vehicle is usually that between the less and the more familiar. He gives us, however, in another passage, the clue both to its provenance and to its evocative effect. It had come, not from ordinary experience only, but from a mingling of something often seen with something encountered in books, by a process which he described thus:

> But when that first poetic faculty
> Of plain Imagination and severe . . .
> Began to have some promptings to put on
> A visible shape, and to the works of art,
> The notions and the images of books
> Did knowingly conform itself, by these
> Enflamed, and proud of that her new delight,
> There came among those shapes of human life
> A wilfulness of fancy and conceit
> Which gave them new importance to the mind . . .
> (*Prel.* VIII.511–22)

One of the illustrations of this mingling of fancy and imagination happens to give the origin of the 'flashing shield':

> There was a Copse
> An upright bank of wood and woody rock
> That opposite our rural Dwelling stood,
> In which a sparkling patch of diamond light
> Was in bright weather duly to be seen
> On summer afternoons, within the wood
> At the same place. 'Twas doubtless nothing more
> Than a black rock, which, wet with constant springs
> Glister'd far seen from out its lurking-place
> As soon as ever the declining sun
> Had smitten it. Beside our Cottage hearth,
> Sitting with open door, a hundred times
> Upon this lustre have I gaz'd, that seem'd
> To have some meaning which I could not find;
> And now it was a burnished shield, I fancied,
> Suspended over a Knight's Tomb, who lay
> Inglorious, buried in the dusky wood . . . (*Prel.* VIII.559–75)

The actual date of this experience, and of the fancies which accompanied it, must have been at some time in his schooldays, for the cottage is certainly that of his 'Dame', Ann Tyson, at Colthouse, about half a mile east of Hawkshead itself. There is nothing like it in *The Vale of Esthwaite*, but it may have been in one of the missing passages of description, and this possibility is the stronger because it occurs in *Descriptive Sketches* which, though nominally about Switzerland, included many images from his own earlier verse. This is the passage:

> 'Tis storm; and hid in mist from hour to hour
> All day the floods a deeper murmur pour,
> And mournful sounds, as of a Spirit lost,[28]
> Pipe wild along the hollow-blustering coast,
> 'Till the Sun walking on his western field
> Shakes from behind the clouds his flashing shield.
> (332–7 [*PW* I, 62])

These lines were composed during Wordsworth's residence in France, in 1791–2. The next version is from *The Borderers*, written in 1796–7:

> Naked was the spot;
> Methinks I see it now – how in the sun
> Its stony surface glittered like a shield . . . (1721–3 [*PW* I, 196])

And the next occurrence of the image is that from which we started, in the first book of *The Prelude*; it was written in January 1799. The image is found very soon afterwards, in the *Michael* drafts of 1800:

So to Helvellyn's side they went
Down looking on that hollow, where the pool
Of Thirlmere flashes like a Warrior's shield
His light high up among the gloomy rocks
With gift of now and then a straggling gleam
To Armath's pleasant fields. (*d.* 9-14 [*PW* II, 483])

It is not found again for fifteen years, and then it reappears in *Artegal and Elidure*, written in 1815:

'And what if o'er that bright unbosoming
Clouds of disgrace and envious fortune passed!
Have we not seen the glories of the spring
By veil of noontide darkness overcast?
The frith that glittered like a warrior's shield . . .
[The Lake that glittered like a sunbright shield *MS*] . . .
(194–8 [*PW* II, 20])

The last use of the image is in the following year, in a poem to a lady *On her First Ascent to the Summit of Helvellyn*:

Lo! the dwindled woods and meadows;
What a vast abyss is there!
Lo! the clouds, the solemn shadows,
And the glistenings – heavenly fair!

And a record of commotion
Which a thousand ridges yield;
Ridge, and gulf, and distant ocean
Gleaming like a silver shield! (9–16 [*PW* II, 286])

This is the whole history of one of 'those arbitrary connections of feelings and ideas with particular words and phrases, from which no man can altogether protect himself'.

It has been easy to trace, because the image of the shield runs through its successive stages. But once the passages in which it occurs have been put together, it becomes apparent at once that they have in common a small group of other words: *gleam* and *flash* in the first, *sparkle*, *light*, *glister*, *lustre*, *burnished* in the second, *flash* again in the third, *glitter* in the fourth, *flash* and *gleam* in the fifth, *glitter* in the sixth, *glisten* and *gleam* in the last. We have been led, it seems, by the particular image to discover one of those clusters of words, of 'words of the same character', near-synonyms which all contribute to and share in that specialisation of meaning which gives them a density which they normally lack. At the level of sensory experience, this special force seems to consist mainly in a heightened contrast between light and dark. Many of these contexts, indeed, contain an antithetical cluster of words making darkness itself more concrete and emphatic: 'lurking-place . . . buried in the dusky wood', 'storm . . . behind the clouds', 'among the gloomy rocks', 'the clouds, the solemn shadows'. As for their more abstract meaning, they all have in common the same tenor, describing a moment of revelation, of enlightenment, against this background of gloom. The history of the shield image, in fact, points towards the history of the word-cluster, of which it turns out to be but a small part.

The really significant difference between the 'shield' image and this larger cluster of words is that while it was essentially localised in its possible range of reference, confined to a very small number of possible repetitions, the word-cluster is capable of forming a constantly widening range of associations, both within itself, with other words embodying the same light–dark contrast, and with a far wider range of contexts. The extent to which it did so can be illustrated by the history of another image which occurred to Wordsworth very early, and also in relation to the setting of the sun. It was first expressed in *The Vale*:

> Yet if Heaven bear me away
> To close the evening of my day,
> If no vast blank impervious cloud
> The powers of thought in darkness shroud,
> Sick, trembling at the world unknown
> And doubting what to call her own,
> Even while my body pants for breath
> And shrinks at the [ ] dart of Death,
> My soul shall cast the wistful view
> The longing look alone on you.
> As Phoebus, when he sinks to rest
> Far on the mountains in the west,
> While all the vale, as dies his beam
> Can never catch one straggling gleam,
> A lingering lustre softly throws
> On the dear hills where first he rose.
>
> (498–513, *alt. reading* 510–11 [*PW* I, 281])

These lines were tidied up, and published as the first of *Poems Written in Youth*:

> Dear native regions, I foretell,
> From what I feel at this farewell,
> That wheresoe'er my steps may tend,
> And whensoe'er my course shall end,
> If in that hour a single tie
> Survive of local sympathy,
> My soul will cast the backward view,
> The longing look alone on you.

Thus, while the Sun sinks down to rest
Far in the regions of the west,
Though to the vale no parting beam
Be given, not one memorial gleam,
A lingering light he fondly throws
On the dear hills where first he rose. (*PW* I, 2)

Wordsworth remained for many years deeply attached to this image, and not unnaturally, for it was associated with what turned out to be the first of the crucial events of his life, leaving the Lakes for the first time in 1787, when he came up to Cambridge. Many years later he told Miss Fenwick the circumstances of its origin:

The beautiful image with which this poem concludes, suggested itself to me while I was resting in a boat along with my companions under the shade of a magnificent row of Sycamores, which then extended their branches from the shore of the promontory upon which stands the ancient, and at that time the more picturesque, Hall of Coniston. (*PW* I, 317)

The next version of the image was written in autumn 1799, and was at that time intended for Book II of *The Prelude*. It describes the sycamores and Coniston Hall, and goes on:

. . . the radiance of the setting sun
Himself unseen, reposing on the top
Of the high eastern hills. And there I said,
That beauteous sight before me, there I said,
(Then first beginning in my thoughts to mark
That sense of dim similitude which links
Our moral feelings with external forms)
That in whatever region I should close
My mortal life I would remember you
Fair scenes! that dying I would think on you
My soul would send a longing look to you:
Even as that setting sun while all the vale
Could nowhere catch one faint memorial *gleam*
Yet with the last remains of his last light
Still linger'd and a farewell *lustre* threw
On the dear mountain tops where first he rose.
(From MSS V and U [Oxford *Prelude*, pp. 582–3])

It was not, however, used anywhere in the 1805 *Prelude*, and the last version appeared in the 1850 text (VIII, 462–75) slightly shortened from the above draft, but retaining exactly what had become the two key phrases, 'memorial gleam' and 'farewell lustre'. This succession of versions of the sunset-image, then, served to strengthen Wordsworth's deep personal feeling for *gleam*, and added *lustre* to the group of significant tautologies around *gleam*. Together with the 'shield' image, it may have played a large part in generating this word-cluster, but not even the most devout admirer of Wordsworth could want still more versions of either of these two images. Their possibilities had been exhausted. The further extensions of the word-cluster itself, however, were almost inexhaustible.

A good early example of another sunset-scene, in which more words are drawn into association with *gleam*, is in *An Evening Walk*, in the course of a description taken from one of the *Guides* to the Lakes of village superstitions about supernatural horsemen chasing a single rider over the mountains:

> A desperate form appears, that spurs his steed,
> Along the midway cliffs with violent speed;
> Unhurt pursues his lengthen'd flight, while all
> Attend, at every stretch, his headlong fall.
> Anon, in order mounts a gorgeous show
> Of horsemen shadows winding to and fro;
> And now the van is gilt with evening's beam
> The rear thro' iron brown betrays a sullen *gleam*;
> Lost gradual o'er the heights in *pomp* they go,
> While silent stands th'admiring vale below;
> Till, but the lonely beacon all is fled,
> That tips with eve's last *gleam* his spiry head.
>
> (*1793*, 179–90 [*PW* I, 22])

The revision of this passage published in 1820 shows how far, in the meantime, this word-cluster had grown. *Pomp* is now firmly associated with it, and *visionary* and *splendour* have been added:[29]

> While silent stands the admiring crowd below,
> Silent the *visionary* warriors go,
> Winding in ordered *pomp* their upward way,
> . . . and every trace is fled
> Of *splendour* – save the beacon's spiry head . . .
>
> (*1849*, 205–10 [*PW* I, 23])

It is not known how long after the publication of the poem in 1793 this revision was made. Wordsworth himself said that most of the work upon the original poem was done very soon after its publication. If this passage was revised at that time, then this important extension of the word-cluster dates from about 1794. The growing tendency to associated recurrence of these words is very well shown by the poem on his brother John's 'grove' in the sequence on *Naming of Places*:

> . . . the steep
> Of Silver-how, and Grasmere's peaceful lake,
> And one green island, *gleam* between the stems
> Of the dark firs, a *visionary* scene!

And while I gaze upon the spectacle
Of clouded *splendour*, on this *dream*-like sight . . .
(VI.90–5 [*PW* II, 122])

Here, the capability for generalisation in the word-cluster is clearly indicated. The association between *gleam* and sunsets is no more than vestigial; the 'image', if it exists at all, if the 'scene' is tacitly likened to sunlight glimpsed through tree-trunks, is perfunctory. The real work of the description is done by the word-cluster, to which has now been added *dream*, in close relation with visionary. In *Ruth*, written in 1799, the near-synonymy is already established: 'Through dream and vision did she sink' (109 [*PW* II, 230]).

In one of the last of the 'shield' passages, there was a late example of *glory* in this word-cluster. A much earlier instance is found in *A Night-piece*, written in 1798:

At length a pleasant instantaneous *gleam*
Startles the pensive traveller
. . . he looks up – the clouds are split
Asunder, – and above his head he sees
The clear Moon, and the *glory* of the heavens. (8–13 [*PW* II, 208])

It is interesting to compare this description with an entry in Dorothy Wordsworth's *Journal* (25 January 1798) describing the same scene: 'At once the clouds seemed to cleave asunder, left her [the moon] in the centre of a black-blue vault.' She observes and records sharply, and sees what her brother sees; but she has not, in this passage at least, caught from him the habit of using, besides the literal description, cumulatively evocative words.

Although *gleam* seems to hold a central position in this word-cluster (and the card-index makes this much clearer than a few quotations), the other words in it were capable of forming their own associations, and of playing important parts in descriptions based on the general contrast of light–dark, without any reference to sun or moon. Thus *flash* and *glory* are found together in two notable passages of *The Prelude*, written in 1804:

Visionary Power
Attends upon the motions of the winds
Embodied in the mystery of words.
There darkness makes abode, and all the host
Of shadowy things do work their changes there,
As in a mansion like their proper home:
Even forms and substances are circumfus'd
By that transparent veil with light divine;
And through the turnings intricate of Verse,
Present themselves as objects recognis'd,
In *flashes*, and with a *glory* scarce their own. (V.619–29)

This passage is remarkable not only for its use of these two words from the cluster, but also because it is attempting to describe in verse the feeling of the power of words, used poetically – the power of words as *things* – which Wordsworth strove to express in his prose writings on imaginative language. As so often with him, the verbal texture of the passage actually illustrates the processes he is trying to describe. And the same is true of the other passage, from Book VI, in which he describes, in very similar terms, the power of 'Imagination':

> Imagination! lifting up itself
> Before the eye and progress of my Song
> Like an unfather'd vapour; here that Power,
> In all the might of its endowments, came
> Athwart me; I was lost as in a cloud,
> Halted, without a struggle to break through.
> And now recovering, to my Soul I say
> I recognise thy *glory*; in such strength
> Of usurpation, in such visitings
> Of awful promise, when the light of sense
> Goes out in *flashes* that have shewn to us
> The invisible world, doth Greatness make abode. (525–36)

Both of these passages illustrate – and the illustration is of much more general importance – how words from these clusters, originating in 'arbitrary' personal experience, could be reinforced and generalised by repetition and association with one another, so that they could contribute a special force to passages of reflective and abstract writing, redeeming them from plain abstractness, and revealing the strength of the link between sensuous and mental experience both in Wordsworth's substance and in his style.

The manner in which this particular word-cluster grew up in the period of Wordsworth's creative writing could be illustrated much further by a long string of quotations, but it is only too probable that this method of presenting their growth has already been used to excess. The extent and complexity of the relations between the words thus clustered can, however, be shown much more concisely, though also more crudely, by a numerical table, based on a card-index which records *all* the uses of *all* the words in poems written before 1820. The number in each square gives the number of passages in which the word at the head of the column is found with the word at the left of each horizontal row. For example, running down the column headed *glory* to the row designated *flash* it is found that these two words occur together four times. What is lacking, of course, in such merely numerical information is some indication of the strength of the association between *glory* and *flash* in

Table x

	gleam	*flash*	*vision*	*visionary*	*pomp*	*glory*	*splendour*	*glimpse*	*sparkling*	*shield*	*glister glisten*	*glimmer*	*lustre*	*light*
gleam	33	5	1	4	5	3	3	2	2	3	2		2	4
flash	5	25	2	2		4				1			1	8
vision	1	2	19			2	1				1			1
visionary	4	2		16	2	1	1							2
pomp	5			1	18	2	1							3
glory	3	4	2	2	2	27				1				2
splendour	2		1	1	1		20					2	1	4
glimpse	2							6						
sparkling	2								6	1				3
shield	3					1			1	8				
glister } *glisten*	2		1						1	2	5			1
glimmer							2					3		
lustre		1					1						5	
light		9	1	2	3	2	3		1	1				28

these four contexts, and of their range of occurrence when not associated with one another. This additional information cannot be summarised neatly, for it depends upon a scrutiny of all the contexts. With the aid of Table x, however, this scrutiny can be made fairly quickly from the Concordance, with occasional use of the actual text.

This array of words suggests certain possibilities of further statistical analysis. It would, for example, be possible to apply to it one or two well-known measuring devices, which would quantify the tendency of these words to occur in close proximity. A figure, in fact, could be placed on the degree of coherence within the word-cluster. The trouble is, however, that this figure by itself would mean nothing. It might acquire some significance only if it were compared with many other figures, based on other word-clusters, some chosen deliberately on the same principles as the *gleam* cluster, others selected at random. Even so, it would not prove very much. Its significance – or, of course, its lack of significance – could only be substantially increased by making similar tests, both chosen and random, on a large number of other texts of about the same size. This task is, of course, quite beyond present resources both of material and processing. For the same reason, it is hardly bearable to contemplate testing, on the members of this group of words, the basic hypothesis described above concerning the relation between the relative frequencies of words and of their different meanings. Most of them are indeed used by Wordsworth far in excess of what would be expected from Thorndike's T List, or from any other similar measure. And in all the cases so far studied, this excess goes with a 'distortion' of the frequencies of meanings, similar to that noted in the uses of *naked* and *bare*. To carry this study, however, to the point at which conclusions might be obtained would require much more hard labour than is justified by the nature of the materials at present available.

Fortunately, Table X suggests, however tentatively, some simpler non-numerical and literary-critical conclusions. It becomes very noticeable, as one handles the hundreds of cards on which the table is based how often parts of the whole cluster are found in poems usually regarded as being typical of Wordsworth at his best. *Gleam*, for example, occurs in the 'spots of time' passage, enforcing the climactic contrast between the 'golden' memories of youth and the 'dreariness' of the same scene as it appeared in the earlier experience of it. It is found twice in *Tintern Abbey*:

> And now, with *gleams* of half-extinguished thought,
> With many recognitions dim and faint,
> And somewhat of a sad perplexity,
> The picture of the mind revives again . . . (58–61 [*PW* II, 261])

> Nor, perchance –
> If I should be where I no more can hear
> Thy voice, nor catch from thy wild eyes these *gleams*
> Of past existence – wilt thou then forget
> That on the banks of this delightful stream
> We stood together . . . (146–51 [*PW* II, 263])

In the 'spots of time' passage, a similar thought and mood is expressed through a word nearly related to *gleam*, *glimpse*:

> I see by *glimpses* now; when age comes on,
> May scarcely see at all . . . (*Prel.* XI. 338–9)

In the *Elegiac Stanzas Suggested by a Picture of Peele Castle*:

> Ah! THEN if mine had been the Painter's hand,
> To express what then I saw; and add the *gleam*,
> The light that never was, on sea or land,
> The consecration, and the Poet's *dream* . . . (13–16 [*PW* IV, 259])

The most striking single example of the massive deployment of this word-cluster is, appropriately enough, in the *Immortality Ode*, which so completely sums up, and so nearly concludes, Wordsworth's great creative period:

There was a time when meadow, grove and stream,
The earth, and every common sight,
To me did seem
Apparelled in celestial *light*,
The *glory* and the freshness of a *dream* . . .

The sunshine is a *glorious* birth;
But yet I know, where'er I go,
That there hath past away a *glory* from the earth . . .

Whither is fled the visionary *gleam*?
Where is it now, the *glory* and the *dream*?

The Youth, who daily farther from the east
Must travel, still is Nature's Priest,
And by the *vision splendid*
Is on his way attended . . .

The homely nurse doth all she can
To make her Foster-child, her Inmate Man,
Forget the *glories* he hath known. . .

Though nothing can bring back the hour
Of *splendour* in the grass, of *glory* in the flower . . .

It is in the *Ode* above all that the essentially incantatory quality of these cumulative tautologies becomes apparent (*PW* IV, 279–85). There is no point whatever in trying to deal with that last line by the methods of imagery analysis, by summoning up one's own impressions, however vivid, of grass and flowers. This 'splendour' and this 'glory' are not of vegetable origin; still less are they ironic. They are words which have become *things* in the long, impassioned meditations of Wordsworth's mind and feelings. And their repetition throughout the *Ode* confers on them the final fullness of their special power, by a principle of composition not very different from that noted above in *The Thorn* and in the 'spots of time' passage from *The Prelude* – it will be found again in *The Leech Gatherer*. It is completely fitting, as it were a rounding of the circle, that the concluding image of the *Ode* should return, though without using any of the clustered words, to those experiences of sunset which had generated both the 'shield' images and the 'memorial gleams':

The Clouds that gather round the setting sun
Do take a sober colouring from an eye
That hath kept watch o'er man's mortality . . .

The experience of another splendid sunset, exactly ten years later, enabled Wordsworth to compose one of the more striking poems of his middle age, *Composed upon an Evening of Extraordinary Splendour and Beauty*. It has little new to say, and is largely reminiscence, momentarily revivified, of his earlier power – very like the 'one straggling beam' throwing 'A lingering lustre . . . On the dear hills where first he rose'. Wordsworth himself added a note, saying that 'Allusions to the Ode entitled "Intimations of Immortality" pervade the last Stanza.' And so they do. These 'allusions' turn out to be mainly words in the cluster which contributed so much to the *Ode*. And perhaps the trouble with the poem, as with so much of his later verse, was that words had turned too thoroughly into *things*, losing too much of their original pressure of thought and feeling, with little capacity for further growth and richness of association. For all that, they cast a moving light on the role which these words had played in his spiritual life:

> Such hues from their celestial Urn
> Were wont to stream before mine eye,
> Where'er it wandered in the morn
> Of blissful infancy.
> This *glimpse* of *glory*, why renewed?
> Nay, rather speak with gratitude;
> For, if a vestige of those *gleams*
> Survived, 'twas only in my *dreams* . . .
> – 'Tis past, the *visionary splendour* fades;
> And night approaches with her shades.
>
> (61–8, 79–80 [*PW* IV, 12–13])

This demonstration of the power of these words, as words alone, and with little objective reference to anything outside his own 'stream of consciousness', suggests a final comment on the line from which this word-cluster emerged – 'Gleams like the flashing of a shield'. All that has been added does not, in any sense, 'explain' that line, still less explain it away. Its relation with childhood memories, and with all the successive repetitions as 'emotion [was] recollected in tranquillity' is something radically different from the relation between poetry and its 'sources' in the usual literary sense. There is no resemblance whatever between this kind of study and – to take a distinguished example – Lowes' brilliant researches into the background of Coleridge's poetry in *The Road to Xanadu*. There, what was involved was the imaginative transformation of material taken mainly from books. Here, the road leads directly back to Hawkshead and Esthwaite. We are concerned with the growth, from intense and personal experiences, of an intensely personal use of language, sometimes 'private' in its origins, but transmuted into words of wide general power by the process of apparent tautology and repetition. And not the least astonishing thing about it, considering the comparative complexity of some of the linguistic processes involved, is that Wordsworth himself should have had so accurate an intuition of the real nature of what he was doing. It was a capacity not unnoticed by his acquaintance. John Stuart Mill, after long conversations with Wordsworth in 1831, wrote to a friend:

> ... when you get Wordsworth on the subjects which are peculiarly his, such as the theory of his own art ... no one can converse with him without feeling that he has advanced that great subject beyond any other man, being probably the first person who ever combined, with such eminent success in the practice of the art, such high powers of generalization & habits of meditation on its principles.[30]

10

> So oft in castle moated round
> In black damp dungeon underground,
> Strange forms are seen that, white and tall,
> Stand straight against the coal-black wall.
>
> *The Vale of Esthwaite* 39–42 (*PW* I, 270–1)

The *gleam* word-cluster came to light from floundering about in the text, the Concordance, and a substantial card-index. But hindsight, in its usual irritating fashion, suggests that it might well have been identified much more calmly and economically by simple statistical methods. Not much more was involved than finding a group of words, more or less closely related in meaning (perhaps from Roget's *Thesaurus*), all of which showed a large excess of occurrences in Wordsworth when compared, say, with Thorndike's T List, or with his general list of word-frequencies. It may be possible to profit by this elementary discovery in future work, for it goes without saying that there are many more word-clusters in Wordsworth than those studied here.

Some of them, however – and some of importance – would slip through the statistical net just described. The number of their occurrences is so small that they would not attract attention in any purely numerical assessment. This is really no bad thing, for in the last resort I should be sorry to have proved that there could be any other basis for the study of Wordsworth than a thorough knowledge of the text itself. The number of words clustered is also very small, not more than four or five at most, and none of them would attract attention by frequency of occurrence. It may well be, indeed, that the hypothesis outlined above about the relation between frequencies of words and the frequencies of their meanings can be extended to these characteristic word-clusters: the smaller the number of occurrences of the whole cluster, the smaller the number of words in it. However that may be, the history of one such small cluster can be briefly told by way of illustration. It began, of course, at Esthwaite, and in the very first week when Wordsworth went to school there, at Whitsuntide in 1779. The experience which generated it does not appear in *The Vale* as we have it, and may well have achieved poetic form for the first time in that momentous winter in Germany in 1798. At that stage, it was designed for inclusion in the first book of *The Prelude*, together with *There was a Boy*, but both eventually found their place in Book V:

> Well do I call to mind the very week
> When I was first entrusted to the care
> Of that sweet Valley; when its paths, its shores,
> And brooks, were like a dream of novelty
> To my half-infant thoughts; that very week
> While I was roving up and down alone,
> Seeking I knew not what, I chanced to cross
> One of those open fields, which, shaped like ears,
> Make green peninsulas on Esthwaite's Lake:
> Twilight was coming on; yet through the gloom,
> I saw distinctly on the opposite Shore
> A heap of garments, left, as I suppos'd,
> By one who there was bathing; long I watch'd,
> But no one own'd them; meanwhile the calm Lake
> Grew dark, with all the shadows on its breast,
> And now and then, a fish up-leaping, snapp'd
> The breathless stillness. The succeeding day,
> (Those unclaimed garments telling a plain Tale)
> Went there a Company, and, in their Boat
> Sounded with grappling irons, and long poles.
> At length, the dead Man, 'mid that beauteous scene
> Of trees, and hills and water, bolt upright
> Rose with his ghastly face; a spectre shape
> Of terror even! and yet no vulgar fear,
> Young as I was, a Child not nine years old,
> Possess'd me; for my inner eye had seen
> Such sights before, among the shining streams
> Of Fairy Land, the Forests of Romance:
> Thence came a spirit hallowing what I saw
> With decoration and ideal grace;
> A dignity, a smoothness, like the works
> Of Grecian Art, and purest Poesy.[31] (*Prel.* V.450–81)

It must have been, despite the idealising aid of fairy tales, a powerful experience, and the more so because Wordsworth himself had found the heap of clothes the night before. But what seems to have emerged from its excitement and complexity for his own memories and their favourite words was simply the posture of the dead man, *bolt upright* – and it is, after all, perhaps the most surprising detail in the whole account. And it was this vivid and curious detail that proved to have the capacity for repeating itself, and the words which described it, in his later life. Just possibly the earliest revival of it – and even so a very partial one – is in the posture of the Gothic spectres in *The Vale*, 'white and tall . . . straight against the coal-black wall' (41–2 [*PW* I, 271]). But however this may be, the upright posture of the drowned man was then, and always remained, closely associated with the words *spectre*, *ghost* and *ghastly*. In one of its earliest occurrences, Peter Bell draws the drowned man out of the river, having twined his staff in the corpse's hair:

> He pulls – and looks – and pulls again
> And he whom the poor Ass had lost
> The man who had been four days dead,
> Head-foremost from the river's bed
> Uprises like a ghost! (576–80 [*PW* II, 358])

This was written at Alfoxden in April 1798. Two months before, he had composed the description of the 'discharged soldier' which eventually found a place at the end of Book IV of the 1805 *Prelude*. This image, the first of the remarkable 'apparitions' which came to Wordsworth in succession with their special 'admonishments', in origin was doubtless a real soldier, encountered one night in 1788, during the first summer vacation from Cambridge. But the encounter had been made impressive beyond any ordinary human contact because this tall figure fitted in so aptly with images long established in Wordsworth's mind, and described in *The Vale*. The main early sources of the soldier's strange 'ghastly' image will be mentioned later, but for the moment it is enough to notice that one of the chief elements in the first startling impression he made was that he was 'upright':

> He was of stature tall,
> A foot above man's common measure tall,
> And lank, and *upright*. (MS *Verse 18A*)

Another such admonitory apparition came to Wordsworth, his sister and Coleridge as they walked on a September morning along the shore of Grasmere, looking at the flotsam and jetsam, the flowers and ferns:

> And feeding thus our fancies, we advanced
> Along the indented shore; when suddenly,
> Through a thin veil of glittering haze was seen
> Before us, on a point of jutting land,
> The tall and *upright* figure of a Man
> Attired in peasant's garb, who stood alone,
> Angling beside the margin of the lake.
> 'Improvident and reckless', we exclaimed,

'The Man must be, who thus can lose a day
Of the mid harvest, when the labourer's hire
Is ample, and some little might be stored
Wherewith to cheer him in the winter time.'
Thus talking of that Peasant we approached
Close to the spot where with his rod and line
He stood alone; whereat he turned his head
To greet us – and we saw a Man worn down
By sickness, gaunt and lean, with sunken cheeks
And wasted limbs, his legs so long and lean
That for my single self I looked at them,
Forgetful of the body they sustained. –
Too weak to labour in the harvest field,
The Man was using his best skill to gain
A pittance from the dead unfeeling lake
That knew not of his wants. I will not say
What thoughts immediately were ours, nor how
The happy idleness of that sweet morn,
With all its lovely images, was changed
To serious musing and to self-reproach.

(*Poems on the Naming of Places* IV.43–70 [*PW* II.116–17])

This passage, alone of those which have the special *upright* posture as a distinguishing feature of a figure on its first, characteristically sudden appearance, has no suggestion of the supernatural. But the 'admonishment' which that sudden revelation of the turned face administered to the three cheerful wanderers is entirely comparable with the last line of another description, the most remarkable and powerful embodiment of that early Esthwaite experience; it is from Wordsworth's account of the anonymous swirling crowds of London:

And once, far-travell'd in such mood, beyond
The reach of common indication, lost
Amid the moving pageant, 'twas my chance
Abruptly to be smitten with the view
Of a blind Beggar, who, with *upright* face,
Stood propp'd against a Wall, upon his Chest
Wearing a written paper, to explain
The story of the Man, and who he was.
My mind did at this spectacle turn round
As with the might of waters, and it seemed
To me that in this Label was the type,
Or emblem, of the utmost that we know,
Both of ourselves and of the universe;
And, on the shape of the unmoving man,
His fixèd face and sightless eyes, I look'd
As if admonish'd from another world.

(*Prel.* VII.607–22)

There are few descriptions in literature so deceivingly simple as these apparitions in Wordsworth. At first sight, they seem to be so little more than factual, sensitive accounts of real encounters. It is only when they are taken together, and with an eye on the rest of his writing, that they are seen for what they really are: meeting-places of some present or recently past sight with much earlier and deeper memories, strange coincidences of different layers of the memory, suddenly brought together by words, even by a word so apparently simple as *upright*. In this last description, not only has the blind beggar that curious upright posture characteristic of blind people, but he is also partly a spectre, like the drowned man drawn up from the lake; and memories of the lake itself return – 'As with the might of waters'. And perhaps as he stood 'propp'd against the wall' he had something too of those 'Strange forms . . . white and tall, . . . straight against the coal-black wall.'

Wordsworth once expressed, in lines almost too hackneyed to be taken to have much meaning, this view of his own history:

> The Child is father of the Man;
> And I could wish my days to be
> Bound each to each by natural piety.
>
> (*My heart leaps up* 7–9 [*PW* I, 226])

His wish was often granted. What he had seen and felt as a child continually entered into what he saw and felt as a man, casting over the later vision a power which is only to be understood in terms of its relation with earlier visions, and with the words which linked all together.

11

> Poetry is the breath and finer spirit of all knowledge; it is the impassioned expression which is in the countenance of all Science.
>
> *Preface* to *Lyrical Ballads* (*PW* II, 396)

It has already been remarked that the words and word-clusters characterising Wordsworth's idiolect are capable of contributing their special force to passages of 'philosophic' or reflective writing, saving them from bareness, and embodying, in the words themselves, the strong links between sensuous and mental experience in his mind and style. This deserves somewhat fuller illustration, and it will be taken from part of Book I of *The Prelude*. The passage is not particularly well known, nor very striking in style, though in content it describes one of the really decisive moments in the development of English poetry: it follows, and comments on, his long search for the apt subject of an epic theme, or some 'philosophic Song':

But from this awful burthen I full soon
Take refuge, and beguile myself with trust
That mellower years will bring a riper mind
And clearer insight. Thus from day to day
I live, a mockery of the brotherhood
Of vice and virtue, with no skill to part
Vague longing that is bred by want of power
From paramount impulse not to be withstood,
A timorous capacity from prudence;
From circumspection, infinite delay.
Humility and modest awe themselves
Betray me, serving often for a cloak
To a more subtle selfishness, that now
Doth lock my functions up in blank reserve,
Now dupes me by an over-anxious eye
That with a false activity beats off
Simplicity and self-presented truth.
– Ah! better far than this, to stray about
Voluptuously through fields and rural walks,
And ask no record of the hours, given up
To vacant musing, unreprov'd neglect
Of all things, and deliberate holiday;
Far better never to have heard the name
Of zeal and just ambition, than to live
Thus baffled by a mind that every hour
Turns recreant to her task, takes heart again,
Then feels immediately some hollow thought
Hang like an interdict upon her hopes.
This is my lot; for either still I find
Some imperfection in the chosen theme,
Or see of absolute accomplishment
Much wanting, so much wanting, in myself,
That I recoil and droop, and seek repose
In listlessness from vain perplexity,
Unprofitably travelling towards the grave,
Like a false Steward who hath much received
And renders nothing back. – Was it for this
That one, the fairest of all Rivers, lov'd
To blend his murmurs with my Nurse's song,
And from his alder shades and rocky falls,
And from his fords and shallows, sent a voice
That flow'd along my dreams? (*Prel.* I.235–76)

Before commenting on the words, attention must be given to the way in which they are ordered – a matter of great importance, necessarily laid aside while we are examining single words and short phrases. This passage demonstrates very clearly one of Wordsworth's greatest technical powers, that of controlling the rise and fall of fairly long and complex sentences, with a sureness and flexibility which has something in common with the draughtsmanship of the great painters. They have freedom and sweep and variety, but no looseness, no encouragement to faltering reproductions of those combinations of pause, pitch and stress which were designed to link the words together. No doubt he was much helped in attaining this quality by his habit of oral composition, and by his tenacious verbal memory. Here, for example, the oxymoron of lines 239–40 is steadily, but not monotonously expanded through the different kinds of conflict described in lines 241–51, at first in short antitheses, 'timorous capacity/prudence', then in longer phrases, still held together in a sequence of half-formal contrasts, 'From circumspection, infinite delay' achieving its climax by sudden reversal of the two elements. Antithesis, of course, is much more than a rhetorical or stylistic trick. One has only to glance at the *Thesaurus* to see that it is a major characteristic of words themselves, and there are few more powerful ways of selecting between the possible meanings of words than placing them in this relationship with one another. Here, it is used powerfully, without the wit of Pope, but also without his occasional monotony or apparent automatism. While he was at St John's College, Wordsworth had a Tutor in Rhetoric. He seems to have benefited at least from this part of his tuition.

As for the words themselves, the most obvious quality, for a modern reader with modern tastes, is a negative one – the absence of striking images and metaphors in the Shakespearean tradition. The solitary exception is 'interdict' (line 262), which looks a little like the legal imagery common in both Shakespeare and Donne, but it is not developed, and is left isolated; it is, in fact, the only use of the word in Wordsworth. For the rest, the images are gentle, almost commonplace. They draw no attention to themselves, and have neither wit nor vivid obscurity: '*mellower* years', '*riper* mind', '*bred* by want of power', '*Betray* me, *serving* often *for a cloak*', '*lock* my functions *up*', '*beats* off / simplicity', '*hollow* thought'. These subfusc colourings are to Shakespearean images as lichen is to bracken and heath in September. And the more complex metaphors and references are as quietly managed: 'recreant' and 'baffled', for example (lines 259–60), which unobtrusively recall the world of chivalry and knighthood, of knights unfaithful to their calling, who were *baffled*, disgraced by having their arms tied upside down over their tents. In the same glancing fashion, the 'false Steward' (line 270) avails itself of one of the parables of the New Testament. It is not here, or in an analysis of this kind, that the real effect of the passage will be found. It is to be sought in the apparent tautologies, in the words repeated here, and many times elsewhere in Wordsworth, gathering with repetition force and clarity, as memories grow in strength when they recur in active meditation.

In line 248, the phrase 'blank reserve' carries the more weight of meaning because it is exceptional in English to find *reserve* used in this sense, indeed in any pejorative sense. It is, as a moral quality, much more usually valued highly, and in all its other uses in Wordsworth it is so valued. The pejorative meaning here is, of course, given to it by *blank*, and it is this that turns out to be distinctive to Wordsworth – idiolectal. Wordsworth used it 34 times. Just before him, Cowper had used it 8 times, and among his contemporaries it occurs thus: Coleridge 13, Shelley 8, Keats 7. These crude figures must, of course, be regarded askance, and with an eye to the problems discussed above arising from differences caused by size of sample-texts. But it is much safer to attach significance to the fact that *blank* occurs in Wordsworth in a special sense, and in several obviously weighty passages, whereas in all the other writers it is used in the simple literal sense, save only for Keats' phrase 'blank splendour' in *Hyperion* and in one poem of Coleridge's mentioned below. These are typical of the contexts in Wordsworth:

> Fallings from us, vanishings;
> Blank misgivings of a Creature
> Moving about in worlds not realized . . .
>
> (*Immortality Ode* 144–6 [*PW* IV, 283])

In Book I of *The Prelude*, the incident with the stolen boat ends with this description of guilty fear:

> my brain
> Work'd with a dim and undetermin'd sense
> Of unknown modes of being; in my thoughts
> There was a darkness, call it solitude,
> Or blank desertion . . . (*Prel.* I.418–22)

And in *The Excursion*, the mood of The Solitary on his way to America is described thus:

> And, in the blank and solitude of things,
> Upon his spirit, with a fever's strength,
> Will conscience prey. (*PW* V, 104)

The only use of the word comparable with contexts like these is in Coleridge's *Dejection* Ode, where it is used to describe his own loss of the faculty of perceiving Nature: 'And still I gaze – and with how blank an eye!' (line 30). It seems that, in a passage which draws a melancholy distinction between

Wordsworth and himself in their attitudes to Nature, he caught instinctively this characteristically Wordsworthian use of this word.

The more positive side of Wordsworth's experience is represented by three notable words, *insight* (*Prel.* I.238), *paramount* and *impulse* (*Prel.* I.242). These notes sketch, very briefly and incompletely, their status in Wordsworth's idiolect.

Insight. This is used by Wordsworth 15 times, not at all by Cowper, Keats or Shelley, and once only in Coleridge's verse. It occurs in that odd little poem *Star-Gazers*, where he reflects on the night-walkers paying their pennies to look through a telescope in Leicester Square, and ejaculates '– what an insight must it be!' (*PW* II, 219). Much more central contexts are found in *The Prelude*:

> If thou partake the animating faith
> That Poets, even as Prophets, each with each
> Connected in a mighty scheme of truth,
> Have each his own peculiar faculty,
> Heaven's gift, a sense that fits him to perceive
> Objects unseen before, thou wilt not blame
> The humblest of this band who dares to hope
> That unto him hath also been vouchsafed
> An insight that in some sort he possesses,
> A privilege whereby a work of his,
> Proceeding from a source of untaught things
> Creative and enduring, may become
> A power like one of Nature's. (*1850* XIII.301–12)

> This love more intellectual cannot be
> Without Imagination, which, in truth,
> Is but another name for absolute strength
> And clearest insight, amplitude of mind,
> And reason in her most exalted mood. (*Prel.* XIII.166–70)

The first of these is from Wordsworth's most remarkable description of the office of the Poet, and the second from his final attempt to describe the Imagination. The association of *insight* with both subjects leaves no doubt that the word was one of high solemnity in Wordsworth's idiolect. The *OED* suggests some further light on its special role, for it shows that the word was common among the theological writers of the seventeenth century, for whom it meant the power of seeing below the appearances of things to their inner essence. The last two quotations are early in the eighteenth century, and then nothing more until Wordsworth himself. It is not possible, of course, to put much weight on the sequence of citations given in the *OED*, and much more extensive search of the likelier contexts would be necessary to prove that this gap in the word's usage really existed. So far as it goes, however, it seems possible that the word had been revived, brought back into English, largely by his agency.

Impulse. This is at once recognised as one of the characteristic Wordsworthian words, because of the awful frequency with which it has been quoted in 'One impulse from a vernal wood'. But it turns out to be strongly idiolectal by more objective standards. He used it 39 times, Cowper 3 times, Coleridge 10 times, Shelley 17 times, and Keats not at all. It does not occur in Shakespeare either, but there are several uses in Milton, to which we will return. Much more important, however, than the mere numbers of occurrences are the relative frequencies of the two chief meanings of the word. And it was Milton who most clearly distinguished between them. On the one hand, he uses the word to describe some internal flurry of the spirit, which usually produces bad actions, as here: 'hurry them by a blind impulse into habitual fornication' (*Christian Doctrine* I.10); 'subdue the primary impulses of the ungovernable age' (*Prolusion* VII); 'no control of his impulses' (*Commonplace Book*). On the other hand, he used it to mean a movement in the spirit directed by God himself, as here: 'Spirit signifies a divine impulse' (*Christian Doctrine* I.6); 'the natural mind and will of man being partially renewed by a divine impulse' (*Christian Doctrine* I.17). And he has, of course, no doubt which is the worthier kind of impulse: 'the greater praise for doing it not upon blind impulse but upon deliberation and design . . . I cannot but think that these things were brought about rather by a divine impulse' (*First Defence* I). Both of these meanings are found in Shelley, Coleridge and Wordsworth, but in markedly different proportions. In Wordsworth alone the first is much more frequent, in the other poets it is rare. The one notable exception is in Coleridge's *Dejection* ode, where it is used of the coming storm:

> Those sounds which oft have raised me, whilst they awed,
> And sent my soul abroad,
> Might now perhaps their wonted impulse give,
> Might startle this dull pain, and make it move and live! (17–20)

In a poem describing the loss of his feeling for Nature, the failure of joy and 'genial spirits', it was entirely apt that he should have used, in just this way, this characteristically Wordsworthian meaning, just as, a few lines later, he falls into the Wordsworthian use of 'blank'.[32] For in Wordsworth himself, the word usually referred to some exercise of an outward power upon the spirit, as it had done in Milton and in other theological writers. And it took on this preferred meaning early, for it is used in this way, not only in 'One impulse from a vernal wood', but more powerfully in a fragment from the *Christabel* Notebook:

> In many a walk
> At evening or by moonlight, or reclined
> At midday upon beds of forest moss,
> Have we to Nature and her impulses
> Of our whole being made free gift . . . (*vi*.8–12 [*PW* v, 343–4])

A word as important as this in Wordsworth's idiolect was not likely to remain isolated, but would tend to form part of a characteristic word-cluster. It is connected, very interestingly, with *influx*, for the line quoted above from the 1850 *Prelude*, 'An insight that in some sort he possesses', had been written in 1805: 'An influx, that in some sort I possess'd'. *Influx* is another word of this group, a near-synonym of *impulse*, related also with *influence* and *power*. And *power* is too central to his vocabulary to be dealt with in passing.

Paramount. This is not a common word in any writer, but is used by Wordsworth 13 times, by Cowper twice, but in simple meanings such as 'paramount lord', 'paramount claims'. It does not appear in Coleridge, Keats, Shelley or Shakespeare. It is found once in Milton, in the phrase 'their mighty paramount', of Satan. In Wordsworth, it links together a number of significant passages. It occurs, for example, in his account of the influence of Euclid on his conception of God:

> from this source more frequently I drew
> A pleasure calm and deeper, a still sense
> Of permanent and universal sway
> And paramount endowment in the mind,
> An image not unworthy of the one
> Surpassing Life, which out of space and time,
> Nor touch'd by welterings of passion, is
> And hath the name of God. (*Prel*. VI.150–7)

Here, the political notion of paramountcy has been applied to a description of the universe. In other passages it is retained within the political sphere, but used in a new way, as in the lesser-known companion-sonnet to 'Milton! thou shouldst be living at this hour', where he compares the French Revolution with the English Civil War:

> France, 'tis strange,
> Hath brought forth no such souls as we had then.
> Perpetual emptiness! unceasing change!
> No single volume paramount, no code,
> No master spirit, no determined road;
> But equally a want of books and men! (*PW* III, 116–17)

Though Wordsworth was in principle a democrat in political theory, his notion of democracy was tempered by an almost Platonic belief in the need for 'guardian' spirits, to lead democracy aright. This conception is found, with *paramount* again, in another passage on the French Revolution, intensely personal, for it explains why he had not himself taken an active part in it, with his friends the Orleanists, against the extremists. 'An insignificant Stranger . . . and little graced with power / Or eloquence even in my native speech,' he had nevertheless perceived that:

> A Spirit thoroughly faithful to itself,
> Unquenchable, unsleeping, undismay'd,
> Was as an instinct among Men, a stream
> That gather'd up each petty straggling rill
> And vein of water, glad to be roll'd on
> In safe obedience, that a mind whose rest
> Was where it ought to be, in self-restraint,
> In circumspection and simplicity,
> Fell rarely in entire discomfiture
> Below its aim, or met with from without
> A treachery that defeated it or foil'd . . .
>
> Well might my wishes be intense, my thoughts
> Strong and perturb'd, not doubting at that time,
> Creed which ten shameful years have not annull'd,
> But that the virtue of one paramount mind
> Would have abashed those impious crests, have quell'd
> Outrage and bloody power . . . (*Prel.* X.131–3, 148–58, 177–82)

It will be noticed that in this passage, the problem described is rather like that of the passage from which this note started out. There, he was explaining his failure to begin writing the great epic or philosophic poem because *circumspection* had become confused with infinite delay, *simplicity* had been 'beaten off', and there had been no 'paramount impulse'; here, he envisages himself much more certainly as having *simplicity*, *circumspection*, and the other qualities of that kind of 'paramount mind' which can act effectively in political crises. It is clear that, at moments of difficult personal choice, the considerations which were turned over in his meditations were often more or less the same, and that the words in which they presented themselves to his thoughts and feelings were very much the same.

There is, however, one word in all these passages which has been unduly neglected, and which is all too easily overlooked, the word *one*, and its near-synonym *single*. In the first of these passages, *paramount* was associated with 'the one / Surpassing Life'; in the second, it ends the phrase 'no single volume paramount', and in the third it is next to *one*, 'one paramount mind'. It looks rather as if 'paramount' were not an isolated element in Wordsworth's idiolect, but rather one of a word-cluster, probably all used to reinforce *one* itself. This much broader meaning, indeed, is strongly suggested by the context of the passage from Book I, for Wordsworth had introduced his long list of epic themes thus:

> Time, place, and manners; these I seek, and these
> I find in plenteous store; but nowhere such
> As may be singled out with steady choice . . . (*Prel*. I.169–71)

And he concludes his survey of these possible themes with the reflection that none has in fact singled itself out – there has been no 'paramount impulse'; none, that is, until this impulse suddenly presents itself in the momentous question of the closing lines, 'Was it for this / That one . . .' The answer to this question was, of course, the answer to his long hesitation.

Before passing on to look more carefully at *one*, a brief comment is needed on the larger context of the passage from which this section started, for the content is, as usual, very closely bound up with the style. This search among possible themes, among times and places and manners, for the subject of an epic had been traditional among English poets since Dryden and Pope. They had failed. And those who thought they had found the themes, like Blackmore and Glover, had failed too. Wordsworth was, in fact, merely the last in a line which stretched back to Virgil – or rather, to Apollonius Rhodius. All of them, century after century, had been led a pretty dance by the *ignis fatuus* of an epic poem, a poem like that which they believed to have been written by Homer, but which no Homer had written, at any rate in the sense they understood. Some such man may have existed, even one of that name, but as only one of the many composers and reciters of the saga-cycles to which this name happened to be affixed, perhaps as late as the time of the Peisistratean redaction. Not only did the precedent upon which the later writers relied not exist, but the quality of the Homeric poems was one which could not, in its very nature, be attained by an individual writer at work in a relatively sophisticated society, concerned with readers rather than hearers, faced by the perplexities of choice between many subjects and many styles, instead of having both prescribed for him by tradition. The Homeric quality, in fact, is necessarily as different from that of the epic imitators as is the quality of the anonymous traditional ballads from those written by Coleridge, Keats, John Crowe Ransom and the rest. It is no wonder that the history of the 'literary' epic is littered with half or wholly ridiculous failures, since failure was inevitable. The only residual problem is to explain why, here and there, a writer came so near to success: Virgil, Milton, Camoëns perhaps – but since I cannot read him in Portuguese, he is placed here by hearsay only.

What Wordsworth does, then, in this momentous passage is to accept defeat, to reconcile himself, however reluctantly, to the realities of this strange piece of literary illusion, and to turn in upon himself asking why he felt that he was a poet, and how this burden of achievement had been laid upon him. In doing this, in returning to the influence of that 'fairest of all Rivers' on his childhood dreams, he was undertaking a task difficult enough, but one not by its nature impossible. It is a moment of self-analysis very like that in *The Vale* when he had turned from Gothic terrors as 'Fond sickly Fancy's idle toys'. But it is more momentous in its consequences, not least for the development of his style. So subjective a subject both demanded and developed an idiolect as an essential condition for its own expression.

Whatever the Homeric language may be, it is certainly not idiolectal. It has, of course, strong dialectal features, which survive the Attic influences of the first reduction to writing. But it has also the overwhelmingly general character of a style from which personal elements have been eliminated, if they ever existed; worn down in the long process of repetition from memory, by many reciters in many places over a long period of time. It is distinguished by the effective use of all those conventional epithets which are so much in place in saga and ballad, and so curiously offensive when encountered in a 'literary' writer. The one thing which these epithets have in common with Wordsworth's use of his idiolectal words is repetition. But with them, the repetition involves no growth or change of meaning. On the contrary, its function, in oral recitation, is to help in fixing the mind of the reciter and his hearers by a standard, readily recognisable expansion of a noun; for this purpose it was necessary that Ἠώς should be always ῥοδοδάκτῦλος, and that Odysseus should always be πολύμητις. In the apparent tautology of the Wordsworthian repetitions, on the other hand, the effect was to strengthen the words by the cumulative force of their contexts, so that feeling came in aid of feeling, to associate them in clusters within which their near-synonymy gained both precision and individuality of meaning, and to enforce a personal, subjective choice among their possible meanings. The words, indeed, may be 'a selection of the language really spoken by men', but the meanings of those words are largely Wordsworth's own, some imposed anew, others recovered from a past stage of the language. And it is this use of words that confers a density of imaginative weight upon passages of argument and reflection, in *The Prelude* especially, sometimes in *The Excursion*, and occasionally in the shorter poems.

12

Here keepest thou in singleness thy state . . .

Prel. 1850, XIV.211

The list of Wordsworth's 'favorite words' given by F. B. Snyder was made after some words had been omitted from the process of counting. Of these some were left out because Snyder himself considered that they were of 'but little significance'; others because they had been disregarded in the Concordance; and others again because only partial lists had been given there. From the statistical point of view, these omissions helped to deprive Snyder's list of any significance it might otherwise have had. But it must be admitted that very few of these words would be of much interest to the ordinary reader or student of Wordsworth. The omitted articles, conjunctions, prepositions and pronouns are all among the very common words in English, and it is very likely that he used most of them in the common way – in a way, that is to say, resulting from the fact that he was writing in English, and not from the fact that he was Wordsworth.

There is, however, at least one notable exception, the word *one*, which the Concordance had listed only partially. Even so, it has 769 occurrences, and would have come well up in Snyder's list of 'favorite words' – unless he himself had decided that it was of 'no particular significance'. Had he done so, many critics would have agreed with him readily, for it seems that they have paid very little attention to the use of numerals in poetry, at least from any broad standpoint. Writing on the ballads, they sometimes say a little about the special prominence of 3, 7 and 9; and there are a few comments on Keats' well-known letter defending the 'kisses four' in *La Belle Dame*. The numerals do not deserve this general neglect. They are interesting in relation to important general principles of vocabulary behaviour, and also because some of them turn out to be unexpectedly significant.

The general problems can best be indicated by a table, and Table XI shows the relative frequencies of occurrence of the numerals from 1 to 19 in Wordsworth and Shakespeare. In the first column are set out the frequencies in the Thorndike–Lorge List. In the fourth are the number of definitions of each of the numerals given in the *SED*. A glance down the columns suggests at once that numbers, considered as words, obey the laws imposed by numbers, mathematically considered, on all other words. The first three columns produce characteristic frequency distributions, and the fourth shows that, with some curious exceptions, the definitions of number-words decrease in proportion with the occurrence of the words themselves.

Table XI

	Thorndike–Lorge	*Shakespeare*	*Wordsworth*	*SED (definitions)*
one	17,569	1909	769 (*partial*)	31
two	5908	639	183	15
three	2873	354	89	12
four	1637	140	24	4
five	1462	127	28	6
six	806	58	23	17
seven	615	71	35	11
eight	657	35	21	4
nine	468	56	10	8
ten	1260	159	50	12
eleven	227	20	2	4
twelve	413	42	18	12
thirteen	92	5	1	5
fourteen	143	25	2	5
fifteen	410	17	3	4
sixteen	194	12	2	5
seventeen	139	6	0	3
eighteen	215	7	3	2
nineteen	109	3	0	3

The first column was based on 4½ million words of text, taken from American magazines between 1927 and 1938. It represents modern usage, in a mixed sample. It shows beyond doubt that the number-words tend to be used in inverse ratio to the numerals they represent, and where this general trend is broken, it is usually for obvious reasons, at any rate in the upper, and therefore more reliable part of the table. One would have expected that the influence of the decimal and duodecimal systems would bring 5, 10 and 12 into surplus, and it does so quite clearly. The numeral 6 does not seem to benefit from being half of 12, though in the last column it has a remarkable surplus of definitions, for no very obvious reason. In the lower part of the table, the frequency of 15 is out of line with the rest, but perhaps this is due to the fact that at this level the problems of small samples and small liabilities of occurrence are in play. The regularity of the decline of frequencies in the upper part of the table is matched by the same cardinals multiplied by 10. They have these frequencies:

twenty: 673 thirty: 341 forty: 283 fifty: 525 sixty: 161 seventy: 59 eighty: 82 ninety: 62

The higher powers of 10 itself, where words exist for them, show the same pattern:

hundred: 1355 thousand: 1240 million: 598 billion: 93

It would seem, then, to be an observable law of linguistic behaviour, at least in English, that words representing small numbers are used more often than those representing large ones, in a very direct ratio. It would not be uninteresting to speculate on the implications of this law for the structure of the universe, and the manner in which the human mind perceives it. But, for the moment, we are concerned with the general law only insofar as it enables us to examine more hopefully the other columns in the table.

The columns of frequencies from Shakespeare and Wordsworth clearly follow the general trend very closely, and do not fail to reflect the decimal and duodecimal surpluses for 5, 10 and 12. They seem to share with the T–L List the one notable evidence of superstition on the use of numbers, for, like it, they have conspicuous deficits for 13. They differ from the general trend, however, in showing marked surpluses for two of the other superstitious numerals, 7, which is in excess for both poets, and 9, which is in excess for Shakespeare, but roughly in its expected place for Wordsworth. The superstitious properties of 3 do not seem to be represented in any of the lists, though a more sophisticated statistical analysis might perhaps reveal their effect.

The last column, showing the number of definitions for each number-word, according to the *SED*, is in general agreement with the linguistic law which states that the frequency of occurrence of any word is in direct ratio with the number of definitions of it given in a good dictionary. It appears to reflect faithfully both the arithmetical surpluses of 10 and 12, and the superstitious ones of 7 and 9. There are, however, obvious oddities in this column. For the numbers 4, 5, 8 and 11 are markedly in deficit, while 6 is in surplus of expectation. For this surplus no reason is apparent, unless it be that the article on 'six' in the *OED* (on which the *SED* was based) was written by an exceptionally fine discriminator of meanings. Certainly the entries under section B in the *SED* entry are more finely drawn than they are in the articles on neighbouring numbers, such as 7. For the deficits, however, an uncomfortable reason may be suggested. They all accompany words which stand high in the alphabet, one in E and four in F. It seems likely that the compilers of the *OED* were less skilful in discriminating meanings in their dealings with the earlier letters than they became, with the benefit of experience, when they came to the lower part of the alphabet. This list is only one of the pieces of evidence pointing in this direction. It is, at any rate, more reasonable to suppose that they gained in skill as they went on with their great task, than that in English words beginning with the letters A to I have fewer meanings than those beginning with J to Z.[33]

From these general considerations of the table, we can now turn to comment on the three numerals which appear to have special relevance to Wordsworth's poetry. The first is 7, and it has an obvious bearing on the poem *We are Seven*. Bearing in mind the figures showing that he attached some special significance to this number, one can see that the poem could hardly have existed as *We are Four*, *We are Eight* – still less *We are Thirteen*. And it may be asked (though without much prospect of an answer) whether the little girl who had this conversation with Wordsworth in 1793 near Goodrich Castle really used this number; if so, whether the number played some part in his deep impression of her family history. Or did she in fact give a different number, such as four or eight, while he changed it to seven for his own sake? Was there, in fact, to be a kind of poetic mathematics, based on a selection of the numbers really used by men?

A more important, and more easily answered question arises over the first line of *Three years she grew*. It has sometimes been supposed that this might refer to an actual date in the life of a particular person – indeed of the mysterious 'Lucy' herself. A glance at the Concordances is enough to show that it had no such 'real' significance. The number is used here simply because it was, and had long been, the conventional date for the end of infancy and the beginning of childhood. Thus Shakespeare:

> Canst thou remember
> A time before we came unto this cell?
> I do not think thou canst; for then thou wast not
> Out three years old. (*The Tempest*, I.2, 38–41)

Believe then, if you please, that I can do strange things. I have, since I was three years old, convers'd with a magician. (*As You Like It*, V.2.58–60)

> He had two sons – if this be worth your hearing,
> Mark it – the eldest of them at three years old,
> I'th' swathing clothes the other, from their nursery
> Were stol'n . . . (*Cymbeline*, I.I.57–60)

And Wordsworth:

> The One, yet unbreeched, is not three birthdays old . . .
> *The Two Thieves* 13 (*PW* IV, 245)

And Coleridge:

> The Wedding-Guest stood still,
> And listens like a three years' child . . . (*The Ancient Mariner* 14–15)

'Three years', then, was chosen because it said that the influence of Nature by her adoption of this favourite child came about at the earliest possible moment, when she had just emerged from swathing clothes and become a human being, a child, not an infant.

Seven and *three*, however, are no great matters. The really important, and really difficult, numeral in Wordsworth is clearly shown by the table. It is *one*. Some idea of its importance can be gained from the great surplus of its occurrences in his poetry, when compared either with the Lorge List or with Shakespeare. In the former, *one* occurs in the ratio 2.9 to *two*, in the latter the same ratio is 2.4. In Wordsworth, on the other hand, even for the partial listing of the word, the ratio is 4.3, already nearly double that in Lorge or in Shakespeare. There can be no doubt that, even when all allowances have been made for differences in sizes of sample, and the special character of the Lorge samples, *one* was a very prominent word in Wordsworth's idiolect. Despite its partial omission from the Concordance, and the prevailing lack of concern with numerals on the part of literary critics, it would seem to be a word worth looking at.

It is also a word which needs to be looked at very carefully, because, over and above its very high relative frequency among the numerals as shown in the table, it has a very high frequency among all words. The Lorge List, for example, places it thirty-first in frequency of occurrence among all the words in English,[34] roughly equal with *all* and *we*, and surpassed only by the commonest of articles, conjunctions, prepositions and auxiliary verbs. It is, for this reason alone, certain to present severe problems of multi-meaning, and the last column of the table shows that it does so. Moreover, the hypothesis outlined above concerning the relation between the relative frequencies of words and the relative frequencies of their separate meanings is likely to apply to it with great force. Because Wordsworth uses it so much more often than most other writers do, he must use it in senses which depart extensively from the more usual frequencies.

The article on *one* in the *OED* fills twelve columns, or four pages, and this mass of information must be simplified before it can be analysed. This can best be done by disregarding, for the moment, the arabic sub-divisions of meaning, and concentrating on the main Roman headings. Six of these are especially significant, and they are characterised below:

I As plain numeral, in simple enumeration, or in slightly more specialised contexts such as 'one man, one vote'.

II As emphatic numeral: one in contrast to two or more: one and no more, one only; a single.

III In pregnant senses: one made up of many components; one in continuity; the same in all parts, at all times or in all circumstances; uniformly the same; one and the same. One in relation to two or more things or persons; one in substance; identical; the same. One in kind; the same in quality or nature. One in mind, feeling, intention, or bearing; in unison, harmonious; at one.

IV In a particularising or partitive sense. One from amongst others; a particular, an individual, as in 'one of'; in antithesis to Another, Other, with or without noun following; 'the one . . . the other'; reciprocally, 'one another'.

V Indefinite pronoun (with genitive *one's*). A person, someone. Defined by a noun in apposition, 'the name of one Boileau'; defined by a clause or phrase, 'one who . . .', 'One above . . .'. Any one of everybody; any one whatever; including (and in later language often specially meaning) the speaker himself.

VI Pronominal or substantival form of *a*, *an*. To avoid repetition of a noun, 'I lose a neighbour and you gain one'. Added after demonstrative and pronominal adjectives, as *the*, *this*, *any*, *each*, *every*, *which* etc. After pronominal and other adjectives, without contextual reference: Person, body, persons; as in *any one*, *every one*, *some one*; *little ones*, *the Holy One*, *the Evil One*, etc.

The first step towards analysing these six classes is to introduce the one vital linguistic feature which dictionaries are, even now, accustomed to omit: varieties of stress when the word is actually used in speech. A lexicographer can perhaps be forgiven for disregarding the fact that the written language is but a poor shadow of the spoken one, having little or no way of representing changes of pitch and stress, or pauses – unless it be that punctuation may imply these features of real speech. He already has a great deal on his mind. But those who merely use a dictionary when all the spade-work has been done can never afford to disregard the importance of the non-verbal features of language. Here, it will be observed that *one*, in its various uses, has three clearly distinguishable strengths of stress. The heaviest is that associated with headings II and III; this is the stress of Milton's

And transgress his Will
For one restraint, Lords of the World besides.

(This is cited by the *OED*, and the metre helps to put the stress beyond doubt.)

> He is made one with Nature.

(*OED* from Shelley. Again the metre is decisive.) The weakest stress on *one* is that associated with heading VI. In all such uses, the preceding word carries the strong stress, as in *any one*, *every one*, *Evil one*. Stress intermediate between the strong and the weak is associated with headings IV and V, and possibly with I also, but the stressing of numerals, when used in the actual process of counting, is to some extent a special case.

These distinctions make it possible to classify the six main headings into two clearly defined groups. Those which use *one* with medium or light stress, IV, V and VI, correspond with its occurrences as a structural word in the language, that is to say a word having no specific lexical meaning of its own, but essential to the composition of utterances because it shows the relations between other structurals and lexical words, those with full meaning. The second group, in which *one* is associated with strong stress, includes headings II and III, in which *one* acts as a lexical word. Heading I is to some extent anomalous, as might be expected, for numerals are perhaps best regarded as combining structural and lexical features, and as constituting a special case.

The distinction between these two groups is very helpful in suggesting a link between the uses of *one* and the basic hypothesis concerning the relative frequencies in headings IV, V and VI would tend to be constant, since it is characteristic of structurals, all of them high-frequency words, to occur with little variation of frequency from one text to another: they are the meanings imposed on the user by the language itself, irrespective of his choice of topic and his personal preferences among words and meanings. On the other hand, we should expect the rates of occurrence in the headings of the second group, II and III, to vary much more widely; for these are the lexical, fully meaningful uses, upon whose frequency choice of topic and personal preference can operate freely. Now since it is clear that Wordsworth used *one* with a frequency much higher than that usually found, it must follow that this excess can only result from a greatly increased use on his part of the lexical meanings in II and III. For the structural meanings, in IV, V and VI, are not open to variation by individual choice. As for heading I, we must keep an open mind: with anomalies, anything can happen. Table XII shows what actually happens to the frequencies of meanings of *one* in Lorge's Semantic Count and in Wordsworth. Under headings IV, V and VI, the number of occurrences,

Table XII

OED heading	no. of meanings expected from L distribution	no. of meanings found in Wordsworth
I	228	38
II	67	269
III	4	115
IV	240	153
V	119	151
VI	111	43
Total	769	769

though not matching closely, has a certain family resemblance in both columns. These are the structural meanings, which can be expected to remain fairly steady in their relative frequencies. Under headings I, II and III, on the other hand, there is a complete misfit between the columns, but fortunately it is one easily understood. The figures for I and II have been very nearly transposed, for, different as they are, their totals are almost the same, 295 and 307. That is to say, in poetry it is only rarely that numbers are used numerically, so that *one* in the sense of 1 is much less frequent than it is in a mixed sample of modern prose. On the other hand, in Wordsworth (whatever other poets may do) there is very often occasion for the emphatic use of *one* meaning *one only*, *single* etc. The figures for III are much the most startling, for they show that in modern prose the main lexical meanings of *one* occur very rarely, while in Wordsworth they are relatively frequent. This high frequency has been obtained, it will be noticed, at the expense of the structural occurrences, of which, taking the three headings IV, V and VI together, 470 examples would be expected, and only 347 are found. The difference almost exactly matches the surplus under heading III. In general, then, the actual figures are remarkably near to what would be expected from the hypothesis concerning the relation between the relative frequencies of words and of meanings. We have a high-frequency word, used by this writer in excess of the usual frequency, and we find that the whole pattern of the frequencies of meanings of the word is distorted, and in the expected direction.

The immediate practical result of applying the hypothesis to this material is to direct our attention to those senses of *one* which fall under headings II and III as being of special significance in Wordsworth – as being his 'favorite' meanings of the word, and also the most meaningful ones. Before coming to examples of meanings under II, here – turning to the Concordance – are two from I, merely to illustrate the difference between plain *one* and emphatic *one*:

> And fiendish faces, one, two, three

> Withered leaves – one – two – and three

Here is a selection of contexts with meanings under II:

> By one soft impulse saved from vacancy

> And in the midst is one particular rock

> – Fair as a star, when only one

> 'This was a work for us; and now, my Son,
> It is a work for me. But, lay one stone –'

> This glade of water and this one green field

> A single beech-tree grew
> Within this grove of firs! and, on the fork
> Of that one beech, appeared a thrush's nest

> and Grasmere's peaceful lake
> And one green island, gleam between the stems

> those fraternal four of Borrowdale,
> Joined in one solemn and capacious grove

> It seems a day
> (I speak of one from many singled out)

> The one only dwelling on earth that she loves

> And one coy Primrose to that Rock

> That thought's return
> Was the worst pang that sorrow ever bore,
> Save one, one only, when I stood forlorn

> One impulse from a vernal wood

> One moment now may give us more

> – But there's a Tree, of many, one,

> The memory of one particular hour

> Let this one temple last, be this one spot
> On earth devoted to eternity

those individual sights
Of courage, or integrity, or truth,
Or tenderness, which there, set off by foil,
Appeared more touching. One will I select

there, in silence, sate
This One Man, with a sickly babe outstretched
Upon his knee

The single sheep, and the one blasted tree

among gleams of sky
And clouds, and intermingling mountain tops,
In one inseparable glory clad,
Creatures of one ethereal substance

These are selected contexts with meanings under heading III, again employing the Concordance:

We all are of one blood

Where earth and heaven do make one imagery

Earth breathed in one great presence of the spring

. . . such delight I found
To note in shrub and tree, in stone and flower,
That intermixture of delicious hues,
Along so vast a surface, all at once,
In one impression, by connecting force
Of their own beauty, imaged in the heart

There are forty feeding like one!

these orchard-tufts,
Which at this season, with their unripe fruits,
Are clad in one green hue, and lose themselves
'Mid groves and copses

That we have all of us one human heart

He travels on, and in his face, his step,
His gait, is one expression

Dust as we are, the immortal spirit grows
Like harmony in music; there is a dark
Inscrutable workmanship that reconciles
Discordant elements, makes them cling together
In one society

did my boat move on;
Leaving behind her still, on either side,
Small circles glittering idly in the moon,
Until they melted all into one track
Of sparkling light

Wordsworthian words

Communing in this sort through earth and heaven
With every form of creature, as it looked
Towards the Uncreated with a countenance
Of adoration, with an eye of love.
One song they sang

More frequently from the same source I drew
A pleasure quiet and profound, a sense
Of permanent and universal sway,
And paramount belief; there, recognised
A type, for finite natures, of the one
Supreme Existence

The unfettered clouds and region of the Heavens,
Tumult and peace, the darkness and the light –
Were all like workings of one mind, the features
Of the same face, blossoms upon one tree;
Characters of the great Apocalypse,
The types and symbols of Eternity,
Of first, and last, and midst, and without end

Living amid the same perpetual whirl
Of trivial objects, melted and reduced
To one identity, by differences
That have no law, no meaning, and no end

                    There is
One great society alone on earth:
The noble Living and the noble Dead

                    save that through a rift . . .
Mounted the roar of waters, torrents, streams
Innumerable, roaring with one voice!

                    the emblem of a mind
That feeds upon infinity, that broods
Over the dark abyss, intent to hear
Its voices issuing forth to silent light
In one continuous stream

And yet a spirit, there for me enshrined
To penetrate the lofty and the low;
Even as one essence of pervading light
Shines, in the brightest of ten thousand stars,
And, the meek worm that feeds her lonely lamp
Couched in the dewy grass

                    among gleams of sky
And clouds, and intermingling mountain tops,
In one inseparable glory clad,
Creatures of one ethereal substance

These two collections differ in one very simple respect. Those which fall under heading II fall quite unambiguously under the section number 7 in the *OED*, most of them under 7*a*, a few under 7*b*; in the total occurrences under this heading, 234 came under 7*a* and 35 under 7*b*. But the only difference between 7*a* and 7*b* is that in the latter, the oneness, in contrast with two or more, is 'Strengthened by *but*, *only*, *single*, *sole*, *alone*'. The only passage seriously in doubt is the last, with its two uses of *one*. The first, in 'one inseparable glory', may just conceivably fall under this definition, since it may be regarded as saying that what might have been two separate 'glories', that of the clouds and that of the mountains, were intermingled into one glory. But the second use, in 'Creatures of one ethereal substance', undoubtedly belongs to III, and within it either to section 13, 'One in kind; the same in quality or nature', or just possibly to 11, 'One in continuity; the same in all parts, at all times, or in all circumstances; uniformly the same; one and the same'. And since the second use is placed in close parallel with the first, it might be better to transfer that too to heading III. With this exception, the meaning of *one* in all these lines can be simply defined. It refers to spots of space or moments of time, or to both together, distinguished, in Wordsworth's perceptions and memories, from space and time in general by some special quality which the contexts describe.

The same definition would cover many of his uses of *single*, which is very nearly synonymous with sense II of *one*, as appears from, for instance, 'A single beech-tree . . . that one beech' above. Here are a few examples:

> Behold her, single in the field,
> Yon solitary Highland Lass!

> There is a Yew-tree, pride of Lorton Vale,
> Which to this day stands single, in the midst
> Of its own darkness . . .
> This solitary Tree!

> A single tree
> With sinuous trunk, boughs exquisitely wreathed,
> Grew there.

> – But there's a Tree, of many, one,
> A single Field which I have looked upon

It is readily apparent from these few examples that *one*, like *naked* and *gleam*, is part of a word-cluster, which includes *solitary* and *single*, and no doubt many more, such as *individual* and *particular*. We are, in fact, touching on another of the lexical groups specially significant in Wordsworth's diction.

But even in the apparent simplicity of the definition which may be given to *one*, and to the words clustered with it, there lurks, by one of those paradoxes which seem to be at the heart of all existence, an unavoidable ambiguity. All isolation, of objects, places and moments, is necessarily relative, and so not wholly isolated from all else. It is a quality, an effect, only to be conceived or perceived against some surroundings in space and time, however remote and shadowy. The effect of painting a black square on a white canvas is to make the white only a little less conspicuous than the black shape within it. This ineradicable implication of oneness, singleness, in a pattern involving other elements is clear in several of the lines quoted to illustrate heading II. The four single trees in Borrowdale make up *one* grove. 'Individual sights . . . set off by foil' appear 'more touching'. In *Michael*, the old father, about to be left to build his sheep-fold in the hills by himself, asks his departing son to lay just one stone from the heap that lies ready, as a pledge of hope for their future; and this enters into an imaginative pattern, as well as a merely physical one, leading up to the final picture of the old man, all hope gone, still labouring at his little building:

> and 'tis believed by all
> That many and many a day he thither went,
> And never lifted up a *single* stone. (464–6 [*PW* II.94])

It is because of this latent and inevitable implication of pattern, group, *Gestalt*, that the word *one* so often slides, by small, greasy degrees, from the meanings of heading II into those of III. If four single trees make up one grove, then earth and heaven can make 'one imagery' and forty cattle can then become as 'one' by their identity of direction and posture, just as easily as the overall colouring of green can make orchards blend with 'groves and copses'. And of course the eddies left by the oars on each side of the boat do in fact, as well as in appearance, melt 'all into one track' in the moonlight. It is but a very short step, yet a very momentous one, from recognition of the concrete relation between the *one* and the background from which it is isolated to the much more abstract conceptions found in many of the lines illustrating heading III. In them, 'the one / Supreme Existence', the 'mind / That feeds upon infinity' is set in the same kind of relationship with all the rest of the universe. Wordsworth himself never went the full dangerous length of adding *the* to *one*, and pairing it off with *the* + *many* – though he uses the second combination three times of people, in contrast with 'the few'. But he came very near it in 'The unfettered clouds . . .', and in 'And yet a spirit . . .', as well as in the whole of the Snowdon passage in Book XIII of *The Prelude*, and in his discussion of 'imagination' in the 1815 *Preface* (*PW* II, 439).

This analysis of Wordsworth's uses of *one* shows that when he used meanings from heading III he moved on slippery, but when from II on firm ground. Objects, places and moments isolated from the rest of space and time seem to have had a clear and special significance in his experience, and in his vocabulary. It so happens that the most general demonstration of this special significance can be given in a final, very brief piece of statistical lexicography. The phrase 'spots of time' has been used very often here, as in all studies of Wordsworth, because it is the least inconvenient way, on the whole, of referring to one of the most remarkable passages in his poetry, at the end of *The Prelude* XI (1805) and XII (1850). But I never use it without regret, for such repetition helps to obscure its full meaning, already heavily hackneyed. And that is the very last quality it should be given, for it is, in itself, enormously surprising, and highly significant precisely because of its rarity. Indeed it has more than rarity. It is unique, being found neither in the *OED* nor anywhere else in Wordsworth – hence the brevity of its lexicography. *Spot* itself and *time* are very high-frequency words; both are in the top thousand of the Thorndike–Lorge List. Both, therefore, have very many definitions in the *OED*, the former 50 odd, the latter about 75. In Wordsworth, *time* is used at about its normal rate. *Spot*, however, is one of his 'favorite words'; from the T List we should expect it to occur about 70 times in his verse, and in fact it is found about 200 times. This excess above the normal is, as usual, accompanied by a violent distortion of the normal frequency of the meanings. The L List shows that in its mixed sample, *spot* was used for 50% of its occurrences in *OED* meaning 8*a*: 'A particular place or locality of limited extent'. In Wordsworth, this is its meaning in 97% of its occurrences. It is used, overwhelmingly, of small localities notable for their 'fairness', or 'loveliness', or for their association with some important experience. In only one other passage is it used of time:

> We summon'd up the honourable deeds
> Of ancient Story, thought of each bright spot,
> That could be found in all recorded time,
> Of truth preserved and error pass'd away . . . (*Prel.* IX.371–4)

Here, however, the association with time is more remote: it was, in any case, written long after the 'spots of time' passage itself. There, the collision, as it were, between the familiar use of *spot* and this altogether exceptional application to time is sudden and correspondingly violent. And the amount of 'information' which it conveys is accordingly maximal: it has the least possible 'redundancy', or level of expectation. It should be read, silently or aloud, with understanding of its exceptional quality, with a slight pause after 'of', and strong stress on 'time'. Taken thus, it is the most compressed imaginable statement of the importance to Wordsworth of the isolated, in space and time; and it makes its statement both of space and time.

It also happens to be an example of the remarkable tenacity of Wordsworth's verbal associations, of that quality which fostered such transformations of meaning by repetition. The passage in *The Vale* on which the 'spots of time' lines are based opens thus:

> No spot but claims the tender tear
> By joy or grief to memory dear. (416–17 [*PW* I, 279])

13

Enough examples have now been given to illustrate the special qualities of a few words often used by Wordsworth, and the tendency of such words to fall into clusters – to illustrate, but not to prove that these qualities are common to a large number of his most characteristic words. For proof, a much wider study would be necessary, and without it, of course, this study of his vocabulary is seriously incomplete, lacking breadth. It is also, however, incomplete in another respect. It lacks depth, for so far words have been treated in relative isolation, as if they were almost autonomous counters which could be manipulated numerically. They may be so, for some limited purposes, and in the course of a provisional analysis. But it remains limited and provisional until its results have been tested against a much more careful study of their contexts, in the whole framework of the thought and feeling of the writer who uses them, and of those other writers with whom he is to be compared. Of the words so far examined, the fullest account has been given of *naked* and *one*. But this account is far from being full enough, unless these words are examined at work in their contexts, in particular passages of Wordsworth, in the broader setting of his poetry, and against the still wider background of the age in which he wrote.

Unfortunately, there has to be a choice at this point between the two kinds of incompleteness, for they cannot be remedied together. The methods of study necessary to each of them are too different. A broader study of the vocabulary would lead on to more figures, more tables; and as they became more numerous, more complex mathematical techniques would become necessary to compare one with another, and to measure their resemblances and differences. It is possible, without any such methods, to reach conclusions about ten or twenty such tables, but not about several hundred. On the other hand, the deeper study of a handful of words in their whole context can only be carried on by the more traditional methods of literary criticism. And in what follows, it may appear that there has indeed been a change of method.

Some change is unavoidable and very desirable. For the method of analysis must necessarily change with the material to be studied, and above all with a change in the perspective. There is no incompatibility, in my view, between linguistic studies and literary criticism. They are, or ought to be, different phases of the same analytic process – complementary, not hostile. For some purposes the one is more effective, for other purposes, the other. There is no good reason why studies which begin with linguistic analysis should not pass into literary criticism, and none why literary criticism should not pass into linguistics. Indeed they should do so. Linguistic studies, especially of texts of great literary quality, cannot afford to stop short of that deeper analysis of thought and feeling which the words themselves serve to convey. And literary critics cannot afford to be ignorant of all that linguistic study can tell them about the words themselves.

While, therefore, it would be desirable to enlarge the field of the linguistic analysis of Wordsworth, and to study many more of his characteristic words, it is just as desirable to take up some of those which have been studied in this way, and to see them in their deeper context. And it so happens that the two which have been examined most fully, *naked* and *one*, are very apt for this purpose. The second leads directly to a study of Wordsworth's manner of experiencing the world, and of his intuitions about its nature, while the first enforces a comparison between his attitudes to it and those of his predecessors – a comparison which turns out to be a forcible contrast, and which throws into much deeper relief his idiolectal use of the word *naked*.

PART III

Involutes and the process of involution

14

> The mind of man is fram'd even like the breath
> And harmony of music . . .
>
> *Prel.* I.351–2

The significance of 'spots of time' in Wordsworth's account of the growth of his own mind (and by clear implication, in the growth of other minds too) lies not in the mere fact of their isolation in space and time, but rather in the process by which they have been isolated from the apparent continuum of experience, and the special effect of 'renovating virtue' (*1850*) which they exert later by their capacity for recurring life in the memory – joined, of course, with those recurrences of word and phrase, 'apparent tautologies', which have come to embody them. These two aspects of them in fact go closely together, for this power over the later life of the mind and spirit is a result of their manner of selection, and Wordsworth gave much thought to exploring this dual problem. Summarily expressed, this experience – for it was that much more than a view or theory – suggested that the mind has a natural 'set' in its dealings with experience, not just passively accepting what is given to it, but actively choosing some elements and, comparatively, neglecting others. And further, that this 'set' is cumulative and self-intensified, continually bringing its separable elements of experience into patterns more and more comprehensive, into larger patterns than themselves, just as the separate notes of music fall into the larger patterns of melody and harmony. It follows, of course, that any of the specially favoured recurrent words in his poetry, any of the 'apparent tautologies', should be capable of expansion into one or more of these larger mental constructs, and in the following chapters a few of these expansions will be attempted.

One of them, it so happens, throws direct light on the manner in which Wordsworth experienced this patterning of experience; its expansion clearly does much to illustrate the general process of expansion itself. It has its starting-point in those meanings of the word *one* which fall under heading II in the *OED* – those which express emphatically the one in particular, the single and individual.

The strength and clarity of Wordsworth's feeling for the significance of isolated objects is well shown by a line from *Yarrow Unvisited.* The poem was written partly as a compliment to Walter Scott, whom Wordsworth and his sister had visited in 1803. In 1805, a copy was sent to Scott, with a letter from

Wordsworth. No doubt this was the best thing to do with it, for the poem has slender merits in itself. Scott amiably included one line from it in his next popular poem, *Marmion*, a copy of which he sent to the Wordsworths in 1806. He was thanked, with something as near insincerity as that abnormally truthful household could manage – they were fond of Scott personally, but not much impressed by his verse. Their gratitude, however was accompanied by Wordsworth's mild addition:

> In the notes you have quoted two lines of mine from memory, and your memory, admirable as it is, has here failed you. The passage stands with you
>
> The swa*ns* on *sweet* St Mary's lake
>
> The proper reading is
>
> The *swan* on *still* St Mary's lake
>
> I mention this that the erratum may be corrected in a future edition. (*MY* 344/123)

The incident is rich in its bearings on the two men, on their relation, and their relative popularity at that time. Scott was immensely successful, as novelist and poet: Wordsworth wholly unsuccessful, by commercial standards, and hounded by the reviewers, many of whom were among Scott's Edinburgh friends. Scott was making a fortune from his writings: Wordsworth was still making nothing. Yet Scott was here doing his best for Wordsworth. Without obvious patronage, he was trying to spare him a little puff from his own gust of publicity. It speaks much for Scott's decency and perception, but tells against his taste. For him, and for his great public, lakes would certainly be 'sweet' rather than merely 'still', and if you were going in for swans, why stick at just one of them? Scott's memory, in fact, has betrayed him, and not merely into an inaccuracy. On the other side, Wordsworth's rather lordly demand that the mistake should be corrected in the next edition is equally typical. Despite the difference in their public standing and their literary fortunes, Wordsworth and his household knew pretty well where Scott stood in the real world, and where he would stand – or eventually fall. Many years later, however, and long after Scott's death, Wordsworth was still carrying on about the enormity of this mistake, still saying all that he had refrained from saying in that letter of 1808. Aubrey de Vere thus reports his conversation in the 1840s:

> 'Scott misquoted in one of his novels my lines on Yarrow. He makes me write –
>
> "The Swans on sweet St. Mary's lake
> Float double, swans and shadow."
>
> but I wrote –

"The *swan* on *still* St. Mary's lake."

Never could I have written "swans" in the plural. The scene when I saw it, with its still and dim lake, under the dusky hills, was one of utter loneliness; there was *one* swan, and one only, stemming the water, and the pathetic loneliness of the region gave importance to the one companion of that swan – its own white image in the water. It was for that reason that I recorded the swan and the shadow. Had there been many swans and many shadows, they would have implied nothing as regards the character of the place, and I should have said nothing about them.'[1]

The reasons which underlay these strong feelings were more fully explored in a sonnet, written before 1804, and in a commentary upon it, designed to explain its real significance. This is the sonnet:

With Ships the sea was sprinkled far and nigh,
Like stars in heaven, and joyously it showed;
Some lying fast at anchor in the road,
Some veering up and down, one knew not why.
A goodly Vessel did I then espy
Come like a giant from a haven broad;
And lustily along the bay she strode,
Her tackling rich, and of apparel high.
This Ship was nought to me, nor I to her,
Yet I pursued her with a Lover's look;
This Ship to all the rest did I prefer:
When will she turn, and whither? She will brook
No tarrying; where She comes the winds must stir:
On went She, and due north her journey took. (*PW* III, 18)

The commentary was provoked because, when the poem was published in the 1807 collection, among *Moods of My own Mind*, a friend of Lady Beaumont's who had 'entered into the spirit' of other poems thought that in this one Wordsworth had 'fallen below' himself. He wrote to Lady Beaumont to demonstrate that this was not so: upon this poem, he observes,

. . . I could say something important in conversation, and will attempt now to illustrate it by a comment which I feel will be very inadequate to convey my meaning. There is scarcely one of my Poems which does not aim to direct the attention to some moral sentiment, or to some general principle, or law of thought, or of our intellectual constitution. For instance in the present case, who is there that has not felt that the mind can have no rest among a multitude of objects, of which it either cannot make one whole, or from which it cannot single out one individual, whereupon may be concentrated the attention divided among or distracted by a multitude? After a certain time we must either select one image or object, which must put out of view the rest wholly, or must subordinate them to itself while it stands forth as a Head:

Now glowed the firmament
With living sapphires! Hesperus, that *led*
The starry host, rode brightest; till the Moon,

Rising in clouded majesty, at length,
Apparent *Queen*, unveiled *her peerless* light,
And o'er the dark her silver mantle threw.[2]

Having laid this down as a general principle, take the case before us. I am represented in the Sonnet as casting my eyes over the sea, sprinkled with a multitude of Ships, like the heavens with stars, my mind may be supposed to float up and down among them in a kind of dreamy indifference with respect either to this or that one, only in a pleasurable state of feeling with respect to the whole prospect. 'Joyously it showed,' this continued till that feeling may be supposed to have passed away, and a kind of comparative listlessness or apathy to have succeeded, as at this line, 'Some veering up and down, one knew not why.' All at once, while I am in this state, comes forth an object, an individual, and my mind, sleepy and unfixed, is awakened and fastened in a moment. 'Hesperus, that *led* The starry host,' is a poetical object, because the glory of his own Nature gives him the pre-eminence the moment he appears; he calls forth the poetic faculty, receiving its exertions as a tribute; but this Ship in the Sonnet may, in a manner still more appropriate, be said to come upon a mission of the poetic Spirit, because in its own appearance and attributes it is barely sufficiently distinguish[ed] to rouse the creative faculty of the human mind; to exertions at all times welcome, but doubly so when they come upon us when in a state of remissness. The mind being once fixed and rouzed, all the rest comes from itself; it is merely a lordly Ship, nothing more:

This ship was nought to me, nor I to her,
Yet I pursued her with a lover's look.

My mind wantons with grateful joy in the exercise of its own powers, and, loving its own creation,

This ship to all the rest did I prefer,

making her a sovereign or a regent, and thus giving body and life to all the rest; mingling up this idea with fondness and praise –

where she comes the winds must stir;

and concluding the whole with

On went She, and due north her journey took.

Thus taking up again the Reader with whom I began, letting him know how long I must have watched this favorite Vessel, and inviting him to rest his mind as mine is resting.

(*MY* 301/75)

As with all observations which are both highly original, without aid from earlier formulations, and also highly personal, with all the inevitable dubieties of introspection, these thoughts are not free from uncertainties and hesitations, both of expression and of substance. It is not quite clear, for example, whether the mind, faced by a multitude of objects, has two quite different possibilities of dealing with them, to make of them 'one whole', or to 'single out one individual', or whether these two apparently different processes are really one and the same, the singling out of the one being the means by which the whole is organised. What is, however, quite clear is that Wordsworth's central point concerns the power of the mind, and its direct influence upon the processes of sensation. The mind is not inert, at any rate when once roused; it imposes patterns of its own upon the stream of sense-data which beat in upon it in the flow of time.

It might seem in some ways remarkable that Wordsworth should have anticipated so clearly the leading principles of that *Gestalt* psychology which became fashionable more than a century later, but it is the less curious if it is recognised that the root causes of these principles lie in the nature of the human eye itself, and in its intimate nervous connection with the brain. 'The eye', as Wordsworth himself had written, 'it cannot choose but see' (*PW* IV, 56). But neither can it choose not to choose what it sees. There are two different kinds of cell in the retina, some of which possess a high degree of discrimination, within a very limited angle of view, while others see more vaguely, but over a very wide angle of view. The human eye, in fact, is a remarkable combination of a telephoto lens and a wide-angle lens, and any act of vision is selective, in the sense that the narrow angle of sharp vision is focussed on one area rather than another, while the more blurred peripheral vision deals with the rest of what is visible. Yet this singling out of one area for sharp focus does not preclude the eye, and the brain behind it, from perceiving the whole view before it, as a whole. Indeed it enhances this perception, because it unavoidably and instinctively organises it into a pattern, in which the relative importance of the various elements of the visible world are put in order. The other human senses have the same automatically selective property, though in a lesser degree. The ear is more directionally sensitive than most microphones: hence the notable differences between what is heard by a human being at a cocktail party, or in a bird-filled wood, and what a tape-recorder would report of the same sounds. 'We cannot bid the ear be still', Wordsworth rightly says (*loc. cit.*): nor can we bid it cease from selecting from the sounds to which it is sensitive, from regarding some few as significant, and the rest as mere noise. Neither Wordsworth nor Coleridge was aware of these physiological properties of the senses and the brain, but they were both convinced, by observation and reflection, that the senses, by continually choosing from the data before them, partly created what they saw and heard, by imposing pattern and order upon it, subordinating one sight or sound, making another 'sovereign' or 'regent'. And it was this observed quality in his own mode of experiencing and perceiving the world that led Wordsworth towards a position of real originality, in tacit and probably unconscious opposition to the accepted theories of the philosophers of the eighteenth century. He was the less likely to become fully conscious of his difference from them because what he was contradicting was not so much their formal doctrines – which he accepted in general – but rather some of the unexpressed assumptions or implications running through their work.

In their determination to show that all ideas, all thoughts, were derived strictly from sensory experience and nothing else, the empirical philosophers from Locke onwards insisted that the mind is essentially passive and inactive in its receptivity. This is the purport of the three revealing images in which Locke variously describes it; first as a kind of show-case, as of specimens of pottery or butterflies: 'The Senses at first let in particular *Ideas*, and furnish the yet empty Cabinet . . .'; secondly, as blank paper: 'Let us then suppose the Mind to be, as we say, white Paper, void of all Characters, without any *Ideas*; How comes it to be furnished?'; thirdly, as a dark room:

> . . . external and internal Sensation, are the only passages I can find of knowledge to the Understanding. These alone, as far as I can discover, are the Windows by which light is let into this *dark Room*. For, methinks, the *Understanding* is not much unlike a Closet wholly shut from light, with only some little openings left, to let in external visible resemblances or *Ideas*, of things without; which would they but stay there, and lie so orderly as to be found upon occasion, it would very much resemble the Understanding of a Man, in reference to all Objects of sight, and the *Ideas* of them.[3]

With these images and their implications, Locke's immediate successors, Hume and Hartley, would not have disagreed. They would have accepted too in a general way his views on the activity of the mind itself, after this initially passive reception of sensory experiences: 'But as the Mind is wholly Passive in the reception of all its simple *Ideas*, so it exerts several acts of its own, whereby out of its simple *Ideas*, as the Materials and Foundations of the rest, the other are framed' (II.xii.1). Even in this activity, however, Locke did not allow the mind much autonomy, for he believed the process of forming more complex ideas from simple ones to be conditioned by certain aspects of sensory experience itself, and chiefly by repetition. For if 'simple ideas' frequently recur together, then 'the one no sooner at any time comes into the Understanding but its Associate appears with it; and if they are more than two which are thus united, the whole gang always inseparable shew themselves together'.[4] In Hume's theory of causality, this dependence of association upon recurrence in conjunction became central. It depended, for him, entirely upon the effect of the 'constant conjunction' of sensations, 'the repetition' whereby 'like objects are constantly plac'd in like relations of succession and contiguity'.[5] And Hartley, in his still more rigorous expression of the processes of association, found recurrence and repetition to be dominant forces in mental activity:

> Let the Sensation *A* be often associated with each of the Sensations *B*, *C*, *D*, &c. . . . *A*, impressed alone, will, at last, raise *B*, *C*, *D*, &c. all together, *i.e.* associate them with one another . . . All compound Impressions $A+B+C+D$, &c. after sufficient Repetition leave compound Miniatures $a+b+c+d$, which recur every now and then from slight Causes.[6]

In all these expositions, it is steadily assumed, though never quite explicitly stated, that sensory experience is continuous and homogeneous, that it flows in upon the mind with undifferentiated force, no one piece of it being in itself more important than another, unless it happens to become so by repetition in conjunction with another piece. Perhaps the closest approach to a statement of this assumption is in Locke's phrase about 'the notice that our senses take of the constant vicissitude of things'.[7] It is this impression of 'constant vicissitude of things' which contrasts so strongly with Wordsworth's 'one impulse'. For the empirical philosophers, there was a constant stream of incoming impulses, one no more forceful than another. For him, the experiencing mind was no passive *tabula rasa*, but itself an active agent, selecting from among its myriad perceptions a few of special significance – a significance conferred by itself, and by its selection in the very act of perceiving them. For him – and for Coleridge – the senses were, so to speak, mindfully active, imposing upon experience their own patterns as a result of their own qualities. And for both of them, this was no merely theoretical departure from a philosophical tradition from which they took much; it was itself an experience, an observation made upon their own mode of experiencing the world around them.

The philosophers had taken many of their premisses from observations of their own experience, but in a manner which can only be called slapdash when compared with Wordsworth's. They throw off phrases like 'How often may a man observe in himself . . .', 'I believe it will not be very necessary to employ many words in explaining this distinction. Every one of himself will readily perceive the difference betwixt feeling and thinking.' Wordsworth, on the other hand, found the process of introspection to be a complex one, involving a condition of something like temporary 'double personality':

> . . . sometimes . . . I seem
> Two consciousnesses, conscious of myself
> And of some other Being. (*Prel.* II.31–3)

There is a certain wariness here, a fuller understanding of the difficulty of using this kind of evidence, which promises a slightly greater skill in using it, and in avoiding its more obvious dangers. This duality of consciousness was well known to Wordsworth, and he had much more to say about it (see pp. 145–7). It is more likely because of this than because his experience was radically different from that of the philosophers that Wordsworth perceived so clearly the active element in all perception. He expressed it in many passages, often making use of the word *create* to do so:

of all the mighty world
Of eye, and ear, – both what they half *create*,
And what perceive . . . (*Tintern Abbey* 105–7 [*PW* II, 262])

Emphatically such a Being lives,
An inmate of this *active* universe;
From nature largely he receives; nor so
Is satisfied, but largely gives again,
For feeling has to him imparted strength,
And powerful in all sentiments of grief,
Of exultation, fear, and joy, his mind,
Even as an agent of the one great mind,
Creates, *creator* and receiver both,
Working but in alliance with the works
Which it beholds. (*Prel.* II.265–75)

One of the most remarkable and concrete descriptions of this active perception is in an extended simile in Book VIII of *The Prelude*. It has been given less attention than it seems to deserve because its application, to his first impressions of London, seems almost trivial:[8]

As when a Traveller hath from open day
With torches pass'd into some Vault of Earth,
The Grotto of Antiparos, or the Den
Of Yordas among Craven's mountain tracts;
He looks and sees the cavern spread and grow,
Widening itself on all sides, sees, or thinks
He sees, erelong, the roof above his head,
Which instantly unsettles and recedes
Substance and shadow, light and darkness, all
Commingled, making up a Canopy
Of Shapes and Forms and Tendencies to Shape
That shift and vanish, change and interchange
Like Spectres, ferment quiet and sublime;
Which, after a short space, works less and less,
Till every effort, every motion gone,
The scene before him lies in perfect view,
Exposed and lifeless, as a written book.
But let him pause awhile, and look again
And a new quickening shall succeed, at first
Beginning timidly, then creeping fast

Through all which he beholds; the senseless mass,
In its projections, wrinkles, cavities,
Through all its surface, with all colours streaming,
Like a magician's airy pageant, parts,
Unites, embodying everywhere some pressure
Or image, recognis'd or new, some type
Or picture of the world. (711–37)

In nothing is this description more typical of Wordsworth's account of his own acts of introspection than in its picture of an ebb and flow, of activity sinking to a passive trance-like state, which opens the way for a still more vivid perception.

As it happens, one of his fullest descriptions of this process comes to us indirectly, in the words of De Quincey: but it bears all the marks of authenticity. The two of them had been waiting late one night for the carrier bringing news of some great engagement in the Peninsular War:

At intervals, Wordsworth had stretched himself at length on the high road, applying his ear to the ground, so as to catch any sound of wheels that might be groaning along at a distance. Once, when he was slowly rising from this effort, his eye caught a bright star that was glittering between the brow of Seat Sandal and of the mighty Helvellyn. He gazed upon it for a minute or so; and then, upon turning away to descend into Grasmere, he made the following explanation: 'I have remarked, from my earliest days, that, if under any circumstances, the attention is energetically braced up to an act of steady observation, or of steady expectation, then, if this intense condition of vigilance should suddenly relax, at that moment any beautiful, any impressive visual object, or collection of objects, falling upon the eye, is carried to the heart with a power not known under other circumstances. Just now, my ear was placed upon the stretch, in order to catch any sound of wheels that might come down upon the lake of Wythburn from the Keswick road; at the very instant when I raised my head from the ground, in final abandonment of hope for this night, at the very instant when the organs of attention were all at once relaxing from their tension, the bright star hanging in the air above those outlines of massy blackness fell suddenly upon my eye, and penetrated my capacity of apprehension with a pathos and a sense of the infinite, that would not have arrested me under other circumstances.' He then went on to illustrate the same psychological principle from another instance; it was an instance derived from that exquisite poem, in which he describes a mountain boy planting himself at twilight on the margin of some solitary bay of Windermere, and provoking the owls to a contest with himself, by 'mimic hootings' blown through his hands. . . . Afterwards, the poem goes on to describe the boy as waiting, amidst 'the pauses of his skill,' for the answers of the birds – waiting with intensity of expectation – and then, at length, when, after waiting to no purpose, his attention began to relax – that is, in other words, under the giving way of one exclusive direction of his senses, began suddenly to allow an admission to other objects – then, in that instant, the scene actually before him, the visible scene, would enter unawares –

'With all its solemn imagery'[9]

It is, of course, possible to doubt whether De Quincey recollected what

Wordsworth had said with complete accuracy – he was writing some thirty years after the event. But it is much harder to doubt that he had remembered vividly both the occasion, and the gist of what Wordsworth had said, for it is so well consonant with what he said elsewhere of these 'spots of time', so entirely in harmony with the most convincing autobiographical passages of *The Prelude*. And in this more prosaic description, the essential isolation of these moments, their difference from the usual texture of experience, emerges with special clearness.

It is hard to resist asking the question, even if it be probably unanswerable, which was the more nearly accurate description of experience, Wordsworth's or the philosophers'. Very possibly, of course, different people tend to experience things in different ways: it is easy to imagine that Locke's tenor of life was pretty different from Wordsworth's. But it is certainly worth remarking that one of the most influential of later observers, Freud, reached substantially the same conclusion as Wordsworth. To him also it became clear – at first much to his surprise – that certain perceptions or sensations had a far greater power on the growth of the spirit than others, that they were comparatively few, but in some cases decisive for its future development. It was lucky for Freud that, together with his own acuteness and intelligence as an observer, Vienna provided him with so many so-called 'neurotics' – of whom, as he said himself, 'there were only too many in our society'.[10] And it was even more fortunate for Wordsworth that the material which fell under his notice was so much more normal, so that he could concern himself with the more rewarding problems of the natural, the undistorted growth of the spirit. Allowing for this difference, however – the difference between using normal and pathological subjects for observation – the agreement in the basic findings is remarkable. One of the earliest and clearest of Freud's tributes to the power of single occurrences was in a paper written in 1892, in collaboration with Breuer:

> The disproportion between the many years duration of an hysterical symptom and the single occurrence which evoked it is similar to that which we are accustomed to see regularly in traumatic neurosis; it was quite frequently in childhood that the events occurred, producing a more or less grave symptom which persisted from that time onwards.[11]

His later works are full of repetitions and enlargements of this discovery, and this will serve to illustrate the many that might be made:

> . . . *our hysterical patients suffer from reminiscences*. Their symptoms are residues and mnemic symbols of particular (traumatic) experiences. . . . Not only do they remember painful experiences of the remote past, but they still cling to them emotionally; they cannot get free of the past and for its sake they neglect what is real and immediate. This fixation of mental life to

pathogenic traumas is one of the most significant and practically important characteristics of neurosis.[12]

Freud, then, has reported unambiguously in the same sense as Wordsworth, that mingled with the normal texture of experience, there are a few experiences of an altogether special character, which may cause long-lasting damage to the personality. His discovery was, in fact, simply the obverse of Wordsworth's – that in the formation of the normal human personality, not all experiences count equally and evenly, but that some 'spots of time' have 'distinct pre-eminence' and 'retain' it.

One of the differences between the normal and the pathological reaction to these moments is suggested by an observation in another of Freud's early papers, on *Screen Memories* (1899):

> . . . there are some people whose earliest recollections of childhood are concerned with everyday and indifferent events which could not produce any emotional effect even in children, but which are recollected (*too* clearly, one is inclined to say) in every detail, while approximately contemporary events, which on the evidence of their parents moved them intensely at the time, have not been retained in their memory. Thus the Henris mention a professor of philology whose earliest memory, dating back to between the ages of three and four, showed him a table laid for a meal and on it a basin of ice. At the same period there occurred the death of his grandmother which, according to his parents, was a severe blow to the child. But the professor of philology, as he now is, has no recollection of his bereavement; all that he remembers of those days is the basin of ice.[13]

There are some notable similarities between this professor and Wordsworth, in their initial situations and in their memories of them. The former had lost all conscious memory of the actual bereavement, the latter can indeed remember it, but mentions it in the barest possible outline, with the minimum of emotion –

> . . . he died,
> And I and my two Brothers, Orphans then,
> Follow'd his Body to the Grave. (*Prel.* XI.366–8)

And even this bare outline is given but once. On the other hand, just as the professor remembered – '*too* clearly' – the table laid for a meal and the bowl of ice, so Wordsworth remembered, with all of the same inexplicable clarity, the single sheep, the whistling hawthorn, the old stone wall and the two misty roads. There are, of course, some differences too. The content of Wordsworth's memory was richer, more apt to make the experience one of 'vivifying Virtue' (*1805*). But the underlying principle is the same. Freud, like Wordsworth, insisted that some few experiences acquire a special importance in the life of the individual; that these experiences are clearly distinguished from the ordinary continuum of life; and that they are marked above all by their capacity to remain vivid in the memory, and to come to life again and again with something like the same vividness, and sometimes with gathered richness of associations from later experiences.

These special experiences are, of course, rather different in quality from those with which the philosophers had been concerned. For Locke and Hume, the main problem had been to account for the presence of abstract ideas in the mind, since they could not be present in it initially, and could be produced only from the data of the senses. And it had seemed to them that there was a clear dividing line between the abstract and the concrete, between ideas and perceptions. It followed, however, from Wordsworth's conviction that the mind was itself active in the processes of perception that, in these specially important experiences, there was no such clear distinction between abstract and concrete aspects. They would contain elements of both, joining some of the original concrete circumstances with more generalised implications. They would also possess – and here Wordsworth is joined by Freud – a strong capacity to be linked with feelings, conscious or unconscious, emotional or moral.

For entities of this kind there are many names – so many that they can safely be regarded as a common element in human experience. In the system of ancient rhetoric, for example, they were in some ways like the enthymeme, the standard unit of rhetorical exposition, as the syllogism was the unit of logic, but distinguished from syllogistic reason in that its purpose was to secure persuasion, not proof. It was, therefore, emotive rather than rational. Another name for roughly the same thing is 'image', but this has been so extensively used in literary criticism for the last generation that its meaning has expanded to, and beyond, bursting-point, and it could be restored to usefulness only after a long process of purgatorial definition. The same is true of 'symbol'. Another name, perhaps too highly personal to be of general use, is the 'epiphany' of James Joyce – though it has the great advantage of stressing the sudden and revelatory quality of these 'spots of time'. Rather than enter upon a long critical account of any one of these terms, I have decided to make provisional use of another in the same series, which happens to have the two advantages of being almost unknown, and yet of being well enough defined to be helpful in actual use. It has the incidental advantage, moreover, of having been formulated by De Quincey, who was, over a few years, thoroughly exposed to Wordsworth's ways of thinking and feeling, and who, in *Confessions of an English Opium-Eater*, produced a work of imaginative autobiography in many ways more like *The*

Prelude than anything else in English – like, at least, in kind, though not in quality.

De Quincey's formulation is slipped in, as are so many of his most enlightening reflections, by way of parenthesis in a description of one of the most profoundly formative moments of his own childhood, when he had crept into the room where lay the body of a dearly loved sister, and had found her bed not where he had expected it to be, and the room full of 'the sun of midsummer at mid-day . . . showering down torrents of splendour'.[14] He is noting in himself a powerful association between death and summer, in the making of which this incident had played a large part, and goes on:

> And, recollecting it, I am struck with the truth, that far more of our deepest thoughts and feelings pass to us through perplexed combinations of *concrete* objects, pass to us as *involutes* (if I may coin that word) in compound experiences incapable of being disentangled, than ever reach us *directly*, and in their own abstract shapes. (p. 39)

It is, I believe, a usable coinage. It does some justice to the essential quality of the 'spots of time' as exercising special importance both in thought and in feeling; it insists that both thought and feeling are involved in the concrete experience, and with one another – 'involuted' in 'compound experiences incapable of being disentangled'; and it is in appropriate contrast with the syllogism, with purely rational organisation of experience. Best of all, it has not yet been knocked about in usage, or had its potential meanings licentiously expanded. It will serve as a convenient short term by which to describe, even to identify by showing where search may be made, those 'harmonies' of the spirit which Wordsworth made of the elements and the recurring words of his chief experiences.

What has so far emerged about Wordsworth's sense of involutes and of the processes of involution in experience has been suggested by a detailed study of his use – or rather, one of his uses – of the word *one*. We have seen that it leads fairly directly to an appreciation of his feeling that some few experiences are of crucial importance in the growth of the spirit, because they are felt as distinct from the ordinary flow of impressions on the senses and the mind, and because they are in themselves organised, as it were, into patterns endowed with order – an order often derived from some powerful *single* perception, to which all other elements are subordinated in a significant fashion. There remains, however, the other sense of *one* which was almost more idiolectal in his verse: that sense which goes beyond the perception of organised pattern in a particular set of impressions, and rises to a feeling for the essential unity of existence itself, including somehow within it both the experiencing spirit and the material of its experience. In exploring his feeling for this more complex kind of *one*-ness, we shall have to reckon with the more difficult aspect of involutes: their involvement in thought and feeling, as well as in perceptions. We shall be concerned not only with shapes and patterns, but even more with emotions and intuitions, with those deeper processes of the mind which are usually beyond the conscious, at least the fully conscious, attention and the directions of the will. And before attempting this more complex exposition, it is very necessary, by way of preparation for it, to study more generally Wordsworth's attitude towards, and use of, these more recondite functions of the hidden and active memory.

15

While terror shapeless rides my soul,
[ ] together are we hurled
Far, far amid the shadowy world.
And since that hour, the world unknown,
The world of shades is all my own.

The Vale of Esthwaite 374–8 (*PW* I, 278)

This was one of Wordsworth's attitudes towards the fashionable Gothic terrors of his time. Another was embodied in the lines already quoted about the 'poor and puny joys / Fond sickly Fancy's idle toys'. And though this apparently renounces the machinery of ghosts and haunted castles, the renunciation was far from complete. It would, indeed, have been surprising had it been so; for it was not Wordsworth's habit to deny the significance of any of his early memories.

The survival of one aspect of the Gothic in his mature poetry is often overlooked, because it was so profoundly transmuted. Its flashier and shallower symbols indeed disappeared, together with the lurid conventional scenery, the stage-properties. But the feeling of awe, of terror, remained, as something positive and meaningful. And it survived not least because such feelings are often the natural accompaniments of involutes, and the process of involution. De Quincey's term tends to emphasise – and valuably – the intimate mingling of concrete and abstract experience in these moments, but it does a little less than justice to the quality of surprise and awe which often accompanies them. Joyce's term, 'epiphany', is the one that most fully recognises in them the element of sudden and astonishing revelation. It seems likely that the perception, or formation of an involute is never achieved by conscious choice, but that it comes of itself, at its own time, and often in that relaxed temper of mind and feeling which Wordsworth so often described as a kind of trance. And coming in this way, it naturally has some of the qualities of the preternatural. It is a cognitive, not a recognitive process. Even though many elements of past experience may be involved in it, their combination and patterning is new, and the effect of this novelty is the usual one of *omne ignotum pro magnifico*.[15]

The importance and pervasiveness of this kind of feeling in Wordsworth has perhaps been obscured a little by the traditional comparisons between him and Coleridge, and above all by the account of their intentions given by Coleridge himself in *Biographia Literaria*. Of *Lyrical Ballads* he says:

> . . . it was agreed that my endeavours should be directed to persons and characters supernatural, or at least romantic; yet so as to transfer from our inward nature a human interest and a semblance of truth sufficient to procure for these shadows of imagination that willing suspension of disbelief for the moment, which constitutes poetic faith. Mr. Wordsworth, on the other hand, was to propose to himself as his object to give the charm of novelty to things of every day, and to excite a feeling analogous to the supernatural, by awakening the mind's attention from the lethargy of custom and directing it to the loveliness and the wonders of the world before us. (Ch. XIV)

If this passage is read at all carelessly, it may easily leave the reader with the impression that a simple distinction is being made – that Coleridge was to deal with the supernatural, Wordsworth with the real world. The two riders are easily missed, but they are vital. Coleridge himself, though beginning, as it were, with the supernatural, was to link it with much that was natural, while Wordsworth, though dealing with things of every day, was to 'excite a feeling analogous to the supernatural' by his manner of handling them. If these riders are given the prominence they deserve, it can be said that both writers achieved what they set out to do. Coleridge succeeded in writing poetry on supernatural themes, as in *Christabel* and *Kubla Khan*, yet without evoking any of those ill-defined and yet definite feelings which are often associated with them, and which go under such vague names as the 'uncanny', the 'eerie'. Wordsworth, however, enveloped many of his dealings with everyday things in precisely this atmosphere. His 'naked pools and dreary crags' are indeed uncanny, eerie, to a degree far beyond that of the river Alph and his measureless caverns. And *The Leech Gatherer* is much more like a ghost-story than *Christabel* or the *Ancient Mariner*. So are parts of *The Thorn*, the meeting with the discharged soldier in Book IV of *The Prelude*, the sight of the blind beggar in Book VII, and many other minor incidents up and down Wordsworth's poetry. He is, in fact, one of the most notable masters in European literature of the eerie, the uncanny.

But while it is easy to make this assertion, it is very difficult to define the quality itself, and to analyse the means by which it is achieved. It happens not to have been a favourite topic with critics and theorists of aesthetics. Tragedy and the tragic they have discussed exhaustingly. Of comedy and the comic they have been more shy, but not wholly reticent. On the supernatural, the preternatural as literary qualities, and on the technical methods for achieving these effects, they have been almost entirely silent. This is the more troublesome because a few moments' thought is enough to deter anyone from wishing to be an innovator in this field. It doesn't even look easy. It should not, then, be surprising that earlier authorities have been earnestly sought out, and that they should prove to be slightly out of the way. The first is a poem by the one great poetess, Emily Dickinson:

> One need not be a Chamber – to be Haunted –
> One need not be a House –
> The Brain has Corridors – surpassing
> Material Place –
>
> Far safer, of a Midnight Meeting
> External Ghost
> Than its interior Confronting –
> That Cooler Host.
>
> Far safer, through an Abbey gallop,
> The Stones a'chase –
> Than Unarmed, one's a'self encounter –
> In lonesome Place –
>
> Ourself behind ourself, concealed –
> Should startle most –
> Assassin hid in our Apartment
> Be Horror's least.
>
> The Body – borrows a Revolver –
> He bolts the Door –
> O'erlooking a superior spectre –
> Or More –

This remarkable poem makes three points, all very helpful for our immediate purpose. First, every stanza is based upon a pithy antithesis between a conventional and ineffective source of 'hauntedness' and a real and powerful one. These conventions are mainly literary, haunted chambers and houses, ghosts, Gothic ruins and unseen horses churning up the stones, but they include also the intruder under the bed, the stranger in the house. They are, in fact, the traditional sources of terror, pretty much as they were shown in *Northanger Abbey* and *Nightmare Abbey*, and they are judged to be no more akin to real terror than Jane Austen and Peacock found them – or than the young Wordsworth found them a generation earlier. Secondly, it is suggested that 'hauntedness' is by no means attached to the same experiences or images in life and in literature. Many things can be described in literature which would be terrifying if they were to be encountered in reality, which in literature are no more than entertaining, and used traditionally as sources of entertainment. Thirdly, and most penetratingly, she suggests that the characteristic source of real 'hauntedness' is one's own self, encountered as something at once internal and separate. She sees it, in fact, as the specific effect of the *Doppelgänger*, the meeting with another self.

All these points are made, of course quite independently, more fully and prosaically – though still with characteristic touches of imaginative intuition – by our second main authority, Freud, in his paper *Das Unheimliche*.[16] He points out, for example, that the 'uncanny' is by no means the same thing in real life and in literature. In fairy-tales, for example, there is a complete lack of correspondence between the two:

> . . . I cannot think of any genuine fairy-story which has anything uncanny about it. We have heard that it is in the highest degree uncanny when inanimate objects – a picture or a doll – come to life; nevertheless in Hans Andersen's stories the household utensils, furniture and tin soldiers are alive and nothing could perhaps be more remote from the uncanny. And we should hardly call it uncanny when Pygmalion's beautiful statue comes to life. (p. 400)

He makes nearly the same point in relation to literary works not classified as fairy-tales, but including more or less substantial elements of the supernatural:

> The story-teller can also choose a setting which, though less imaginary than the world of fairy-tales, does yet differ from the real world by admitting superior spiritual entities such as daemonic influences or departed spirits. So long as they remain within their setting of poetic reality their usual attribute of uncanniness fails to attach to such beings. The souls in Dante's *Inferno*, or the ghostly apparitions in *Hamlet*, *Macbeth* or *Julius Caesar*, may be gloomy and terrible enough, but they are no more really uncanny than is Homer's jovial world of gods. We order our judgement to the imaginary reality imposed on us by the writer, and regard souls, spirits and spectres as though their existence had the same validity in their world as our own has in the external world. And then in this case too we are spared all trace of the uncanny.
> (pp. 404–5)

This is at least a large part of the reason for the absence of the uncanny in Coleridge's supernatural poems; the admission of the spiritual entities and influences is imposed on his imaginary world, and so on the reader, without any complication greater than is readily accepted by the ordinary 'suspension of disbelief for the moment, which constitutes poetic faith' (*Biog. Lit.*,

Ch. XIV). This is not, of course, to imply that these poems are inferior on this account; it is only to distinguish them from the very different effect often found in Wordsworth.

Freud also takes the same view as Emily Dickinson of the close relation between the uncanny and the *Doppelgänger* effect, and examines it much more fully, for it is the basis of his own theory of the genesis of the uncanny:

> The idea of the 'double' does not necessarily disappear with the passing of the primary narcissism, for it can receive fresh meaning from the later stages of development of the ego. A special faculty is slowly formed there, able to oppose the rest of the ego, with the function of observing and criticizing the self and exercising a censorship within the mind, and this we become aware of as our 'conscience'. In the pathological case of delusions of being watched this mental institution becomes isolated, dissociated from the ego, and discernible to a physician's eye. The fact that a faculty of this kind exists, which is able to treat the rest of the ego like an object – the fact, that is, that man is capable of self-observation – renders it possible to invest the old idea of a 'double' with a new meaning and to ascribe many things to it. (pp. 387–8)

The link between this doubleness in the structure of the human personality and the 'uncanny' is supplied by a principle which Freud believed he had established as generally true, to which he gave the name *repetition-compulsion*. This dynamic feature of unconscious mental processes he regarded as instinctive, and powerful enough to over-rule the normal desire for pleasant experiences and memories, by enforcing the recurrence, either directly or in disguised and symbolic forms, of certain earlier experiences in themselves unpleasant or even terrifying. 'Whatever reminds us', he says, 'of this inner *repetition-compulsion* is perceived as uncanny.' In this way, the special feeling of the uncanny is closely associated with the phenomenon, noted by many other psychologists, of *déjà vu*, the eerie sensation of having seen all this before – 'I've been in this situation before', 'I've been through this already.' Anyone who has a wide experience of nightmares will not need to be reminded of this feeling, and will all too readily perceive its close relationship with that kind of double personality common in dreams, where the dreamer both acts and suffers, and somehow observes himself acting and suffering. Freud thus summarises the central points in his definition:

> In the first place, if psycho-analytic theory is correct in maintaining that every emotional affect, whatever its quality, is transformed by repression into morbid anxiety, then among such cases of anxiety there must be a class in which the anxiety can be shown to come from something repressed which *recurs*. This class of morbid anxiety would then be no other than what is uncanny, irrespective of whether it originally aroused dread or some other affect. In the second place, if this is indeed the secret nature of the uncanny, we can understand why the usage of speech has extended *das Heimliche* into its opposite *das Unheimliche*; for this uncanny is in reality nothing new or foreign, but something familiar and old-established in the mind that has been estranged only by the process of repression. (p. 394)

Yet again, then, in this study of Wordsworth, we are unexpectedly brought up against the significance of *recurrence*: and this time, not directly by any observation of his own, but at the suggestion of a completely independent source.

In applying Freud's hypotheses to the study of Wordsworth's uncanniness, there is good reason to feel that they carry the more weight because they are based on completely different material – they have not been fudged up to solve just this problem, like so many of the hypotheses which keep literary criticism going. But it must also be noticed that this independence is itself a remarkable fact: the fact that Freud, well read as he was in the literatures of Europe, sufficiently interested in Shakespeare to have made himself not the least notable of his critics, was nevertheless unfamiliar with Wordsworth. In this, of course, he was in an enormous boat, which contains the vast majority of Europeans, and a very large number of Britons too. The reason for the inability of nearly all 'foreigners', and of so many of his own countrymen, to 'understand' Wordsworth is at the heart of the problems we are now examining. His use of language in general, and his ways of attaining the effect of the uncanny in particular, are so subtle that they are simply inaccessible to anyone who has a command of English in the least degree deficient; and since they are beyond the reach of so many whose native language is English, it is not to be wondered at that they are quite untranslatable, and that his European reputation should be so absurdly smaller than his real value. But for this, Freud would surely have discovered in him the most complete and perceptive of all the forerunners of his own theories.

This deserves a little further comment, in view of Freud's mention of Dante above, for a comparison between Wordsworth and Dante is illuminating in this particular context. *La Divina Commedia* and *The Prelude* are the two major verse autobiographies in European literature, and despite the large interval of time between them, and the even larger gap in poetic tradition, they have much in common. Dante's poem is largely made up of an account of his meetings with spirits, some of whom he had known in this world, some of whom belonged to history or fable; Wordsworth's poem also has its encounters, sometimes with people, though not always known to him save by chance, and sometimes with patterns of circumstance, 'spots of time', in which human beings (apart from himself) played no part. They are most alike when, in the course of these significant, providentially destined meetings, words are uttered to them which carry to their own minds and spirits a flash of enlightenment, an immediately perceptible advance in their own understanding both of themselves and of the human condition. Thus when Dante encounters Brunetto Latini, his old teacher, or Forese, with whom he had shared a period of dissipation, he hears words spoken which are, in their special significance, comparable with the providential utterances of Wordsworth's discharged soldier or the Leechgatherer; when Dante contemplated the ultimate end of Ulysses, even though it was probably his own imagination that presented it to him, he saw in it the same kind of enormous import that Wordsworth found in the sight of the blind beggar and his label among the swirling crowds of London. But the knowledge needed by the reader to appreciate the full significance of these encounters is very different in the two cases. Dante was indeed drawing upon knowledge, as it were public knowledge, of history, of real persons, and of what we might call myths, which to him were barely distinguishable from history. Wordsworth was drawing upon private experience and knowledge, some of it partly hidden even from himself. For the deeper study of Dante we go to the notes; for the understanding of Wordsworth we must refer ourselves, as usual, to other passages of Wordsworth. And it is for this reason that Dante is rarely uncanny; the personages he encounters are not related to lost regions of his own memory which recur of their own volition, and without his full realisation of what they are. Brunetto, Forese and Ulysses exist for him as persons clearly remembered or authoritatively vouched for by history. It is characteristic that the only passage in his poem which approaches – perhaps reaches – the 'uncanny' is Canto XXV of the *Inferno*, which describes the horrifying transmutations of the thieves in the ditch; and that the commentators can tell us very little about these men – and also that we need to know nothing about them to understand the Canto. It is because the sources, the materials of Wordsworth's encounters, are partly derived from earlier memories of his own, and from their recurrences, that his effect is uncanny.

Finally, it must be noted that this effect in Wordsworth is so very different from the supernatural of Coleridge, or the stones a'chase in haunted Abbeys, because it is at once eerie and realistic: eerie in its quality of feeling, yet realistic inasmuch as this is the manner in which the uncanny is actually felt in real life, and this is how it is produced. For the river Alph and its caverns, some suspension of disbelief is necessary, at least in an adult reader. For the uncanny quality of some of Wordsworth's central involutes, no such suspension is needed, for we experience them exactly as adults (at least some adults) experience similar feelings of *déjà vu*, of situations which *feel* as if they have been met before, either in life or in dreams. The adult, however, while in the midst of such experiences, retains his capacity of disbelief, and continues to exercise it. He does not stop feeling, nor does he cease to think. He does both and for the time being there is a kind of 'doubleness' in the experience. Wordsworth did not fail to notice this state of mind. On the contrary, he was deeply interested in it, and wrote much about it.

16

I look for ghosts; but none will force
Their way to me . . .

The Affliction of Margaret 57–8 (*PW* II, 49)

Wordsworth never saw a ghost – never, at least, let on that he had seen one. But he saw many sights which he described as ghostly. Of him, indeed, Emily Dickinson's profound aphorism was profoundly true: 'One need not be a Chamber – to be Haunted'. Yet his intelligence, skill in introspection, that wary solidity of mind which made the infamous Lockhart remark 'that he would have been an admirable country attorney',[17] and above all his characteristic northern determination not to be fooled – all these qualities made him treat these gleams and glimpses of what might have been the supernatural with a steady scepticism, even at the very moments when he was most nearly haunted. It was this not very common combination that made him so vivid a reporter of the stranger moods of his own mind, and of everyone's mind.

A simple but striking example of this tense balance of belief and disbelief is found in one of the 'Lucy' poems. It was sent in this form to Coleridge by Dorothy Wordsworth from Goslar, with the comment 'The next poem is a favorite of mine – i.e. of me, Dorothy':

1

Once, when my love was strong and gay,
And like a rose in June,
I to her cottage bent my way,
Beneath the evening Moon.

2

Upon the moon I fixed my eye
All over the wide lea:
My horse trudg'd on, and we drew nigh
Those paths so dear [to] me.

3

And now I've reached the orchard-plot,
And as we climbed the hill,
Towards the roof of Lucy's cot
The moon descended still.

4
In one of those sweet dreams I slept,
  Kind nature's gentlest boon,
And all the while my eyes I kept
  On the descending moon.

5
My horse moved on; hoof after hoof
  He raised and never stopped,
When down behind the cottage roof
  At once the planet dropp'd.

6
Strange are the fancies that will slide
  Into a lover's head,
'O mercy' to myself I cried
  'If Lucy should be dead!'

7
I told her this; her laughter light
  Is ringing in my ears;
And when I think upon that night
  My eyes are dim with tears. (*EL* 89/105)

The first five stanzas describe, without comment or interruption, a minor involute. In the sixth, and just before the natural climax, is interjected a sceptical caveat about the strangeness of the fancies that will slip sidelong into a lover's head. Yet even after this recognition that the whole involute was no more than a fancy, it is resumed, and the final apparent absurdity is reported. And this delicate, wavering mixture of belief and self-mockery is entirely characteristic of such experiences. They involve, generally, the making of little private omens, especially upon occasions emotionally charged. More concretely, they may be described as things that we all do, and never mention, partly because we are – afterwards – a little ashamed of them. One waits for a long time: and she does not come; one waits again, and still she does not come. Despondent, hopeful, despondent again, then a blend of both: 'if she hasn't come by the time that piece of paper has blown past the trees, she won't come at all' – 'as long as that one attic light burns, she may still come. If it goes out . . .' This, in his own form, is the common experience which Wordsworth is describing, doing justice both to the strength of the feelings involved in it, and to his own awareness that it is strange and fanciful. In the version published later, this awareness has been strengthened by a sceptical introduction:

Strange fits of passion have I known:
And I will dare to tell,

But in the Lover's ear alone,
What once to me befell. (1–4 [*PW* II, 29])

The self-criticism of the original sixth stanza is also strengthened in this final version, into 'What fond and wayward thoughts will slide / Into a Lover's head!', and the last verse has been omitted altogether, so that the poem may, by a reader given to melancholy, be interpreted in the elegiac mode, and so incorporated in the 'Lucy' myth.

Another example of the same delicate balance between imaginative and self-critical impulses is in the sestet of one of his best-known sonnets:

The world is too much with us; late and soon,
Getting and spending, we lay waste our powers;
Little we see in Nature that is ours;
We have given our hearts away, a sordid boon!
This Sea that bares her bosom to the moon;
The winds that will be howling at all hours,
And are up-gathered now like sleeping flowers;
For this, for everything, we are out of tune;
It moves us not. – Great God! I'd rather be
A Pagan suckled in a creed outworn;
So might I, standing on this pleasant lea,
Have glimpses that would make me less forlorn;
Have sight of Proteus rising from the sea;
Or hear old Triton blow his wreathèd horn. (*PW* III, 18–19)

The balance is established here between the outburst 'I'd rather be / A Pagan' and its instant check with the phrase 'a creed outworn'. Yet, though the impossibility of the imaginative impulse has been thus recognised, he goes on, just as in *Strange fits*, to indulge in it, to round it off with a triumph of mythical persons, one from Spenser and one from Milton, with a fine roll of proper names – an effect of which he was very sparing. It is as if the incantatory force of the myths, with his own knowledge of the particular embodiments in two of his most deeply respected predecessors, had enabled him to prolong the glimpses for a few moments longer. But there had been no self-deception. The vision, however consoling, had been known for a vision even while it was at its strongest.

The same type of rhetorical climax, based on an incantation of proper names, is found in a less well-known sonnet, in which the same basic theme is handled, but from outside. In it, Wordsworth is contemplating the possible value of superstition, of ghosts and apparitions, in the life of an old countryman well known to him – his name was Mitchell:

Though narrow be that old Man's cares, and near,
The poor old Man is greater than he seems:

For he hath waking empire, wide as dreams;
An ample sovereignty of eye and ear.
Rich are his walks with supernatural cheer;
The region of his inner spirit teems
With vital sounds and monitory gleams
Of high astonishment and pleasing fear.
He the seven birds hath seen, that never part,
Seen the SEVEN WHISTLERS in their nightly rounds,
And counted them: and oftentimes will start –
For overhead are sweeping GABRIEL'S HOUNDS,
Doomed, with their impious Lord, the flying Hart
To chase for ever, on aërial grounds! (*PW* III, 34)

The mythology here is not classical, but home-grown and -spun. Wordsworth had met with something like it in the Lakes, or at least in the *Guides* to the Lakes. The seven whistlers and the supernatural hunt are embodiments, of course, of a strange honking and whistling sounds made by some birds, mainly migratory geese, a little before dawn. The balancing element of scepticism here is contained in that flash of humorous observation, 'and counted them', one of those touchingly absurd assurances which the countryman will give as he indulges in high astonishment of one sort or another: 'Now it's the truth what I'm telling you – you ask my wife what's sitting there if it isn't. I'm not telling you no lie now. I counted every one of 'em as they passed.' And Wordsworth, though he knows that these are nothing more than myths, shares with the old man a moment's imaginative relish for them, and insists that their importance in his life, in anyone's life, is much more than momentary. The presence of the central word of the *gleam*-cluster should not be missed in this sonnet, any more than *glimpses* in the one quoted before it.

The most generalised and weighty statement of this balance between scepticism and credulity, and of the role of myths in the life of the mind, is in a part of the fourth book of *The Excursion* which much influenced Keats:

'. . . Who thinks, and feels,
And recognizes ever and anon
The breeze of nature stirring in his soul,
Why need such man go desperately astray.
And nurse "the dreadful appetite of death?"
If tired with systems, each in its degree
Substantial, and all crumbling in their turn,
Let him build systems of his own, and smile
At the fond work, demolished with a touch;
If unreligious, let him be at once,
Among ten thousand innocents, enrolled
A pupil in the many-chambered school,
Where superstition weaves her airy dreams.

'Life's autumn past, I stand on winter's verge;
And daily lose what I desire to keep:
Yet rather would I instantly decline
To the traditionary sympathies
Of a most rustic ignorance and take
A fearful apprehension from the owl
Or death-watch: and as readily rejoice,
If two auspicious magpies crossed my way; –
To this would rather bend than see and hear
The repetitions wearisome of sense,
Where soul is dead, and feeling hath no place;
Where knowledge, ill begun in cold remark
On outward things, with formal inference ends;
Or, if the mind turn inward, she recoils
At once – or, not recoiling, is perplexed –
Lost in a gloom of uninspired research;
Meanwhile, the heart within the heart, the seat
Where peace and happy consciousness should dwell,
On its own axis restlessly revolving,
Seeks, yet can nowhere find, the light of truth.'

(IV.598–630 [*PW* V, 128])

Thus Wordsworth salutes the splendour of superstitions, even while recognising them as superstitious: he sees the kernel in the husk.

This balancing, or rapid alternation between contradictory attitudes can easily (above all by those 'Lost in a gloom of uninspired research') be made to look like more of an act than it is in practice. It is far from being an acrobatic feat of mind and memory. On the contrary, it is one of the most natural results of reviving memories of past thought and feelings, and so of being forced to compare the mood in which they were originally experienced with that in which they are now surveyed. If the reader will inquire within, and remind himself of some very distant memory, let him try to make out who is the central figure in it, who is doing the remembering and the experiencing. Is it himself, as he is now? Or a slighter figure, differently clothed? Or some mingling of the two? Dickens perceived the contrast in *David Copperfield*, described it vividly, but – as one might expect – with less subtlety than Wordsworth. For example, in a passage on the later part of David's school-days:

My school-days! The silent gliding on of my existence – the unseen, unfelt progress of my life – from childhood up to youth! Let me think, as I look back upon that flowing water, now a dry channel overgrown with leaves, whether there are any marks along its course, by which I can remember how it ran.

A moment, and I occupy my place in the cathedral, where we all went together, every Sunday morning . . . The earthy smell, the sunless air, the sensation of the world being shut out, the resounding of the organ through the black and white arched galleries and aisles, are wings that take me back, and hold me hovering above those days, in a half-sleeping and half-waking dream.

I am not the last boy in the school. I have risen, in a few months, over several heads. But the first boy seems to me a mighty creature, dwelling afar off, whose giddy height is unattainable . . .

I am higher in the school, and no one breaks my peace . . .

A blank, through which the warriors of poetry and history march on in stately hosts that seem to have no end – and what comes next! *I* am the head boy now! I look down on the line of boys below me, with a condescending interest in such of them as bring to mind the boy I was myself, when I first came there. That little fellow seems to be no part of me; I remember him as something left behind upon the road of life – as something I have passed, rather than have actually been – and almost think of him as of some one else.

(Ch. XVII, 'A Retrospect')

There is a characteristic difference between the main images used by Dickens and by Wordsworth to describe the process of retrospection. Dickens has the flowing stream, with its dried-up channels; Wordsworth also uses the image of a river and its windings (as in the opening of Book IX of *The Prelude*), but his most careful and revealing comparison is this:

As one who hangs down-bending from the side
Of a slow-moving Boat, upon the breast
Of a still water, solacing himself
With such discoveries as his eye can make,
Beneath him, in the bottom of the deeps,
Sees many beauteous sights, weeds, fishes, flowers,
Grots, pebbles, roots of trees, and fancies more;
Yet often is perplex'd, and cannot part
The shadow from the substance, rocks and sky,
Mountains and clouds, from that which is indeed
The region, and the things which there abide
In their true dwelling; now is cross'd by gleam
Of his own image, by a sunbeam now,
And motions that are sent he knows not whence,
Impediments that make his task more sweet;
Such pleasant office have we long pursued
Incumbent o'er the surface of past time
With like successes . . . (*Prel.* IV.247–64)

Dickens' image is perfunctory, even superficial; he is concerned with the flow of time only so far as it is needed to provide a framework for the purely human description, for the facts themselves, and the deeper observation on the apparent duality of the remembering personality is made with little slackening of the tempo. With him – and naturally enough – the flow is the thing, the pace must not fail. Wordsworth's image is concerned with a retrospect apparently more static, in depth and of still water. Yet movement comes to it, of a more dynamic kind: the tensions of perplexed minglings of past and present, of real memory and present alteration to it, and of memories that transform themselves under the sway of invisible undercurrents. The image ends, indeed, by expressing the very close resemblance between what Wordsworth had both experienced and observed and what Freud was later to describe as the dynamic quality of memory. The same duality is described more succinctly, though less richly, here:

> A tranquillising spirit presses now
> On my corporeal frame: so wide appears
> The vacancy between me and those days
> Which yet have such self-presence in my mind
> That, sometimes, when I think of them, I seem
> Two consciousnesses, conscious of myself
> And of some other Being. (*Prel.* II.27–33)

When the mind is in this literally 'reflective' mood, seeing both the mirror and the image, it is not difficult for it to believe and to disbelieve, to see ghosts or the memories of them, and at the same time to know that they are not, and cannot be, ghostly. The internal simulacrum of the older but simpler self reproduces the early experience, while the older and more sophisticated present self watches with wary interest; and now and then it may happen that the interest grows so intense that the wariness forgets itself, the memory resumes its full life of feeling and vividness, and will hardly pass away again in quite the same form.

Wordsworth's own experience thus led him to a description of the life of the mind very different from that of the empirical philosophers, not only in his insistence on the actively selective powers of perception, but perhaps even more in his recognition of the far-reaching effects of memories revived, re-lived, not as passive traces of old perceptions, capable only of mechanical combination and association, but as new elements of experience, able to grow and change in their own fashion, not once, but repeatedly. And this still living, constantly modified repetition of memories is, of course, the inward reality corresponding with the apparent tautologies, the repetitions of his special poetic style and use of words.

17

> . . . dire faces, figures dire,
> Sharp-kneed, sharp-elbowed, and lean-ankled too
> With long and ghostly shanks . . .
> *The Ruined Cottage* MS B, 182–4 (*PW* v, 383)

In two of Wordsworth's uncanny involutes, that of the discharged soldier and that of the blind beggar, we have already noted the presence – the recurrence – of earlier memories. The sight of the drowned man as he rose from the lake, 'bolt upright', seems to have come to life again in the 'upright face' of the beggar, and in the 'upright' lank leanness of the soldier. But these are not the only recurrences which help to confer their special quality on these two descriptions. At least one more obvious and powerful recurrence can be traced back, through an intermediate stage, to the same source of imagery and feeling which, according to Wordsworth himself in *1805* prevented him from feeling a merely 'vulgar fear' when, not yet nine years old, he had seen that spectre rise from the waters. He had, even then, seen it before, or something sufficiently like it to make this no new experience, but a recurrence of one already experienced, and so already embedded in the 'set' of his mind and spirit, already determining the way in which he would experience such things again, not as a blank *tabula rasa*, but as an active, even a dominating force:

> . . . my inner eye had seen
> Such sights before, among the shining streams
> Of Fairy Land, the Forests of Romance:
> Thence came a spirit hallowing what I saw
> With decoration and ideal grace;
> A dignity, a smoothness, like the works
> Of Grecian Art, and purest Poesy. (*Prel.* v.475–81)

The other significant reference to his childhood reading of fairy-tales is in his description of the upbringing of the Pedlar, a figure who was, in part, autobiographical: 'I am here called upon freely to acknowledge that the character I have represented in his person is chiefly an idea of what I fancied my own character might have become in his circumstances' (*PW* v, 373). So he wrote in the long Fenwick Note on *The Excursion*, in Book I of which *The Ruined Cottage* and its frame, *The Pedlar*, were first published. We may, therefore, take the following as obliquely referring to to his own childhood:

> . . . and here and there
> A straggling volume torn and incomplete
> Which left half-told the preternatural tale,
> Romance of giants, chronicle of fiends,
> Profuse in garniture of wooden cuts
> Strange and uncouth; dire faces, figures dire,
> Sharp-kneed, sharp-elbowed, and lean-ankled too
> With long and ghostly shanks – forms which once seen
> Could never be forgotten.
>
> (*The Ruined Cottage* MS B, 177–85 [*PW* I, 383)

The quality of the feeling here strikingly confirms Freud's suggestion that the real fairy-tale (as opposed to literary creations in the same convention) is not uncanny. All that we encounter here is the frank use of supernatural machinery to awaken wonder and simple terror. And it is the same quality of feeling, conventionally terrifying, but quite free from the real uneasiness of uncanny writings of experiences, which we find in the recurrence of this same singularly lean personage, as one of the Gothic apparitions in *The Vale of Esthwaite*:

On tiptoe, as I lean'd aghast
Listening the hollow-howling blast
I started back – when at my hand
A tall thin spectre seem'd to stand
Like two wan wither'd leaves his eyes. . .

. . .

His bones look'd sable through his skin
As the pale moonbeam wan and thin
Which through a chink of rock we view
On a lone sable blasted eugh;
And on one branded arm he bore
What seem'd the poet's harp of yore;
One hand he wav'd – and would have spoke,
But from his trembling shadow broke
Faint murmuring – sad and hollow moans
As if the wind sigh'd through his bones.

(325–39 [*PW* I, 277–8])

It was about a year after writing these lines, and presumably upwards of ten years after seeing the woodcuts of those lanky giants and fiends, that Wordsworth was walking back to Colthouse from Windermere, after a late party celebrating one of the Regattas which, according to the guide-books, played a great part in Lakeland social life at that time. And there, on the deserted road, he saw in the moonlight just such a figure as he had seen before in the woodcuts, and had re-created in his imagination. But now according to his account, it was really there; and he encountered it in precisely that mood of relaxation after excitement which, as he told De Quincey, had always been typical of those experiences which we are calling, for the moment, involutes:

While thus I wander'd, step by step led on,
It chanc'd a sudden turning of the road
Presented to my view an uncouth shape
So near, that, slipping back into the shade
Of a thick hawthorn, I could mark him well,
Myself unseen. He was of stature tall,
A foot above man's common measure tall,

Stiff in his form, and upright, lank and lean,
A man more meagre, as it seem'd to me,
Was never seen abroad by night or day.
His arms were long, and bare his hands; his mouth
Shew'd ghastly in the moonlight; from behind
A milestone propp'd him, and his figure seem'd
Half-sitting and half-standing . . .
. . . From his lips, meanwhile,
There issued murmuring sounds, as if of pain
Or of uneasy thought; yet still his form
Kept the same steadiness; and at his feet
His shadow lay, and mov'd not . . .
I wish'd to see him move; but he remain'd
Fix'd to his place, and still from time to time
Sent forth a murmuring voice of dead complaint,
Groans scarcely audible . . . (*Prel.* IV.400–32)

The mingling of things seen with things remembered shows itself most clearly in the tautologies themselves, in the words which recur with the recurrent images, forming a small word-cluster of their own: *lean*, *tall*, *thin*, *murmuring*. And when at last Wordsworth left the shade of the hawthorn and hailed the man, this real figure replied with 'a lean and wasted arm / In measur'd gesture lifted to his head' (437–8), just as the Gothic ghost had waved one hand. The interference of past and present experience with one another is seen in the slight contradictions of the accounts of the soldier's posture. Entirely consonant with the present of reality and observation is his position half-sitting and half-standing on the milestone. He is ill and weary, and when addressed 'Slowly from his resting-place / He rose' (436–7); and slightly inconsistent with this attitude, but wholly in harmony with the past of memory is his stiffness and uprightness. The strange harmony of these physically contradictory features is established nowhere other than in Wordsworth's own spirit, and in the force of the words already, and for so long, associated with the spectres of his childhood, from lakes or from books.

One of the odder verbal links between the soldier, the blind beggar and the Leechgatherer too is that all three are 'propp'd' in their singular immobility, the first on the milestone, the second 'against a Wall' (*Prel.* VII. 612), the third 'Upon a long grey staff of shaven wood' (*PW* II, 257). The coincidence is the more striking because the word only occurs seven times in Wordsworth's poetry, so that if the association with these three rather similar figures is fortuitous, it is by a very long chance indeed. The only possible hypothesis which suggests itself concerning the early memories which determine this feature of the three descriptions takes its point of departure from the use of the word in this passage:

> Humanity, delighting to behold
> A fond reflection of her own decay,
> Hath painted Winter like a traveller old,
> Propped on a staff, and, through the sullen day,
> In hooded mantle, limping o'er the plain,
> As though his weakness were disturbed by pain:
> (*The French Army in Russia* 1–6 [*PW* III, 140])

This description leads back directly enough to one of his earliest poems in his mature style, *The Old Cumberland Beggar*, written at almost exactly the same time as the description of the discharged soldier:

> He travels on, a solitary Man . . .
> . . . Poor Traveller!
> His staff trails with him; scarcely do his feet
> Disturb the summer dust; he is so still
> In look and motion . . . (44, 58–61 [*PW* IV, 235–6])

It seems at least possible, though far from demonstrable, that all three of the uncanny figures bear some memory-traces of that actual old Cumberland beggar often seen by Wordsworth in his childhood before he went to Hawkshead, as he later said 'with great benefit to my own heart'.[18] Their images are linked with his by their age or infirmity, and by their need to prop or propel themselves by a staff. All four, also, are indigent, objects of pity, and needing help and sympathy.

Two rather difficult questions arise from this suggestion that these three uncanny figures owe much of their effect to the fact that they mingled past and present perceptions together. First, how far was Wordsworth himself aware of this mingling? And second, how far is a knowledge of it directly relevant to the reader – is the effect on him just as great without any such knowledge? Neither is easy to answer with any certainty, but both can perhaps be a little illuminated by recourse to Freud's essay. It is central to his hypothesis about the nature of the uncanny that the recurrence of an older memory in a slightly altered form is *not* consciously connected with the present experience, and that it cannot be, since it has been, in his own terminology, 'repressed', made unavailable to the conscious memory. It is the emotional affect originally attached to the earlier experience which, by transfer to the present experience, generates the emotional tension of the uncanny. It is certainly worth noting, in passing, that this hypothesis belongs to that part of Freud's theory which can readily be re-stated in the terms of a very different, and on the whole less controversial kind of psychology; one has only to think of it in terms of a reflex conditioned by some previous stimulus, perhaps reinforced and slightly generalised, stimulated again by a rather similar stimulus. This would suggest that, had Wordsworth been consciously aware of the many similarities between these three figures and his memories of the drowned man, of the fairy tales, the Gothic ghost, and the old beggar, he would have felt very differently, and much less mysteriously, about their presence. He would not have been troubled, or enriched, by the feeling of *déjà vu*.

This view is, on the whole, confirmed by the early drafts of the description of the discharged soldier. In all of them, one feature of the actual experience is very prominent:

> He frets me sore I do not know
> What 'tis that ails him but I think the dog
> Howls to the murmur of the village stream
>
> (*Alfoxden* MS, fragment (a) [Oxford *Prelude*, p. 537])

> And every second moment rang a peal
> Felt in my very heart. I could have thought
> His wrath was bent on me – there was no noise
> Nor any foot abroad – I do not know
> What ail'd him but it seem'd as if the dog
> Howl'd to the murmur of the village stream
>
> (*Alfoxden* MS, fragment (b) [Oxford *Prelude*, *loc. cit*])

> . . . but all the while
> The chained mastiff in his wooden house
> Was vexed and from among the village trees
> Howled in the stillness . . .
> I felt myself at ease and much reliev'd
> But that the village mastiff fretted me
> And every second moment rang a peal
> Felt . . . *etc. as above*
>
> (*Christabel* MS and MS *Verse 18A* [Oxford *Prelude*, p. 538])

These rather elaborate descriptions of the barking dog, on which so much work had been done in the *Alfoxden* and *Christabel* manuscripts and in *18A*, were completely dropped from the passage in 1805, but it is very difficult not to believe that they had been part of the original experience, so persistently did Wordsworth dwell on them in these earlier versions. No doubt he was right to drop them in the final version, for that wretched mastiff would have distracted the reader from the real business of the passage, as it seems to have fretted Wordsworth in the real encounter. But perhaps it had served its purpose, quite unknown to him, of establishing an unconscious link between the soldier and the old Cumberland beggar:

> . . . he is so still
> In look and motion, that the cottage curs,
> Ere he has passed the door, will turn away,
> Weary of barking at him. (60–3 [*PW* IV, 236])

Professor de Selincourt suggests in his note on these drafts that this dog was the one recorded by Dorothy Wordsworth in the Alfoxden *Journal* (27 January 1798) as belonging to a manufacturer and having a 'strange, uncouth howl': 'It howls at the murmur of the village stream.' This is, I believe, one of those instances in which it is impossible to discover whether she quoted this line from a poem on which Wordsworth was then working, or whether he took it from her *Journal*. All that matters is that the dog was something of a nuisance. But it may be a slight consolation to those town-dwellers who move to the country in search of unattainable rural peace, to reflect that wakefulness is sometimes productive of better things than itself. The Alfoxden dog was surely not the same as the Esthwaite dog, but its barking served the very useful purpose of activating Wordsworth's memories both of the 'cottage curs' who barked at the old beggar in Cockermouth, and the 'chained mastiff' who barked so insistently at the passing of the discharged soldier, before Wordsworth came upon him – and what was still more productive, the purpose of linking together, in some respects, these two figures. Having done this, all the dogs had served their purposes, and were as well out of the final version where, important as they might have been in rousing and modifying Wordsworth's memories, they would have been of no use to the reader. In all this, however, one gets a fairly strong impression that Wordsworth was rather being manipulated by his memories than consciously manipulating them. The same impression is given by a fine simile in the drafts which happens to pick up the two striking lines in *The Vale* about the spectre's bones:

> His bones look'd sable through his skin . . .
> But from his trembling shadow broke
> Faint murmuring – sad and hollow moans
> As if the wind sigh'd through his bones. (330–9 [*PW* I, 277–8])

The *Christabel* and *18A* MSS have these lines about the soldier:

> There was in his form
> A meagre stiffness. You might almost think
> That his bones wounded him. (Oxford *Prelude*, p. 537)

It does not seem very likely that Wordsworth, had he been conscious of the connection between his earlier memories and the former poem, still less had he been consciously exploiting this connection in his description, would have omitted from the final version any reference to the figure's bones – especially so striking a one as this.

The answer to this first question, however, tends to merge in the second problem: how far the descriptions can have their uncanny effect upon the reader who does not know of the manner in which these earlier experiences are linked with the present ones. This can at once be recognised as no more than one of the special cases of a much more general problem: how can any reader understand, let alone be deeply moved by, experiences which he has not himself experienced? And the speciality of this case lies in the fact that the experiences underlying these descriptions appear to be so intensely personal – a particular book of fairy-tales, an unusual childhood witnessing of a drowning, an ageing beggar, a barking dog. The answer lies in Wordsworth's own contention, so urgently pressed in the *Preface* to *Lyrical Ballads*,[19] that the experience on which poetry is based is not in any way special in kind, though it may be in degree and intensity of feeling and above all in activity of memory. When this contention is joined with that other conviction of his, that the tone-row on which the composition of each spirit is based lies in the experiences of 'simple childhood', we are brought very much nearer to Freud's central theory that, even in their unconscious minds, human beings are far more alike than they themselves usually suppose. Or rather, it might be better to say, they combine individuality with common likenesses, and can do so because they are not simple and unitary entities, but complex associations of many different elements. Human beings are, in this respect, rather like the hands dealt out in a game of cards. Each hand, taken as a whole, is different from each of the others, and it is, in terms of the game, a good one or a bad one, or something in between; yet it will, in the great majority of deals, contain spades, hearts, diamonds and clubs, and in this respect it will resemble all the other hands. So human beings, especially in childhood, are likely to resemble one another in respect of many simple experiences and feelings, though they may differ considerably in their reactions to them.

It must be admitted that Freud himself sometimes, and his followers uncomfortably often, have pushed this view to an unlikely extreme, and have supposed – or appeared to suppose – that it was possible to define, as it were, the pack of cards upon which all the individual hands of the human personality are based, to construct a kind of dictionary of symbolism or equivalences between elements of experience and the feelings associated with them. Thus the snake was defined as a male sexual symbol, and the ladder as a symbol for sexual activity, so that the old nursery game of snakes and ladders became a rather sinister affair. But it happens all too often that the excesses to which a theory may be pushed are allowed to obscure its essential validity. And in this case, though a dictionary of symbols cannot be constructed, the principle of which it is an exaggeration is both useful and useable. And it is most likely to be valid when it is applied, not to particular objects like snakes and ladders, but to broader categories of human experience. Freud makes such an application at the close of his essay on the uncanny, when he points to the general association between it and three such broad categories: 'Concerning the factors of silence, solitude and darkness, we can only say that they are actually elements in the production of that infantile morbid anxiety from which the majority of human beings have never become quite free.'[20] Thus broadly defined, the common elements of childhood experience which, recurring in association with later experiences, produce the feeling of uncanniness are plain enough, at least in these descriptions of Wordsworth's. True, the only one which has a background of shadow and darkness is the discharged soldier, but all three are very strongly associated with solitude, silence – and, we must add, as a natural cœnæsthetic companion of silence, a preternatural immobility in living creatures. These qualities, at least, are not bounded by individual experience. They are felt by most of us in our childhood, and are therefore capable, under suitable stimuli, of recurring in later life so as to produce the sensation of the uncanny. Thus, to take the shortest of the three descriptions, the blind beggar in London stood, apart from the swirling crowds, in the solitude of his own darkness,

> And, on the shape of that unmoving man,
> His fixèd face and sightless eyes, I look'd . . . (*Prel.* VII.620–1)

The Leechgatherer had the same immobility:

> Upon the margin of that moorish flood
> Motionless as a cloud the old Man stood,
> That heareth not the loud winds when they call;
> And moveth all together, if it move at all.
>
> . . .
>
> While he was talking thus, the lonely place,
> The old Man's shape, and speech – all troubled me:
> In my mind's eye I seemed to see him pace
> About the weary moors continually,
> Wandering about alone and silently.
>
> (74–7, 127–31 [*PW* II, 237, 240])

As for this uncanny silence, the crucial message of the blind beggar was conveyed, of course, without the use of any words, by the silent symbolic force of the 'written paper' on his chest (*Prel.* VII.613). The Leechgatherer actually speaks far less than a casual reader of the poem might suppose. Four verses are, it is true, given up to describing his utterance, but they give it by report, not directly – and in a report which gradually shades off into a kind of monologue inside Wordsworth's own mind, so that

> . . . his voice to me was like a stream
> Scarce heard; nor word from word could I divide . . . (107–8 [*PW* II, 239])

The Leechgatherer himself speaks only three lines in *oratio recta*, and it is this sudden climactic breaking of his silence that confers on this utterance the high emphasis which it needs, as the preternatural 'admonishment' which he appeared to have been sent to convey:

> 'Once I could meet with them on every side;
> But they have dwindled long by slow decay;
> Yet still I persevere, and find them where I may.' (124–6 [*ibid.*])

No reader of Dante will fail to recognise the resemblance between this tremendous utterance, so brief and reticent that it scarcely breaks the silence, so tense with implication, and the utterances of the damned, the purging, and the blessed.

But it is in the description of the soldier especially that the effects of solitude, immobility and silence are brought to bear on the reader's – and on Wordsworth's own – sense of the uncanny. There is the long introductory description, while Wordsworth watches from the shade of the hawthorn, marking the man's strange height, stiffness, leanness, the 'mouth ghastly in the moonlight', and his utter loneliness:

> He was alone,
> Had no attendant, neither Dog, nor Staff,
> Nor knapsack; in his very dress appear'd
> A desolation, a simplicity
> That seem'd akin to solitude. (*Prel.* IV. 415–19)

In the drafts, this loneliness was even more emphatic, and expressed in terms which hinted even more strongly at the unearthly quality of his isolation:

> His face was turn'd
> Towards the road yet not as if he sought
> For any living spirit [thing *18A*]: he appeared
> Forlorn and desolate, a man cut off
> From all his kind, and more than half detached
> From his own nature . . .
>
> . . . I think
> If but a glove had dangled from his hand
> It would have made him more akin to man . . .
> (*Christabel* MS and MS *Verse 18A* [Oxford *Prelude*, p. 538])

The immobility also is stressed:

> . . . Long time
> Did I peruse him with a mingled sense
> Of fear and sorrow. From his lips, meanwhile,
> There issued murmuring sounds, as if of pain
> Or of uneasy thought; yet still his form
> Kept the same steadiness; and at his feet
> His shadow lay, and mov'd not. . . .
> I wish'd to see him move; but he remain'd
> Fix'd to his place, and still from time to time
> Sent forth a murmuring voice of dead complaint . . .
> (*Prel.* IV.419–25, 429–31)

The drafts do even better with one detail: they make his form keep 'the same awful' or 'the same fearful' steadiness. As for the soldier's silence, it is broken, in the earlier part of the description, only by his faint murmurs, 'Groans scarcely audible'. And even when Wordsworth at last steps from his hiding-place and addresses him, his long reply, and all their later conversation, except for a few words from Wordsworth himself, is in *oratio obliqua*, just as in *The Leech Gatherer*, and with the same eerie effect. In his tone, in his speech, as reported to us, there is the same lack of concern for himself and of personal interest in what he is saying as if he were already dead, already ghost:

> and when, erelong,
> I ask'd his history, he in reply
> Was neither slow nor eager; but unmov'd,
> And with a quiet, uncomplaining voice,
> A stately air of mild indifference,
> He told, in simple words, a Soldier's Tale . . .
> Nor, while we journey'd thus could I forbear
> To question him of what he had endur'd
> From hardship, battle, or the pestilence.
> He, all the while, was in demeanour calm,
> Concise in answer; solemn and sublime
> He might have seem'd, but that in all he said
> There was a strange half-absence, and a tone
> Of weakness and indifference, as of one
> Remembering the importance of his theme
> But feeling it no longer. (*ibid.* 440–5, 469–78)

And so, through the long slow walk through the wood towards the cottage where he is to shelter, the 'tall / And ghastly figure' moved by Wordsworth's side – and strangely enough, now with a staff, which had slipped from his slackened hand as he leaned on the milestone. Through the 'shades, gloomy and dark', they came to their parting, and Wordsworth entreated the man in future to seek the help he needed – and so to the talismanic utterance which this soldier had been sent to make, the first and only words spoken by himself, not merely reported: the only moment at which, to the reader, he breaks silence:

> 'my trust is in the God of Heaven
> And in the eye of him that passes me.' (*ibid.* 494–5)

These, I believe, are some, but still not quite all, of the very complex, or at least well-hidden, means by which this description is invested with that eeriness which ends by conferring such force upon these simple words – and they seem indeed to have belonged to reality, to a real soldier, for they are present in the early drafts, exactly as they stand in the final version. If the point of this analysis has been made at all, it hardly needs to be laboured. It is directed only against those who have been brought up to believe, or who bring up others to believe, that Wordsworth was merely a descriptive and moralising writer, or that his imagination could deploy itself only upon 'Nature'. It would be a pardonable, because useful, exaggeration to claim that he is incomparably the greatest of English writers in the Gothic mode. Even Jane Austen could not have laughed off this soldier or the blind beggar. As for the Leechgatherer, there is a little more to be said.

18

Have sight of Proteus rising from the sea . . .[21]

And when he has risen, he will put on one of the most fascinating and eerie of all mythological performances, that of changing shape into all manner of creatures and objects, of both losing and yet keeping his own identity, of being a constantly shifting *Doppelgänger* to his own successive selves. It is no accident that the one passage in Dante, in Canto XXV of the *Inferno*, which approaches, or attains, the effect of the uncanny is one in which such changes and exchanges of shape are described, with horrifying precision. Proteus, the Shape-Shifter as he appears in works on folk-lore and mythology, has not escaped the attention of Freud, or the imagination of Wordsworth. He is, in part, the discharged soldier, who turns from a milestone into a man: in part, too, the blind beggar, dehumanised against the wall, as if inanimate; and most of all the Leechgatherer. And the complex processes of his creation, as it happens, can be studied the more fully because we know more about them, perhaps, than about any other poem of Wordsworth's. His own comments on the poem, both in the course of writing it, of changing from the early to the final draft, and by way of explanation many years after it was written, are among the most revealing that he ever made – and that is saying a great deal, for, as Mill noted, he had an ability far beyond that of most writers to perceive and explain his own creative processes.

It will be as well to make clear at once what he did *not* perceive: any relation between the figure of the Leechgatherer and the mythical Proteus. This was neither conscious, nor specific, for the connection between them is not that between two things, but rather that between constituent parts of the same whole. Both Proteus and the Leechgatherer are embodiments, and independent embodiments, of the same general pattern of imagination and myth. To this pattern, Freud mentions in passing a very useful key. Quoting from what he calls 'a fertile but not exhaustive paper by E. Jentsch', he says: 'Jentsch has taken as a very good instance [i.e. of the uncanny] "doubts whether an apparently animate being is really alive; or conversely, whether a lifeless object might not be in fact animate".'[22] It happens that this kind of ambiguous image was one which had its appeal to Wordsworth. The earliest example is found, as usual, in *The Vale of Esthwaite*:

. . . I the while
Look'd through the tall and sable isle
Of firs that to a mansion led
With many a turret on its head;
And while the wild wind rav'd aloud,
And each his grim black forehead bow'd,
And flung his mighty arms around
That clang'd and met with crashing sound,
They seemed unto my fear-struck mind
Gigantic Moors in battle joined;
While each with hollow-threatening tone
Claim'd the hoar castle as his own. (210–21 [*PW* I, 274–5])

The same ambiguity of tree and human being is found in one of the more effective passages of *The Borderers*:

To the spot
I hurried back with her. – Oh save me, Sir,
From such a journey! – there was a black tree,
A single tree; she thought it was her Father. –
Oh Sir, I would not see that hour again
For twenty lives. The daylight dawned, and now –
Nay; hear my tale, 'tis fit that you should hear it –

As we approached, a solitary crow
Rose from the spot; – the Daughter clapped her hands,
And then I heard a shriek so terrible
The startled bird quivered upon the wing. (2065–75 [*PW* I, 211])

Similar ambiguities in the interpretation of lonely shapes are found in Wordsworth's poetry between rocks and human beings. Thus in the *Michael* drafts:

There is a shapeless crowd of unhewn stones
That lie together, some in heaps, and some
In lines, that seem to keep themselves alive
In the last dotage of a dying form. (MS 2, fragment (a) [*PW* II, 482])

And the confusion is still more dramatically used in *The Thorn*:

'Twas mist and rain, and storm and rain:
No screen, no fence could I discover;
And then the wind! in sooth, it was
A wind full ten times over.
I looked around, I thought I saw
A jutting crag, – and off I ran,
Head-foremost, through the driving rain,
The shelter of the crag to gain;
And, as I am a man,
Instead of jutting crag, I found
A Woman seated on the ground . . .' (177–87 [*PW* II, 246–7])

It is in *The Leech Gatherer*, however (*PW* II, 235–40), that this confusion between the animate and the inanimate is most elaborately introduced and developed. The elaboration of the introduction lies in its concentration of so many indications of uncanniness in a very few lines of stanza VIII. First, what is to come, before it is described at all, is given as something preternatural – probably, but not quite certainly; Wordsworth's power of at once indulging in superstition and withholding full credit to it is very clear here:

Now, whether it were by peculiar grace,
A leading from above, a something given,
Yet it befell that, in this lonely place,
When I with these untoward thoughts had striven . . .

We still have no idea what is to come: we know only that it is to be something of almost divine providence, a special guidance for his mood, his anxieties. 'Leading' was a word used in this way by Milton, lately revived by Burke in his phrase 'men . . . of light and leading', and widely used by the Quakers. Next the characteristic scene is briefly set, 'Beside a pool bare to the eye of heaven . . .' The reader already knows that this is all hapenning 'on the moors'; now there is a pool, but nothing else whatever. It is 'bare to the eye of heaven', a 'naked pool', like that on the 'bare common' by the border 'Beacon' in the 'spots of time' involute. And now at last the apparition itself: 'I saw a Man before me unawares . . .' In the earlier draft, this had been handled with even greater inexplicability:

> I to the borders of a Pond did come
> By which an Old Man was, far from all house or home. (*PW* II, 540)

Wordsworth's own comment on the early draft, defending it against some criticisms by Sara and Mary Hutchinson, insists on the semi-supernatural nature both of the old man's sudden appearance, and of his own introduction:

> I consider the manner in which I was rescued from my dejection and despair almost as an interposition of Providence. Now whether it was by peculiar grace, A leading from above – A person reading this Poem with feelings like mine will have been awed and controuled, expecting almost something spiritual or supernatural. What is brought forward? 'A lonely place, a Pond', 'by which an old man *was*, far from all house or home': not *stood*, not *sat*, but *was* – the figure presented in the most naked simplicity possible. This feeling of spirituality or supernaturalness is again referred to as being strong in my mind in this passage. *How came he here?* thought I, or what can he be doing? I then describe him . . . (*PW* II, 535)

It is, perhaps, a pity that he altered that blank and eerie 'was', but the other alterations made to meet the objections felt by Sara Hutchinson were notable improvements. The early draft had gone on:

> He seem'd like one who little saw or heard
> For chimney-nook, or bed, or coffin meet,

and this had led on to three stanzas describing him further, and perhaps reporting some of his own account of his past. All this has been deferred, in the final version, in favour of a complex image:

> As a huge stone is sometimes seen to lie
> Couched on the bald top of an eminence;
> Wonder to all who do the same espy,
> By what means it could thither come, and whence;
> So that it seems a thing endued with sense:
> Like a sea-beast crawled forth, that on a shelf
> Of rock or sand reposeth, there to sun itself . . .
>
> . . .
>
> Such seemed this Man, not all alive nor dead,
> Nor all asleep – in his extreme old age:
>
> . . .
>
> Motionless as a cloud the old Man stood,
> That heareth not the loud winds when they call;
> And moveth all together, if it move at all

This is, I suppose, one of the more striking 'images' in Wordsworth, and he himself was so impressed by it that he commented on it at some length in the 1815 *Preface*, as an example of what happens when all the powers of 'Imagination' work together. It is indeed an interesting explanation, but it may be questioned whether it is a complete account of it, either when it had been written, or when it was in the process of being written:

> In these images, the conferring, the abstracting, and the modifying powers of the Imagination, immediately and mediately acting, are all brought into conjunction. The stone is endowed with something of the power of life to approximate it to the sea-beast; and the sea-beast stripped of some of its vital qualities to assimilate it to the stone; which intermediate image is thus treated for the purpose of bringing the original image, that of the stone, to a nearer resemblance to the figure and condition of the aged Man; who is divested of so much of the indications of life and motion as to bring him to the point where the two objects unite and coalesce in just comparison. After what has been said, the image of the cloud need not be commented upon.
> (*PW* II, 438)

Though this is skilful enough – few modern imagery-analysers could do much better – and true enough, as far as it goes, it remains at the level of intelligent criticism after the event. It falls a good way short of explaining either the processes by which it was composed, or its whole effect on the reader. The crucial difference between this and the earlier draft is that here only one line, 'The oldest man he seemed that ever wore grey hairs', separates the opening hints of supernatural intervention from the series of Protean images. The uncanniness is not interrupted, as it had been in the first version, by much biographical detail, but is immediately reinforced, and not only by the shape-shifting. For the description of the stone, the sea-beast, and the old man himself also gains in force from many of the 'apparent tautologies' with which all these supernatural involutes are associated. The 'bald top of an eminence' is no more, and no less, than the 'naked rock', 'naked crag', 'summit', etc., which has already been studied. The single huge stone couched on it establishes the impression of solitude. The old man is 'propped', of course, like the discharged soldier and the blind beggar; and through the simile of the cloud he is made motionless, as they are on the milestone and against the wall in London. The effect of the shape-shifting images, against this established background of tautologies, is not one of ingenuity, of logical modification of stone to sea-beast, and of man to both. It is to reinforce the impression of the uncanny, by maintaining for as long as possible a kind of uneasiness as to whether the old man is animate or inanimate.

This effect is still further intensified by the old man's actual silence, so far as the reader is concerned. Though Wordsworth addresses him, and cites his own actual greeting in *oratio recta*, the Leechgatherer answers in *oratio obliqua*, just as the soldier had done to a similar greeting. His actual words are reserved for the climax of the encounter. And this climax matches the greater complexity of the imagery, and the suggestions of the uncanny, by Wordsworth's representation of himself as continuing to hesitate between the two ways of regarding this lonely figure, either as a real man, old and poor, or as a supernatural creature, sent by providence to guide him. Thus in stanza XVI:

> The old Man still stood talking by my side;
> But now his voice to me was like a stream
> Scarce heard; nor word from word could I divide;
> And the whole body of the Man did seem
> Like one whom I had met with in a dream;
> Or like a man from some far region sent,
> To give me human strength, by apt admonishment.

Abstracted from the actual presence of the old man, Wordsworth's 'former thoughts returned', his memories of what had happened to other poets, his perplexity for himself, and bursting from this miserable reverie, he again asked the old man how he lived, and what he did. In reply to this repeated question, and with a smile, the old man at last utters his real message:

> 'Once I could meet with them on every side;
> But they have dwindled long by slow decay;
> Yet still I persevere, and find them where I may.'

Wordsworth has indeed heard, but not yet with understanding. For the last time, the supernatural aspect of the Leechgatherer is evoked:

> While he was talking thus, the lonely place,
> The old Man's shape, and speech – all troubled me:
> In my mind's eye I seemed to see him pace
> About the weary moors continually,
> Wandering about alone and silently.

Loneliness, solitude, silence, in a weary landscape, plying, like the old Cumberland beggar, a 'weary journey' (53 [*PW* IV, 235]): is this the real, the effective version of the Leechgatherer? Or do we remember him and the encounter in this light – the light of the last verse?

> While I these thoughts within myself pursued,
> He, having made a pause, the same discourse renewed.
>
> And soon with this he other matter blended,
> Cheerfully uttered, with demeanour kind,
> But stately in the main; and when he ended,
> I could have laughed myself to scorn to find
> In that decrepit Man so firm a mind.
> 'God,' said I, 'be my help and stay secure;
> I'll think of the Leech-gatherer on the lonely moor!'

The question may, of course, be put in an even simpler form. What are we to call the poem? Wordsworth himself, when it was published in 1807, firmly entitled it *Resolution and Independence*: it was a descriptive poem above all important for its 'moral'. But the first draft had been called *The Leechgatherer*, and his sister used this title in her journal while he was writing it. No one, either in his own family or outside it, has ever thought of calling it anything else. It is indeed a moral poem, but its weight turns less upon the moral itself, which is worthy but comparatively trivial, than upon the uncanniness of the encounter, and the preternatural quality of the old man. It need not, of course, be a matter of choice; one could very well maintain that the 'moral' and the old man were inseparable, the one lending significance to the other, the combination all-important. This could indeed be said. But the fact is that many generations of Wordsworthians have not hesitated for a moment in their choice of a title.

And they are largely justified by Wordsworth's own comments on it, in the letter replying to Sara Hutchinson's well-meant and well-taken criticisms of the earlier draft. There Wordsworth gives his most vivid description in prose of what it felt like to be in the midst of an involute, to be in the grip of a strongly reacting and interacting cluster of words, memories, thoughts and feelings:

> I then describe him, whether ill or well is not for me to judge with perfect confidence, but this I can *confidently* affirm, that, though I believe God has given me a strong imagination, I cannot conceive a figure more impressive than that of an old Man like this, the survivor of a Wife and ten children, travelling alone among the mountains and all lonely places, carrying with him his own fortitude, and the necessities which an unjust state of society has entailed upon him. You say and Mary (that is you can say no more than that) the Poem is *very well* after the introduction of the old man; this is not true, if it is not more than very well it is very bad, there is no intermediate state. You speak of his speech as tedious: everything is tedious when one does not read with the feelings of the Author – '*The Thorn*' is tedious to hundreds; and so is the *Idiot Boy* to hundreds. It is in the character of the old man to tell his story in a manner which an *impatient* reader must necessarily feel as tedious. But Good God! Such a figure, in such a place, a pious self-respecting, miserably infirm and [ ] Old Man telling such a tale!
>
> My dear Sara, it is not a matter of indifference whether you are pleased with this figure and his employment; it may be comparatively so, whether you are pleased or not with *this Poem*; but it is of the utmost importance that you should have had pleasure from contemplating the fortitude, independence, persevering spirit, and the general moral dignity of this old man's character. Your feelings upon the Mother, and the Boys with the Butterfly, were not indifferent: it was an affair of whole continents of moral sympathy. (*EL* 132/172)

The prose account of the involute, like the verse account, does not clearly distinguish between – indeed it is pre-eminently an involute because it so inextricably mingles – the supernatural and the moral aspects of the old man.

But it is very significant that, when he set about altering the draft which had failed to convince these two critics, both fully accepted as having the right to criticise because they were in close sympathy with his poetry, he reduced that element in the poem which might be called 'Resolution and Independence', and enlarged that which must be called 'The Leechgatherer'. In his own way, he chose between the two titles, the two aspects. And in doing so, especially in the addition of the Protean similes, he brought into play, or at least into much greater play, one of the great resources of the uncanny, the temporary ambiguity of the central figure. But both in the prose and in the renewed act of creation (it is no less) that it provoked, it is clear that he was working, not by conscious intentions, but in response to his own revived memories, and to the words which embodied their recurrences and their successive modifications. Though unconscious of all that he was doing in this particular instance, he was obeying that general law of composition which he was to describe two years later – and his description is based, of course, on this piece of composition and re-composition, besides many others of a similar kind:

> Visionary Power
> Attends upon the motions of the winds
> Embodied in the mystery of words.
> There darkness makes abode, and all the host
> Of shadowy things do work their changes there,
> As in a mansion like their proper home:
> Even forms and substances are circumfus'd
> By that transparent veil with light divine;
> And through the turnings intricate of Verse,
> Present themselves as objects recognis'd,
> In flashes, and with a glory scarce their own. (*Prel.* v.619–29)

This passage is quoted elsewhere, for another purpose (pp. 83–4). Like many, if not all, of the best pieces of his verse, it compels a serious commentator to view it from more than one perspective. From this necessity arise certain inconveniences and apparent repetitions, irritating to the commentator and to his reader. Yet they are largely unavoidable, for it must be recognised that they arise from the remarkable density, so to speak, of Wordsworth's best poetry; from the fact that it brings into play, simultaneously, so many memories, thoughts and feelings – or, to say the same thing more succinctly, so many of his characteristic tautologies. Here what is being said (besides some other things) is that the hidden workings of words bring about their own shadowy perceptions and combinations, so that when next glimpsed at the level of consciousness they are only partly recognised, and correspondingly made more powerful. The tautologies of the *gleam* cluster are, in fact, applied exactly to the complex processes of memory and of vocabulary which brought so much of his experience to bear on the less tangible, the more uncanny, aspects of the Leechgatherer.

19

> . . . huge and mighty Forms that do not live
> Like living men mov'd slowly through my mind
> By day and were the trouble of my dreams. (*Prel.* I.425–7)

In defending the first draft of *The Leech Gatherer* to Sara Hutchinson, Wordsworth himself had placed it in close association with *The Thorn*. The old man's original speech had struck her as 'tedious', but so had the retired sea-captain's speech seemed 'tedious to hundreds'. Yet this second defence was conducted very differently from the first, and the differences illustrate the progress made by Wordsworth in the interval, the firmer grasp of his own real aims, and the methods of achieving them. Whereas in the first case, he had thought of persisting in his original vague notion of a loquacious mariner, even of writing an addition to the poem introducing him more fully, in the second case, he drastically reduced the merely biographical detail in the description of the Leechgatherer. These lines have gone: 'He seem'd like one who little saw or heard / For chimney-nook, or bed, or coffin meet' (*PW* II, 540), and they are just as well away, for they greatly weaken the semi-supernatural aspect of the old man's appearance. The three stanzas telling of the loss of his wife and ten children, so faithfully recorded in Dorothy's note of the actual meeting, have gone too. And it is perhaps worth noting that Dorothy herself had been removed from the actual scene even in the first draft. All these changes move with certainty in one direction. They reduce the element of mere actuality in the encounter, and enhance its eeriness.

The second part of the defence of *The Thorn*, that which defined for the first time the role of repetition and apparent tautology, is not repeated. Nor did it need to be. By the time he came to write *The Leech Gatherer* this method of using words, of building a poem or a passage in a long poem around a small cluster of idiolectal words, had become his normal style, and it so happens that *The Leech Gatherer* is a particularly striking example of this process at work. The way was opened for it – and for that slight resemblance with *The Thorn*, which perhaps prompted Wordsworth to make the two poems neighbours in all editions from 1815 onwards – by the handling of metre and language.

Although the stanza seems to have been taken from Chatterton, the metre itself is handled in a manner entirely characteristic of Wordsworth himself, and it manages to combine, as the matter and mood require, the qualities of the ten-syllable line in which his growing experience of writing *The Prelude* was giving him mastery, and also of the simpler ballad-like rhythms of the earlier 'little Rhyme poems'. Lines like these might well have come from *The Prelude*:

> As if all needful things would come unsought
> To genial faith, still rich in genial good . . .

On the other hand, there are several lines with a strong caesura after the sixth syllable which fall naturally into a ballad-like metre of couplets, with three stresses in one line, two in the other:

> From pond to pond he roamed,
> From moor to moor.

The nineteenth stanza has many such lines – and it is the stanza which, in its substance, most resembles a ballad. This suggestion of the ballad tone is greatly strengthened by a fitful use of the archaic *-th* endings for the third person of verbs – a usage which was generally avoided by Wordsworth. The first example is in line 14, which makes its suggestion the more strongly because it is placed in parallel with the more usual ending in *-s*: 'Runs with her all the way, wherever she doth run'. Thereafter, spread through the poem, are 'chanceth', 'heareth', 'moveth', and an unusually wide use of the 'expletive' forms of the present and past tenses with 'do' and 'did'. These archaisms are not systematic or deliberate, but they are frequent and striking enough to cast over the whole poem an air, a distinct reminiscence, of the ballad style, and so to distance it from later diction – with a distance which reinforces its supernatural atmosphere. Something of the same kind is done by scattered archaisms in one of the best of all modern versions of the ballad, John Crowe Ransom's *Captain Carpenter*.

The technical similarities between *The Leech Gatherer* and *The Thorn*, however, are even stronger in the use of tautology and repetition. They are readily revealed by a 'skeletal' version. For example, the first three stanzas are built around repetitions almost as strictly cumulative and retroactive as those in *The Reverie of Poor Susan*:

> roaring in the wind all night
> rain came heavily
> birds . . singing in the distant woods
> pleasant noise of waters
>
> all things that love the sun
> sky rejoices

grass bright with rain-drops
hare running races
mist . . . glittering in the sun

upon the moor
the hare that raced about with joy
the woods and distant waters roar
pleasant season

Just as, in the second part of the 'spots of time' involute, the whistling hawthorn was metamorphosed into the 'bleak music of that old stone wall', so here the 'roaring in the wind' and the 'birds . . . singing in the distant woods' turn into 'heard the woods and distant waters roar'. These are not visual pictures or descriptions; they are incantations, and provided the incantatory words are there, it matters little how they are applied. The main development of the poem, with its wavering double climax, its close economy of means, is very clearly shown by a skeleton of stanzas VIII to XIX:

lonely place
pool bare to the eye of heaven
a Man before me unawares
The oldest Man

a huge stone
bald top of an eminence
a sea-beast
shelf / Of rock or sand

this Man, not all alive nor dead
extreme old age
bent double

propped, limbs, body and pale face
Upon a long grey staff
Upon the margin of that moorish flood
Motionless as a cloud the old Man

himself unsettling, he the pond
stirred with his staff . . . did look
Upon the muddy water
I . . . to him did say
'a glorious day'

the old Man
courteous speech . . . slowly drew
I thus bespake
'What occupation . . .
This a lonesome place for one like you.'
flash of mild surprise
sable orbs of his yet-vivid eyes

words came feebly
but each in solemn order
lofty utterance,
choice word and measured phrase
a stately speech

to these waters . . . come
To gather leeches, being old and poor
Many hardships
From pond to pond he roamed,
from moor to moor

old Man . . . talking
voice . . . like a stream / Scarce heard
the whole body of the Man did seem
Like one . . . met with in a dream
Or like a man from some far region sent
to give . . . admonishment

former thoughts returned . . . fear
cold, pain, and labour and all fleshly ills
mighty Poets in their misery dead
longing to be comforted
my question . . . 'How is it that you live?'

with a smile did then his words repeat
gathering leeches, far and wide
He travelled, stirring thus about his feet
The waters of the pools
'Once . . . on every side
But . . . dwindled . . . slow decay
Yet still I persevere'.

the lonely place
The old Man's shape, and speech
I seemed to see him pace
About the weary moors continually
alone and silently

It is, perhaps, some excuse for using this method of demonstration that the only others which offer themselves are even more cumbrous and on the whole less effective. The main repeated elements could, of course, be listed, each with its number of occurences – *man* 4 times, *old man* 5, *moor* 7, *pool* and *pond* 6, and so on. But this leaves out too much: the rhythm of iteration in its sequence, the actual pattern of the repetitions. No doubt this too could be represented by a more sophisticated mathematical analysis, as a Markhov chain perhaps, or some other kind of stochastic process. Yet this would convey little, unless it could be compared with many other similar data from other poets, and from Wordsworth himself. All that can be said with reasonable certainty at the moment is that Wordsworth would certainly, other poets would but doubtfully, yield much material of this kind.

The special role of the main tautologies in Wordsworth is more easily demonstrated by a notable peculiarity in his typography. In the course of the eighteenth century, the use of capital letters for all nouns had been abandoned, but apparently in a haphazard fashion, according to the whims of printers and perhaps writers too. At the end of the century, they were used regularly for proper names, and irregularly for other nouns. It is impossible to read much Wordsworth, especially up to 1807 or so, without realising that he felt (or consciously believed) such capitalisation to be a very useful means of marking the special emphasis intended for the main tautologies of any poem or passage in which their role was important. Thus the manuscripts of *The Leech Gatherer* show capitals for Old, Man, Pool and Pond. In *The Thorn*, we find Woman and Thorn throughout. As for *The Prelude*, it is enough to open Professor de Selincourt's edition at any crucial passage, and note the use of capitals in the 1805 version, together with their absence in 1850. Thus in the description of the stolen boat, we find many times over Skiff, Boat, Lake, Steep and Cliff; in the first part of the 'spots of time' we have Common, Pool, Beacon, Girl, Pitcher, Eminence, Woman. This use of capitals to mark the main tautologies is the more remarkable – and the more likely to have been deliberate – since they are not found in the early manuscript drafts, where these exist. Certainly in the *Longman* manuscript we find Wordsworth adding capitals to Sara Hutchinson's fair copy of the *Immortality Ode*, as though for emphasis, at a point demonstrably between draft composition and publication.

A long and tedious investigation would be needed to establish the full significance of Wordsworth's use of capitals, but there is clearly a *prima facie* case for supposing that they were, at any rate up to about 1807, one of the idiolectal features of his style (very likely related with his use of emphasis in oral composition and delivery) which corresponded with his remarkable use of tautology and repetition. And without any further investigation, it can be said that this style, with all that is implied in it concerning mode of composition and approach to its subjects, is found just as much when Wordsworth is writing about Nature as when he writes about Man, and *vice versa*. It is the characteristic style of the great boyhood involutes of crags, cliffs and mountains, and also of the discharged soldier, the blind beggar in the London street, and the Leechgatherer. Stylistically, there are not two

Wordsworths: there is one only, all of a piece. What makes most for his homogeneity of style and of effect is that sense of the literally 'awe-full', of the numinous, which suffuses his descriptions of mountains and men. Though it may have had its dim and murky origins in his early indulgence in Gothic terrors, it had been transformed, by the time when he became a mature writer, into a quality of emotion fully compatible with maturity, with enough of wary scepticism and self-criticism to cut away all that might have been superficial or operatic in it, leaving what was left tempered to a dense solidity. His rememberings, and the tautologies through which they successively modified and strengthened their initial materials, finally expressed themselves in a version of the preternatural so harmonious with the natural that its full effect is accessible even to minds which have grown out of fairy-tales, and are uneasy with the more prosaically expressed versions of pantheism. It is a mood of the mind less negative than Coleridge's 'suspension of disbelief', for it allows a kind of belief, however provisional and for the moment, of the involute of which it forms a part; its momentariness matters the less because it is so surely destined to revive again, with the involute of which it is a part. And it is with this mood in mind that we resume our further exploration of Wordsworth's idiolectal uses of the word *one*.

20

> The Soul of Beauty and enduring life
> Was present as a habit, and diffused,
> Through meagre lines and colours, and the press
> Of self-destroying, transitory things
> Composure and ennobling Harmony. (*Prel.* VII.736–40)

There is every reason to believe that in every human being there is a strong tendency to organise sensory experience into ordered structures, ephemeral or persistent, and that this shaping power often operates by singling out a leading element which establishes hierarchic relations for all the other elements around it. And as we have seen, this tendency was, in Wordsworth, so strongly developed that it became a settled habit, and left its mark upon his uses of the word *one* in poetry. This habit in turn, practised from early years and – as he firmly believed – upon an array of objects specially apt to suggest a sense of order and hierarchy, further modified his modes of perceiving and feeling, so that his sense of oneness, and his use of the word *one* itself, were moved on from that meaning of 'one singled out from a group' to that still more 'pregnant' meaning, headed III in the *OED*, of 'Making up a larger whole, uniform in all its parts'. The 'harmony' of the perceived *Gestalt* was extended, by an intuition based upon habit, to a profounder harmony of larger scale. This is very clearly expressed in prose, in the course of an acute criticism of Ossian:

> Having had the good fortune to be born and reared in a mountainous country, from my very childhood I have felt the falsehood which pervades the volumes imposed upon the world under the name of Ossian. From what I saw with my own eyes, I knew that the imagery was spurious. In nature everything was distinct, yet nothing defined into absolute independent singleness. In Macpherson's work it is exactly the reverse; everything (that is not stolen) is in this manner defined, insulated, dislocated, deadened, – yet nothing distinct. It will always be so when words are substituted for things. (*Essay, Supplementary to the Preface* [*PW* II, 423–4])

The clarity of this exposition, however, comes from the fact that these were by then familiar thoughts. They are perhaps less clear, but more forceful – for they are still warm from the hammer – in *The Prelude*, where this same property of mountain-scenery is described as creating a feeling for 'Harmony' so firm that it counter-balanced the swarming shapelessness of London:

> Oh, blank confusion! and a type not false
> Of what the mighty City is itself . . .
> But though the picture weary out the eye,
> By nature an unmanageable sight,
> It is not wholly so to him who looks
> In steadiness, who hath among least things
> An under-sense of greatest; sees the parts
> As parts, but with a feeling of the whole . . .
> . . . Attention comes,
> And comprehensiveness and memory,
> From early converse with the works of God
> Among all regions; chiefly where appear
> Most obviously simplicity and power.
> By influence habitual to the mind
> The mountain's outline and its steady form
> Gives a pure grandeur, and its presence shapes
> The measure and the prospect of the soul
> To majesty; such virtue have the forms
> Perennial of the ancient hills; nor less
> The changeful language of their countenances
> Gives movement to the thoughts, and multitude,
> With order and relation. . . .
> This did I feel in that vast receptacle.
> The Spirit of Nature was upon me here;
> The Soul of Beauty and enduring life
> Was present as a habit, and diffused,
> Through meagre lines and colours, and the press

Of self-destroying, transitory things
Composure and ennobling Harmony. (*Prel.* VII.695–740)

Once this 'harmony', this ordering of experience, had been felt both within himself and his perceptions, and also as a quality of the outside world, it was a short and natural step to link the two, into a larger pattern which embraced both the inner and the outer worlds. This was taken, however, not by any act of logical reflection, but in an experience, an intuition, which must rank as the most central of all the characteristically Wordsworthian involutes – as in a sense, *the* involute.

The special significance of this involute is shown by the fact that he never quite managed to express it completely, and was driven to make, as it were, a whole series of sketches of it, none of them quite final, but all together leaving no doubt about the character of these recurring moments of vision. It is, oddly enough, more clearly expressed in some of its prose versions, indirect as their reports of it are, than in the verse. The most authentic of them, the only one coming directly from himself, is in the Fenwick note to the *Immortality Ode*:

> I was often unable to think of external things as having external existence, and I communed with all that I saw as something not apart from, but inherent in, my own immaterial nature. Many times while going to school have I grasped at a wall or tree to recall myself from this abyss of idealism to the reality. (*PW* IV, 463)

This is an account given by a man in his seventies of an experience of his boyhood, and it has the defects which might be expected – which he himself would have foreseen, for he was not given to reckless reliance on introspection. In the third book of *The Prelude* he notes cautiously about his memories of his early years:

Of these and other kindred notices
I cannot say what portion is in truth
The naked recollection of that time,
And what may rather have been call'd to life
By after-meditation. (*Prel.* III.644–8)

Here, it is certain that the phrase 'abyss of idealism' was no part of his schoolboy experience, but a product of after-meditation – not least of the kind recorded in the Snowdon involute in the last book of *The Prelude*.[23] The same is true of the phrase 'transcendental world' in this account given by a friend of his later years, the Rev. R. P. Graves of Windermere:

> I remember Mr. Wordsworth saying that, at a particular stage of his mental progress, he used to be frequently so rapt into an unreal transcendental world of ideas that the external world seemed no longer to exist in relation to him, and he had to reconvince himself of its existence *by clasping a tree*, or something that happened to be near him.[24]

A third account, also from a friend of his later years, is this:

> The venerable old man raised his aged form erect; he was walking in the middle, and passed across me to a five-barred gate in the wall which bounded the road on the side of the lake. He clenched the top bar firmly with his right hand, pushed strongly against it, and then uttered these ever-memorable words: 'There was a time in my life when I had to push against something that resisted, to be sure that there was anything outside of me. I was sure of my own mind; everything else fell away, and vanished into thought.'[25]

It is certainly the same theme, but it would seem that even in his conversational reports of what he had felt, he had not reached final formulation of it, only a series of slightly varying versions.

The fourth prose account, however, is in a different position. It stands below the others in authority, for it was at third hand. It was given to the painter, Constable, when he visited Wordsworth in Grasmere in 1806; it was not, however, until 1807 that Constable repeated it at a dinner-party in London, where another painter, Joseph Farington, was struck by it, and entered it in his *Diary*: it had passed through two memories, and a considerable lapse of time. On the other hand, it gains something in credibility because it was given by Wordsworth himself so much earlier in his life than the other prose descriptions:

> He told Constable that while He was a Boy going to Hawkshead School, His mind was often so posessed (*sic*) with images so lost in extraordinary conceptions, that He has held by a wall not knowing but he was part of it.[26]

The radical difference between this version and the others is that the clutch at the wall is presented not as a means of re-establishing a sense of external reality, but quite the contrary, as the outward manifestation of a feeling of identity with it, so that in these moments the normal boundaries between the inner and outer worlds were obliterated.

Possibly the report of Wordsworth's behaviour and explanations while waiting for the coach given by De Quincey on p. 129 above should be regarded as a much diluted account of the same experience – or rather as one fragment of it. What is there made plain is that these moments of special perception and obliteration of the normal boundaries of self and non-self were always closely associated with 'the very instant when the organs of attention were all at once relaxing from their tension'. The eye and the ear for a moment cease their activity, and it is in an almost trance-like state that the visible scene would enter unawares, 'With all its solemn imagery'. This cessation of normal sensory activity is conspicuously present in all the verse reports of these 'spots of time'. The earliest of them is a sonnet published in 1802, with the apologetic sub-title 'Written in very early Youth'. Previous drafts of it may indeed have gone back to Hawkshead, but the manuscript in which it is found belongs to the period 1795–7:

> On the [ ] village Silence sets her seal
> And in the glimmering vale the last lights die
> The kine obscurely seen before me lie
> Round the dim horse that crops his later meal
> Scarce heard; a timely slumber seems to steal
> O'er vale and mountain; now while ear and eye
> Alike are vacant, what strange harmony
> Home-felt, and home-created, seems to heal
> That grief for which the senses still supply
> Fresh food; for only then, when memory
> Is hush'd, am I at rest. My Friends! restrain
> Those busy cares that must renew my pain;
> Oh! leave me to myself, nor let me feel
> The officious touch that makes me droop again. (*PW* I, 3, variants)

It is, of course, very obviously work from the early, the derivative phase. It looks like little more than a variation on the mood of the opening verses of Gray's *Elegy*, strengthened a little by that finely described 'dim horse' – which, however, was taken from one of Wordsworth's favourite poems, the Countess of Winchilsea's *Nocturnal Reverie*. And like so many other poems of that early period, it has a 'respectable-tame conclusion'. Yet in the first eight lines, there is also much that is not only individual, but which also made up the stuff of much of the finest later poetry. There is the description of the trance-like state, in which both eye and ear are 'vacant'; the 'slumber' of the poet extends to the scene itself; and in both, in the inner world and the outer, there is 'harmony / Home-felt, and home-created'.

It so happens that another Hawkshead memory of a horse seen at dusk gave the material for a similar involute, though it seems not to have been written down until 1804, when it was drafted for, and then excluded from, *The Prelude*. It is vivid in itself, and interesting because here Wordsworth perceives the trance-like state, not in himself, but in an outside creature: it is, I suppose, what is sometimes called an 'objective correlative':

> One evening, walking in the public way,
> A Peasant of the valley where I dwelt[27]
> Being my chance Companion, he stopp'd short
> And pointed to an object full in view
> At a small distance. 'Twas a horse, that stood
> Alone upon a little breast of ground
> With a clear silver moonlight sky behind.

With one leg from the ground the creature stood
Insensible and still, – breath, motion gone,
Hair, colour, all but shape and substance gone,
Mane, ears, and tail, as lifeless as the trunk
That had no stir of breath; we paused awhile
In pleasure of the sight, and left him there
With all his functions silently sealed up
Like an amphibious work of Nature's hand,
A Borderer dwelling betwixt life and death,
A living Statue or a statued Life. (MS *W* [Oxford *Prelude*, p. 624])

Despite the difference in standpoint, the objectification of what was more often his own mood, the resemblance is clear enough. The horse's senses are suspended in a kind of trance, 'sealed up', as the village had been 'sealed' by 'Silence' in the early sonnet. And in this state, the animal is intermediate, or rather intermediary between the living world and Nature, partaking of both. This remarkable passage never found its way into *The Prelude*, and it has been quoted here a little out of its strict chronological order, because it is so closely connected with the horse of the early sonnet. But the trance-like state of perception, in Wordsworth's own experience of it, and the intuition of oneness between inner and outer worlds, was the subject of a number of those sketches in blank verse made at Alfoxden, leading up to the writing of *The Prelude* itself in Germany. Here are the best of them:

To gaze
On that green hill and on those scattered trees
And feel a pleasant consciousness of life
In the impression of that loveliness
Until the sweet sensation called the mind
Into itself, by image from without
Unvisited, and all her reflex powers
Wrapped in a still dream [of] forgetfulness.

I lived without the knowledge that I lived
Then by those beauteous forms brought back again
To lose myself again as if my life
Did ebb and flow with a strange mystery.
(*Alfoxden* MS, fragment *iv* [*PW* v, 341])

Of unknown modes of being which on earth,
Or in the heavens, or in the heavens and earth
Exist by mighty combinations, bound
Together by a link and with a soul
Which makes all one. (*Ibid. iii* [*PW* v, 340–1])

These fragments are, so to speak, whole fragments, written separately in the Notebook; that is to say, Wordsworth was treating his attempts to describe this experience in some sense as units, not as incidental episodes in some larger composition. It is treated in the same fashion in the *Christabel* Notebook, which preserves some of the early drafts towards *The Prelude* written in Germany in 1798–9. In them, the involute is expressed in many variations, trying out, one after another, extensions of feeling and phrasing, yet all unmistakably dealing with the same central theme. Together, they offer perhaps the most enlightening example of the way in which the cumulative clarification of experience went hand in hand with the building-up of a cluster of apparent tautologies – and also, of course, of the accumulation of power in the words as they were repeated in the successive formulations. This can best be shown by dismembering the fragments, and re-arranging their members into the four main elements into which the experience may be resolved.

The first is the quietness and steadiness of the outward scene which is the more concrete aspect of the involute:

> The leaves stir not,
> They all are steady as the cloudless sky;
> How deep the Quiet: all is motionless . . .
>
> Oh 'tis a joy divine on summer days
> When not a breeze is stirring, not a cloud,
> To sit within some solitary wood,
> Far in some lonely wood, and hear no sound . . .
>
> The clouds are standing still in the mid heavens;
> A perfect quietness is in the air;
> The ear hears not . . .
>
> In many a walk
> At evening or by moonlight, or reclined
> At midday upon beds of forest moss . . .
>
> . . . I turned
> Towards a grove, a spot which well I knew,
> For oftentimes its sympathies had fallen
> Like a refreshing dew upon my heart;
> I stretch[ed] myself beneath the shade . . .
>
> Long had I stood and looked into the west,
> Where clouds and mountain tops and gleams of light,
> Children of glory all [ ]
> Made one society and seemed to be
> Of the same nature . . .

(*Christabel* MS, fragments *ii–iv, vi–vii* [*PW* v, 343–4])

The second recurring element is the description of a state of mind in which it reflects the calm of the outer world, by its own cessation of activity:

. . . all is motionless,
As if the life of the vast world was hushed
Into a breathless dream.

. . . or reclined
At midday upon beds of forest moss,
Have we to Nature and her impulses
Of our whole being made free gift, and when
Our trance had left us . . .

I stretch[ed] myself beneath the shade
And soon the stirring and inquisitive mind
Was laid asleep . . . (*Ibid. ii, vi–vii*)

This trance-like state of the mind is associated with a cessation of the ordinary activity of the senses, which nevertheless leaves some after-impression with an inner life of its own:

. . . and hear no sound
Which the heart does not make, or else so fit[s]
To its own temper that in external things
No longer seem internal difference . . .

The ear hears not; and yet, I know not how,
More than the other senses does it hold

A manifest communion with the heart.
And soon the stirring and inquisitive mind
Was laid asleep; the godlike senses gave
Short impulses of life that seemed to tell
Of our existence, and then passed away. (*Ibid. iii, iv, vii*)

Finally, there are the various attempts to express this state of consciousness, of the mind itself, in which the boundaries of inner and outer worlds have been blurred or obliterated:

No longer seem internal difference
All melts away, and things that are without
Live in our minds as in their native home.

There is creation in the eye,
Nor less in all the other senses; powers
They are that colour, model, and combine
The things perceived with such an absolute
Essential energy that we may say
That those most godlike faculties of ours
At one and the same moment are the mind
And the mind's minister.

. . . and when
Our trance had left us, oft have we, by aid

Of the impressions which it left behind,
Looked inward on ourselves, and learned, perhaps,
Something of what we are. Nor in those hours
Did we destroy [ ]
The original impression of delight,
But by such retrospect it was recalled
To yet a second and a second life,
While in this excitation of the mind
A vivid pulse of sentiment and thought
Beat palpably within us, and all shades
Of consciousness were ours. (*Ibid. iii, vi*)

The word 'sketches' has been used of these fragments rather deliberately, for they share many of the qualities and purposes of those quick, free-hand drawings which painters make before committing themselves to a final version. Often enough they have one touch or other of lucid brilliance which is not to be found in the finished piece; and in the same way here, there are phrases and lines more illuminating than anything to be found in *The Prelude* itself, or in *Tintern Abbey*, which had so largely anticipated the expression of this involute. Yet none of them is thoroughly impressive as a whole; their lucidities are mingled with weaker passages, and they are not yet firmly articulated in a potentially larger framework of thought and feeling. They are, like sketches, useful not as products, but as processes which lead on to larger products. Their purpose is to develop skills of perception and of expression, to surmount minor problems so that in the larger work the major difficulties can be taken on with free hands.

Wordsworth seems to have paused for eight or nine months before going on with *The Prelude*, in which these sketches were to receive their final expressions.[28] And there is, as might be expected, a considerable difference between it and them. No doubt further meditations had intervened, very probably further drafts, so that the main versions of the involute found in Book II are not, verbally, very close to the early drafts. But there is no mistaking the close similarity of scene, of mood and of more intellectual content. They are even more like that most successful of all the earlier versions, in *Tintern Abbey*, written at the time when the *Alfoxden* Notebook was in use, and just before the journey to Germany when the *Christabel* Notebook takes over from it. Well known as they are, these passages must be quoted here, so that the fullest expressions of the involute can be studied along with the sketches, both in prose and in verse:

My morning walks
Were early; oft, before the hours of School

I travell'd round our little Lake . . .
Nor seldom did I lift our cottage latch
Far earlier, and before the vernal thrush
Was audible, among the hills I sate
Alone, upon some jutting eminence
At the first hour of morning, when the Vale
Lay quiet in an utter solitude.
How shall I trace the history, where seek
The origin of what I then have felt?
Oft in those moments such a holy calm
Did overspread my soul, that I forgot
That I had bodily eyes, and what I saw
Appear'd like something in myself, a dream,
A prospect in the mind. (*Prel.* II.348–71)

I, at this time
Saw blessings spread around me like a sea.
Thus did my days pass on, and now at length
From Nature and her overflowing soul
I had received so much that all my thoughts
Were steep'd in feeling; I was only then
Contented when with bliss ineffable
I felt the sentiment of Being spread
O'er all that moves, and all that seemeth still . . .
O'er all that leaps, and runs, and shouts, and sings,
Or beats the gladsome air, o'er all that glides
Beneath the wave, yea, in the wave itself
And mighty depth of waters. Wonder not
If such my transports were; for in all things
I saw one life, and felt that it was joy.
One song they sang, and it was audible,
Most audible then when the fleshly ear,
O'ercome by grosser prelude of that strain,
Forgot its functions, and slept undisturb'd. (*Prel.* II.413–34)

Nor less, I trust,
To them I may have owed another gift,
Of aspect more sublime; that blessed mood
In which the burthen of the mystery,
In which the heavy and the weary weight
Of all this unintelligible world,
Is lightened: – that serene and blessed mood,
In which the affections gently lead us on, –
Until, the breath of this corporeal frame
And even the motion of our human blood
Almost suspended, we are laid asleep
In body, and become a living soul:

While with an eye made quiet by the power
Of harmony, and the deep power of joy,
We see into the life of things. (*Tintern Abbey* 35–49 [*PW* II, 260])

No doubt these passages thoroughly deserve the attention they receive from readers of Wordsworth. They are more finished, and more forceful than any of the earlier sketches, though they do not manage to include all the *aperçus* and minor felicities found in them. On the more concrete side of the involute, it is perhaps to be regretted that he never brought into the verse that detail so telling in the reported prose, the sudden grasp at a tree or wall, to assure himself either of the existence of an external world, or of his momentary identity with it. It has that quality of vivid memorability which – to take a remote parallel – is possessed by the print of a human foot in the sand in *Robinson Crusoe*, and it is curious that it should have recurred so often in Wordsworth's oral descriptions of the involute, but have been left out of all the written ones.

There are a few other attempts to express it in verse,[29] mostly of lesser importance. But one of them is worth mentioning because of one superb phrase, which links this central involute with the powerful word-cluster associated with *gleam*. It is in a sonnet written at some time before 1804, which Wordsworth himself described to Crabb Robinson as almost his only sonnet 'of pure fancy'. The comment is intelligible, for the octave describes one of those curious natural growths of two shrubs together, one clinging to the other and climbing up through it so as to rise above it. He describes a wild rose thus rising 'tip-toe upon hawthorn stocks', and then compares it – and no doubt here is the fancifulness – with a girl acrobat balancing on a clown's head at a fair. The sestet, however, is of very different quality, for it is a version, not very powerful but unmistakable, of the central involute:

Verily I think,
Such place to me is sometimes like a dream
Or map of the whole world: thoughts, link by link,
Enter through ears and eyesight, with such gleam
Of all things, that at last in fear I shrink,
And leap at once from the delicious stream. (*PW* III, 21)

He does indeed leap, and very abruptly. But that phrase 'gleam / Of all things' has great power, not only because it links these thoughts with the 'visionary' gleams, flashes etc. of the word-cluster, but also because it expresses with such breathtaking compression the intuition of a harmony between the inner and outer world and their ultimate unity.

It was on this side, that of its more abstract implications, that the involute was open-ended, as it were, and capable of deeper if calmer explorations. Two of them are found in drafts never published, one for *The Prelude*, the other for *The Recluse*. The first is in a long passage originally written for the eighth book of *The Prelude*, but never used; and if, as some of his readers are apt to complain, Wordsworth published much verse unworthy of him, he also left unpublished much of very high quality. This passage in particular not only has some very fine lines, but as a whole it summarises with great force the whole pattern of the spirit's progress from childhood to maturity. It is, one might reasonably say, something like a Prelude within *The Prelude*, and it is invaluable as a commentary on this book, with its vitally important function of a *Retrospect*, in the form finally adopted. The extension of the central involute to a more general intuition is given in these lines:

> And now
> The first and earliest motions of his life,
> I mean of his rememberable time,
> Redound upon him with a stronger flood;
> In speculation he is like a Child,
> With this advantage, that he now can rest
> Upon himself; authority is none
> To cheat him of his boldness, or hoodwink
> His intuitions, or to lay asleep
> The unquiet stir of his perplexities;
> And in this season of his second birth . . .
> He feels that, be his mind however great
> In aspiration, the universe in which
> He lives is equal to his mind, that each
> Is worthy of the other; if the one
> Be insatiate, the other is inexhaustible.
> Whatever dignity there be [ ]
> Within himself, from which he gathers hope,
> There doth he feel its counterpart the same
> In kind before him outwardly express'd,
> With difference that makes the likeness clear,
> Sublimities, grave beauty, excellence,
> Not taken upon trust, but self-display'd
> Before his proper senses . . . (Oxford *Prelude*, pp. 575–6)

The other passage, from *Home at Grasmere*, is more compressed, and makes even clearer the abstract reflections developed from the involute:

> Paradise and groves
> Elysian, fortunate (islands) fields like those
> In the deep ocean wherefore should they be
> A History or but a dream, when minds

Once wedded to this outward frame of things
In love find these the growth of common day.
I, long before the blessed hour arrives,
Would sing in solitude the spousal verse
Of this great consummation, would proclaim
Speaking of nothing more than what we are
How exquisitely the individual Mind,
And the progressive powers perhaps no less
Of the whole species to the external world
Is fitted, and how exquisitely too,
Theme this but little heard of among men,
The external world is fitted to the mind
And the creation, (by no lower name
Can it be call'd), which they with blended might
Accomplish: this is my great argument . . . (754– [*PW* v, 338–9])

This deep sense of the harmony between Man and the universe, of the essential homogeneity of all existence, is the fundamental intuition upon which Wordsworth based his views of both morality and politics. It was also – as the criticism of Ossian quoted above shows – the basis of his aesthetic and literary criticism. If there is one thing more than another in the modern world of which he would have disapproved (this is the only occasion in this book in which I allow myself to make such a guess about his attitudes), it is science fiction, with its cultivated picture of strange creatures and stranger worlds in outer space. He would – and this is merely part of the same surmise – have regarded this unnatural picture as the inevitable product of an urbanised fancy, alienated from any true feeling for the universe because alienated from natural life on this earth. It must have followed, from all his deepest convictions, that wherever men may travel, to whatever distance, they will find themselves still at home, still in a world which matches their own minds.

The one passage on this harmony and homogeneity which has not yet been cited is the one which was at once recognised, and has ever since been recognised, as perhaps his most characteristic passage. It is from *Tintern Abbey*, and properly concludes this array of examples of *the* involute:

And I have felt
A presence that disturbs me with the joy
Of elevated thoughts; a sense sublime
Of something far more deeply interfused,
Whose dwelling is the light of setting suns,
And the round ocean and the living air,
And the blue sky, and in the mind of man:
A motion and a spirit, that impels
All thinking things, all objects of all thought,
And rolls through all things. (93–102 [*PW* ii, 261–2])

The open-ended possibilities of this central intuition were capable of two distinct developments. They might be made the basis of a doctrine concerning the nature of reality. Or they might be used as a ground for certain ethical doctrines. Wordsworth himself was clear which use he wished to make of them. The passage just quoted goes on to say that this view of Nature will serve as 'The anchor of my purest thoughts, the nurse, / The guide, the guardian of my heart, and soul / Of all my moral being.' But some of his more philosophically-minded readers have taken the first path. One of the latest of them, Melvin Rader, introduces these same lines by a description of Spinoza's very interesting monism:

> . . . we find in Spinoza a monistic pantheism, or (as some would prefer to say) panentheism; God is not an external contriver, but an immanent, all-pervading, and indivisible presence.
>
> These ideas are reflected in Wordsworth's poetry, whether he derived them from Spinoza or not.[30]

If Wordsworth had indeed derived ideas from Spinoza, there might be some point in saying that his poetry 'reflected' them. But if not, not. And it is abundantly clear, from every page that has been written here, that these 'ideas' came, not from Spinoza at all, but from sundry trees and stones around Hawkshead and from the mountains above them and the clouds still higher. It is, therefore, a singularly unpromising enterprise to discuss whether they are pantheistic, or panentheistic: whether they are Platonic, or transcendental, or Deist, theist, Hylozoist, mystical. One might as well consider whether they were Manichaean, with a touch of the Bogomile about them. Wordsworth's theory of the structure of the universe was reached in his own terms, bit by bit, with his own experience as its material, and the only philosopher from whom he might have derived occasional confirmations of what he already knew was that walking – or rather staggering – compendium, Coleridge.

If sources and analogues must be hunted down, it would be more sensible to look for them among those writers of the eighteenth century with whom Wordsworth felt himself to be akin, most of all Thomson, who could write, sometimes, like this:

> 'Tis harmony, that world-embracing power
> By which all beings are adjusted, each
> To all around, impelling and impelled
> In endless circulation, that inspires
> This universal smile. Thus the glad skies,
> The wide-rejoicing earth, the woods, the streams
> With every life they hold, down to the flower
> That paints the lowly vale, or insect-wing
> Wav'd o'er the shepherd's slumber, touch the mind,

To nature tuned, with a light-flying hand
Invisible, quick-urging through the nerves
The glittering spirits in a flood of day.[31]

It is unlikely, in fact, that Wordsworth knew these lines, for Thomson had not included them in the final edition of *The Seasons* – perhaps because their feeling was too 'enthusiastic', too much like the dangerous warmth of Shaftesbury, for his respectable patrons, especially Lord Lyttelton. And it was, so far as we know, only the final edition that came into Wordsworth's hands. But the general similarity between these lines and those last quoted from *Tintern Abbey* is both a pointer to the importance of this poetic tradition for Wordsworth, and a measure of the extent to which he had risen above and beyond it.

PART IV

Wordsworth and the 'picturesque'

The 18th century was over-dressed.

21

IMAGINATION AND TASTE, HOW IMPAIRED AND RESTORED.

title of Book XII of *The Prelude* (1850)

The importance of any writer, of any poet, may be assessed in several different ways, among which are the personal, and the national – or indeed the international. Any writer is personally important to those readers who find that his work reveals either parts of their own experience not yet clearly realised, or extensions of it not yet achieved; but he may possess this kind of importance, for many readers generation after generation, and still be without the larger importance. For this, there must be some profound coincidence between his own personal history in thought and feeling and the whole spiritual and intellectual development of the culture within which he writes; and if this culture is itself spread beyond the bounds of one nation, his importance will be, at least potentially, international. It follows, of course, that this broader kind of importance is very laborious to demonstrate, for it perforce depends upon establishing the relations between the particular work and a large, complex movement of thought and feeling. And demonstrations of this kind are not to be accomplished without running the gauntlet of many large generalisations, and the gaunt risk of imposing superficial interpretations upon large masses of material. But in such cases such risks must be accepted. And Wordsworth's is such a case.

Oddly enough, the broad national development with which his own experience so intimately and profoundly linked his work is shown in brief outline by his idiosyncratic use of the word *naked*. Here are three contexts in which the same word is used, with very different ranges of response, in the preceding century. The earliest is from Charles Cotton's poem *The Wonders of the Peake*, published in 1681, and it is part of his description of Chatsworth:

> The *Groves*, whose curled *Brows* shade ev'ry *Lake*
> Do ev'rywhere such waving *Landskips* make,
> As *Painter's* baffled *Art* is far above,
> Who *Waves* and *Leaves* could never yet make *move* . . .
> To view from hence the glitt'ring Pile above . . .
> Environ'd round with Nature's Shames and Ills,
> Black Heath, Wild Rock, bleak Craggs, and naked Hills,
> Who is it, but must presently conclude,
> That this is *Paradise*, which seated stands
> In midst of Desarts, and of barren *Sands*?[1]

There is no mistaking the emotional equivalence of the string of epithets, *black*, *wild*, *bleak*, *naked*; and the notion that they are 'Nature's Shames and Ills' is natural enough for a contemporary of Bishop Burnet, who believed that mountains and such-like roughnesses were one of the penalties imposed on earth by the Fall of Man. The essential accuracy of Cotton's 'prospect' of the great house and its surrounding gardens is amply illustrated by a 'perspective view' made in 1699 by a Dutch engraver. It shows – with natural exaggeration – a vast area of geometrical designs, avenues, paths, symmetrical plantations, many of the squares and oblongs filled with formal beds and parterres. This is 'Paradise', a pattern of vegetation imposed by man on the horrid wildness of Nature. Even the slight winding Derwent in front of the great house has been hidden by a perfectly straight artificial canal, and the hills behind are reduced and distanced in tactful defiance of all geography. Their 'nakedness' is not felt to be a possible source of pleasing 'horror' or grandeur, not even a welcome contrast with the rest of the landscape. It is simply distasteful.[2]

The second context is from Addison's *Remarks on Several Parts of Italy*, published in 1705. It is a description of the view from Albano:

> It takes in the whole *Campania*, and terminates in a full View of the Mediterranean. You have a Sight at the same time of the *Alban* Lake, that lyes just by . . . and, by reason of the continu'd Circuit of high Mountains that encompass it, looks like the *Area* of some vast Amphitheatre. This, together with the several Green Hills and naked Rocks, that lye within the Neighbourhood, makes the most agreeable Confusion imaginable. (p. 379)

There is no doubt that the feeling for nakedness in rocks has completely changed, and that it is now a welcome element in the composition of a landscape. Professor Manwaring, who cites this passage (*Italian Landscapes*, p. 11), notes that Addison was much more alert to the scenic effects of mountainous districts when he had spent some time in Rome, and had seen the collections of paintings by Claude, Poussin and Salvator Rosa. He is, in fact, an early example of the profound effect of these painters on the English eye and sensibility. When he passed through the Alps on his way to Italy, he had chiefly remarked on the discomfort of travelling over them. On his return, he saw them differently, and round Geneva enjoyed the contrast between hills 'cover'd with Vineyards and Pasturage' and the 'huge Precipices of naked Rocks rising up in a Thousand odd Figures'.

The third context is from *A Survey of the Lakes* published in 1787 by James Clarke. It is part of a brief discussion of the habit of painters of introducing human figures, even waggons and chaises, in their treatment of mountainous solitudes. This example is given of a drawing which was free from such unnatural accompaniments:

I have seen a drawing of Dun-Dornadilla, in the North-Highlands, which seemed to me excellent in its kind: there was a pensive loneliness about that ruined pile which corresponded well with the dreary nakedness of the vast hills that rose around it. (Introduction, p. xxxv)

Here, the nakedness of the hills, even their dreariness, is welcomed as part of the landscape, not in contrast with more obviously attractive elements in it, but for their own sake. Clarke indeed describes the effect more fully:

. . . the solemnity of those vapours which hang upon mountains in drizzly and gleamy weather, the shades which they occasion, their silent mixing and rolling together, their magnifying effects, with the tops of the mountains peeping above, as it were in another world, lead away the mind from scenes of cultivation, and present ideas of a new, but not less pleasing kind.

It is easy enough to decide which of these three uses of 'naked' applied to rocks is nearest to Wordsworth's. It is certainly the third, as one would expect; for it is contemporary with him, and it may be added that Clarke's *Survey* was a book which influenced Wordsworth in several notable passages both in the early poems and in *The Prelude*. What is much more difficult to make out is the extent to which the three widely differing reactions to naked rocks are individual variations, and the extent to which they are more or less typical of the times at which they were written. Certainly it cannot be assumed lightly that these few samples are representative of three clear-cut stages in fashion, for it is easy enough to find examples which run counter to all of them. For example, Clarke was writing only ten years after Johnson's *Journey to the Western Islands of Scotland*, where there is a reaction to 'nakedness' in landscape as unappreciative as Cotton's: he writes of the Highlands:

They exhibit very little variety; being almost wholly covered with dark heath, and even that seems to be checked in its growth. What is not heath is nakedness . . . An eye accustomed to flowery pastures and waving harvests is astonished and repelled by this wide extent of hopeless sterility. The appearance is that of matter incapable of form or usefulness dismissed by nature from her care . . . and left in its original elemental state. (London, 1775, p. 84)

It was not that Johnson was incapable of feeling with his age about rocks and mountains and grandeur. It was that he did not like them naked. In his account of his journey into Wales in the preceding year, he had written very fashionably in praise of the estate of Sir Rowland Hill at Hawkestone:

. . . a large tract of rocks and wood; a region abounding with striking scenes of terrifick grandeur. We were always on the brink of a precipice or at the foot of a lofty rock; but the steeps were seldom naked; in many places, oaks of uncommon magnitude shot up from the crannies of stone; and where there were not tall trees, there were underwoods and bushes.

This dislike for 'nakedness' in rocks and mountains, this preference for a vegetable vesture over the hard bones of the creation, clearly distinguishes Johnson's sensibility from Clarke's. And we shall find that the same distinction is central to the difference between Wordsworth's feeling for landscape, and the main fashion of his age.

At this point, we are compelled to take into account that whole movement of English culture in the eighteenth century, through poetry and painting, gardening and touring, which is commonly associated with its own favourite terms, the Sublime, the Beautiful, and the Picturesque. Nor can we be concerned with this movement merely in general terms; it is essential to recognise that the Lakes played a special and even central part in the formation of taste, at the very moment when Wordsworth became acquainted with the fashions of the great world outside the place of his birth and education. His personal circumstances, in fact, linked him in a very remarkable – though not unique – manner with one of the dominant fashions of taste in his age. It is this that makes his own relationship with the Lakes so much more complex than is generally understood. And this is but another way of saying that his relationship with Nature was more complex than is generally understood. To understand it better, we must look at the broad fashion, so far as it can be summarised in a few pages, and also at the role of the Lakes within it, and specially that of the four *Guides* to the Lakes which influenced Wordsworth directly.

It may make the following pages easier to understand if two or three large misunderstandings between Wordsworth and the modern reader are put – not wholly out of mind – but very much to one side, where they belong. The first arises from that kind of literary history which goes to work with the aid of abstractions like Classical and Romantic, and which, having classified Wordsworth among the Romantic poets (first generation), develops explanations of his intentions and estimates of his quality from whatever definition of 'Romantic' happens to have been adopted for the moment. It ill becomes dog to eat dog, and critic to belabour critic. I refrain, therefore, from uttering my private thoughts about this method of criticism in general, and about the endless series of definitions of Romanticism in particular. But I cannot, for the sake of my own kind of criticism, refrain from saying, and with unrestrained emphasis, that the classification of Wordsworth as a 'Romantic' poet has no meaning, or has too many possible meanings to be of any value, and that it promotes a large and damaging misunderstanding of his relations with the broad patterns of English culture and literature. It was, however, a misunderstanding for which he was himself partly responsible. Many of the poems which he contributed to *Lyrical Ballads* were indeed experimental and novel – possibly in some vaguely Romantic fashion. And much of what he said in defence of them, in the *Preface*, is directed to the explanation of this novelty –

though it never occurred to him to describe himself as a 'Romantic'. On the other hand, there is also much in the *Preface* which is not specifically directed to the novel element in his poetry, but which expounds his views on poetry in general. And there is also some poetry in *Lyrical Ballads* which is obviously of a kind quite different from the 'little Rhyme poems', as he called them (*EL* 89/105), and which belonged, with some characteristic but minor differences, to the traditional modes of poetry of the eighteenth century – which arose, in fact, directly out of Wordsworth's main literary inheritance. The most notable example is *Tintern Abbey*. This, like his earlier poems *An Evening Walk* and *Descriptive Sketches*, belongs in general to that abundant stream of topographical and meditative poetry which flowed so strongly, yet so gently, from its springs in Denham's *Cooper's Hill*, Dyer's *Grongar Hill*, and Thomson's adaptation of the *Georgics* to English needs and scenery in *The Seasons*. It is, of course, different in the quality of its thought and feeling from all this topographical meditation, but it is a poem of the same kind, if not of the same quality. It was not even the first poem about Tintern Abbey, nor was he one of the earliest visitors there. On the contrary, it was a well-known tourist attraction years before he was born; he was not creating a fashion, but following it – with a difference, or with many differences. And the differences are most readily apparent to the few who have read, in *The Weekly Miscellany: or, Instructive Entertainer* for 1780 an anonymous poem called '*On seeing the beautiful* RUINS of TINTERN ABBEY, *in* Monmouthshire.'[3]

The Prelude is on its much larger scale a characteristic poem of the eighteenth-century kind, though not of the eighteenth-century quality. What was largely original about it was the broad design of an autobiographical poem; what was traditional was the linking of topographical memories with moral meditation. While there is no close precedent for *The Prelude* as a whole, many of its most striking parts are of the tradition, at least in subject. That tribute to 'the fairest of all Rivers' which opens the real subject of *The Prelude* had been dimly sketched by Thomson:

> the Tweed (pure parent stream,
> Whose pastoral banks first heard my Doric reed,
> With, silvan Jed, thy tributary brook) . . .
>
> (*Autumn* 899–91 [Robertson ed., p. 165])

And after him, scores of topographical and Georgic poets had repeated and amplified their debts to rivers, to early memories, and their apprenticeship to verse – in which, to say the truth, none of them advanced much beyond apprenticeship. Indeed the very river which ran at the foot of the Wordsworths' garden had been poetically celebrated long before he wrote about it. A row by moonlight on a lake surrounded by mountains, boys skating on the ice, the themes of two of Wordsworth's most vivid descriptions were already conventional when he wrote of them. As for the sight from the top of Snowdon, of a low-lying mist through which the mountain peaks rose clear, with strange sounds from below, we shall see later that the conventional element in it is so strange that it may help to explain its relative weakness, compared with the other crucial experiences described in the poem. On the other hand, there is, to my knowledge, nothing even remotely similar to the two 'spots of time' descriptions; they, and many other parts of *The Prelude*, seem to owe nothing to traditional themes, and to be entirely personal. It is this mingling of the traditional and the personal in Wordsworth's poetry that makes it dangerous to classify him simply as Romantic, or merely as 'eighteenth-century'. His originality was of the less obvious kind that springs in part from tradition, but even more from an individual leap ahead, an advance on tradition. The two strands are intertwined, and must be seen both in their intimate relations with one another, and separately. None of this is visible to those who mistake the more revolutionary aspects of *Lyrical Ballads* for the whole of Wordsworth, still less to those who have accustomed themselves to see his poetry in the light of vast literary categories, instead of its own actual background.

It is very probable that the originality of most great writers tends to be exaggerated, because their later readers know little or nothing of all the lesser writers who wrote before them. It is only rarely that greatness consists largely in sheer novelty; much more usually, it consists in doing very much better what had been done before, or in making certain combinations of qualities which had never been effectively combined before. One of the chief effects of lapse of time is to throw the greatness of the great writers into this illusory isolation. But it is an illusion which is very hard to destroy in most cases, because its destruction necessarily depends on gaining an acquaintance with much writing which time has consigned to oblivion, and rightly. Even such a perfunctory and unsystematic recovery of Wordsworth's eighteenth-century background as will be attempted here would not be worth undertaking merely to show that his originality was of a kind rather different from that with which he is usually credited. It is only worth the kind of attention which will distinctly illuminate the quality which marks his thought and feeling off from what had gone before him, and what was still going on around him. What follows, therefore, is an exercise, not in scholarship, but in impressionistic summary.

22

For Addison, as we have seen, a visit to the great collections of landscape painting in Rome was, in the fullest sense, an eye-opener. It educated his capacity to see grandeur and beauty in landscape, and indicated the possibility of a quite new use for painting. Until that time, and for some way beyond it, the English painters made their money out of portraits, and English painting was confined to the profitable recording of the faces and persons of the nobility, with their wives and dogs. But they were by no means incapable of other ambitions, and felt the influence of the Roman collections as one tourist after another brought back news of them. One of the earliest to show this influence was Jonathan Richardson, who succeeded Kneller as the fashionable portrait-painter. He was unable to make the Italian tour himself, though touchingly anxious to do so: 'O Rome!' he wrote, 'thou happy repository of so many stupendous works of art which my longing eyes have never seen, nor shall see . . .'[4] But he collected engravings and drawings, and sent his son to Italy, compiling from his notes *An Account of the Statues, Bas-Reliefs, Drawings and Pictures in Italy, &c.*[5] It contains the first clear outlines of the new fashion for landscape painting:

> Landskips are in Imitation of Rural Nature, of which therefore there may be as many kinds, as there are Appearances of This sort of Nature . . . This Sort of Painting is like Pastoral in Poetry; and of all the Landskip-Painters, *Claude Lorrain* has the most Beautiful, and Pleasing Ideas; the most Rural, and of our own Times. *Titian* has a Style more Noble. So has *Nicolas Poussin*, and the Landskips of the Latter are usually Antique, and is seen by the Buildings and Figures . . . *Salvator Rosa* has generally chosen to represent a sort of Wild, and Savage Nature; his Style is Great, and Noble. (pp. 186–7)

Besides this widely influential *catalogue raisonée*, Richardson published essays on painting and 'connoissance', and his writings roused in Reynolds, then a boy, the ambition to become a painter. He had pupils too, and among them John Dyer, who happened to be rambling about in South Wales, where he had been born, sketching in the double capacity as apprentice-painter and poet. It so happened that he failed in the former, and almost accidentally succeeded in the latter, with *Grongar Hill*, published in 1726, one of the most widely influential of all short poems in English, for it translated into the idioms of verse the coming fashion for landscape:

Ever charming, ever new,
When will the landskip tire the view!
The fountain's fall, the river's flow,
The woody vallies, warm and low;
The windy summit, wild and high,
Roughly rushing on the sky!
The pleasant seat, the ruin'd tow'r,
The naked rock, the shady bow'r;[6]
The town and village, dome and farm,
Each give each a double charm . . .

That last line, for all its apparent simplicity, reveals one of the most powerful links between the kinds of poetry and of painting with which Dyer and his readers were familiar. The 'double charm' of contrast, within a highly formal framework based on that feeling for bilateral symmetry which seems to be innate in man (consider the symmetry of houses, trees and people in children's drawings) is the basis of the heroic couplet on the one hand, and of the landscape picture on the other. Though Dyer is writing in octosyllabics, his antitheses are no less formal than in the couplets of his time: 'woody vallies' against 'windy summit', 'warm and low' against 'wild and high', 'pleasant seat' against 'ruin'd tow'r', 'rock' and 'bow'r', 'naked' and 'shady', 'town' against 'village', 'dome' against 'farm'. There is something almost comically mechanical about this knack of composition, but it faithfully reflected the entirely comparable design of the landscape painters. Through the middle of the picture, entering it in the foreground, would wind a road or a river or a valley; and its windings would produce a succession of receding diagonals, one behind the other. And on these diagonals would be placed ruins of castles or abbeys or temples, trees, sheep and human figures, relieving the bilateral symmetry with a variety of decoration. It is not, after all, surprising that so simply forceful a combination of poetic and pictorial fashions should have made *Grongar Hill* so immensely influential on landscape poetry for the next century. And its immense influence, taken with its slight weight, very clearly illustrates the extent to which the two fashions might dominate an age lacking in direction and integrity of taste.

In the same year as *Grongar Hill*, Thomson published the first of his *Seasons*, *Winter*. It is almost entirely lacking in landscape poetry, but in the other parts of the poem, and in the revised version of *Winter* itself, this deficiency was made good, and the final version of 1746 contained many hundreds of lines of landscape, all in the most fashionable style. In the meantime, Thomson had himself made the great Italian tour – as 'tutor' to a young nobleman – and it did not fail to impress him in the expected manner. His plainest record of it, and of his rapidly acquired mastery of the taste of the age, is in *The Castle of Indolence*:

> Sometimes the pencil, in cool airy halls,
> Bade the gay bloom of vernal landskips rise,
> Or Autumn's varied shades imbrown the walls:
> Now the black tempest strikes the astonished eyes;
> Now down the steep the flashing torrent flies;
> The trembling sun now plays o'er ocean blue,
> And now rude mountains frown amid the skies;
> Whate'er Lorrain light-touched with softening hue,
> Or savage Rosa dashed, or learnèd Poussin drew.
>
> (Canto I, xxxviii [Robertson ed., p. 265])

Nothing could be more characteristic of the period than that Thomson should have filled out the landscape in his later verse, not from his own remembered sights of his native Scotland, but from his impressions of the paintings he had seen in Rome, or in the growing collections of his noble patrons in England. The eye-opening education of the paintings had done much more for his imagination than had the Tweed or the 'silvan Jed'. And if this stanza from *The Castle of Indolence* is compared with the three lines from *Autumn* quoted above it will be seen how much more powerful the painted reality was than observation and personal imagination, just as the lines from *Grongar Hill* arise rather from what Dyer had learned as a painter than from what he had experienced of his native country. It is, however, only in this subjection of the poetic imagination to the painters that Dyer and Thomson are comparable. In many other ways, they are unlike. Dyer's poem is a slight, if charming, piece which happened to crystallise out the fashion of the moment. Thomson's *Seasons* is a work on the grand scale, concerned with permanent issues, and including much more than pictorial effects. Two of its other main elements must be noted, for they lead us to the deeper and more serious aspects of the landscape fashion.

Thomson was one of the earliest poetic disciples of Shaftesbury, that philosopher who has never been rated highly by philosophers, but who influenced both poets and novelists throughout the eighteenth century, and of whom Wordsworth said that he was 'unjustly depreciated'.[7] This passage from *The Moralists* will suffice to explain both the verdict of the philosophers and the admiration of the poets:

> . . . the deep shades of the vast Wood; which closing thick above, spreads Darkness and eternal Night below. The faint and gloomy Light looks horrid as the Shade it-self . . . Here *Space* astonishes. *Silence* it-self seems pregnant; whilst an unknown Force works on the Mind, and dubious Objects move the wakeful Sense. Mysterious *Voices* are either heard or fancy'd; and

various Forms of *Deity* seem to present themselves, and appear more manifest in these sacred Sylvan Scenes; such as of old gave rise to Temples, and favour'd the Religion of the antient World.[8]

The direct influence of this passage is found, most evidently, twice in *The Seasons*:

> Still let me pierce into the midnight depth
> Of yonder grove, of wildest largest growth,
> That, forming high in air a woodland quire,
> Nods o'er the mount beneath. At every step,
> Solemn and slow the shadows blacker fall,
> And all is awful listening gloom around.
> These are the haunts of meditation, these
> The scenes where ancient bards the inspiring breath
> Ecstatic felt, and, from this world retired,
> Conversed with angels and immortal forms,
> On gracious errands bent . . .
>
> (*Summer* 516–26 [Robertson ed., pp. 72–3])

> Oh! bear me then to high, embowering, Shades;
> To twilight Groves, and visionary Vales;
> To weeping Grottos, and to hoary Caves;
> Where Angel-Forms are seen, and Voices heard,
> Sigh'd in low Whispers, that abstract the Soul,
> From outward Sense, far into Worlds remote.
>
> (*Winter* [1726] 74–9 [*ibid.*, pp. 229–30])

Even these short passages will suffice to illustrate the power and accuracy with which Thomson had represented Shaftesbury's enthusiastic and genial, if imprecise, Deism in verse. They will also explain Wordsworth's two main comments on the poem: 'It is a work of inspiration; much of it is written from himself, and nobly from himself . . . notwithstanding his high powers, he writes a vicious style; and his false ornaments are exactly of that kind which would be most likely to strike the undiscerning.'[9] There is obviously much in the substance and in the feeling of *The Seasons*, at its best, which is very like the substance and feeling of Wordsworth; but only very rarely is it expressed, for more than a line or two, without the use of that kind of artificial diction against which Wordsworth argued so rightly in the *Prefaces*.

The second and still more important element in Thomson lacking in Dyer was his deep sense of a Virgilian perspective. In the *Preface* which he wrote to the second edition of *Winter*, he briefly explains his ambitions and intentions: to restore poetry to its proper place by 'the choosing of great and serious subjects', among which none could be 'more elevating, more amusing; and more ready to awake the poetical enthusiasm, the philosophical reflection, and the moral sentiment, than the works of Nature' (*ibid.*, pp. 240–1). After a rather awkward passage of prose rhapsody on the beauty and variety of Nature and of the seasons of the year, he gives this Virgilian defence of his own work:

> For this reason the best, both ancient, and modern, Poets have been passionately fond of retirement, and solitude. The wild romantic country was their delight. And they seem never to have been more happy, than when, lost in unfrequented fields, far from the little busy world, they were at leisure, to meditate, and sing the Works of Nature.
>
> The book of Job, that noble and ancient poem, which, even, strikes so forcibly through a mangling translation, is crowned with a description of the grand works of Nature; and that, too, from the mouth of their Almighty Author.
>
> It was this devotion to the works of Nature that, in his Georgics, inspired the rural Virgil to write so inimitably; and who can forbear joining with him in this declaration of his, which has been the rapture of ages?
>
> Me vero primum dulces ante omnia Musae . . .[10]
>
> Which may be Englished thus:—
>
> Me may the Muses, my supreme delight!
> Whose priest I am, smit with immense desire,
> Snatch to their care; the starry tracts disclose,
> The sun's distress, the labours of the moon:
> Whence the earth quakes: and by what force the deeps
> Heave at the rocks, then on themselves reflow:
> Why winter-suns to plunge in ocean speed:
> And what retards the lazy summer-night.
> But, lest I should these mystic-truths attain,
> If the cold current freezes round my heart,
> The country me, the brooky vales may please
> Mid woods and streams unknown. (*Ibid.*, pp. 241–2)

This is all that Thomson has to say about his poetic intentions. The rest of the *Preface* is no more than a polite address to friends and patrons. But in leaving so much to Virgil, and to this passage above all, he was doing something that would be thoroughly well understood, and taken for much more than its face value. Like Thomson himself, his literate readers would have read this passage first before they were ten years old, would have translated it not once, but many times in their remaining years at school and university. Around it would have gathered associations of other similar passages, and the innumerable imitations which it had excited in more modern poetry. Its immediate setting, at the end of the second *Georgic*, is one of the central generative passages of all European poetic conventions, contrasting the pleasures, simplicity and peace of country life with the luxury, corruption and ferocity of city life. Its grip on the imagination of the five centuries after the Renaissance is difficult, probably impossible, for the modern reader to recapture, partly because it has not formed part of his basic education, and partly because the style of natural description has, in the last two centuries, changed in such a way as to leave Virgil looking rather abstract and stilted.

Thomson was in part responsible for initiating this change of style, and its general direction is shown very clearly by the contrast between the more or less literal translation given above and the free adaptation of the same passage which concludes his *Autumn*:

O Nature! all-sufficient! over all
Enrich me with the knowledge of thy works;
Snatch me to heaven; thy rolling wonders there,
World beyond world, in infinite extent
Profusely scattered o'er the blue immense,
Show me; their motions, periods, and their laws
Give me to scan; through the disclosing deep
Light my blind way: the mineral strata there;
Thrust blooming thence the vegetable world;
O'er that the rising system, more complex,
Of animals; and, higher still, the mind,
The varied scene of quick-compounded thought,
And where the mixing passions endless shift;
These ever open to my ravished eye –
A search, the flight of time can ne'er exhaust!
But, if to that unequal – if the blood
In sluggish streams about my heart forbid
That best ambition – under closing shades
Inglorious lay me by the lowly brook,
And whisper to my dreams. From thee begin,
Dwell all on thee, with thee conclude my song;
And let me never, never stray from thee!

(*Autumn* 1352–73 [*ibid.*, pp. 180–1])

It is Virgil modernised, certainly. The list of natural phenomena has been significantly extended (much under the influence of Shaftesbury) to include animals, and the mind and passions of man. But even so, it is far from being modern, and hardly satisfies a modern taste better than its original. The language remains too general and abstract, especially in its descriptions: the 'closing shades' and the 'lowly brook' carry no conviction of reality. Somewhere between Thomson and ourselves, the feeling for such things, the poetic conventions which convey them, has been changed – and we are, in fact, beginning on an inquiry into the nature and timing of this change. But we shall only understand it better if we make a kind of imaginative reconstruction, within which we recognise that there was, for other readers than ourselves, a profound and powerful meaning in this central passage of Virgil, and in all its later transformations. And this effort of imagination will be the easier if we admit the idea that the manner of seeing Nature and of describing it is not, after all, the central theme of this tradition of verse. This central theme is the contrast between the quality of human life as it is lived in the country, and as it must be lived in towns, and this contrast, so far from being a convention of any age, or of one or two ages of European history, is of immediate and urgent concern to all ages, most of all our own. It is this broad consideration that makes it necessary, and useful, to study in this kind of detail the views of 'Nature', and of town and country life, which were so fully explored by the two Augustan ages, even if in idioms of thought, feeling and language not our own.

And it is the same broad consideration, of course, which establishes the deeper similarity between the two Augustan ages, that of Virgil and that of Thomson. In the first, the growth of the cities, of Rome above all, reached the critical point at which the quality of life within them decisively worsened, in terms of comfort, decency and safety – the point at which corruption of all kinds, the unrestrained pursuit of wealth, luxury and violence, all that follows when human beings are so crowded together that competition between them becomes altogether more powerful than co-operation, all these join together to urge on less corrupted citizens the need to withdraw to the country. The rapid growth of London towards the end of the seventeenth century had created the same conditions in England, and it was this basic similarity of social conditions, rather than mere literary tastes and fashions, which gave force and reality to the rediscovery of Virgil and the *Georgic* attitudes. But these attitudes were not, of course, in themselves sufficient to meet all the needs of the second Augustan age. London was not Rome, nor England Italy, nor the eighteenth century the same as the first. There was needed much adaptation and addition, of which the passage of Thomson just quoted is but a fractional illustration. In one sense, the whole movement of thought and feeling which it concerns is one of remoulding the earlier Augustan traditions to suit a new level of intensity in the basic town–country contrast, and the many other material and social changes which clearly differentiate England from Rome. But great as these differences are, it is necessary to see them in their relation to the original Augustan situation. Not only was this a persistent starting-point for the eighteenth century, but it serves as a constant reminder that the problem which concerned both ages is one that concerns ourselves, and in a still more urgent degree of intensity.

23

One great difference between the Roman background of *The Georgics* and the English background of *The Seasons* was that the Roman villa, though in some respects comparable with the English estate, was more for use than decoration and ostentation. Virgil had written – as tradition suggests on the instructions of Augustus himself – to encourage the Roman gentry to return to their villas, not only to escape the corruption of the capital, but also to grow food and raise animals. It is a far more practical and didactic work than *The Seasons*. The English nobleman had little need to make his estates profitable, since his income came, in the main, from political jobbery, commercial speculation and banking. And his interests were best served by making his house, gardens and estates a conspicuous advertisement of his wealth and success. Critics, connoisseurs and even demi-philosophers were not wanting to suggest the desirability of it, and before long practitioners appeared who could do for a nobleman's estate what the portrait-painters did for his person, and his wife and children and dogs and horses. They were, however, practitioners of a new, and for long a purely English art, not of gardening, but of landscape-gardening, and they moved rapidly away from the geometrical designs like that which Cotton had admired at Chatsworth only a generation before.

As so often, Addison and Shaftesbury were in the forefront of those who announced the new taste. Shaftesbury described it in general terms, linking it with his preference for 'Nature' as against 'art':

I shall no longer resist the Passion growing in me for Things of a *natural* kind; where neither *Art*, nor the *Conceit* or *Caprice* of Man has spoil'd their *genuine Order*, by breaking in upon that *primitive State*. Even the rude *Rocks*, the mossy *Caverns*, the irregular unwrought *Grotto's*, and broken *Falls* of Waters, with all the horrid Graces of the *Wilderness* itself, as representing NATURE more, will be the more engaging, and appear with a Magnificence beyond the formal Mockery of Princely Gardens.[11]

Addison puts the same view, but more aesthetically:

The Beauties of the most stately Garden or Palace lie in a narrow Compass, the Imagination immediately runs them over, and requires something else to gratifie her; but, in the wide Fields of Nature, the Sight wanders up and down without Confinement, and is fed with an infinite variety of Images . . . we find the Works of Nature still more pleasant, the more they resemble those of Art . . . We are pleased as well with comparing their Beauties, as with surveying them, and can represent them to our Minds, either as Copies or Originals. Hence it is that we take Delight in a Prospect which is well laid out, and diversified with Fields and Meadows, Woods and Rivers . . . But why may not a whole Estate be thrown into a kind of Garden by frequent

Plantations, that may turn as much to the Profit, as the Pleasure of the Owner? . . . a Man might make a pretty Landskip of his own Possessions.[12]

The first of the artists in this new medium, Bridgeman, was at work within a few years, and his was the clever notion of using a fence sunk in a ditch (a device of French and military origin) to secure privacy, while allowing the eye to take in wide prospects of fields and woods. His more eminent successor, William Kent, was an unsuccessful painter, but a notable maker of landscapes, some of which still remain. The quality of his painting may be guessed from his frontispiece to Thomson's *Spring* in 1730. It has a winding path in the centre, leading to a winding lake; on the receding diagonals are trees (one shaggily moribund in the manner of Salvator Rosa),[13] a large classical villa, a castle, groves, and a mountain as background. A rainbow rises to the sky from the middle distance, leading to clouds on which a number of chubby allegorical figures dance round a half-hidden sun. Considerable traces of his landscaping survive at Stowe, Euston and Holkham; and it was of this last that Robert Potter wrote, in 1774:

Can the verse paint like nature? Can the pow'r,
That wakes to life free fancy's imag'd store,
Boast charms like hers? Or the creative hand
In blended tints such beauteous scenes command,
Tho' learned Poussin gives each grace to flow,
And bright Lorrain's ætherial colours glow?[14]

The interlacing of influence and media so characteristic of the whole period is well shown here and the only element of the convention lacking at Holkham is the 'savagery' of Salvator Rosa, no doubt because the rather flat coast of north Norfolk is unpropitious for effects of that kind.

Holkham seems to have been Kent's own favourite among his creations, but it was from the kitchen-garden at Stowe that the next great landscape-gardener emerged. This was Lancelot Brown, usually called Capability Brown, partly because of his efficiency, partly because his usual remark to a prospective employer was that his estate had 'great capabilities', and partly because it was convenient so to distinguish him from another eminent man of the same surname, John Brown, who was usually called Estimate Brown, after the title of his most successful book, *An Estimate of the Manners and Principles of the Times* (London, 1757). The first major display of Capability Brown's abilities was made at Blenheim, where he was very great in the management of water, for which, as he himself boasted, the Thames would never forgive him. He took over and 'improved' well over a hundred large estates, and a few smaller ones, sometimes extending the work of Kent, sometimes obliterating it. Perhaps no single individual has contributed as much to the English landscape as we still see it, and on the whole for the good: perhaps we are, even today, so influenced by his conception of what it ought to be that we take it for granted, and mistake thousands of acres of Brown for England. It was Joseph Warton who paid him the appropriate tribute:

> I think it neither exaggeration nor affectation to call Mr. Brown a great painter, for he has realised
>
> Whate'er Lorrain light-touched with softening hue,
> Or savage Rosa dash'd, or learned Poussin drew.

In the idiom of the age, and quoting Thomson,[15] what could be said fairer than that?

Brown's large practice and reputation passed into the hands of the next major landscape-gardener, Humphrey Repton, in 1783, when Brown died, his work incomplete. Shortly before his death a group of Irish noblemen made him a very handsome offer to take over the improvement of Ireland, but he refused, saying that he had not yet finished England. His next task was, of course, eminently foreseeable, even before his death. A minor practitioner of the same art, Richard Owen Cambridge, had once remarked to him, 'Mr Brown, I very earnestly wish I may die before you.' 'Why so?' asked Brown in natural surprise. 'Because I should like to see heaven before you had improved it.'

Repton did not enjoy such a commanding position as his predecessor, largely because competition was growing, and of two kinds, closely related. From the middle of the century onwards, much was written on the theory of landscape-gardening, both in prose and in verse. And this new kind of criticism was not slow in developing conflicts of ideas, and a search for novelty. Even before his death, Brown was often criticised, and there seems to have been a slight change of taste in the direction of still wilder imitations of Nature than he had usually employed. Some of these writers were themselves landed proprietors, and felt quite confident that they could take in hand their own improvements at a higher aesthetic level than the professional earth-shifters. The two most notable of these were neighbouring squires in the West, Uvedale Price and Richard Payne Knight. They were both 'connoisseurs' in the fullest sense of their time, collectors of paintings from Italy, patrons of the English imitators of the Italian style, by now numerous, old friends of Repton, but afraid that he would perpetuate what they had come to feel was a certain insipidity in the notions of Brown. Together they introduced a new fashion, both in practice and in theory, for more roughness, more of shaggy nature, in landscape gardens. What they had in common is well expressed in Knight's poem *The Landscape, a Didactic Poem . . . Addressed to Uvedale Price, Esq.* published in 1794:

> Hence let us learn, in real scenes, to trace
> The true ingredients of the painter's grace;
> To lop redundant parts, the coarse refine,
> Open the crowded, and the scanty join.
> But, ah! in vain: – see yon fantastic band,
> With charts, pedometers, and rules in hand,
> Advance triumphant, and alike lay waste
> The forms of nature, and the works of taste!
> T'improve, adorn, and polish, they profess;
> But shave the goddess, whom they come to dress;
> Level each broken bank and shaggy mound,
> And fashion all to one unvaried round . . .
> Shav'd to the brink, our brooks are taught to flow
> Where no obtruding leaves or branches grow;
> While clumps of shrubs bespot each winding vale,
> Open alike to ev'ry gleam and gale . . .
> Hence, hence! thou haggard fiend, however call'd,
> Thin, meagre genius of the bare and bald;
> Thy spade and mattock here at length lay down,
> And follow to the tomb thy fav'rite Brown:
> Thy fav'rite Brown, whose innovating hand
> First dealt thy curses o'er this fertile land . . .
>
> (Book I, 257–68; 277–80; 283–8)

For at least a decade after the publication of Knight's poem, a vigorous controversy went on between Knight himself, Uvedale Price, Repton, and many others, in which the aesthetic principles underlying their practical differences were explored, often with great subtlety and skill. It is perhaps a justifiable simplification to describe it as centering on the definitions between this quality and the Beautiful and the Sublime, which had been the dominant aesthetic terms of the mid eighteenth century, not only in Burke's well-known treatise, but in hundreds of other works on painting and landscape, in prose and in verse. It is worth noting that this vigorous and much-publicised discussion proceeded throughout the period when Wordsworth was most active as a writer, and that he could hardly have failed to hear something of it when he was in London in 1795. And if he did not hear of it then, he certainly learned of it from Coleridge, two years later, for Knight had meddled extensively with the 'Imagination', and may well have contributed to concentrate Coleridge's attention on this central problem in aesthetic theory. But direct traces of any connection between Wordsworth's ideas and those involved in the Price–Knight controversies have not yet been found. It is a very different matter with the work of the writer who had, ten years earlier, popularised the word 'picturesque', though without the theoretical complexities of the aestheticians. This was William Gilpin, and he is the effective meeting-point between Wordsworth, especially the Wordsworth of *The Prelude*, and the whole of this current of eighteenth-century thought and taste. He is also a focal point in complicating Wordsworth's reactions to the Lakes.

24

The education of the English in landscape began with Italian paintings, and in the first half of the eighteenth century it was associated with people wealthy enough to buy these paintings, and to make the Grand Tour to Italy itself, where they could see not only the paintings, but also the Alpine and Appennine scenery upon which it had been based. It was, in the first place, a fashion for noblemen like Burlington, Leicester, Pelham, Bathurst, Temple, and for the more successful and socially acceptable writers, such as Addison, Pope and Thomson. But a fashion so massively successful, in an age so deeply devoted to social climbing, was bound to spread quickly and widely. In the second half of the century, the middle classes were finding ways of joining in it, and since their resources were more limited, they contracted the Grand Tour into the cheaper pastime of touring in Britain, in search of landscape-gardens, the picture-galleries of the great mansions, and of scenery which, in its own way, could offer what the Italian mountains offered to wealthier travellers.

As usually happens, this rapidly growing demand for tourism created the facilities which made it still more fashionable. Methods of transport were improving, not only for this reason, but for more material ones. Roads were being extended and improved, and coaches were readily available, for those who could pay for them. At the same time, the rapidly increasing size and noisomeness of large towns, above all London, gave the wealthier part of the middle classes a strong reason for seeking their holidays in an environment as different as possible from that in which they lived and worked. It was at this time, indeed, that the modern holiday, inseparably connected with an absence from 'home', replaced the older conception of a holyday as a period of rest from work, often associated with religious observance, but spent at home. It was the period of the great inland spas, like Bath and Tunbridge Wells, of the watering places along the south coast, like Brighton, Teignmouth and

Lyme Regis, and it saw also the discovery of British scenery in Derbyshire, Wales, the Lakes and the Highlands. It was in the 1780s that the word 'tourist' entered the English language.

Only one account of such a tour is now widely read. It is that taken by Elizabeth Bennet to Derbyshire, with her uncle and aunt, in *Pride and Prejudice*.[16] So skilfully is it worked into the main patterns of the novel that its accuracy as a social observation, and a comment on reigning fashion, probably escapes the notice it deserves. The uncle, Mr Gardiner, was engaged in some kind of trade, and lived in Gracechurch Street, 'within view of his own warehouses' (II.ii). It is a district, as Elizabeth frankly explains to her aunt, which no wealthy and well-born young man would think of visiting: 'Mr. Darcy may perhaps have *heard* of such a place as Gracechurch Street, but he would hardly think a month's ablution enough to cleanse himself from its impurities, were he once to enter it' (II.ii). Mr Gardiner himself, however, was a 'sensible gentlemanlike man' (II.ii), and evidently regarded Gracechurch Street as suitable enough for his business, but not for a holiday. When Elizabeth was invited to 'accompany her uncle and aunt in a tour of pleasure which they proposed taking in the summer' (II.iv), they hoped to go to 'the Lakes', and her reactions were in accordance with the fashion:

> 'My dear, dear aunt,' she rapturously cried, 'what delight! what felicity! You give me fresh life and vigour . . . What are men to rocks and mountains? Oh! what hours of transport shall we spend! And when we *do* return, it shall not be like other travellers, without being able to give one accurate idea of anything. We *will* know where we have gone – we *will* recollect what we have seen. Lakes, mountains, and rivers, shall not be jumbled together in our imaginations; nor, when we attempt to describe any particular scene, will we begin by quarrelling about its relative situation. Let *our* first effusions be less insupportable than those of the generality of travellers.' (II.iv)

If this book were on Jane Austen, there would be leisure enough to consider how far this passage is serious, and how far it is ironic; but the task would need leisure. For the present purpose, all we need note is that, whether seriously or mockingly, there is reference to the idea that contact with wild Nature, with rocks and mountains, is of special spiritual benefit – one of the characteristic doctrines of the 'picturesque' tourists. And, mockingly without doubt, there is the suggestion that this spiritual benefit is not the main purpose of the tourists. They are much more concerned with accumulating prestigious topics of conversation against their return home, and they ominously foreshadow the modern miseries of the slide-show and holiday film.

Unfortunately for Elizabeth (but very luckily for the conduct of the novel), Mr Gardiner found that he could not spare the six weeks needed for a tour in the Lakes, and the month's holiday at his disposal was enough only for a more 'contracted tour' into Derbyshire – where, of course, Mr Darcy's estate of Pemberley was situated (II.xix). It would have been an opportunity for a lesser writer to work in a fashionable tour, but Jane Austen rejects it, just as she so often rejected the chance to report meaningless conversation:

> It is not the object of this work to give a description of Derbyshire, nor of any of the remarkable places through which their route thither lay; Oxford, Blenheim, Warwick, Keneilworth, Birmingham, &c. are sufficiently known. (II.xix)

Indeed they were more than 'sufficiently known'. This was exactly the route followed in one of William Gilpin's most influential 'picturesque tours', that to the *Mountains, and Lakes of Cumberland, and Westmoreland.*[17] Section II describes the country about Oxford and Blenheim, Section III describes mainly Warwick and Kenilworth castles, and Section IV conducts the tourist to Birmingham. Section I has already made it clear that if a 'contracted tour' has to be taken, Derbyshire is the place, for there 'the first mountainous country begins' (I, i, p. 3).

The conduct of the visit to Pemberley itself is illustrative of the social conventions of the time. We are now, perhaps, rather prone to suppose that the custom of visiting 'stately homes' is a modern one. All that is modern about it, however, is that the owner deliberately encourages such visits, and charges for entrance. In the eighteenth century, he was generally willing to have the visitors – for what other purpose had he 'improved' his estate than to impress as many people as possible? He left them, however, to reward suitably the housekeeper who showed them round the house, and the gardener who exhibited the grounds. No doubt it was so at Pemberley, though the transaction is not mentioned; Mr Gardiner was too 'gentlemanlike' to allow his wife and niece to see the money changing hands. Or perhaps Jane Austen was too lady-like to record such things.

As for the scenery of Derbyshire, Jane Austen, as always, confined her descriptions to what she knew and understood. The grounds of Pemberley itself were certainly in a state of Brownian improvement, with a river, hanging woods, and hills of some size and steepness. But Elizabeth found that things had not been overdone, or subjected to any of the more extreme fashions of the time. Where, for example, a bridge was needed over the river, it was 'simple . . . in character with the general air of the scene' (III.i). It might, after all, have been ostentatiously rustic, Gothic, or even Chinese. It was, in fact, the estate of a man of taste, and of such extent that it hardly needed the minor adornments of mere fashion; its circumference, as the gardener told the visitors when they expressed a wish to walk all round it, was ten miles. So far, Jane Austen could carry her description, giving the impression of Mr Darcy which she intended to give, through the medium of his estate and the kind of good manners which had made it, or left it, as it was. The wilder scenes of Derbyshire, however – those rocks and deep vales for which the tourists came – she did not attempt, and turned her very refusal to good dramatic account. For when Elizabeth found herself for a few minutes alone with Mr Darcy, and much at a loss for subjects, considering all that had previously passed between them, 'she recollected that she had been travelling, and they talked of Matlock and Dove dale with great perseverance' (III.i). They could hardly have done better, for by that time the picturesque tourists had said all that could possibly be said of both places, Gilpin among them, and all that was needed – all that was possible – was to rehearse their opinions and the more notorious differences between them. A perfect topic for a difficult moment.

In Jane Austen's attitude to landscape-gardening and to the 'picturesque', there is something not unlike her attitude to religion. She treats them as matters in which she is not expert, and which, therefore, she cannot assess or discuss directly and in terms of their own qualities. She is, however, expert in the manners and characters of those who profess, or who do not profess, religion, of those who talk much of landscape-gardening and of the 'picturesque'. And her verdict, no less certain for being indirect, and all the more damning, is given in terms, not of the qualities of the things themselves, but of the qualities of those who are much concerned with them. Landscape-gardening comes off badly. It is discussed extensively in *Mansfield Park* by the buffoon, Mr Rushford, who is boasting of his intention to have his estate improved by Repton himself, and by the villain, Henry Crawford, who has some taste and education, but no real 'principle', and who sees 'improvement' solely in terms of social ostentation. This is how he advises the 'hero', Edmund, on the 'capabilities' of his parsonage at Thornton Lacey:

> The air of a gentleman's residence therefore you cannot but give it, if you do any thing. But it is capable of much more . . . By some such improvements as I have suggested . . . you may give it a higher character. You may raise it into a *place*. From being the mere gentleman's residence, it becomes, by judicious improvement, the residence of a man of education, taste, modern manners, good connections. All this may be stamped on it; and that house receive such an air as to make its owner be set down as the great land-holder of the parish, by every creature travelling the road; especially as there is no real squire's house to dispute the point. (II.vii)

Crawford's attitude to landscape-gardening is thus made into a clear demonstration of his lack of real principle, and so of real taste. Edmund himself has no such ambitions for his parsonage, and firmly announces that he will accept none of the proposed improvements.

The 'picturesque', on the other hand, is handled with some respect. Its attractions are recognised, especially for impressionable and sensitive young ladies. In *Love and Freindship*, written in her teens, Jane Austen describes Augusta as a young lady with a 'considerable taste for the Beauties of Nature', who is lured to Scotland after reading William Gilpin's tour in the Highlands (Letter 14). And in *Sense and Sensibility* a similar young lady, Marianne, the embodiment of 'sensibility', is a devotee of the 'picturesque'. The villain, Willoughby like Henry Crawford, is equipped with all the latest fashions in taste, and at his first meeting with Marianne they establish their complete agreement on poetry – enthusiasm for Cowper and Scott, no more than proper admiration for Pope. Her more sensible sister, Elinor, comments on the headlong speed of their sympathies:

> But how is your acquaintance to be long supported, under such extraordinary dispatch of every subject for discourse? You will soon have exhausted each favourite topic. Another meeting will suffice to explain his sentiments on picturesque beauty, and second marriages, and then you can have nothing further to ask. (I.x)

A little later there is a full-dress discussion between Marianne, Elinor, and one of the 'heroes', Edward Ferrars, a young man of good sense, in which the comparative complexity of Jane Austen's attitude to the 'picturesque' is fully explored. Edward has been walking in the countryside, and praises it when he returns to the two sisters:

> Edward returned to them with fresh admiration of the surrounding country; in his walk to the village, he had seen many parts of the valley to advantage; and the village itself, in a much higher situation than the cottage, afforded a general view of the whole, which had exceedingly pleased him. This was a subject which ensured Marianne's attention, and she was beginning to describe her own admiration of these scenes, and to question him more minutely on the objects that had particularly struck him when Edward interrupted her by saying, 'You must not inquire too far, Marianne – remember I have no knowledge in the picturesque, and I shall offend you by my ignorance and want of taste if we come to particulars. I shall call hills steep, which ought to be bold; surfaces strange and uncouth, which ought to be irregular and rugged; and distant objects out of sight, which ought only to be indistinct through the soft medium of a hazy atmosphere. You must be satisfied with such admiration as I can honestly give. I call it a very fine country – the hills are steep, the woods seem full of fine timber, and the valley looks comfortable and snug – with rich meadows and several neat farm houses scattered here and there. It exactly answers my idea of a fine country, because it unites beauty with utility – and I dare say it is a picturesque one too, because you admire it; I can easily believe it to be full of rocks and promontories, grey moss and brush wood, but these are all lost on me. I know nothing of the picturesque.'
>
> 'I am afraid it is but too true,' said Marianne; 'but why should you boast of it?'
>
> 'I suspect,' said Elinor, 'that to avoid one kind of affectation, Edward here falls into another. Because he believes many people pretend to more admiration of the beauties of nature than they

really feel, and is disgusted with such pretensions, he affects greater indifference and less discrimination in viewing them himself than he possesses. He is fastidious and will have an affectation of his own.'

'It is very true,' said Marianne, 'that admiration of landscape scenery is become a mere jargon. Every body pretends to feel and tries to describe with the taste and elegance of him who first defined what picturesque beauty was. I detest jargon of every kind, and sometimes I have kept my feelings to myself, because I could find no language to describe them in but what was worn and hackneyed out of all sense and meaning.'

'I am convinced,' said Edward, 'that you really feel all the delight in a fine prospect which you profess to feel. But, in return, your sister must allow me to feel no more than I profess. I like a fine prospect, but not on picturesque principles. I do not like crooked, twisted, blasted trees. I admire them much more if they are tall, straight and flourishing. I do not like ruined, tattered cottages. I am not fond of nettles, or thistles, or heath blossoms. I have more pleasure in a snug farm-house than a watch-tower – and a troop of tidy, happy villagers please me better than the finest banditti in the world.' (I.xviii)

It is an impertinence to this admirable passage to comment upon it briefly, for it is, apart from *The Prelude*, the most penetrating criticism of the fashion for the 'picturesque' made while that fashion was still reigning. Indeed it is a classically clear exposition of the nature of fashion itself, of its appeal to some temperaments, who feel it in part sincerely, while still recognising that it has become exaggerated into insincerity, and of its rejection by tempers of mind more slow and sober, because of this social cachet, though they may find something in it akin to their own real tastes. But for the moment all that concerns us is Marianne's reference to 'the taste and elegance of him who first defined what picturesque beauty was'. There was no need to name him, for every reader would name him without hesitation. There was but one man who answered this description, William Gilpin. And to understand what Jane Austen was saying, and what Wordsworth was saying at almost the same time, it is necessary to know a little of William Gilpin.

25

It was by one of those fortunate coincidences between individual men and their times which make it so hard to lay down general principles of historical development that the Lakes came to hold a pre-eminent position in the fashion for the 'picturesque'. William Gilpin's birthplace, the family into which he was born, the character of his father and the group which gathered round him, all played a remarkable part in directing his tastes and in reinforcing them by an early exposure to the main tendencies of thought and feeling which we have just sketched.

He was born in 1724, in the half-ruined castle of Scaleby a few miles north-west of Carlisle. It was a prophetically appropriate birthplace for a man who was to write much about ruins, real and artificial, and to use hundreds of them as objects of interest on the innumerable diagonals of his landscape drawings. When he visited it half a century later, he wrote:

> What share of picturesque genius Cromwell might have, I know not. Certain however it is, that no man, since Henry the eighth, has contributed more to adorn this country with picturesque ruins. The difference between these two masters lay chiefly in the style of ruins, in which they composed. Henry adorned his landscape with the ruins of abbeys; Cromwell, with those of castles. I have seen many pieces by this master, executed in a very grand style; but seldom a finer monument of his masterly hand than this.[18]

Readers of Jane Austen's *History of England* will recognise this as the source of her observation that Henry VIII abolished the monasteries, and left them to 'the ruinous depredations of time' for the purpose of improving the landscape.

His father, Captain Gilpin, was the younger son of the Recorder of Carlisle (himself an amateur painter and patron of local talent). He married young, and went into the army, where the height of his achievement was to become commander of one of the two 'Companies of Invalids' which garrisoned Carlisle in 1738. He and his family were by then living in the town, at the Deanery, which had been placed at his disposal by his friend, the Dean. There he was able to devote much of his time to drawing and painting, and to 'connoisseurship' of the kind that went with it. He was a musician, as well as a painter, and the circle which came to gather round the Deanery included one man who was later to achieve a national reputation, Dr John Brown of the *Estimate*, then the bishop's chaplain. The only disturbance of this pleasant and cultured life was the appearance of the Jacobite army before Carlisle in 1745. Those ominously named 'Companies of Invalids' proved to be worthy of their name, and after the surrender Captain Gilpin removed his family to safety in Whitehaven. William was then at Oxford, and seems to have taken no part in the disturbance. Dr Brown preached the assize sermon in the cathedral when the time came to deal with the rebels.

There was much more to Brown than the *Estimate*, though this was his only really successful enterprise. He too was a musician, active in drawing landscapes in the local style, and something of a poet. His two tragedies, *Barbarossa* and *Athelstan*, were performed by Garrick in 1754 and 1756, but without lasting success. He was a temperamental and quarrelsome man – 'very unpleasant to live with' as William Gilpin told Samuel Rogers long after his death. Like many other clergymen, he was in search of preferment, but had a ruinous tendency to quarrel with possible benefactors. From 1756 to

1760 he held a living near Colchester, and in 1761 he returned to the north as Vicar of St Nicholas, Newcastle, where the organist, Charles Avison, was another member of the Gilpin 'circle', and had gained some reputation by a work on music which, entirely in the taste of the time and place, made some very curious parallels between choral music and landscape painting. Horace Walpole, in 1758, saw Brown 'singing the Stabat Mater with the Mingotti behind a harpsichord at a gt concert at my Lady Carlisle's' in 'last Passion week', and noted that this hardly seemed consistent with his denunciation of opera. He thought that Brown must be a little mad.[19] And Warburton, Pope's protégé and literary executor, who took Brown under his wing for a time, recorded that he was 'rarely without a gloom and sullen insolence on his countenance'.[20] In 1766, after a strange transaction in which Catherine the Great invited him to Russia to reform education, Brown took his own life by cutting his throat.

In his earlier days at Carlisle, however, Brown seems to have been less disturbed by temperamental difficulties, and to have lived with some comfort and happiness in the circle of Captain Gilpin, to whose children he may have acted as tutor. Certainly he formed a friendship with William Gilpin and, when William was at Oxford, they corresponded fairly regularly. It was in this correspondence that they first began to discuss the relative merits of the landscapes of Oxfordshire and Cumberland. Gilpin seems to have raised the subject, but we hear of it first in a letter of Brown's at the end of 1741:

> . . . you tell me you are sometimes tempted to make a Comparison of Oxford & the north, at which times the last appears in dismal Colours – this paragraph I read in a pretty large Company: after many debates upon the Subject, Cumberland was at last proved to be a finer Country than Oxfordshire; but as you are I suppose by this time an experienced Logician (& consequently can easily get the better of Truth) I shall not trouble you with the Reasons upon which this opinion was founded.[21]

Brown evidently disagreed with Gilpin's preference, as he was likely to do, for he was himself a Cumberland man, and had been educated, like Gilpin and Wordsworth, at one of the remarkably good grammar schools in the region, at Wigton. It is likely that he returned to the subject in letters now lost, for about six weeks later he records a change of opinion on Gilpin's part:

> Yes indeed, I think you are entirely right when you prefer our Cumberland Prospects (some of them at least) to your Oxford ones.[22]

Brown continued, however, to give some of the reasons on which, in his view, this opinion should be founded, and they show how widely their discussion of landscape was based:

In doing this you prefer the Beauties of Nature to those of Art; and that is certainly a true Judgment. Now, Sir, I wou'd beg leave to transfer this Principle to another Subject. I find you admire Virgil – and I think very justly – but you prefer him to Homer – there I differ from you. Homer's Works I take to be a very transcript of Nature, drawn out with the utmost Beautie and Simplicity: Virgil is majestic, grave, elegant and correct, but then there is in him an appearance of Art, which is not so pleasing in Poetry.[23]

Brown goes on to apply this mainly to the descriptions of people in the *Aeneid* and the *Iliad*, and says nothing of landscape. But what he has done, in the terms of his age – and they were terms which Gilpin certainly understood – was to broaden the discussion of two kinds of scenery so as to include two of its central preoccupations. One was with the classical poets, who formed the basis of all education, and so did much to determine the taste of the age in landscape. If Gilpin preferred Virgil to Homer, it was certainly because he found in him much more description of scenery than in the Greek epic. In his later writings, he claimed that Virgil had been 'a great master' in landscape,[24] frequently quoted from him to illustrate English scenery, and even projected an elaborate examination of Virgil as a 'picturesque' writer.[25] It was to prove of the first importance that these two, in this early discussion of English landscapes, were already drawing upon that classical education which was the common ground of all 'connoisseurs'.

The second notable extension of the discussion was that implied in the contrast between 'Nature' and 'Art'. The argument about the relation between these two large abstractions was, and had long been, one of the great commonplaces of discussion among philosophers and critics, and Brown's recourse to it in this letter may well have been no more specific than that. But it is also possible that he already had in mind the special prominence which Shaftesbury had given to the same contrast. What is certain is that in the next few years he became deeply interested in Shaftesbury, and so did Gilpin. In 1751 Brown published the first full-scale discussion of Shaftesbury's *Characteristicks*, in a book composed of four *Essays* on them. It is a curious work, often critical of its subject on the ground that Shaftesbury's ideas were incompatible with orthodox Christianity, yet showing a kind of fascination with many aspects of it. Exactly the same attitude is found in Gilpin a little earlier, for in about 1748 he wrote (and never published) some 'Letters of Advice to an Undergraduate at Oxford' one of which has this comment:

Ld. Shaftesbury I know in Oxford is reckoned an infidel, & though indeed I should be far from subscribing to all his opinions, yet there are some parts of his works which I think it is scarce possible to read without panting after virtue.[26]

But even earlier than this, Gilpin had been given direct personal experience of the influence of Shaftesbury, for one of the most brilliant of his contemporaries at Queen's, George Potter, had suddenly thrown up his prospects at Oxford, to attend at Glasgow the lectures of Francis Hutcheson, then the leading exponent of Shaftesbury's ideas. Gilpin thus describes Potter's reaction to his new education:

At Glasgow he was first introduced to the writings of Lord Shaftesbury; whose refined ideas were intirely adapted to his own. He adopted them with his usual warmth; & even carried them farther, than his master, under whom he studied, would authorize. Lord Shaftesbury was his great apostle; & from his tenets he formed his creed.

In the year 1746 the rebellion in Scotland was at its height; and that military spirit, which was then diffused over the kingdom, seized, and took entire possession of this animated youth. He became a mere enthusiast in the cause of liberty: his conversation on this subject was almost rhapsody. He expressed his inclination . . . to go into the army . . .[27]

Brown too encountered this young enthusiast, and after they had met in Carlisle he wrote to Gilpin: 'Your Friend Potter is a very pretty Fellow as any I have seen: By pretty Fellow I don't mean a modern Fop, but a man form'd for engaging.'[28]

It is clear that through this devoted disciple of Shaftesbury's, both Gilpin and Brown were introduced to his ideas, and to the potential strength of his influence. And this influence extended to the discussion of landscape, for in one of his earliest published works, *A Dialogue upon the Gardens . . . at Stow* (London, 1748), Gilpin conducts his description and comment by means of a dialogue in which Potter and himself are the disputants, though each of them is concealed by an elaborate Greek pseudonym.[29] In this speech especially Potter expounds the central doctrine of Shaftesbury's ethics, that virtue is based upon an innate 'taste' for good conduct, and that this taste may be cultivated by discipline in the fine arts:

. . . can it be considered as a Work entirely of a private Nature, for a superior Genius to exert itself in an Endeavour to fix a true Standard of Beauty in any of these allowed and useful kinds of Pleasure? In the Way of Gardening particularly, the Taste of the Nation has long been so depraved, that I should think we might be obliged to any one that would undertake to reform it. While a Taste for Painting, Music, Architecture, and other polite Arts, in some measure prevailed amongst us, our Gardens for the most Part were laid out in so formal, aukward, and wretched a Manner, that they were really a Scandal to the very Genius of the Nation; a Man of Taste was shocked whenever he set his Foot into them. But *Stow*, it is to be hoped, may work some Reformation: I would have our Country Squires flock hither two or three times in a Year, by way of Improvement, and after they have looked about them a little, return Home with new Notions, and begin to see the Absurdity of their clipped Yews, their Box-wood Borders, their flourished Parterres, and their lofty Brick-walls. – You may smile, but I assure you such an Improvement of public Taste, tho' there is no Occasion to consider it as a matter of the first

Importance, is certainly a Concern that ought by no means to be neglected. Perhaps indeed I may carry the Matter farther than the generality of People; but to me I must own there appears a very visible Connection between an *improved* Taste for Pleasure, and a Taste for Virtue: When I sit ravished at an Oratorio, or stand astonished before the Cartoons, or enjoy myself in these happy Walks, I can feel my Mind expand itself, my Notions enlarge, and my Heart better disposed either for a religious Thought, or a benevolent Action: In a Word, I cannot help imagining a Taste for these exalted Pleasures contributes towards making me a better man.
Polyphthon. Good God! what an Enthusiast you are! Polite Arts improve Virtue! an Assertion indeed for a Philosopher to make. (*ibid.*, pp. 48–9)

It followed naturally enough from this concern for virtue and 'benevolence', that *Callophilus* found the greatest pleasure in gentle, prosperous southern landscapes, which bespoke the general prosperity of their inhabitants. *Polyphthon*, on the other hand, prefers a wilder kind of scenery, and his description of it is one of the fullest of the early tributes to the region later called 'the Lakes' – though it so happens that he does not mention the Lakes themselves:

As we are got into the North, I must confess I do not know any Part of the Kingdom that abounds more with elegant natural Views: Our well-cultivated Plains, as you observed before, are certainly not comparable to their rough Nature in point of Prospect. About three Years ago I rode the Northern Circuit: The Weather was extremely fine; and I scarce remember being more agreeably entertained than I was with the several charming Views exhibited to me in the northern Counties. Curiosity indeed, rather than Business, carried me down: And as I had my Time pretty much to myself, I spent it in a great measure in hunting after beautiful Objects. Sometimes I found myself hemmed within an Amphitheatre of Mountains, which were variously ornamented, some with scattered Trees, some with tufted Wood, some with grazing Cattle, and some with smoaking Cottages. Here and there an elegant View likewise was opened into the Country. – A Mile's riding, perhaps, would have carried me to the Foot of a steep Precipice, down which thundered the whole Weight of some vast River, which was dashed into Foam at the Bottom, by the craggy Points of several rising Rocks: A deep Gloom overspread the Prospect, occasioned by the close Wood that hung round it on every Side. – I could describe to you a Variety of other Views I met with there, if we *here* wanted Entertainment in the Way of Landskip. One, however, I cannot forbear mentioning, and wishing at the same time that his Lordship had such Materials to work with, and it could not be but he would make a most noble Picture. – The Place I have in view is upon the Banks of the River *Eden* (which is indeed one of the finest Rivers I ever saw). I scarce know a fitter Place for a Genius in this Way to exert itself in. There is the greatest Variety of garnished Rocks, shattered Precipices, rising Hills, ornamented with the finest Woods, thro' which are opened the most elegant Vales that I have ever met with: Not to mention the most enchanting Views up and down the River, which winds itself in such a manner as to shew its Banks to the best Advantage, which, together with very charming Prospects into the Country, terminated by the blue Hills at a Distance, make as fine a Piece of Nature, as perhaps can any where be met with. (*Ibid.*, pp. 24–5)

The *Dialogue* was fairly successful, being reprinted two or three times in the next few years. But it marked no new fashion, for it had moved towards novelty only very tentatively. It was most original, moreover, where it was least Gilpin's, and where it depended most on Potter's enthusiastic insistence on the potential moral effects of the new art of landscape-gardening. But as to the art itself, Gilpin did not go beyond the accepted view that Stowe was a very fine example of it. His regional patriotism went no further, as yet, than the suggestion that the northern landscape of Cumberland would provide better, more impressive raw material for the landscape-artists. He was still a long way from the notion that some landscapes needed no gardening, and that in their natural state they could fulfil much better than Stowe the moral purposes which Shaftesbury had envisaged.

This further step was taken, at some time within the next decade, by Brown, the older and more forceful man of the two. And it was made possible by an experience which happened to symbolise, as it were, the change of feeling for Nature and landscape which distinguished the earlier from the later part of the century. It started with a visit to Hagley, Lord Lyttelton's famous estate, now largely engulfed in Birmingham, but then newly laid out with lawns, pastures, hanging woods, artificial ruins, temples, and a stream with which pains had been taken to make it gurgle in its channel through the lawns. Not only was it a show-piece of landscape-gardening, but it was also the very place where Thomson had revised and partly rewritten *The Seasons*. A place had been specially prepared from which he could take his prospects of Nature at his ease – he had grown to be stout by then – and this too was one of the noteworthy sights of the place. Gilpin described it when he saw it a few years later:

> *Thompson*'s seat exhibits a noble display of scenery. You look across a spacious valley of a mile in extent; the whole a pasture, winding at both ends from the eye. The opposite bank, which conducts the sweep, is hung with wood. At one end of the valley is a distant view into the country; terminated by the Malvern hills. At the other, the woody bank is adorned by a modern ruin, which stands well, but is an object too minute for the scene.[30]

From this highly wrought piece of landscape-gardening and its distinguished literary associations, Brown went first to Dovedale and then to Keswick, on his way back to Carlisle. The letter which he wrote to Lord Lyttelton about this tour remained unpublished until after his death, but once it had appeared in a widely-read miscellany[31] it achieved that talismanic influence which an emerging fashion often confers upon a comparatively minor production. Just as Dyer and Thomson, a generation earlier, had hit off so aptly the fashion for landscape which was just coming in, so Brown's tour from Hagley to Keswick hit off the passing of that fashion, and the coming-in of a new one, for wild and dramatic scenes instead of gentle and cultivated, from the peacefully artificial to the violently natural.

His *Letter* begins:

> In my way to the north from Hagley, I passed through Dovedale; and, to say the truth, was disappointed in it. When I came to Buxton, I visited another or two of their romantic scenes; but these are inferior to Dovedale. They are but poor miniatures of Keswick; which exceeds them more in grandeur than I can give you to imagine; and more, if possible, in beauty than in grandeur.
>
> Instead of the narrow slip of valley which is seen at Dovedale, you have at Keswick a vast amphitheatre, in circumference above twenty miles. Instead of a meagre rivulet, a noble living lake . . . The rocks indeed of Dovedale are finely wild, pointed, and irregular; but the hills are both little and unanimated; and the margin of the brook is purely edged with weeds, morass, and brushwood. – But at Keswick, you will on one side of the lake, see a rich and beautiful landscape of cultivated fields, rising to the eye, in fine inequalities, with noble groves of oak, happily dispersed, and climbing the adjacent hills, shade above shade, in the most various and picturesque forms. On the opposite shore you will find rocks and cliffs of stupendous height, hanging broken over the lake in horrible grandeur . . . steep and shaggy sides . . . dreadful heights . . . waterfalls tumbling in vast sheets from rock to rock in rude and terrible magnificence. (p. 36)

Having completed this general description, Brown clinches the comparison by bringing it into direct relation with the words around which the fashion for scenery had gathered, from Addison onwards, and with the standard trio of the picturesque painters:

> Were I to analyse the two places into their constituent principles, I should tell you, that the full perfection of Keswick, consists of three circumstances, beauty, horror, and immensity united; the second of which is alone found in Dovedale . . . But to give you a complete idea of these three perfections, as they are joined in Keswick, would require the united powers of Claude, Salvator Rosa, and Poussin. The first should throw his delicate sunshine over the cultivated vales, the scattered cots, the groves, the lake, and wooded islands. The second should dash out the horror of the rugged cliffs, the steeps, the hanging woods, and foaming water-falls; while the grand pencil of Poussin should crown the whole with the majesty of the impending mountains. (p.37)

What is above all typical of the age here is the intimate mingling of what Brown had actually seen, and known – presumably – for much of his life, with what he had been taught to look for, as a man of education, taste and fashion in the style of the time. Both elements are perfectly genuine, and this makes the mixture in some ways even more odd to a modern reader. It would be more natural for us to admire the painters for giving vivid impressions of landscapes than to admire landscapes because they reproduced the effects of painters. But this was the essence of the eighteenth-century fashion. The eye carried with it everywhere the strong traces of its education, just as the mind and feeling behind the eye carried with them impressions of Shaftesbury, Addison, Virgil and Milton. And this mixture of observation and education is central to an understanding of Wordsworth's use of his predecessors, and of his ultimate rejection of them.

The distinction can be illustrated, as it happens, from his comments on the other work of Brown's which entered at once into the tradition of Lakes landscape, a verse *Fragment*, published in 1776. The prose *Letter* had ended with a description of the endless variety of the Keswick scenery, as light and colour changed, as clouds and winds came and went, and as the whole scene was sometimes mirrored in the perfectly calm water. The conclusion was a pair of contrasting 'prospects', the first from a high point, where the mountains in the distance, 'craggy and broken', can only be described by the 'image of a tempestuous sea of mountains' (p. 39) – it was an image that was very often repeated in the later literature. The second scene had an even more distinguished progeny. It was a night-piece:

> Let me now conduct you down again to the valley and conclude with one circumstance more; which is, that a walk by still moon-light (at which time the distant waterfalls are heard in all their variety of sound) among these inchanting dales, opens such scenes of delicate beauty, repose, and solemnity, as exceed all description. (*Ibid.*)

Brown seems to have been his own imitator here, for the verse *Fragment* is an elaboration of this simple piece of prose:

> Now sunk the sun, now twilight sunk, and night
> Rose in her zenith; not a passing breeze
> Sigh'd to the grove, which in the midnight air
> Stood motionless, and in the peaceful floods
> Inverted hung: for now the billows slept
> Along the shore, nor heav'd the deep; but spread
> A shining mirror to the moon's pale orb,
> Which, dim and waning, o'er the shadowy cliffs,
> The solemn woods, and spiry mountain tops,
> Her glimmering faintness threw: now every eye,
> Oppress'd with toil, was drown'd in deep repose,
> Save that the unseen Shepherd in his watch,
> Propp'd on his crook, stood listening by the fold,
> And gaz'd the starry vault, and pendant moon;
> Nor voice, nor sound, broke on the deep serene;
> But the soft murmur of swift-gushing rills,
> Forth issuing from the mountain's distant steep,
> (Unheard till now, and now scarce heard) proclaim'd
> All things at rest, and imag'd the still voice
> Of quiet, whispering in the ear of night.

Wordsworth quotes the *Fragment* in his own *Guide* to the Lakes,[32] and very cordially introduces Brown as 'one of the first who led the way to a worthy admiration of this country' (p. 84). In a footnote he adds:

. . . it is pleasing to notice a dawn of imaginative feeling in these verses. Tickel, a man of no common genius, chose, for the subject of a Poem, Kensington Gardens, in preference to the Banks of the Derwent, within a mile or two of which he was born. But this was in the reign of Queen Anne, or George the First. Progress must have been made in the interval; though the traces of it, except in the works of Thomson and Dyer, are not very obvious. (*Ibid.*)

This 'progress', however, he clearly regarded as limited. In Brown's verses he found no more than the 'dawn' of imaginative feeling. And the footnote states exactly what was still lacking:

Dr. Brown . . . was from his infancy brought up in Cumberland, and should have remembered that the practice of folding sheep by night is unknown among these mountains, and that the image of the Shepherd upon the watch is out of its place, and belongs only to countries, with a warmer climate, that are subject to ravages from beasts of prey. (*Ibid.*)

What Wordsworth is saying is that Brown's shepherd is not a Cumberland figure, but one carried into his lines along with the classical commonplace of night and creatures in repose – a Virgilian or Horatian shepherd. And the difference was the more important to him because, as he records in Book VIII of *The Prelude*, his own first strong impression of human beings was of the shepherds he met among the mountains. And in the same book, he distinguishes them elaborately and carefully from their Arcadian counterparts in classical literature. In short, it was not enough to admire the scenery of Cumberland; it was necessary too to know what went on within it, and to admire that too.

These deficiencies, however, were not ones to trouble the thoughts of the new tourists, and upon them both the *Letter* and the *Fragment* had an immediate effect, once they were published. It was the *Letter* that sent Gray on his tour of the Lakes in 1769, and though his journal of the tour was not published until 1775, it served at once to reinforce the rapidly growing reputation of the Lakes. The publication of Gray's *Journal* also served to bring Gilpin's *Tour* of the Lakes to public notice. And by that time, Gilpin too had advanced far beyond the rather tentative descriptions of the *Dialogue on Stow* which he had discussed with Brown. After holding several curacies in London, he had, in 1752, taken over the management of a private school at Cheam, and for several years was too occupied with its affairs – which he took very seriously – to spend much time on drawing, or any on travelling. In 1769, however, he found leisure to make the first of his 'picturesque tours'. Others followed over the next seven or eight years. All that was novel about the 'picturesque' tour was a combination of activities which had all existed separately, and which all happened to be within Gilpin's own powers. The tourist travelled from one great estate to another, viewing the improvements and the galleries, criticising each with politeness but with honesty, and he ended in some wilder country, where Nature predominated over Art. Each evening, Gilpin made quick notes of what he had seen and thought, and whenever opportunity offered he made very quick rough sketches of scenery. During the winter, back at his school in Cheam, both kinds of sketches were polished into better order, but with this vital difference: the verbal account was literal and veracious, in the manner of a guide-book, but the drawings were not even intended to be topographical. They were, designedly and deliberately, an idealised version of the chief features of each landscape, natural, but improving on Nature for the sake of composition and pictorial effect. They were, in fact, an imaginary 'improvement' of the actual landscape of mountains, rivers, abbeys and castles, of just such a kind as the landscape-gardeners had applied to smaller and more tractable areas of countryside.

There was at first no question of publishing the finished product, for no means existed of reproducing the drawings effectively. The manuscripts were circulated among friends, in a rapidly growing circle, and they were at once welcomed warmly by the established connoisseurs. The first tour, down the Wye, fell into the hands of Gray just before his death in 1771, and received his influential accolade. It was with the encouragement of William Mason, Gray's friend and editor, that Gilpin undertook a similar tour to the Lakes in 1772, and when Mason published Gray's journal of his tour to the Lakes three years later, he inserted a handsome tribute to Gilpin's work. He claimed that Gray had done everything that could be done with language alone, but admitted that words often needed to be supplemented by drawings, and went on:

> I have seen one piece of verbal description which compleatly satisfies me, because it is throughout assisted by masterly delineation. It is composed by the Rev. Mr. Gilpin, of Cheam in Surry; and contains, amongst other places, an account of the very scenes which, in this tour, our author [Gray] visited. This Gentleman, possessing the conjoined talent of a writer and a designer, has employed them in this manuscript to every purpose of picturesque beauty, in the description of which a correct eye, a practised pencil, and an eloquent pen could assist him. He has, consequently, produced a work *unique* in its kind at once. But I have said it is in manuscript, and, I am afraid, likely to continue so; for would his modesty permit him to print it, the great expence of plates would make its publication almost impracticable.[33]

This commendation, in such a place, established Gilpin's *Tour* as part of the rapidly growing canon of Lakes literature. Though it was not published until 1786, largely because of the difficulty of providing plates, the manuscript with its drawings was widely circulated among the nobility and the connoisseurship. Queen Charlotte and the Duchess of Portland asked to see it twice. Lord Harcourt and Horace Walpole seem to have been contented with one inspection.

Within a year or two of Wordsworth's birth, the two connoisseurs of Carlisle had established that special mingling of local patriotism and the whole eighteenth-century tradition of landscape which made the Lakes pre-eminent as a place for the picturesque tourist. They had recruited Gray to their cause, and had set the fashion on its long and distinguished course. While Wordsworth was still a child, or a schoolboy at Hawkshead, other *Guides* appeared, and by the time he went to Cambridge, there was already an extensive body of writing on the Lakes. So far from 'discovering' the special quality of the region, he was faced by its discovery by others, some of them men of real ability and sensibility, all of them embodying the authority of a central trend in the thought and feeling of the century. Through them, and the massive weight of tradition which they embodied, his own 'Taste' for his own region, and for Nature herself, was first 'Impaired'; and then, by an arduous process of development and self-criticism, it was 'Restored'. The details of both impairment and restoration are best studied in relation to his own work, and to that of his younger brother Christopher. But this exploration will be made easier if we start with a general impression of those previous writings which most directly influenced him. The *Guides* to the Lakes are now largely forgotten, and it might easily be assumed that they were nothing more than would be expected of similarly titled modern works. This expectation is not borne out by reading them. They were, in their different ways, notable pieces of writing, and four of them, those of Gray, Gilpin, West and Clarke, together represent what Wordsworth was up against – and also what they had to offer him.

26

Gray's *Journal* is remarkable in one respect. It is the only piece of writing on the Lakes of this period which makes no mention of Lorrain, Salvator Rosa and Poussin. The omission was not due to ignorance, of course; Gray was an accomplished connoisseur. It was rather that his journal was written in a familiar style, a low key, intended, not for publication, but for the private amusement of his friend Wharton, who had been prevented from accompanying him on the tour. Nevertheless, Gray's approach to the scenes he visited was very much that of a landscape-painter, and though he did not himself attempt any drawings, he was assisted in viewing them by a simple optical device which was just then coming into fashion, a Claude, or landscape-glass. This was a plano-convex mirror, about 4 inches in diameter, often of violet-coloured glass. It had two remarkable effects on any landscape. First, it reduced a stretch of many miles in width to the compass of 4 inches, and the user could readily include or exclude certain parts of the scene, until he had found a perfect 'prospect'. Secondly, the coloured glass cast over the whole scene just that 'browner shade' which had been typical of the Italian paintings, especially as they grew older. This brown colouring was so much valued by both connoisseurs and painters that they were quite unable to believe Constable when he claimed that it was merely the effect of ageing varnish, and that when first painted there was some green visible, even in Poussin. Wordsworth's friend, Sir George Beaumont, is said to have carried among his painting equipment an old violin, which helped him to get his grass just to the right colour. And he once asked Constable in a puzzled way about one of his landscapes, 'And where is your brown tree?'

The one slight inconvenience in using these glasses is that the user must turn his back towards the view he wishes to see in them. It is very typical of their attitude to Nature that such a position should have seemed desirable. The posture was not without its dangers, too, as Gray found at Keswick:

> Dined by two o'clock at the Queen's Head, & then straggled out alone to the *Parsonage*, fell down on my back across a dirty lane, with my glass open in one hand, but broke only my knuckles.[34]

This accident occurred on Gray's first night in Keswick. He was more careful on the remaining four days of his stay, and records many more successful uses of his glass:

> From hence I got to the *Parsonage* a little before Sunset, & saw in my glass a picture, that if I could transmitt to you, & fix it in all the softness of its living colours, would fairly sell for a thousand pounds. this is the sweetest scene I can yet discover in point of pastoral beauty. the rest are in a sublimer style.[35]

Gray, then, though not troubling himself to mention the names of painters, accepted entirely the convention of the time, that landscapes must be looked at as if they were paintings – and even priced in the same way. Granted that this was his object, the brisk pace of his tour was natural enough: one day's excursion from Penrith to Ullswater, four days at Keswick, one day's ride in a chaise round Bassenthwaite, a trip to Grange and a little way into Borrowdale; then a ride in one day by Thirlmere to Grasmere and Ambleside, where the 'best bed-chamber' at the inn was so dark and damp that he decided to make for Kendal at once.[36]

This brisk pace was characteristic of the tourists. It did not, after all, need much time to savour any one prospect. After a few minutes, it was more amusing to search for the next. Gray described what he saw well, with few of the affectations and elaborations of his time, but his tour was both hasty and superficial. The only human beings with whom he had any contact were his landlord at the Queen's Head, who acted as his guide to Borrowdale, and a farmer at Grange who provided some wonderful butter and milk, with 'thin oaten cakes, & ale' for a picnic on cold tongue.[37] The same farmer gave Gray an account of plundering an eagle's nest, and thereafter some such feat entered into the regular canon of Lakeland *Guides*. It may have contributed slightly to Wordsworth's description of his own plundering of the raven's nest in Book I of *The Prelude*: not by offering details of the operation – Wordsworth was far more expert in such work than Gray – but rather by suggesting that such things had an imaginative value. Gray's special contribution, in fact, to the tourist tradition was not one of detailed description, but one of prestige. He helped the age to take the Lakes seriously, and did it with good taste and honesty.

West, the next of the guide-book writers to publish,[38] had no prestige to give, but some to gain. He was a Scot by birth, and had been converted to Roman Catholicism. He had studied on the Continent and become a Jesuit. On his return to a parish in Westmorland, presumably under the protection of the Stricklands, an old Catholic family of some position there, he gave much of his time to the study of local antiquities, and, according to prefatory matter in the second edition of his *Guide*, '*frequently accompanied genteel parties on the* Tour of the Lakes'. From these two interests, his *Guide* emerged naturally enough. And it may perhaps be added that his religious training also contributed its own very characteristic colouring. For his book is curiously like a form of religious service, or ritual, and the second edition included a kind of collection of the earlier scriptures of the founding fathers. In a number of Appendices we find Brown's *Letter*, Gray's *Journal*, with extracts from the few poems which had already been written about the Lakes. It was almost certainly from West that Wordsworth himself first learned of these writings, and in his own *Guide* he pays a not unhandsome tribute to West, as an 'authority . . . whose Guide to the Lakes has been eminently serviceable to the Tourist for nearly fifty years' (de Selincourt ed., pp. 146–7).

In his brief preface, West indicated that for some, at least, of his 'genteel parties', the tour might have a religious significance, as a sort of pilgrimage:

Such as spend their lives in cities, and their time in crouds will here meet with objects that will enlarge the mind, by contemplation, and raise it from nature to nature's first cause. Whoever takes a walk into these scenes must return penetrated with a sense of the creator's power in heaping mountains upon mountains, and enthroning rocks upon rocks. And such exhibitions of sublime and beautiful objects cannot but excite at once both rapture and reverence.

(3rd ed., p. 4)

Perhaps the most striking peculiarity of his *Guide* is its use of the word 'Stations' to indicate the precise spots from which the best views could be obtained. West did not invent the use of the word in this sense, for it occurs occasionally in Gray's *Journal*, for example here:

oh Doctor! I never wish'd more for you; & pray think, how the glass played its part in such a spot, wch is called *Carf-close-reeds*: I chuse to set down these barbarous names, that any body may enquire on the place, & easily find the particular station, that I mean.[39]

What West did was to organise these stations into a regular series, partly by correcting previous accounts of them, as here:

The late Mr. *Gray* was a great judge of landscapes, yet whoever makes choice of his station at the three mile stone from *Lancaster*, on the *Hornby* road, will fail in taking one of the finest afternoon rural views in *England*. The station he points out is a quarter of a mile too low, and somewhat too much to the left. The more advantageous station, as I apprehend, is on the south side of the great, or Queen's road, a little higher than w[h]ere Mr. *Gray* stood.

(3rd ed., pp. 6–7)

The 'Stations' round the main lakes were similarly defined, and numbered in Roman numbers, so that there could be no mistake about the order in which they should be visited. It is possible that West had in mind the Catholic use of the word 'stations' to indicate stopping-places on a pilgrimage.[40] Certainly the effect of his careful numbering was to make viewing the Lakes very like a sort of lay-pilgrimage, and it lasted, as a continuous tradition, until my own childhood, when tours were conducted by wagonettes drawn by four horses. We used to bowl out of Keswick at a great rate, until the road began to rise. Then the pace became slower, the smell of hot horses more pungent. After a further slow climb, they would come to a halt without any sign from their driver, by a gate or a stile in the wall. We would all descend through a small door at the back of the contraption, pass through the gate or climb over the stile, and follow a well-worn track to the 'station' itself, a worn piece of dry grass upon which generations had stood in turn. There we would all stand for a few minutes, the adults reverently, the children – I speak for myself at least – a little puzzled, because it was rather like being in church. Then the party would return quietly to the waggonette, the horses would resume their slow progress, until they reached their next resting-place, and the next station in our pilgrimage.[41] The bus and the motor-car have, of course, put an end to these quaint survivals. The modern tourists stop wherever they can find room for their folding tables and chairs. And they pass through the country at a rate never dreamed of by Gray and West, seeing nothing, and apparently feeling even less.

West's chief concern was with 'picturesque' scenes, and like Gray, he relied on the glass and a right choice of 'station' to obtain them. His usual style is well represented by this passage, on 'Station V' on Windermere:

> These are the finest stations on the lake for pleasing the eye, but are by much too elevated for the purpose of the artist, who will find the picturesque points on the great island, well suited to his intention of morning and evening landscape, having command of fore-ground, the objects well ascertained, grouped and disposed in the finest order of nature. A picture of the north end of the lake, taken from this island, will far exceed the fanciful production of the happiest pencil. – This may be easily verified by the use of the convex reflecting glass. (3rd ed., p. 70)

The word 'verified' there is specially typical of West's practical approach and of his sense of an established orthodoxy. The pilgrim was hardly to be trusted to use his own eyes, either for choosing his 'station' or for looking at the view when he had found it. The purpose of this *Guide* was to save him from the trouble of doing so, and from possible mistakes; 'the writer has here collected and laid before [the traveller], all the select stations and points of view, noticed by those authors who have last made the tour of the lakes, verified by his own repeated observations' (3rd ed., p. 2).

From this strictly pictorial concern, West rarely digresses. Sometimes he adds brief notes on the history of one place or another, and it so happens that one of his notes, about the old haunted ruin of Calgarth, was of special interest to the Wordsworths. More often he gives select quotations of verse to illustrate the beauties of particular places. Gray had done the same, but there is an interesting difference in their choice of poets. Gray, writing to a friend almost as learned as himself, quotes from Virgil, Milton and Dante. West, writing for 'genteel parties', also quotes from Virgil and Ovid, but adds many passages from recently fashionable poets, Pope, Armstrong, Beattie, and one of the writers on the beauties of Killarney, which had entered the picturesque-beauty competition a few years earlier. It is in a quotation from Richard Cumberland's *Ode to the Sun* that West makes the essential obeisance to the painters.[42] Cumberland thus expressed his preference for Ullswater above all other lakes:

> For neither Scotish *Lomond*'s pride,
> Nor smooth *Killarney*'s silver tide,
> Nor aught that learned *Poussin* drew,
> Or dashing *Rosa* flung upon my view,
> Shall shake thy sovereign undisturbed right,
> Great scene of wonder and sublime delight! (p. 155)

It is an apt summary of West's reaction to the landscape, and a perfect statement, in consequence, of the stage the 'picturesque' had reached.

Gilpin's book, interestingly, was not presented as a *Guide*. Its full, and fully intended title, was *Observations, relative chiefly to Picturesque Beauty, Made in the Year 1772, On several Parts of England; Particularly the Mountains, and Lakes of Cumberland, and Westmoreland*. It was in two volumes, and was a much more expensive production than West's *Guide*, chiefly because of the plates. Wordsworth noted this twice, in relation to his own copy, together with that of Gilpin's Scottish Tour:

I hope you have preserved the catalogue of my books left at Montagu's. You would oblige me much by calling there; and desiring Jones to procure a box sufficient to contain them. See that they are nailed up in it. Gilpin's tour into Scotland, and his northern tour, each 2 vols., ought to be amongst the number. Montagu either did lend, or talked of lending, one of these to Miss Roby. Pray request that he would take care to have it returned immediately. I am the more solicitous on this account as the books, having been very expensive, are the *less likely* to be returned. (*EL* 54/60)

This was in 1796. Two years later he wrote to his Bristol bookseller and publisher, Cottle: 'They are expensive books, and I should like to dispose of them. Could you assist me in getting them off my hands?' (*EL* 83/96) He was, at the time, in need of money for the German visit, but he would hardly have decided to sell his Gilpins had they not already served whatever purpose they could serve with him.

About half of the two volumes is devoted to the Lakes themselves, and the descriptions are on the usual lines. In his description of Derwentwater Gilpin shows a nice sense of his debt to his father's circle, to Brown and his friend Avison, the musician of Newcastle:

Of all the lakes in these romantic regions, the lake we are now examining, seems to be most generally admired. It was once admirably characterized by an ingenious person, ['The Late Mr. Avison, organist of St. Nicholas at Newcastle upon Tyne': *Gilpin's note*], who, on his first seeing it, cried out, *Here is beauty indeed – Beauty lying in the lap of Horrour*! We do not often find a happier illustration. Nothing conveys an idea of *beauty* more strongly, than the lake; nor of *horrour*, than the mountains; and the former *lying in the lap* of the latter, expresses in a strong manner the mode of their combination. The late Dr. Brown, who was a man of taste, and had seen every art of this country, singled out the scenery of this lake for it's peculiar beauty.
(2nd ed. [London, 1788] I.xiii [p. 191])

Gilpin's approach to the scenery is, of course, different from that of Gray and West, for he is rather more concerned to discuss the principles of the 'picturesque' itself than to give exact topographical descriptions. The chapters on the Lakes are introduced by a long disquisition on the general properties, almost the 'capabilities', of mountains, lakes, rocks, cascades and so forth. But Gilpin then goes on to explain that these are rather the raw materials of the 'picturesque' than the thing itself:

In the mean time, with all this magnificence and beauty, it cannot be supposed, that every scene, which these countries present, is *correctly picturesque*. In such immense bodies of rough-hewn matter, many irregularities, and even many deformities, must exist, which a practised eye would wish to correct. Mountains are sometimes crouded – their sides are often bare, when contrast requires them to be wooded – promontories form the water-boundary into acute angles – and bays are contracted into narrow points instead of swelling into ample basons.

(*Ibid.*, I.ix [p. 127])

In such cases, the 'imagination' steps in, and corrects what is deficient in nature itself. Mountains are altered in shape, removed or added: 'Upon yon bald declivity, . . . may be reared a forest of noble oak' (*ibid.*, p. 128), and so on. Thus it 'composes a landscape, as the artist composed his celebrated Venus, by selecting accordant beauties from different originals' (p. 129). If there was one word which characterised Gilpin's sense of the 'picturesque' amid its many rather loose definitions, it was 'roughness'. Here, the 'bare' or 'bald' mountain is the one to be avoided and modified by the imagination.

Apart from these chapters on the theory of landscape, Gilpin's mode of description is direct, easy-going, and rarely impressive, largely because it so often turns aside into rather scrappy speculations on one aspect or another of scenic beauty, into comments on the merits of roughness in sketches, or on Burke's theories of the Sublime and the Beautiful. He does, however, allow himself to mention much more of the human side of the Lakes than West had done. He writes, not always, but sometimes, as a native of the region, with a knowledge of how people lived there. For example, in one of his criticisms of smoothness in a mountain-scene, he falls into a very important contrast between the demands of the 'picturesque' and the effect of these bare slopes on those who live among them:

Three broad mountains, sloping into each other, formed a tripartite valley, centering in one point. The surface of each mountain was smooth to it's very summit; except that, here and there, a few large stones lay scattered about . . . The whole was a peculiar and novel scene; but neither interesting, nor picturesque.

These smooth-coated mountains, tho of little estimation in the painter's eye, are however great sources of plenty. They are the nurseries of sheep; which are bred here, and fatted in the vallies.

But the life of a shepherd, in this country, is not an Arcadian life. His occupation subjects him to many difficulties, in the winter especially, when he is often obliged to attend his flock on the bleak side of a mountain, which engages him in many a painful vigil.

(*Ibid.*, pp. 222–3)

While he is talking of shepherds, Gilpin moves in the same world as Wordsworth:

> . . . Shepherds were the men who pleas'd me first.
> Not such as in Arcadian Fastnesses
> Sequester'd, handed down among themselves,
> So ancient Poets sing, the golden Age . . .
> There 'tis the Shepherd's task the winter long
> To wait upon the storms . . . (*Prel.* VIII. 182–5 and 359–60)

But when he talks of the mountains themselves, he is in his own world, prettier but less real. The 'naked' and the 'bare' effects are useless to his eye, and unmanageable for his rapid calligraphic pencil. There is, in his next publication, *Three Essays*, a contrasting pair of prints to illustrate this central point in the theory of landscape drawing.[43] One print shows the spur of a mountain entering on the right foreground, sloping down to the left; behind it another spur enters from the left, and slopes down behind the first. In the angle between them is a plain, by way of middle distance, and it is bounded by the background, a distant arc of mountain, quite smooth, like those in the foreground. The only relief in this very strict composition is a bright misty light to the left of the furthest mountain. In the second print, Gilpin has taken the same basic design, but has broken the smooth line of all three mountains. The nearest is now surmounted by trees, then dips into a rocky cliff, which ends among bushes and fallen rocks. The second is now surmounted by a ruined castle, and much decorated with trees and declivities. A third diagonal has been added before we reach the plain in the middle distance, mainly to define the winding road which enters the foreground, and serpentines through the middle of the composition. The background mountain has had two large slices scooped out of it, to produce two asymmetrical pinnacles. And to complete the picturesque effect, two figures are placed on the road, not quite in the foreground. Gilpin was weak in figure-drawing, and knew it, but comparatively few of his landscapes lack these two figures; they were known to his intimates as 'the two friends'. This second print is, in its way, charming enough. But the first is impressive. It is, moreover, remarkably like the landscape of Wordsworth's poetry, in its naked and barren simplicity. Yet Gilpin's comment on it is:

> In a mountain-scene what composition could arise from the corner of a smooth knoll coming forward on one side, intersected by a smooth knoll on the other; with a smooth plain perhaps in the middle, and a smooth mountain in the distance? The very idea is disgusting. Picturesque composition consists in uniting in one whole a variety of parts; and these parts can only be obtained from rough objects. (*Ibid.*, p. 19).

It would, of course, be easy to make a large collection of quotations from Gilpin against smoothness, in favour of roughness, but one more will be enough to show how totally he differed from Wordsworth in his feeling for rocks. It is from his *Tour* down the Wye:

> The *rocks*, which are continually starting through the woods, produce another *ornament on the banks* of the *Wye*. The rock, as all other objects, though more than all, receives its chief beauty from contrast. Some objects are beautiful in themselves. The eye is pleased with the tuftings of a tree: it is amused with pursuing the eddying stream; or it rests with delight on the shattered arches of a Gothic ruin. Such objects, independent of composition, are beautiful in themselves. But the rock, bleak, naked, and unadorned, seems scarcely to deserve a place among them. Tint it with mosses, and lychens of various hues, and you will give it a degree of beauty. Adorn it with shrubs, and hanging herbage, and you still make it more picturesque. Connect it with wood, and water, and broken ground, and you make it in the highest degree interesting.[44]

It is in passages like this – and therefore in all his work, for it is all like this – that Gilpin shows the consistency of his approach to landscape. It is significant, not in itself, not for the sake of the people who live in it, but simply for the painter. Its appeal is to the eye, and if to anything deeper in human experience, only through the eye.

When Wordsworth, five years after finishing *The Prelude*, came to write his own *Guide* to the Lakes, his approach was the opposite one. He begins with a characteristic declaration, much more startling than it appears to be until one has reflected on it:

> In preparing this Manual, it was the Author's principal wish to furnish a Guide or Companion for the *Minds* of Persons of taste, and feeling for Landscape. (de Selincourt ed., p. 35)

But nothing, after all, could be more characteristically Wordsworthian than this insistence that the real importance of mountain scenery was not visual, but mental – and nothing more thoroughly antithetical to Gilpin's approach to the same scenes. In at least two notable passages in his *Guide*, Wordsworth briefly indicates the mental effects for which he values the nakedness and bareness of living rock. In the first, he is suggesting something like a geographical basis for the two qualities, so often distinguished in the eighteenth century, in so many different definitions, of sublimity and beauty; and in particular he is commenting on the margins of the lakes:

> That uniformity which prevails in the primitive frame of the lower grounds among all chains or clusters of mountains where large bodies of still water are bedded, is broken by the *secondary* agents of Nature, ever at work to supply the deficiencies of the mould in which things were originally cast. Using the word *deficiencies*, I do not speak with reference to those stronger emotions which a region of mountains is peculiarly fitted to excite. The bases of those huge barriers may run for a long space in straight lines, and these parallel to each other; the opposite sides of a profound vale may ascend as exact counterparts, or in mutual reflection, like the

billows of a troubled sea;[45] and the impression be, from its very simplicity, more awful and sublime. Sublimity is the result of Nature's first great dealings with the superficies of the earth; but the general tendency of her subsequent operations is towards the production of beauty; by a multiplicity of symmetrical parts uniting in a consistent whole. (*Ibid.*, p. 69)

This variety, he goes on to explain, is produced by the masses of rock that have fallen from the heights, and by the constant action of brooks which deposit soil and gravel, and so make promontories of varying size, and help to create 'meandering shores' (p. 70). The variety is visual, and is regarded as pleasing very much in the tradition of Hogarth and his 'serpentine line of beauty', but for Wordsworth the most important source of emotion is the sense of the contrast between the primeval forms of the creation and the minor dilapidations of time and weather. The same contrast is more concretely described in a passage on the proper manner of planting trees in this country:

As to the management of planting with reasonable attention to ornament, let the images of Nature be your guide . . . in rocky districts, a seemly proportion of rock left wholly bare, and other parts half-hidden . . . woods surmounted by rocks utterly bare and naked, which add to the sense of height, as if vegetation could not thither be carried, and impress a feeling of duration, power of resistance, and security from change! (*Ibid*, p. 125)

But though Wordsworth's feeling for naked and bare rock is opposite to Gilpin's and is based on a wholly different approach to the business of looking at landscape, he is nevertheless of the same age, and in many ways of the same world. He refers, in his own *Guide*, and with approval, to Gilpin's condemnation of white-painted houses as disastrous in a landscape or in a picture (pp. 115–16).[46] His observations on the management of planting are wholly in the landscape-gardening tradition, and in his *Guide* he takes part in the long battle which has raged between the writers on the Lakes and the owners of the main island on Windermere (pp. 103–27). Gray had apparently not noticed what they were up to, perhaps because he passed along the lake more briskly than devoutly. But Gilpin himself had seen what was going on in 1772, and had reprobated it. Before his tour was published, he learned that the island 'had been under the hands of improvement. The proprietor, I have been told, spent six thousand pounds upon it; with which sum he has contrived to do almost every thing, that one would wish he had left undone'. William Hutchinson, in 1774, was driven to crude gibes at the proprietor's background, and the source of his wealth. There was 'a narrow foot path', he says, round the edge, 'laid with white sand, resembling the dusty paths of foot passengers over Stepney fields, or the way along which the owner has often heyed to Hackney'.[47] The trouble was, of course, that this Cockney tradesman had created a formal garden, in the old Dutch style, in a very unsuitable place.

West uttered reproofs with more restraint, and expressed the hope that the unfortunate Mr English would 'restore the island to its native state of pastoral simplicity, and rural elegance,' by having his garden removed (*Guide*, 3rd ed., p. 60). Wordsworth, though writing twenty years later, held loyally to the tradition of his predecessors, and asked 'Could not the margin of this noble island be given back to Nature?' (*Guide*, ed. de Selincourt, p. 106).

The only one of the early writers of *Guides* to be recalcitrant about this island was James Clarke, an eminent Surveyor and another Cumberland man, who wrote a *Survey of the Lakes* in 1787. He regretted that the proprietor had taken some notice of the earlier criticisms, and removed his fruit garden. Clarke gave the very practical reason for his view that he had enjoyed eating the fruit when he visited the place (p. 139). Clarke's *Survey* was the most impressively produced of all these books, being a handsome volume in folio. But since it had no pictorial plates, it may well have cost less than the Gilpin volumes. It affects a certain disdain for the 'picturesque' fashion, directly criticises Gilpin, and records local traditions to the effect that Gray had been so frightened of the mountains on some parts of his tour that he had pulled down the blinds of his carriage, and ordered his driver to hasten past them. Nevertheless, he joins in the business of defining 'stations', moving the older ones so much to the right or left, a few yards up or down – never, however, going to the superb lengths of Wordsworth himself, who suggested that the best possible point from which to view the Lakes as a whole would be 'the top of either of the mountains, Great Gavel, or Scawfell; or, rather, let us suppose our station to be a cloud hanging midway between those two mountains, at not more than half a mile's distance from the summit of each, and not many yards above their highest elevation' (p. 55). The special importance of Clarke for the Wordsworths, however, was not as a describer of scenery, but as a collector of local superstitions and antiquities, and a recorder of the way of life characteristic of the region. Unlike all the others, he was concerned as much with the people of the Lakes as with their country; the past, present and possible future concerned him, and he wrote well about them. Though his *Survey* contributed something to the landscape tradition, it contributed more to that other side of the Lakes which was, in the end, so much nearer to Wordsworth's real concerns.

Clarke also continues the tradition of the earlier *Guides* in introducing substantial quotations, often those which had become part of the Lakeland ritual, and mostly from English writers. But here the most luxuriant user of verse quotations was certainly Gilpin. And though he quoted often from English writers, chiefly Milton, Spenser and Thomson, he made even greater use of Virgil and Ovid.[48] In his writings, more clearly than in any of the others, the essential relation between the discovery of the Lakes and the main tradition of Augustan landscape is demonstrated – that is to say, the relation between the *Guides* and the tradition of thought and feeling which united Virgil and Ovid with Shaftesbury and Thomson, Lorrain, Salvator Rosa and Poussin, landscape-gardening and the picturesque. There was a real weight of culture and tradition in these books which made them much more than topographical manuals. And it is the less surprising that they should all, in their own ways, have influenced deeply not only Wordsworth, but also his sister Dorothy, and his brother Christopher.

27

'My Brother John I imagine sailed for India on Saturday or Sunday . . . William is at Cambridge, Richard in London, and Kitt at Hawkshead, how we are squandered abroad' (*EL* 8/8). So wrote Dorothy Wordsworth from Norfolk in 1790. And this break-up of the family was, of course, the main result of the death of their father in 1783. It meant that there was no longer any one home for them, in the Lakes or anywhere else. It exiled them from their native region for many years, some of them for ever. But they were rather differently affected by the timing and manner of their exiles.

Of the three who concern us here, Dorothy was least a native of the Lakes, for she left Cockermouth after her mother's death when she was but seven, and there is no reason to suppose that before this time she had seen more than distant glimpses of the mountains. Most of her exile was spent in Halifax and in Norfolk, and on her visits to her grandparents at Penrith there was no chance for her to wander far. She was not to see the mountains and the lakes for herself until 1794 when, at the age of twenty-three, she walked among them with her brother William, and stayed for some weeks at a farmhouse above Keswick. Though a native of the country, she returned to it as a tourist. The emotional effect of her return was great, but it was simple; she had no vivid earlier memories to mingle with what she saw, and what she expected to see from her reading of the *Guides* and her acquaintance with the new fashion for the Lakes. In a letter which she wrote from the farmhouse, she rejoices because 'From the window of the room where I write I have a prospect of the road winding along the opposite banks of this river.' The word was from the characteristic vocabulary of tourism. Many years later, Wordsworth remembered that the farmer's wife – 'a shrewd and sensible woman' – once exclaimed in his hearing, 'Bless me! folk are always talking about prospects: when I was young there was never sic a thing neamed.'[49] It is not at all unlikely that this exclamation was provoked by Dorothy's attitude to the view from the windows. It was – and is – a very good view, but in describing it, Dorothy shows little of that talent for vivid description which appeared later in her letters and journals. She was still seeing largely through the eyes of others – and perhaps even more through the words of others. She had read Gray's *Journal* (probably in West's *Guide*), and notes that he had called the vale of Keswick 'the Vale of Elysium'. And she goes on: 'This vale is terminated at one end by a huge pile of grand mountains in whose lap the lovely lake of Derwent is placed' (*EL* 1/1). It sounds rather as if she had been looking at her brother's copy of Gilpin's *Tour of the Lakes*, and had remembered, or half-remembered, the exclamation of the Newcastle organist about '*Beauty lying in the lap of Horrour*!'

Christopher Wordsworth became as it were a tourist in his own country because the new fashion for the Lakes caught up with him while he was still at Hawkshead school. By the time he was sixteen, he was already familiar with the *Guides*, and spending part of his school holidays in walking-tours with his friends. He was no doubt in possession of his own memories of the country, his own unspoiled childish reaction to it, but these earlier reactions blended without any break into his more cultivated and fashionable response to it.

Wordsworth himself – and he alone – was in a more complicated position, through the accidents of time and place. His early memories of the Lakes were both vivid and personal, unaided or unspoiled by the tourist fashion, which seems not to have touched Hawkshead itself while he was at school. Perhaps this was because it lay a little aside from the main tourist route down Windermere, and possibly tourists would be less noticeable in the village because it was visited by strangers for quite other reasons. Clarke, in his *Survey*, had observed that the school was 'very beneficial both to the town and to the neighbourhood, by the number of gentlemens sons boarded there; it also makes this place much resorted to by the families who visit their children here in Summer' (p. 146). There is no trace, either in his youthful writings or in his later memories of his youth, of any tinge of consciousness that he was living in a region of special note in public taste, however notable it seemed to his private experience of it. But when he left it and came to Cambridge, it was a different matter. There he heard of the fashion, and by the time he left Cambridge he was thoroughly familiar with the *Guides*, with Gray's *Journal*, Brown's *Letter*, Gilpin's *Tour*, West, and Clarke. To him alone was presented, with the utmost force of contrast, two utterly different ways of seeing the Lakes, one public, documented, already much adorned with words and phrases, the other entirely private, the material of his own vision and feeling. His 'Imagination' was at first 'Impaired' because it was for a time overwhelmed by the public vision of the Lakes. It was eventually 'Restored' because he decisively and consciously rejected the public vision, and returned to his private memories.

The evidence bearing on the period of impairment, of subjection to the Lakeland fashion and the 'picturesque', is plentiful enough. The most direct is in his first published poems, *An Evening Walk* and *Descriptive Sketches* (*PW* I, 4–39, 42–91). The title of the former has its ancestry in Gray's *Journal* – 'In the evening I walked alone down to the lake'[50] – and in Brown's recommendation that Keswick should be viewed by moonlight. The prose summary with which it is prefaced is clearly meant to 'place' the poem in the tradition of Lake tours: 'General Sketch of the Lakes – Author's Regret of his Youth passed amongst them'. The footnotes deliberately strengthen this view of the poem. For example, a 'cascade' described in lines 71–84 has a footnote:

> The reader, who has made the tour of this country, will recognize, in this description, the features which characterize the lower waterfall in the gardens of Rydale.

The crude crosses of wall on the mountain-side in line 117 are also explained:

> These rude structures, to protect the flocks, are frequent in this country: the traveller may recollect one in Withburne, another upon Whinlatter.

Other footnotes explain local words, comment on the abundance of woodcock in winter, draw attention to a Druid monument near Broughton 'of which I do not recollect that any tour descriptive of this country makes mention' (line 171). And one of the most elaborate passages, on the 'strange apparitions' which make up local superstitions, has this reference to Clarke's *Survey*:

> See a description of an appearance of this kind in Clark's 'Survey of the Lakes', accompanied with vouchers of its veracity that may amuse the reader. (Line 187)

Less obvious, but no less certain, are some of the descriptions closely imitated from the writers on the Lakes. The poem ends, for example, with another night-piece, in the manner of Brown's verses quoted above (p. 219):

> The song of mountain streams unheard by day,
> Now hardly heard, beguiles my homeward way . . .
>
> (*An Evening Walk*, 433–4)

And the penultimate line seems to have been taken from Gray's *Journal*:

> The distant forge's swinging thump profound
> (*An Evening Walk*, line 445)

> The calmness and brightness of the evening, the roar of the waters, and the thumping of huge hammers at an iron-forge not far distant, made it a singular walk.[51]

An Evening Walk is, in fact, a very conventional poem: and the conventions which it embodied above all were those of the Lakes version of the 'picturesque', the most immediately active and fashionable version of Augustan landscape. As for *Descriptive Sketches*, it is enough to contemplate the full title to see how fully it conformed with the same conventions: 'DESCRIPTIVE SKETCHES IN VERSE TAKEN DURING A PEDESTRIAN TOUR *&c.*' Nothing could be more subtly and certainly characteristic of the fashion for the 'picturesque' than that particular use of the verb 'take' together with 'sketches'. Either with the pencil, or the brush, or with prose, or with verse, 'sketches' were then 'taken' as we 'take' photographs today. But Wordsworth himself puts the closeness of the connection beyond any doubt, for in a footnote to line 347 he says that he 'had once given to these sketches the title of Picturesque'.

Evidence of Wordsworth's subjection to the 'picturesque' fashion a little less direct, but much more detailed, is found in a remarkable notebook published in 1958 by Z. S. Fink. It turned up – naturally in America – among a collection of Wordsworth family papers, and was recognised at once as containing some very early drafts of lines by Wordsworth himself, probably from his schooldays, together with rough sketches for a poem in Latin on the Lakes in the hand of Christopher Wordsworth. There are good reasons for believing that these sketches were made late in 1790 or in 1791, just before Christopher came up to Cambridge. It was about at this time when Dorothy noticed that Christopher's

> disposition is of the same cast as William's, and his inclinations have taken the same turn . . . William has a great attachment to poetry; indeed so has Kitt, but William particularly, which is not the most likely thing to produce his advancement in the world; his pleasures are chiefly of the imagination, he is never so happy as when in a beautiful country. (*EL* 14/14)

It was also the one time at which relations between William and Christopher were close enough for them to be in regular correspondence – or, as William cautiously and no doubt more truthfully phrased it, 'almost upon terms of regular correspondence' (*EL* 10/10). There was a gap of four years in their ages, and while they had been at school together, this must have separated them widely in their interests; but four years later it would have narrowed greatly, and the close similarities in their early surroundings, above all the influence of Hawkshead, must have brought them more nearly together. Fink has shown, in his admirable commentary on Christopher's part of the notebook, that he echoes – or finds for himself – a number of thoughts also found in poems by his brother, and he refrains, with scholarly caution, from speculating on the reasons for these coincidences. He is, however, undoubtedly right in his main contention that the real importance of the notebook is that it shows how deeply both brothers were influenced by the new literature of the Lakes, and how they drew upon it for the materials of their poems and projected poems. It is, as Fink rightly claims in his title, a notable addition to our detailed knowledge of *The Early Wordsworthian Milieu*.

Christopher's notes for his poem, which was to be in praise of the Lakes, have sent Fink directly to the fashionable literature, and he has traced precisely the uses made of Gray, Brown, Gilpin, West and Clarke. Here are two extracts from the many which demonstrate this aspect of the notes:

This exordium. then descrip
tion of the Lakes, Mountains, Vallies,
Cascades. Rydal particular etc etc etc.
when read the Georgics
of a maniac.
A Tale relative to Grasmere
of ning
Hawkshead. School. Praise of ler
Windermere. Echo. A Narration of
the drowning of some person
to inquire of Mrs. T. abot this.[52]
Rydal Lowdore. King of Patter
dale. Read Guide to the Lakes
G[r]ays & Dr Browns Letters.

(from Page 2 of the *Notebook* [Fink, 77])

Autumn. Storm. ~~No. 8.15~~
~~16.20.30~~ Thompson's
Seasons p. 126. 148.88.
Gilpin
Georgics.
Mists. Beatties Min. Seasons. 139.

(from Inserted Leaf 1, *recto* [Fink, 97])

These short extracts demonstrate, not only the pressure on the 'early Wordsworthian milieu' of the literature of the Lakes fashion, but also the close relation between this fashion itself and the main stream of Augustan verse about country life and scenery, with the *Georgics* as its chief model. But besides the *Georgics*, the notebook has frequent references to other Latin poets, to Milton as well as Thomson; and Denham's *Cooper's Hill* is mentioned once, as is Dyer's *Grongar Hill*. Christopher had, in fact, laid eager and competent hands on the whole hagiology of Augustan landscape, in its more general as well as in its Lakeland version. And there is every reason to suppose that he had done so in close contact with William, and to some extent with William's help.

What is, then, specially illuminating about this little notebook, and about Fink's admirable annotations, is the demonstration that the 'impairment' of Wordsworth's imagination – we can now forget the fate of Christopher's – was achieved not by a shallow obeisance to the fashions of the age, but by an extensive study of the literature which had embodied and clarified them; and not only of that literature which was concerned chiefly with the Lakes and the 'picturesque', but also of the weightier writers, from the original Roman and the later English Augustan ages. The 'restoration' of imagination and taste, in the face of a tradition so long, so weighty, and in many ways so attractive, was no light or easy affair. It was far beyond Christopher's more ordinary powers, and in achieving it, Wordsworth defined his essential power and originality, not only within the tradition of English thought and feeling, but within that of European culture in its broadest sense.

28

Thus placed against its whole Augustan background, Wordsworth's 'restoration' of 'imagination and taste' was indeed a severe and magnificent task. It was not to be accomplished easily, or quickly: had it been easy and quick, it would not have been of much importance. And it would not have been accomplished at all, save under the strong pressure of personal need, a clear sense of the ways in which it was deficient (all the clearer because he had, for a time, shared its characteristic 'impairment'), and the urgent necessity of finding ways of thought and feeling to replace it.

This strong necessity arose, of course, not from the deficiencies of the 'picturesque' approach to Nature only, but from the whole shape of Wordsworth's life and experience. His fullest discussion of his own 'picturesque' period, and of the 'impairment' of his 'Imagination and Taste', follows immediately on his long account of his state of mind after his return from France, his growing disillusion, first with France itself, then with Godwinism, and most of all, perhaps, with the quality of human life as he had seen it lived in cities, both English and French. This crowded period of his life, from 1789 to 1793, is precisely the period of his absence from the North of England, and from the Lakes. According to Milton, a man who was to write well 'in laudable things ought himself to be a true poem, that is, a composition, and pattern of the best and honourablest things' (*Apology for Smectymnuus*). Wordsworth's life had at least one vital characteristic of 'composition'; it had a clearly marked beginning, a middle, and an end. The beginning had been in his childhood and schooldays, when he was a pure native of the Lakes and of Nature; the middle was this period of exile both from the Lakes and from Nature, save insofar as memories of her were present to him; and the end was his restoration, first to Nature, and finally to the Lakes again. It is this simplest and strongest of all the possible patterns for a large composition which governs *The Prelude* itself, and it is clearly announced at the beginning of the book which deals with the impairment and recovery of imagination:

> Long time hath Man's unhappiness and guilt
> Detain'd us; with what dismal sights beset
> For the outward view, and inwardly oppress'd
> With sorrow, disappointment, vexing thoughts,
> Confusion of opinion, zeal decay'd,
> And lastly, utter loss of hope itself,
> And things to hope for. Not with these began
> Our Song, and not with these our Song must end. (*Prel*. XI. 1–8)

Yet the beginning and the end were by no means the same; the 'Nature' of the first period was not felt in the same way as the 'Nature' of the last. It was modified, and profoundly, by the experience of the middle phase of his life:

> So neither were complacency nor peace
> Nor tender yearnings wanting for my good
> Through those distracted times; in Nature still
> Glorying, I found a counterpoise in her,
> Which, when the spirit of evil was at height
> Maintain'd for me a secret happiness;
> Her I resorted to, and lov'd so much
> I seem'd to love as much as heretofore;
> And yet this passion, fervent as it was,
> Had suffer'd change; how could there fail to be
> Some change, if merely hence, that years of life
> Were going on, and with them loss or gain
> Inevitable, sure alternative. (*Prel*. XI. 29–41)

It was within this firmly designed composition, both poetic and autobiographical, that Wordsworth set his own analysis of the 'picturesque', and of his own period of subservience to its fashion – and he showed it as belonging, not to the earlier or the later periods of his life, but to that disturbed middle period of inevitable change, of loss and gain.

The Prelude here, as it usually does, gives the fullest account of what Wordsworth had felt and thought, but it does not supply dates, and they have to be obtained from elsewhere in his writings. In this case, a reaction against the 'picturesque' can be dated with some certainty by the footnote, already mentioned, to *Descriptive Sketches*, outlining his earlier intentions for the title:

> I had once given to these sketches the title of Picturesque; but the Alps are insulted in applying to them that term. Whoever, in attempting to describe their sublime features, should confine himself to the cold rules of painting would give his reader but a very imperfect idea of those emotions which they have the irresistible power of communicating to the most impassioned imaginations. The fact is, that controuling influence, which distinguishes the Alps from all other scenery, is derived from images which disdain the pencil. Had I wished to make a picture of this scene I had thrown much less light into it. But I consulted nature and my feelings. The ideas excited by the stormy sunset I am here describing owed their sublimity to that deluge of light, or rather of fire, in which nature had wrapped the immense forms round me; any intrusion of shade, by destroying the unity of the impression, had necessarily diminished it's grandeur.
>
> (Note to line 347 [*PW* I, 62])

Two things are clear in this note. First, the reaction had come at some time before 1793, when the note was published; the duration of his subjection to the fashion, therefore, was not more than about five years, though the effects of that subjection doubtless lingered. Secondly, the main reason for Wordsworth's rejection of the 'picturesque' was central to the tradition: the ideal of *ut pictura poesis*, which had been accepted by all the Augustans from Dryden and Addison onwards, and which had been made into a reality by the enormous influence of the Italian painters on the English sense of landscape. Wordsworth goes at once to the heart of the matter, with the statement that the 'rules of painting' are 'cold', and that the most powerful influences of this landscape 'disdain the pencil'. But at this stage of his rejection, he was still unable to discern or formulate clearly any positive principles of poetic description apart from those suggested by the analogy with painting. All that he can do is to claim that, having taken the evidence of Nature and his own feelings, the chiaroscuro effects so essential to any kind of painting were here inappropriate, unfaithful to what he actually saw in the Alpine sunset. He has, however, relied on a kind of picture – a kind which Turner was to paint often enough in the following generation.

In the much longer analysis of the deficiencies of the 'picturesque' in *The Prelude*, he had progressed far beyond this central, but simple criticism. In one of his longest and subtlest passages of self-analysis, he records the double crisis of thought and feeling which ended the middle period of his life. There had been, he says, an abandonment of all the sources of his earlier strength, in favour of 'syllogistic words, / Some charm of Logic' (*Prel.* XI.82–3) and reliance upon a kind of 'Reason':

> There comes (if need be now to speak of this
> After such long detail of our mistakes)
> There comes a time when Reason, not the grand
> And simple Reason, but that humbler power
> Which carries on its no inglorious work
> By logic and minute analysis
> Is of all idols that which pleases most
> The growing mind. (*Prel.* XI.121–8)

It had been this kind of 'Reason' which had led him to base his hopes for the brotherhood of man in a better future upon the syllogisms of Godwin, and to forget for the time being those 'mysteries of passion' upon which this brotherhood and these hopes are really based (*ibid.*, 84–92). And by another effect of the same addiction to the lower kind of 'Reason', he was deprived, when he most needed it, of the ability to rejoice fully in the 'visible universe' (*ibid.*, 115–20). This lower 'Reason', in fact, led him into his Godwinian phase, and when he lost trust in Godwinism, the same 'Reason' deprived him of anything like his old, full communion with Nature, having once imposed upon him the fashion for the merely 'picturesque'.

So much has been written – much of it very well – about the Godwinian side of Wordsworth's intellectual crisis in the middle years that little remains to be said, except this, that it was for him inseparable from the emotional crisis of the 'picturesque'. It so happens that the passages in *The Prelude* which explain this inseparability are among the most difficult in the whole poem. They have often been misread, even by devoted readers, and I am afraid that they were wrongly punctuated, at a vital point, by that most devoted and best of editors Professor de Selincourt. Even Wordsworth himself seems to have found them difficult – for every writer is his own first reader, as well as often his last. In the 1850 version of the poem, he omitted about fifty lines of the earlier text, and replaced them by five lines which, though less illuminating and detailed, at least serve to make clear the essential connection between Godwinism and the 'picturesque', and help to unravel the more complex account given in 1805. These are the lines:

> What wonder, then, if, to a mind so far
> Perverted, even the visible Universe
> Fell under the dominion of a taste
> Less spiritual, with microscopic view
> Was scanned, as I had scanned the moral world? (XII.88–92)

Of the omitted lines from the earlier version, some have just been quoted; they are those defining the lower and higher kinds of 'Reason' above. Here are the others: they follow immediately on the description of the loss of faith in Man, in his history, even in poetry, which resulted from the arid addiction to Godwinian theories:

> What then remained in such eclipse? what light
> To guide or chear? The laws of things which lie
> Beyond the reach of human will or power;
> The life of nature, by the God of love
> Inspired, celestial presence ever pure;
> These left, the Soul of Youth must needs be rich,
> Whatever else be lost, and these were mine,
> Not a deaf echo merely, of the thought
> Bewilder'd recollections, solitary,
> But living sounds. Yet in despite of this,
> This feeling, which howe'er impair'd or damp'd,[53]
> Yet having been once born can never die,[54]
> 'Tis true that Earth with all her appanage
> Of elements and organs, storm and sunshine,
> With its pure forms and colours, pomp of clouds
> Rivers and mountains, objects among which
> It might be thought that no dislike or blame,
> No sense of weakness or infirmity
> Or aught amiss could possibly have come,
> Yea, even the visible universe was scann'd
> With something of a kindred spirit, fell
> Beneath the domination of a taste
> Less elevated, which did in my mind
> With its more noble influence interfere,
> Its animation and its deeper sway. (*Prel.* XI. 96–120)

The taste for the 'picturesque' was, then, a kind of corruption of his earlier response to the visible world, and it was surprising to him that so blameworthy an infirmity could have intervened in this way between him and Nature.

So far, the main advance on his earlier rejection of the 'picturesque' in the footnote to *Descriptive Sketches* is that he has clearly associated it with the lower kind of 'Reason', argumentative and syllogistic; and he has more dimly foreshadowed a description of its ill effects in obscuring Nature's 'noble influence... / Its animation and its deeper sway'. These general terms are to be caught up again in the next eddy of the argument, and gradually expanded and clarified:

> Oh! soul of Nature, excellent and fair,
> That didst rejoice with me, with whom I too
> Rejoiced, through early youth before the winds

And powerful waters, and in lights and shades
That march'd and countermarch'd about the hills
In glorious apparition, now all eye
And now all ear; but ever with the heart
Employ'd, and the majestic intellect;
Oh! Soul of Nature! that dost overflow
With passion and with life, what feeble men
Walk on this earth! how feeble have I been
When thou wert in thy strength! Nor this through stroke
Of human suffering, such as justifies
Remissness and inaptitude of mind,
But through presumption, even in pleasure pleas'd
Unworthily, disliking here, and there,
Liking, by rules of mimic art transferr'd
To things above all art. But more, for this,
Although a strong infection of the age,
Was never much my habit, giving way
To a comparison of scene with scene
Bent overmuch on superficial things,
Pampering myself with meagre novelties
Of colour or proportion, to the moods
Of time or season, to the moral power
The affections, and the spirit of the place,
Less sensible.

(138–64)

Here much that had been left undefined in the other passages on the 'picturesque' is brought to relative clarity, though there remain some touches of uncertainty in the expression. In the more negative part of the criticism, the phrase 'rules of mimic art transferr'd / To things above all art' obviously functions as Wordsworth's most concise point against the whole 'picturesque' tradition, yet its meaning is not quite beyond doubt. Does 'mimic art' mean something like 'imitative art', with the implication that painting necessarily involves a more simply representational kind of creative activity than poetry? And how far do the pejorative overtones of 'mimic' (derivative, counterfeit etc.) operate within the phrase? But there can be no doubt about the strong pejorative effect of the metaphor in 'a strong *infection* of the age', or about the general condemnation both of the fashion and of his own temporary indulgence in it. The deficiencies of the 'picturesque' are now, however, much more clearly defined by being opposed to the characteristics of a less superficial and self-indulgent approach to Nature. It is presented as a response of the whole personality, not merely that of the eye, or even of the senses:

> now all eye
> And now all ear; but ever with the heart
> Employ'd, and the majestic intellect . . .

This 'majestic intellect' is clearly another name for 'the grand and simple Reason' which had just been contrasted with 'that humbler power' which works by 'logic and minute analysis'. Wordsworth is saying that, just as the more inclusive and majestic 'intellect' would find a much broader basis for the political hopes of mankind than could be found in Godwin's tight syllogisms, so it would produce an approach to Nature much more comprehensive than the speculations of Gilpin – or of Uvedale Price and Knight. And what it would include is further defined in the last lines of the passage –

> the moral power
> The affections, and the spirit of the place –

all qualities which are clearly beyond the reach of direct expression in painting or drawing, and which therefore place a true approach to Nature quite beyond the reach of 'mimic art'.

In the next stage of his analysis, Wordsworth picks up again the notion that a true response to Nature is one involving not one of, but all, the senses:

> Nor only did the love
> Of sitting thus in judgment interrupt
> My deeper feelings, but another cause
> More subtle and less easily explain'd
> That almost seems inherent in the Creature,
> Sensuous and intellectual as he is,
> A twofold Frame of body and of mind;
> The state to which I now allude was one
> In which the eye was master of the heart,
> When that which is in every stage of life
> The most despotic of the senses gain'd
> Such strength in me as often held my mind
> In absolute dominion. Gladly here,
> Entering upon abstruser argument,
> Would I endeavour to unfold the means
> Which Nature studiously employs to thwart
> This tyranny, summons all the senses each
> To counteract the other and themselves,
> And makes them all, and the objects with which all
> Are conversant, subservient in their turn
> To the great ends of Liberty and Power.
> But this is matter for another Song . . . (164–85)

That other song, of course, was never written, but in this idea of inter- and counteraction of the senses, and of their domination, together with that of their sensory objects, by an over-riding internal power, Wordsworth happens to have made a very penetrating observation on his own poetic practice. It is exactly this ready interchangeability, as it were, of sensory powers and objects which we have noticed already in the descriptions of the 'spots of time' passage, and in *The Leech Gatherer*. In the 'variations' of the former, the 'whistling' of the hawthorn turned into 'the bleak music of that old stone wall'; in the latter, the 'roaring in the wind all night' turned into the 'roar' of 'woods and distant waters'. It would be easy to analyse a hundred other descriptions in the same way, and to show that it was entirely characteristic of Wordsworth to involve in them all the senses, and something beyond the senses – 'the moral power / The affections, and the spirit of the place'.

The whole analysis is completed by another very characteristic Wordsworthian turn of mood and mind. Having recognised all the deficiencies of the 'picturesque', and condemned himself both roundly and subtly for his indulgence in it, he allows himself nevertheless to return, in memory and imagination, to the feelings which had once been so strong. It is that turn of mind which we have seen before in his dealings with beliefs which he found attractive but untenable –

> I'd rather be
> A Pagan, suckled in a creed outworn;
> So might I, standing on this pleasant lea,
> Have glimpses that would make me less forlorn . . .

Now he gives what is almost a tribute to the 'picturesque'; and now, of course, that he has so firmly placed it, and placed it behind him, he can afford to recognise its power over himself, and perhaps over the age which it 'infected':

> Here only let me add that my delights,
> Such as they were, were sought insatiably,
> Though 'twas a transport of the outward sense,
> Not of the mind, vivid but not profound:
> Yet was I often greedy in the chace,
> And roam'd from hill to hill, from rock to rock,
> Still craving combinations of new forms,
> New pleasure, wider empire for the sight,
> Proud of its own endowments, and rejoiced
> To lay the inner faculties asleep. (*Prel.* XI. 186–95)

This passage has often been compared with some lines in *Tintern Abbey*, and they are indeed comparable. Yet for all their basic similarities, it is still more interesting to relish their differences. By a further lapse of time, Wordsworth has more firmly distanced his 'picturesque' phase, has become more careful to condemn it, and much more subtle in his analysis of the reasons for which it deserved to be condemned. In the passage from *Tintern Abbey* he speaks less of these things, more – and more freshly – of the positive side of his indulgence:

> like a roe
> I bounded o'er the mountains, by the sides
> Of the deep rivers, and the lonely streams,
> Wherever nature led: more like a man
> Flying from something that he dreads than one
> Who sought the thing he loved. For nature then
> (The coarser pleasures of my boyish days,
> And their glad animal movements all gone by)
> To me was all in all. – I cannot paint
> What then I was. The sounding cataract
> Haunted me like a passion: the tall rock,
> The mountain, and the deep and gloomy wood,
> Their colours and their forms, were then to me
> An appetite; a feeling and a love,
> That had no need of a remoter charm,
> By thought supplied, nor any interest
> Unborrowed from the eye. – That time is past,
> And all its aching joys are now no more,
> And all its dizzy raptures. (67–85 [*PW* II, 261])

One significant change between the two passages deserves comment. In the earlier one he feels himself to have been almost hunted, like a roe bounding over the mountains, 'like a man / flying from something that he dreads'. In the later, he has become himself the hunter, 'greedy in the chace'. And this second image, it so happens, is one which had been a favourite with Gilpin in all his writings on the 'picturesque'. As early as the *Dialogue on Stow* it is quite elaborately deployed: 'as I had my Time pretty much to myself, I spent it in a great measure in hunting after beautiful Objects' (p. 241). More often, it is glancingly embodied in phrases like 'the pursuit of the picturesque' or in this phrase from the *Observations on the River Wye* (which we know Wordsworth to have read): 'The following little work proposes a new object of pursuit' (p. 1). But on at least one occasion he develops the image – even over-develops it. This is in his *Three Essays*, published in 1792:

> The first source of amusement to the picturesque traveller, is the *pursuit* of his object – the expectation of new scenes continually opening, and arising to his view . . . Every distant horizon promises something new; and with this pleasing expectation we follow nature through all her walks. We pursue her from hill to dale; and hunt after those various beauties, with which she every where abounds.

The pleasures of the chase are universal. A hare started before dogs is enough to set a whole country in an uproar . . .

And shall we suppose it a greater pleasure to the sportsman to pursue a trivial animal, than it is to the man of taste to pursue the beauties of nature? (pp. 47–8)

There is, so far as I know, no direct evidence that Wordsworth had read the *Three Essays*. But they were published just at the time when he was most involved in the 'picturesque', and they were immediately popular. If he had even glanced at the book, it is likely enough that this image of the 'chase' for the 'picturesque' would have made some mark on his memory, even if an unconscious one. For the passage is conspicuous in the even, flat tenor of Gilpin's agreeably undistinguished prose. A few years after *The Prelude* was written, it caught the roughly perceptive eye of William Combe, whose *Tour of Doctor Syntax, in Search of the Picturesque* was an immensely popular skit on Gilpin's *Tours*. In Canto 13, Dr Syntax thus replies to an invitation to join in a hunt:

Your sport, my Lord, I cannot take,
For I must go and hunt a lake;
And while you chase the flying deer,
I must fly off to *Windermere*.
Instead of hallowing to a fox,
I must catch echoes from the rocks.
With curious eye and active scent,
I on the picturesque am bent.
This is my game; I must pursue it,
And make it where I cannot view it.[55]

But it matters little whether Wordsworth had picked up this hunting image from Gilpin himself. However he had come by it, it expresses with authentic vividness the self-consciousness and fashionable urgency with which he had allowed himself to follow the trend of the age, and so deprived himself of real contact with Nature at the very time when he most needed it.

What he had come to understand most clearly, and above all in this passage of self-analysis, was the more negative side of his intellectual and moral crisis. It is always easier to define what is lacking than to suggest what should be put in its place. There is a real sense in which most of his greatest poetry is a continued, and ever varied attempt to express the more positive side of his criticism of the 'picturesque' – to show more fully what it omitted, how it distorted, by putting in its place a much deeper feeling for Nature and its relation with human perception. To some extent, this attempt was never quite completed. The highest kind of originality is always liable to this partial incompleteness of realisation and expression, perhaps because no exploration can ever be quite completed, and the sense, however dim, of what remains to be explored makes all combinations of words fall a little short of what is aimed at. All that is possible is a series of sketches and approximations, none definitive, but taken together very nearly so. We shall return to some of the more central of these attempts to express the processes by which imagination was eventually 'Restored' to him, but for the moment we may pause to see in its whole perspective his account of the manner in which it had been 'Impaired', and not only for him.

It has been repeatedly stressed that the fashion for the 'picturesque', as Wordsworth encountered it above all in the literature on the Lakes, on his own native region, was far from being mere local topography. It was the latest development of a movement of feeling, perception and thought which ran powerfully through the whole of eighteenth-century culture, and for powerful reasons. The growth of urban centres, at a suddenly increased rate, had revived, naturally enough, the imaginative and social attitudes of the original Augustan period in Rome itself. Virgil and Horace appealed so strongly to Englishmen, not only because of their merits, not only because they were the basis of all education, but even more because they 'spoke to their condition', expressed much of what they felt, reflected the same problems. But what Wordsworth had to say, and because he had experienced it himself, was that this revived Augustan attitude to Nature was a poor, thin thing. It would not solve the problems of an ever-increasing urbanisation, because it was shallow, self-conscious, self-regarding, and served only to cut men off from the real sources of power in man's relation with the universe. The Sabine farm of Horace, the villas of Virgil, Claude, Poussin and Salvator Rosa, Thomson and Dyer, Gray and Gilpin – none of these, nor all taken together, were of any avail. And not only useless, but high obstacles. In modern terms, he was saying that the family party sitting in folding chairs round their folding table within a few feet of their car, the collection of holiday snapshots, the transparency, the film, the bus tour through the Lakes or the Alps, the beaches of the Costa Brava – that none of these, nor all taken together, and much more besides of the same kind, amount to anything at all in terms of restoring that deeper relation with Nature which has been ever more grossly impaired since Wordsworth's day by the unchecked and constantly accelerating lapse into urbanism, with its steady erosion of the quality of life. Not only do they contribute nothing to this restoration, but they are insurmountable obstacles in its path.

29

This long detour through a large tract of eighteenth-century landscape was suggested, in the first place, by the necessity to explore Wordsworth's apparently idiosyncratic use of the word *naked*, and to discover how far it was peculiar to him, or if shared with others, with what kinds of thought and feeling it was associated. In the course of the detour, the word has cropped up often enough, but it will be as well to underline more systematically the main findings about its broader uses before we return to a more detailed survey of the Wordsworthian involutes in which it plays so central a part.

That it should be a word of central importance will now seem much less surprising, for it has turned out that in the 1790s a very pervasive and powerful fashion in landscape had been based upon those qualities which were obviously opposite to nakedness and bareness. The 'picturesque' was essentially everything in scenery that was rough, broken, detailed, varied. These were the qualities that called for the quick, often graceful calligraphy of the pencil, and caught the play of light and shade. In rejecting the 'picturesque', and in selecting bare and naked scenes, Wordsworth was of course running counter to this predominant fashion. But he was doing so, not only for the more deliberate reasons just examined, but also – and much more deeply – because his own early and formative experiences of Nature had been with the bare, rocky, sparse landscape of the mountains. His rejection of the 'picturesque', in fact, was predetermined at Hawkshead. And it led to the revival of his Hawkshead experiences, with a new richness of power and association.

These experiences dominate the early drafting of *The Prelude*, and the landscape against which they were placed is clearly shown by this summary:

Snaring woodcock:	Cliffs, smooth Hollows, open turf, heights, silent . . . turf (I.309–32)
Raven's nest:	lonesome peaks, mountains, slippery rock, naked crag, perilous ridge (*Ibid.* 333–50)
Stolen boat:	rocky Cave, hoary mountains, rocky Steep, craggy ridge, craggy Steep, huge Cliff (twice) (*Ibid.* 452–89)
Skating:	precipices, icy crag, solitary Cliffs (*Ibid.* 452–89)
'Spots of time':	bare Common, naked Pool, hills, Beacon on the summit, naked Pool, Beacon on the lonely Eminence, naked pool, dreary crags, melancholy Beacon . . .
	crag, an Eminence, highest summit, naked wall, whistling hawthorn, crag, blasted tree, old stone wall (XI.258–389)

With the exception of the 'blasted tree', sole relic of the manner of Salvator Rosa this was a landscape not merely unpicturesque, but anti-picturesque. It was stronger, more pungent, sparse and broadly outlined.

In the more reflective passages which explore the deeper implications of these experiences, it is evident that Wordsworth was profoundly concerned with one of the other pervasive conceptions of the eighteenth century: the distinction between the two qualities usually called the Sublime and the Beautiful, and the possible relationships between them. The names varied from one writer to another, especially for the Sublime, which might be 'the great', 'grandeur', but the broad contrast remained the same. Beauty was taken to be pleasing in the obvious, the common manner, while the Sublime was taken to be a stronger, more complex feeling, in which fear played a large though paradoxical part. One of the earliest expressions of this feeling is said to be in an account by a very minor seventeenth-century poet, John Dennis, of his feelings among the Alps:

> . . . the impending Rock that hung over us, the dreadful Depth of the Precipice, and the Torrent that roar'd at the bottom, gave us such a view as was altogether new and amazing. On the other side of that Torrent, was a Mountain that equall'd ours . . . Its craggy Clifts, which we half discern'd thro the misty gloom of the clouds that surrounded them, sometimes gave us a horrid Prospect. And sometimes its face appear'd Smooth and Beautiful . . . In the very same place Nature was seen Severe and Wanton. In the mean time we walk'd upon the very brink, in a litteral sense, of Destruction . . . The sense of all this produc'd different motions in me, *viz.* a delightful Horrour, a terrible Joy, and at the same time, that I was infinitely pleas'd, I trembled.[56]

But these feelings were hardly a discovery of Dennis': they were already in the air, and they soon received a further impulse from a renewed interest in Longinus' treatise *On the Sublime.* Addison, in his *Essay on the Pleasures of the Imagination* in 1712, formulated the three sources of imaginative pleasure as 'the Sight of what is *Great*, *Uncommon*, or *Beautiful*'.[57] Of these, the second tended (though slowly) to drop out, leaving the other two in a more or less antithetical relationship, and this was given a new clarity and popularity by the publication, apparently in 1757, of Burke's *Philosophical Enquiry into the Origin of our Ideas of the Sublime and Beautiful.* In the later part of the century, in the writings on the 'picturesque', the Lake *Guides*, and Wordsworth himself, there are many references to 'the sublime' and 'the beautiful', either under those names, or with slight variations.

The most important of these variations of nomenclature arise from Burke's systematic attempt to explain sublimity and beauty in terms of human feelings. The former, he believed, is derived from 'Whatever is fitted in any sort to excite the ideas of pain, and danger, that is to say, whatever is in any sort terrible, or is conversant about terrible objects, or operates in a manner analogous to terror'. Beauty, on the other hand, is 'that quality or those qualities in bodies by which they cause love, or some passion similar to it'. Under the pervasive influence of these formulations, 'sublimity' was replaceable not only by the older words such as 'grand', 'great', 'grandeur', but also by 'horror', 'terror', 'fear', and so on; while 'beauty' was – at any rate for those who had read Burke with any attention – meaningfully synonymous with such words as 'lovely', 'loveliness'. It is, of course, a simple variation on this set of antonyms which provided the organist of Newcastle with his memorable description of Keswick, '*Beauty lying in the lap of Horrour!*' And it is from the same pervasive set of ideas that the writers of the *Guides* drew many of their descriptions. Thus one of the founding fathers of the fashion for the Lakes, Brown, had described Derwentwater as 'beauty, horror and immensity united'. Gray had found that view worth a thousand pounds as a picture to be 'the sweetest in point of pastoral beauty', while 'the rest are in sublimer style'. West had expected his 'genteel parties' to benefit morally by the 'Exhibition of sublime and beautiful objects'. Gilpin – to quote from the Lakes *Tour* alone – has references of this kind:

As we seek among the wild works of nature for the sublime, we seek here for the beautiful.

About Levens, a seat of the earl of Suffolk, there is a happy combination of every thing that is *lovely* and *great* in landscape.

In this part grandeur gives way to beauty.[58]

And Gilpin also refers to, and quotes from, Burke's *Enquiry*.

Despite this abundance of usage, none of the other *Guides* to the Lakes (relative to their size) uses this pair of words as often as Wordsworth's:

. . . the sublime and beautiful region (p. 54)

. . . from the circumference to the centre, that is, from the sea or plain country to the mountain stations specified, there is – in the several ridges that enclose these vales, and divide them from each other, I mean in the forms and surfaces, first of the swelling grounds, next of the hills and rocks, and lastly of the mountains – an ascent of almost regular gradation, from elegance and richness, to their highest point of grandeur and sublimity. (p. 58)

. . . the influences of light and shadow upon the sublime or beautiful features of the landscape (p. 59)

. . . the house does not deign to look upon the natural beauty or the sublimity which its situation almost unavoidably commands. (p. 101)

Now, every one knows that from amenity and beauty the transition to sublimity is easy and favourable, but the reverse is not so; for, after the faculties have been elevated, they are indisposed to humbler excitement. (p. 132)

Hence on the score even of sublimity, the superiority of the Alps is by no means so great as might hastily be inferred; and, as to the *beauty* of the lower regions . . . (p. 137)

. . . lamenting to see a decaying and uncomfortable dwelling in a place where sublimity and beauty seemed to contend with each other. (p. 156)

These are the passages in which 'beauty' and 'sublimity' are mentioned closely together, and in opposition to one another. There are many other passages in which they are more loosely contrasted, or handled separately, notably in those definitions of Sublimity and Beauty in relation to Nature's early and late dealings with the face of the earth already quoted.

But though this pair of qualities is so often mentioned in the *Guide*, it dominates the main reflective passages of *The Prelude* even more, and there takes on the character of a constantly recurring and eddying argument, leading gradually to a striking climax. At the outset in Book I, the effect of the crucial experiences of childhood is expressed in variations of the two qualities. They are, indeed, those which formally open the first passage of reflection at line 305:

Fair seed-time had my soul, and I grew up
Foster'd alike by beauty and by fear . . .

There follow the three scenes against the landscape of rocks and crags – snaring woodcock, robbing the raven's nest, and stealing the boat. And in all of them, both as experiences, and in the reflections which follow them, it is above all the element of fear, terror even, which is emphasised:

Ah me! that all
The terrors, all the early miseries,
Regrets, vexations, lassitudes, that all
The thoughts and feelings which have been infus'd
Into my mind, should ever have made up
The calm existence that is mine when I
Am worthy of myself! . . .
But I believe
That Nature, oftentimes, when she would frame
A favor'd Being, from his earliest dawn
Of infancy doth open out the clouds,
As at the touch of lightning, seeking him
With gentlest visitation; not the less,
Though haply aiming at the self-same end,
Does it delight her sometimes to employ
Severer interventions, ministry
More palpable, and so she dealt with me. (355–71)

Wisdom and Spirit of the universe!
. . . not in vain,

By day or star-light thus from my first dawn
Of Childhood didst Thou intertwine for me
The passions that build up our human Soul,
Not with the mean and vulgar works of Man,
But with high objects, with enduring things,
With life and nature, purifying thus
The elements of feeling and of thought,
And sanctifying, by such discipline,
Both pain and fear, until we recognize
A grandeur in the beatings of the heart. (428–51)

In these three experiences, and in the reflections on them, the dominant feeling is that of fear, the main effect sublimity, and the landscape of naked rock. The point of balance, as it were – the point at which beauty and fear are nearly equal – comes in the description of skating (lines 465–89). It begins in the rocky landscape, the crags tinkling with ice, with 'an alien sound' from the hills 'Of melancholy, not unnoticed'. It ends with that sudden change of mood, when the skater stopped short, and 'the solitary Cliffs / Wheeled by me . . .', moving as the 'huge Cliff' had done in the stealing of the boat. But this time their motion unlike that of the 'huge Cliff' striding after him, grew 'feebler and feebler' – 'Till all was tranquil as a dreamless sleep'.

It is at once a characteristic and a great advantage of an argument conducted partly, or largely, through involutes that the links between one set of thoughts and feelings and another can be expressed as well – often better – by a transitional involute as by an abstract and apparently logical proposition. From this point onwards, Book I turns to the exploration of beauty, rather than fear, though still continuing to hold the two passions in their traditional pairing. Thus the immediate reflection of the skating description exactly matches the content of the imagery, by putting the more positive emotions more emphatically than the negative:

Ye Presences of Nature, in the sky
Or on the earth! Ye Visions of the hills!
And Souls of lonely places! can I think
A vulgar hope was yours when Ye employ'd
Such ministry, when Ye through many a year
Haunting me thus among my boyish sports,
On caves and trees, upon the woods and hills,
Impress'd upon all forms the characters
Of danger or desire, and thus did make
The surface of the universal earth
With triumph, and delight, and hope, and fear,
Work like a sea? (490–501)

. . . even then,
A Child, I held unconscious intercourse
With the eternal Beauty, drinking in

A pure organic pleasure from the lines
Of curling mist, or from the level plain
Of waters colour'd by the steady clouds. (588–93)
. . . and thus
By the impressive discipline of fear,
By pleasure and repeated happiness,
So frequently repeated, and by force
Of obscure feelings representative
Of joys that were forgotten, these same scenes,
So beauteous and majestic in themselves,
Though yet the day was distant, did at length
Become habitually dear, and all
Their hues and forms were by invisible links
Allied to the affections. (630–40)

In the second book of *The Prelude*, this change of emphasis continues, and both the descriptions and the reflective passages develop more amply the mood of tranquillity, as of a 'dreamless sleep', with which the skating passage had ended. The phrase 'discipline of fear' now gives place to 'the discipline of love' (II.251), in a passage on the relations between an infant and his mother. A little later, there is a brief reminder of the kind of experience recorded in Book I, but its purpose here is rather to reinforce the significance of the gentler kind of 'discipline', in which the scenery of rocks is replaced by one of tranquillity:

. . . and I would stand,
Beneath some rock, listening to sounds that are
The ghostly language of the ancient earth,
Or make their dim abode in distant winds.
Thence did I drink the visionary power.
I deem not profitless those fleeting moods
Of shadowy exultation: not for this,
That they are kindred to our purer mind
And intellectual life; but that the soul,
Remembering how she felt, but what she felt
Remembering not, retains an obscure sense
Of possible sublimity, to which
With growing faculties she doth aspire,
With faculties still growing, feeling still
That whatsoever point they gain, they still
Have something to pursue.
And not alone,
In grandeur and in tumult, but no less
In tranquil scenes . . . (II.326–43)

Throughout the middle books, those which describe the period of

Wordsworth's exile from Nature, from the Lakes and almost from himself, references to beauty and sublimity, love and fear, are rare and almost incidental; yet this central theme is never quite dropped. In Book V, for example, the description of the drowned man on Esthwaite has an interesting variation on the theme of beauty and horror:

> At length, the dead Man, 'mid that beauteous scene
> Of trees and hills and water, bolt upright
> Rose with his ghastly face; a spectre shape
> Of terror even! and yet no vulgar fear . . .
> Possess'd me (V.470–5)

The last of the books before the period of exile is the sixth, and it ends with the clearest of all Wordsworth's reflections on the two disciplines, the one of fear, the other of love. It summarises their effects upon his mind and feelings in childhood and youth, and prepares the way for their further development after the period of 'impairment', as part of the 'restoration' of imagination, and does so with an exactness of view, both backwards and forwards, which is more typical of *The Prelude* than is often supposed: it is easy enough for the casual reader to follow the exposition so far as it is simply chronological, less easy to do full justice to the coherence of the more reflective and argumentative structure. Here Wordsworth remarks, with entire accuracy, that in this first period of his development, the discipline of fear, with its feelings of sublimity and grandeur, had been more powerful in its effects upon him than the opposite discipline of love and tenderness; but at the same time he predicts, as it were, that the larger development yet to come will be with the latter:

> Finally whate'er
> I saw, or heard, or felt, was but a stream
> That flow'd into a kindred stream, a gale
> That help'd me forwards, did administer
> To grandeur and to tenderness, to the one
> Directly, but to tender thoughts by means
> Less often instantaneous in effect;
> Conducted me to these along a path
> Which in the main was more circuitous (VI.672–80)

In writing of the middle period of his exile, in London and in France, this theme naturally recedes, though it does not quite disappear. Two notable passages describe the persistence of his earlier feelings towards grandeur and beauty with some elaboration. In the first, they enter into his reflections as a counterpoise to the 'blank confusion' of London:

> Attention comes,
> And comprehensiveness and memory,

From early converse with the works of God
Among all regions; chiefly where appear
Most obviously simplicity and power.
By influence habitual to the mind
The mountain's outline and its steady form
Gives a pure grandeur, and its presence shapes
The measure and the prospect of the soul
To majesty; such virtue have the forms
Perennial of the ancient hills; nor less
The changeful language of their countenances
Gives movement to the thoughts, and multitude,
With order and relation . . .
This did I feel in that vast receptacle.
The Spirit of Nature was upon me here;
The Soul of Beauty and enduring life
Was present as a habit, and diffused,
Through meagre lines and colours, and the press
Of self-destroying, transitory things
Composure and ennobling Harmony. (VII.716–40)

These lines, and by no accidental chance of meandering composition, conclude the book called *Residence in London*. They serve to explain both his sense of the utter confusion, the annihilating vacuity of life as he had seen it there, and also his own capacity to observe it and measure it without being in danger of surrender to its apparent power and variety of impact.

The second of these passages from the middle years is in Book VIII, *Retrospect*, where, with a characteristically eddying movement, with some complexity of sequence, yet no confusion, his whole development in the earlier part of his life is reviewed, with an emphasis which looks forward to what is still to come. In these lines, he is completing a review of all that had been said more largely in Book IV about the influence of a growing interest in mankind, as well as in Nature, on his thoughts and feelings. Now he notes that this influence was far from being 'pre-eminent', for his concern with Man was still subordinate to Nature:

. . . her awful forms
And viewless agencies: a passion, she!
A rapture often, and immediate joy,
Ever at hand; he distant, but a grace
Occasional, an accidental thought,
His hour being not yet come. Far less had then
The inferior Creatures, beast or bird, attun'd
My spirit to that gentleness of love,
Won from me those minute observances
Of tenderness, which I may number now

With my first blessings. Nevertheless, on these
The light of beauty did not fall in vain,
Or grandeur circumfuse them to no end. (VIII.485–97)

Here, as in the passage from Book V quoted above, he is looking backward, but also forward, and to that period of recovery, of restoration, which followed on his experiences in France, and those in relation to France after his return.

A part, and a vital part, of this recovery was his emergence from the influence of the 'picturesque' in his attitude to Nature. But another part, no less vital, was played by his more mature concern for Man, as well as for Nature. Here too, as in his attitude to words and to the workings of the senses, he was profoundly aware of a mutuality, a reciprocity of influence. It was not merely that he himself took a greater interest in human beings: it was also that they much more profoundly influenced him. In the last book, the *Conclusion* of *The Prelude*, there is the final attempt to express the positive side of the relationship with Nature which he had recovered; and it is, at the same time, a final comment on the relations between the sublime and the beautiful – a comment which decisively reverses the emphasis given to each of them in his earlier days:

To fear and love,
To love as first and chief, for there fear ends,
Be this ascribed; to early intercourse,
In presence of sublime and lovely Forms,
With the adverse principles of pain and joy,
Evil as one is rashly named by those
Who know not what they say. (XIII.143–9)

This is a remarkable formulation of the issues. Remarkable for its clarity and comprehensiveness, for in thus associating the 'sublime' with the 'principle of pain' and 'beauty' with that of 'love', Wordsworth was exactly and concisely summarising the whole tradition of a century's thought and feeling on these qualities and their association: Dennis on the Alps, Brown's *Letter* on Keswick, the *Guides* to the Lakes, the Newcastle organist, and Burke himself. And though he is expressing the conclusion that 'beauty' and 'love' are, after all, more fundamental to human life than 'pain' and the 'sublime', he does not disown his own past, of rocks and naked crags, the discipline of fear. So far as this brief formulation can achieve it, he disowns only the traditional antithesis between the two qualities in experience and the passions on which they rest:

From love, for here
Do we begin and end, all grandeur comes,
All truth and beauty, from pervading love,
That gone, we are as dust. (149–52)

There is, he goes on, one kind of love, real enough, like that between a lamb and its mother, or that between human lovers; but this is not all:

> . . . thou call'st this love
> And so it is, but there is higher love
> Than this, a love that comes into the heart
> With awe and a diffusive sentiment;
> Thy love is human merely; this proceeds
> More from the brooding Soul, and is divine. (160–5)

This higher, more intellectual love cannot exist without Imagination, which is 'clearest insight, amplitude of mind / And reason in her most exalted mood'. And this highest of all human qualities must of necessity be a lonely, indeed a solitary achievement:

> . . . Here must thou be, O Man!
> Strength to thyself; no Helper hast thou here;
> Here keepest thou thy individual state:
> No other can divide with thee this work,
> No secondary hand can intervene
> To fashion this ability; 'tis thine,
> The prime and vital principle is thine
> In the recesses of thy nature, far
> From any reach of outward fellowship,
> Else 'tis not thine at all. But joy to him,
> Oh! joy to him who here hath sown, hath laid
> Here the foundations for his future years!
> For all that friendship, all that love can do,
> All that a darling countenance can look
> Or dear voice utter to complete the man,
> Perfect him, made imperfect in himself,
> All shall be his: and he whose soul hath risen
> Up to the height of feeling intellect
> Shall want no humbler tenderness, his heart
> Be tender as a nursing Mother's heart;
> Of female softness shall his life be full,
> Of little loves and delicate desires,
> Mild interests and gentlest sympathies. (188–210)

There follows, with complete appropriateness, the last and fullest of his tributes to his sister Dorothy, and her influence upon him. But it is something more than that. It is also a final statement on his own history, and of his relations with fear and love. Indeed it is something even more than that: for it turns from abstract statement into an 'involute', within which Wordsworth sees into the nature of his early days, perceives himself as a rock among rocks, but one now softened from fear and grandeur into a symbol of love and beauty. It is a passage which shows both his own power to control a large design, an eddying mass of related, yet separate ideas, and also the inherent power of the involute as a form of expression in which the concrete and the abstract can find a fusion of fuller consciousness than either might reach by itself:

> Child of my Parents! Sister of my Soul!
> Elsewhere have strains of gratitude been breath'd
> To thee for all the early tenderness
> Which I from thee imbibed. And true it is
> That later seasons owed to thee no less;
> For, spite of thy sweet influence and the touch
> Of other kindred hands that open'd out
> The springs of tender thought in infancy,
> And spite of all which singly I had watch'd
> Of elegance, and each minuter charm
> In nature and in life, still to the last
> Even to the very going out of youth,
> The period which our Story now hath reach'd,
> I too exclusively esteem'd that love,
> And sought that beauty, which, as Milton sings,
> Hath terror in it. Thou didst soften down
> This over-sternness; but for thee, sweet Friend,
> My soul, too reckless of mild grace, had been
> Far longer what by Nature it was fram'd,
> Longer retain'd its countenance severe,
> A rock with torrents roaring, with the clouds
> Familiar, and a favorite of the Stars;
> But thou didst plant its crevices with flowers,
> Hang it with shrubs that twinkle in the breeze,
> And teach the little birds to build their nests
> And warble in its chambers. (211–36)

If it were to be regarded merely with the eye, it would seem that the aboriginal crag had been made picturesque, very much as Gilpin would have had it. But the difference, a vital one, depends upon the fact that this is not merely a visual impression. Flowers, shrubs and birds are here, not for decoration, not to exercise the eye or the calligraphic pencil. They are here as symbols of a group of feelings which have transformed the rock, and all feelings for the rock.

Yet despite this profound transformation, there remained always something craggy about Wordsworth, even about his countenance. Haydon – not a bad authority on it, for he was a painter of sorts – recorded in his *Diary*: 'His head is like as if it was carved out of a mossy rock, created before the flood.'[59] And Henry Taylor, a close friend of Wordsworth's in his later years, wrote in his *Autobiography*: 'It was a rough grey face, full of rifts and clefts and fissures, out of which, someone said, you might expect lichens to grow.'[60] It was not even the head and face alone that reminded people of rocks: there was something in the voice, above all the poetic voice, which came close to 'The ghostly language of the ancient earth' (*Prel.* II.328). Canon Rawnsley, in his collection *Reminiscences of Wordsworth among the Peasantry* reports one of his informants as saying:

> And he hed a way of standin' quite still by t' rock there in t' path under Rydal, and fwoaks could hear sounds like a wild beast coming frat' rocks, and childer were scared fit to be dëad a'most.[61]

There is something permanently and deeply true in these impressions. Yet if it should ever happen that the profile of a crag or cliff should be found to resemble Wordsworth's head (not improbably, for he saw something very like it himself on the cliffs near Whitby), and if – by a much stronger stretch of the imagination – this rocky visage should, by some more than Aeolian freak, begin to give utterance in a roaring, gusty fashion to *The Prelude*, one can be quite sure that the wonder of it would not last much beyond nine days. Television would make much of it at first. A film would be made, mainly about the affair with Annette. But the mystery would remain, like so much in this poet's genius, 'too far above the snowline', in a naked landscape of rocks and ice, beyond the ken of all but a very few eyes and minds.

PART V

Ecolect and inmatecy

30

There is a sense in which all that Wordsworth wrote, after his return to his native region in 1799, was an attempt, a long series of attempts, to explain more fully the positive side of his reunion with Nature, once the fashion for the picturesque had been overcome. In one way and another, he tried to describe the essence of that 'naked' landscape which is the characteristic scene of his experiences, a landscape freed from prettiness and decoration of a painterly and scenic kind, sparsely inhabited by prophetic personages, mingling the 'fear' of his early experiences with the 'love' of his recovery, peopling the rocks and barren moors with softer symbols and 'the spirit of the place'. But this new strength of 'love' also brought about a profound change in the quality of his life. And this in turn led to a notable change in his poetry. Until this time, he had been, at least since the death of his father and the break-up of the family, a lonely man and a wanderer, with no fixed home or residence. From this time onwards, he recovered both his kith and kin, and lodged himself in the house where he was to live for many years, and the place where he spent the rest of his life. This end to his loneliness and wandering was the more vital to him because he had, for nearly ten years, been unfixed and solitary.

It is likely enough that none of the great human achievements, in the arts or the sciences or in practical life, are ever purely individual. Though the individual must be the executant, he owes much to his environment, and especially to those who are most closely connected with his great work, whatever it may be. Thus while Shakespeare beyond question wrote the plays and poems attributed to him, he certainly owed very much to his friends – who were many – and most of all to his partners and fellow-actors in the theatre where he spent his working life. The plays are, in this sense, not merely his: they are a product of the Globe, and perhaps of the Blackfriars too. Wordsworth's circle was smaller, and correspondingly more intensely linked with his work. It was, in the crucial period of his writing, made up of his sister, his cousin Mary – later his wife – and Coleridge. These were the 'inmates' of Grasmere while the great poetry was being written, the first two steadily, Coleridge more fitfully, but always felt to be a gap in the household while he was absent. The contribution of the two women to the actual composition of the poems was partly, and most visibly, in the fair copies which they made. Not only are these now the basic manuscript records: their existence reminds us of the extent to which the labours of Dorothy and Mary enabled Wordsworth to persist in his custom of composing and revising orally, as well as on paper – a habit of composition which contributed enormously to his strength of phrasing and his control of long and complex periods in verse. As for the less tangible contributions of the household to the poetry itself, and to the man himself, they are acknowledged in *The Prelude*, and not merely by way of expressing gratitude. Each of the three 'inmates' of Grasmere was used by Wordsworth as it were thematically, especially in the later part of the poem. Each of them had a role to play as a standard of comparison, by which he clarified for himself his own development, and explained it more clearly. The whole poem, of course, is addressed to Coleridge; and at several crucial points the comparison between his own life and Coleridge's is the essence of its spiritual exploration. His special debt to Dorothy is expressed more than once, but most weightily in the passage just quoted, bearing on his final release from the craggy mood of his earlier years. Mary too has her obvious acknowledgements. But I believe that some readings of *The Prelude* itself, and of other poems related to it, do much less than justice to her role in his life at this time. Both she herself, and his marriage with her, have been pushed into a kind of weak domestic background, partly by the vulgar interest in the affair with Annette, but even more by the deeper reticences which accompany any real marriage.

So far were these reticences taken that they have made possible a total misunderstanding of the unfinished, but still illuminating, set of drafts in which Wordsworth tried to define what was most positive in his return to Nature, in terms of a comparison between himself, Dorothy and Mary. These writings, all closely associated with the poem published in the 1800 *Lyrical Ballads* as *Nutting*, were written in Germany in 1798, in that formative period when *The Prelude* was taking its first shape, and were at that time intended to be part of it. It deserves to be noted that, as early as this, Wordsworth was preparing to turn from the loneliness of his youthful experiences, with their inevitable appearance of self-centredness, if not of egotism, to a mode of thought and feeling and writing which was in essence dramatic, for it involved the deliberate contrasting of one character with another, and of conflicting impulses within yet another. And so far from being self-centred or egotistical, the main tenor of these drafts is one of self-criticism – the note which, indeed, dominates the whole of his account of his own subjection to the 'picturesque'.

Unfinished as they are, the drafts nevertheless point unequivocally to a simple dramatic plan. Two women are involved, one who, in the excitement of the chase, has broken some hazel boughs in her efforts to pluck their nuts, and the other so gentle that 'the unnoticed heath . . . Lives in her love'. And there is Wordsworth himself, as a boy who had once broken hazel boughs for the same reason, with the same savagery, and who had instantly repented of it. The exordium was to have been this description of the first 'maiden':

> Ah! what a crash was that! with gentle hand
> Touch these fair hazels – My beloved Friend!
> Though 'tis a sight invisible to thee
> From such rude intercourse the woods all shrink
> As at the blowing of Astolpho's horn.
> Thou, Lucy, art a maiden 'inland bred'
> And thou hast known 'some nurture'; but in truth
> If I had met thee here with that keen look
> Half cruel in its eagerness, those cheeks
> Thus [ ] flushed with a tempestuous bloom,
> I might have almost deem'd that I had pass'd
> A houseless being in a human shape,
> An enemy of nature, hither sent
> From regions far beyond the Indian hills –
> Come rest on this light bed of purple heath,
> And let me see thee sink into a dream
> Of gentle thoughts, protracted till thine eye
> Be calm as water when the winds are gone
> And no one can tell whither. – See those stems
> Both stretch'd along the ground, two brother trees
> That in one instant at the touch of spring
> Put forth their tender leaves, and through nine years,
> In the dark nights, have both together heard
> The driving storm – Well! blessed be the powers
> That teach philosophy and good desires
> In this their still Lyceum, hand of mine
> Wrought not this ruin – I am guiltless here –
> For, seeing little worthy or sublime
> In what we blazon with the pompous names
> Of power and action I was early taught
> To look with feelings of fraternal love
> Upon those unassuming things which hold
> A silent station in this beauteous world. (*PW* II, 504–5)

In the drafts, this passage is followed by an address to the powers of Nature, 'Ye gentle Stewards of a Poet's time!', which was later woven into the proem to Book XI of *The Prelude*. And this, after a score of lines, leads into the poem published under the title *Nutting*, about which Wordsworth told Miss Fenwick: 'Written in Germany; intended as part of a poem on my own life, but struck out as not being wanted there'. It tells of his own experience as an over-eager gatherer of hazel-nuts. At first, his mood had been one of joyful holiday, in clothes so ragged that even the risks of nutting could damage them no further, and he had gone to one special 'dear nook', where 'not a broken bough / Drooped with its withered leaves, ungracious sign / Of devastation'. There he had rested, his cheek on a mossy stone, listening to the murmuring stream –

> In that sweet mood when pleasure loves to pay
> Tribute to ease; and, of its joy secure,
> The heart luxuriates with indifferent things,
> Wasting its kindliness on stocks and stones,
> And on the vacant air. Then up I rose,
> And dragged to earth both branch and bough, with crash
> Of merciless ravage: and the shady nook
> Of hazels, and the green and mossy bower,
> Deformed and sullied, patiently gave up
> Their quiet being: and unless I now
> Confound my present feelings with the past,
> Ere from the mutilated bower I turned
> Exulting, rich beyond the wealth of kings,
> I felt a sense of pain when I beheld
> The silent trees, and saw the intruding sky. –
> Then, dearest Maiden, move along these shades
> In gentleness of heart; with gentle hand
> Touch – for there is a spirit in the woods. (39–56 [*PW* II, 212])

So far, the drafts are clearly aiming at a poem in which two 'violators of Nature' are described. One of them is Wordsworth himself as a boy: the other is the maiden addressed as 'Lucy'. And the first sequence ends with a record of the feeling of penitence which had come upon him after the act of violence, and an exhortation to the maiden to feel likewise, and to act upon her feelings. This seems to lead to a more general set of reflections on the proper attitude of mankind towards the humbler creatures, especially plants and flowers. And this includes a tribute to 'one beloved maid' who exemplifies this attitude so completely that she could never have been guilty of the kind of violation of a hazel-grove described in the other two:

> I would not strike a flower
> As many a man will strike his horse; at least,
> If, from the wantonness in which we play
> With things we love, or from a freak of power,
> Or from involuntary act of hand
> Or foot unruly with excess of life,
> It chanc'd that I ungently used a tuft
> Of meadow-lillies, or had snapp'd the stem

Of foxglove bending o'er his native rill,
I should be loth to pass along my way
With unreprov'd indifference, – I would stop
Self-question'd, asking wherefore that was done.
And ye who, judging rashly, deem that such
Are idle sympathies, the toys of one
More curious than need is, say, have ye not
Your gardens with their individual flowers
Which ye would spring to rescue from the hand
Of any rude destroyer *with the same*
Instinctive eagerness as if a child,
Your own, were sleeping near a lion's mouth?
Ye have my wishes for a recompense
The best which your devotion can bestow;
But some there are, and such as I have known
Far happier, chiefly one beloved maid;
For she is Nature's inmate, and her heart
Is everywhere; even the unnoticed heath
That o'er the mountains spreads its prodigal bells
Lives in her love; friends also more than one
Are hers who feed among the woods and hills
A kindred joy. And blessed are your days
That such delights are yours. (Oxford *Prelude*, p. 612)

It is needful to pause for a moment on the phrase 'But some there are', for one of the most skilled of all Wordsworth's readers, Professor de Selincourt, did not feel that it established a contrast between one kind of person and another. He did not, in fact, attach to the word *but* what dictionaries call 'adversative force'. He believed that the lines which follow it were yet another description of Dorothy, and that there was no contrast intended between this 'beloved maid' and the two violators of the hazel-groves, since she was herself one of them. Helen Darbishire, whose authority is second only to Professor de Selincourt's in this field, disagreed with him – it was perhaps the most striking disagreement between them. She believed that this 'beloved maid' was Mary Hutchinson, not because she sees the overall design of these drafts as involving a contrast between the two 'violators' and the 'beloved maid', but because the description of 'her placid character fits Mary and not Dorothy'.[1] But while Helen Darbishire was right in her identification, the word by which she chose to define the contrast between Mary and Dorothy was in some ways misleading. Dorothy had, indeed, an element of wildness about her, but to dismiss Mary as merely 'placid' is an error which has persisted for far too long.

The nature of the error is shown very clearly in the passage about Mary which was developed from the *Nutting* draft and placed in formal contrast with the account in *The Prelude* of Wordsworth's own addiction to the 'picturesque', his 'thraldom' to a too-exclusive pleasure in the sense of sight. It is just such a contrast as he had begun, but not quite finished, in the *Nutting* drafts:

> 'twas a transport of the outward sense,
> Not of the mind, vivid but not profound:
> Yet was I often greedy in the chace,
> And roam'd from hill to hill, from rock to rock,
> Still craving combinations of new forms,
> New pleasure, wider empire for the sight,
> Proud of its own endowments, and rejoiced
> To lay the inner faculties asleep.
> Amid the turns and counter-turns, the strife
> And various trials of our complex being,
> As we grow up, such thraldom of that sense
> Seems hard to shun; and yet I knew a Maid,
> Who, young as I was then, conversed with things
> In higher style, from Appetites like these
> She, gentle Visitant, as well she might,
> Was wholly free, far less did critic rules
> Or barren intermeddling subtleties
> Perplex her mind; but, wise as Women are
> When genial circumstance hath favor'd them,
> She welcom'd what was given, and craved no more.
> Whatever scene was present to her eyes,
> That was the best, to that she was attuned
> Through her humility and lowliness,
> And through a perfect happiness of soul
> Whose variegated feelings were in this
> Sisters, that they were each some new delight:
> For she was Nature's inmate. Her the birds
> And every flower she met with, could they but
> Have known her, would have lov'd. Methought such charm
> Of sweetness did her presence breathe around
> That all the trees, and all the silent hills
> And every thing she look'd on, should have had
> An intimation how she bore herself
> Towards them and to all creatures. God delights
> In such a being; for her common thoughts
> Are piety, her life is blessedness. (*Prel.* XI.188–223)

'Placidity' falls some way short of doing justice to this maid. She was also an 'enthusiast', 'wise', with a 'perfect happiness of soul', a creature radiating and receiving love, endowed with an unfailing piety – with that simplicity and consistency of daily experience which Wordsworth desired so much for himself:

And I could wish my days to be
Bound each to each by natural piety.
(*My heart leaps up* 8–9 [*PW* I, 226])

The phrase 'Nature's inmate', moreover, not only links this maid with Nature, but does so in one of the most intimate and significant of all relationships, and through a word which was one of the most highly characteristic of Wordsworth's 'favorite words': we shall return to it later. For the moment, it is enough to observe that this 'maid' has qualities much more positive and more significant to Wordsworth himself than are included in the usual meaning of 'placid' – unless, indeed, the user is very mindful of the proverb about the profundity of still waters.

The weight which Wordsworth himself attached to Mary's character, both before and after his marriage to her, is indeed weightily demonstrated by the place which she holds in the structure of *The Prelude*. For it is here, at the climax of his attempt to explain how he had erred into the merely 'picturesque', and what he had found out about the shallowness of that aberration, that he revives and amplifies that dramatic contrast between Mary on the one hand, and Dorothy and himself on the other, which had first been attempted in the *Nutting* drafts. From this second version, Dorothy has disappeared. The contrast is between himself and Mary alone, and it is used to strengthen and clarify his most extended piece of self-criticism, by stressing her natural superiority to himself in certain qualities which he highly values – almost envies. This superiority, too, he sees as a natural result of the differences between her life and his own. For her, there had been no break in the link of 'natural piety' between her days, no period of exile from their common native region, no French Revolution, no Godwinism, no deviation into the 'picturesque'. She had always been what he had been as a boy, and what he had, with such struggle and effort of imagination, become again as a man – and as a man married to her. This, in plain and deliberately rather over-simplified prose, is the meaning of the passage which both concludes his own long self-analysis, and links it to the last two 'spots of time' from his boyhood which, by offering a climax before the end, come near to weakening the whole plan of *The Prelude* as a large composition:

Even like this Maid before I was call'd forth
From the retirement of my native hills
I lov'd whate'er I saw; nor lightly lov'd,
But fervently, did never dream of aught
More grand, more fair, more exquisitely fram'd
Than those few nooks to which my happy feet
Were limited. I had not at that time

Liv'd long enough, nor in the least survived
The first diviner influence of this world,
As it appears to unaccustom'd eyes;
I worshipp'd then among the depths of things
As my soul bade me; could I then take part
In aught but admiration, or be pleased
With any thing but humbleness and love;
I felt, and nothing else; I did not judge,
I never thought of judging, with the gift
Of all this glory fill'd and satisfi'd.
And afterwards, when through the gorgeous Alps
Roaming, I carried with me the same heart:
In truth, this degradation, howsoe'er
Induced, effect in whatsoe'er degree
Of custom, that prepares such wantonness
As makes the greatest things give way to least,
Or any other cause which hath been named;
Or lastly, aggravated by the times,
Which with their passionate sounds might often make
The milder minstrelsies of rural scenes
Inaudible, was transient; I had felt
Too forcibly, too early in my life,
Visitings of imaginative power
For this to last: I shook the habit off
Entirely and for ever, and again
In Nature's presence stood, as I stand now,
A sensitive, and a creative Soul.

There are in our existence spots of time . . . (*Prel.* XI.224–58)

That Wordsworth should have used this contrast between Mary and himself to introduce his final comment upon his period of exile, and his final description of his homecoming, is proof enough of the significance of her personality for him. But it raises something of a problem. Why, if she represented – for him – so much that was positive, do we read so little about her in the works of biography and criticism, and so much about Dorothy and Annette Vallon? To a serious inquirer, it is evident that poor Annette contributed very little positively to Wordsworth's life and growth; it was not, after all, very likely that an ardent Royalist could have influenced deeply a passionately convinced young Republican. More negatively, her existence, and that of their daughter, certainly weighed upon him. He was not made to take such responsibilities lightly. The case of Dorothy is, of course, quite different. She was a powerful influence upon him, and above all in the period of his recovery from the 'picturesque'; then, and both earlier and later, she was as formative for him as she was herself formed by him. There is no doubt whatever about the complete accuracy of his many tributes to her, and their significance has been amply and rightly demonstrated, not least by Professor de Selincourt. She was, moreover, a vivid writer herself, and her *Journals* hold their own place in literature, in their own right. Mary, on the other hand, was no authoress – though it should not be overlooked that two lines of poetry are to her credit, and that they are the most frequently quoted lines of one of his best-known poems. It was she who added

They flash upon that inward eye
Which is the bliss of solitude

to 'I wandered lonely as a cloud', that almost too-well-known poem about daffodils (*PW* II, 216–17). But having left no other written record of her quality (save for some letters, mainly from the later part of her life[2]), she comes down to us from the records of others, and most vividly, but also most misleadingly, from De Quincey's brilliant account of his first introduction to the Dove Cottage household in 1807.

Its brilliance is of two kinds, fictional and technical. It is fiction, in the sense that while it purports to give his first impressions – and indeed does so – of the two ladies who greeted him at that unassuming door, while Wordsworth himself made his politenesses to Mrs Coleridge in the carriage a few yards away, it weaves in with this account all that he was to learn about both of them in the next few years, first as an inmate of the Cottage, then as a tenant of it himself, a difficult neighbour, sunk under opium, debt and the local awkwardness of a forced marriage with the daughter of a small farmer down the road. The technical brilliance depends largely upon his superb command of antithesis, both strategic and tactical. The two portraits are deliberately contrasted. Dorothy is 'wild' and 'startling': Mary is 'soft' and quiet. Dorothy was awkward in carriage, Mary was 'lady-like' etc., etc. As he comments, with engaging frankness, they were as different 'in personal characteristics as could have been wished for the most effective contrast'.[3] This is the general strategy, but the local tactics are also antithetical, and they are like nothing so much as Pope's 'Atticus' portrait of Addison, both in method and in effect. Praise is indeed given – though some of it is faint; and immediately upon its heels comes the hesitation of dislike, the hint of a fault, and the praise and blame combine to give such an impression of the blame much more strongly than if it had never been so equitably mixed with praise. Mary was 'sweet', 'angelic', a young woman who exercised 'all the practical fascinations of beauty', and yet when you came to look at her she was 'generally pronounced very plain'. Her eyes were 'Like stars of twilight fair' indeed – yet she was also cross-eyed, and 'much beyond that slight obliquity which is often supposed to be an attractive foible in the countenance'. As for her intellect, she had, of course, 'enjoyed such eminent advantages of training, from the daily society of her husband and his sister' that she could hardly have 'failed to acquire some power of judging for herself, and putting forth some functions of activity. But undoubtedly that was not her element: to feel and to enjoy in a luxurious repose of mind – there was her *forte* and her peculiar privilege.' There, indeed, was 'placidity', and to the utmost. As for her conversation, De Quincey praises the 'simplicity', the 'womanly self-respect and purity of heart speaking through all her looks, acts and movements. *Words*, I was going to have added; but her words were few. In reality, she talked so little that Mr. Slave-Trade Clarkson used to allege against her that she could only say "*God bless you*!"' The reasons which led De Quincey to give this elaborately but clandestinely hostile portrait can only be surmised,[4] but there can be no doubt at all of its deadly influence upon all subsequent pictures of its subject, and all attempts to understand the significance of the marriage, and the long wooing before it, in Wordsworth's life and poetry. To the few facts which bear on the deeper importance of this relationship, we shall return. Here, however, it remains to add a note on another of Wordsworth's 'favorite words', both because it deserves attention as a specially characteristic part of his vocabulary, and also because it throws more light on his view of Mary's personality than might be thought possible, for a single word.

This is the word *inmate*, in the phrase 'For she was Nature's inmate'. It is of considerable antiquity, and of remarkable complexity. First recorded in the later sixteenth century, it may have been derived either from 'in' or from 'inn', and seems first to have been used predominantly of one who merely lodged in a household or a place; there were laws against harbouring 'inmates', since they might become a burden on the parish arrangements for the poor. It was not, outside this context, a very common word, not occurring in Shakespeare or Spenser, and but once in Donne. In the course of the sixteenth century, it lost something of its application to an 'outsider', and took on more of its later sense as an 'indweller', 'one received into the household'. Its two occurrences in Milton, and four in Dryden, show it veering to this meaning. But it remained uncommon; it is not found in Pope and only twice in Cowper. In Wordsworth it occurs no less than twenty-one times. And in his use it has completely lost any tinge of its earlier sense of 'outsider', and has taken on the full force of 'intimate inhabitant of a household, either kith and kin, or close friend'. Indeed in one of its most powerful contexts it is specifically placed in opposition to the word 'outcast':

> No outcast he, bewilder'd and depress'd;
> Along his infant veins are interfus'd
> The gravitation and the filial bond
> Of nature, that connect him with the world.
> Emphatically such a Being lives,
> An inmate of this *active* universe . . . (*Prel.* II.261–6)

It is used yet again of Nature's 'inmates' in the *Immortality Ode*, 'her Foster-child, her Inmate Man' (83 [*PW* IV, 281]), and here in a general context which in some ways remarkably resembles that from *The Prelude*, in other ways quite as remarkably differs from it.[5] Twice (in *Michael* and in *The Excursion*) it is used of the children of the household. It had, in fact, for Wordsworth a highly emotive force, and one utterly different from the more modern use, which applies it especially to the 'inmates' of institutions, where there is precisely that absence of intimacy, of sharing in a household of kith and kin, which was central to Wordsworth's sense of 'inmatecy'.

His use of the word is, then, another clear example of the general principle outlined in an earlier chapter, that any word used by one writer with much more than its usual frequency is likely to bear in his usage a meaning very different from its common ones. And in particular, it is significant, not only of his feeling for Mary herself, but also of those values which he attached to the small group of persons who made his household, his kith and kin, together with Coleridge. It is the very word that embodies most forcefully this intense appreciation of the quietness of his own hearth:

> To sit without emotion, hope, or aim,
> In the loved presence of my cottage-fire,
> And listen to the flapping of the flame,
> Or kettle whispering its faint undersong.
> (*Personal Talk* 11–14 [*PW* IV, 73])

Thus his specially powerful use of *inmate* both reflects and strengthens that sense of communal, or rather household, achievement which was noted at the beginning of this chapter. And it raises another possible linguistic problem. So far, it has been assumed (mainly for the sake of simplicity of exposition) that Wordsworth's idiolect was individual to himself. No doubt some parts of it were exclusive – he did not, after all, share all his own qualities with even his most intimate friends and relations. But it is certainly possible that some of his 'favorite words' were indeed shared by his kith and kin, even by his neighbourhood.[6] One notable example happens to be mentioned by De

Quincey, in the rather malicious comment repeated from Mr Slave-Trade Clarkson. If Mary Wordsworth said little more than 'God bless you', she was at least making use of one word which occurs with exceptional frequency in Wordsworth's poetry, and often in very powerful contexts:[7]

> I bless Thee, Vision as thou art,
> I bless thee with a human heart . . .
>
> (*To a Highland Girl* 17–18 [*PW* III, 73])

> that blessed mood
> . . . that serene and blessed mood
>
> . . .
>
> Our cheerful faith, that all which we behold
> Is full of blessings. (*Tintern Abbey* 37 etc. [*PW* II, 260, 262–3])

> Thus blindly with thy blessedness at strife . . .
>
> (*Immortality Ode* 126 [*PW* II, 283])

> Oh there is blessing in this gentle breeze . . .
>
> (the opening line of *The Prelude*)

> I, at this time
> Saw blessings spread around me like a sea. (*Prel.* II.413–14)

> A more than Roman confidence, a faith
> That fails not, in all sorrow my support,
> The blessing of my life, the gift is yours,
> Ye mountains! thine, O Nature! (*Prel.* II.459–62)

These few examples leave little doubt that in Wordsworth's idiolect, 'bless' and its derivatives and compounds were very closely associated with all that Nature had done for him, as a boy and as a returning exile.

Moreover, certain other contexts show how profoundly the same word was woven into what might be called the *ecolect* of those who were 'inmates' to him.[8] Of his sister Dorothy he wrote:

> The Blessing of my later years
> Was with me when a boy . . .
>
> (*The Sparrow's Nest* 15–16 [*PW* I, 277])

And of Mary Wordsworth he declared:

> for her common thoughts
> Are piety, her life is blessedness. (*Prel.* XI.222–3)

It is not enough, of course, to speak of an ecolect if the word concerned is used only by one member of the family group; in such a case, it remains an idiolect. But quite apart from Mr Slave-Trade Clarkson's testimony, so obligingly repeated by De Quincey (though hardly with the intent of obliging anybody), there is evidence that both Dorothy and Mary used the word to and of

Wordsworth, as he used it of them. It is found in one of the most intimate of all the household letters preserved for us by chance, one consisting of fragments added by Dorothy and Mary to a letter of De Quincey's which they were forwarding from Grasmere to London in 1806; towards the end of her addition, Dorothy slips into the second person singular, clearly in response to a sense of intimacy and affection:

The wind is howling away the rain beats. Oh my dear William that thou wast humming thy own songs in time to it and untying thy many strings or resting thy hands upon thy knees as thou art used in musing while work pauses . . . God bless thee.

And Mary, though remaining with the second person plural, uses the word which concerns us still more emphatically and ecolectically:

Good night my blessing . . . God love you for ever and ever. (*MY* 249/12)

What seems to emerge from this over-brief study of these two words is an intimation that Wordsworth's sense of the 'household', of a small group of kith and kin, with a very few other intimates, was indeed strong; and that this 'household' in all probability had its own ecolect, which was embodied, partly at least, in his writing. And it is against this general intimation that we should see his tributes both to Dorothy and to Mary. What Dorothy had given him, throughout his life, was a 'blessing' almost exactly of the same kind as that which 'Nature' had given him; she had been, in a sense, another 'Nature' for him. As for Mary, when he called her 'Nature's inmate', he was using a term of such force that neither criticism nor linguistic statistics can begin to measure it. Only against the context of his long self-analysis, and of the humble contrast drawn between his own aberration into the 'picturesque' and of her unwavering habitation of their native region and of Nature herself can it begin to be understood. She was, as it were, the representative in *The Prelude* and in his life too of the being who had never experienced the Fall from Nature; and the being who therefore represented for him most decisively his own redemption from his own fall from grace.

But it is not enough to see her relationship with him in this light only. In the 1850 version of *The Prelude*, and in an earlier draft of the same passage dating from 1816–19, he extended her 'inmatecy' still further:

Thereafter came
One who in friendship had been early pair'd
No more an apparition to ador[n]
A moment, but an Inmate of the heart . . .

(*Prel.*, *app. crit.* for XIV.266–9 [1850])

This is, of course, no more than an adaptation of his description of Mary in *She was a phantom of delight*. But neither is it any less, and the full force of his feeling for 'inmatecy' can be understood only with reference to that poem, and to his whole relationship with her.

It may, perhaps, be added that the chief reason why so little attention has been paid to Mary is that the marriage was so deeply satisfactory. A glance at the world of men and women, and above all of married men and women, is enough to inform the most casual observer that the partners in unsatisfactory marriages are tolerably free in their comments on one another; and that the deeper and more successful a marriage, the more surely it imposes on both of them a reticence, a privacy, which forbids them to say very much about it, save to each other and in private. It is almost, if not quite, a kind of bad manners for a really happy husband to praise his own wife: it has something of an appearance of boasting. It was, no doubt, something of this kind which prevented De Quincey from seeing very far into the Wordsworths' marriage, and which leaves Wordsworth himself as the only veracious, though reticent, authority upon it.

31

So close is the parallel that can be drawn between Wordsworth's relationship with Mary Hutchinson, and his relationship with Nature and his native region, that one can only be suspicious of it – in the same way that a statistician, in using the χ^2 test for the significance of an association between one group of data and another will have an eye open for those parts of the tables (at the 95% and 99% levels) which indicate too much agreement, and suggest that the data may have been 'cooked' so as to provide too succulent an answer. The material on which the parallel is based, however, cannot be subjected to this, or any other statistical test, and all that can be done is to draw it, and let it take its chance.

In broad outline, it amounts to this: that Wordsworth's first acquaintance with her was in his childhood, for she was his cousin, and he seems to have been a schoolmate of hers for a time at Penrith. He came to know her much better towards the end of his schooldays, and while he was at Cambridge, and at this time not only regarded himself as being in love with her, but 'breathed my first fond vows' to her, and wrote poems about and to her. Then came a gap in their relationship, coinciding with his own period of exile from his native region and from Nature herself – the period of the wanderings in the south of England, in France, and of the affair with Annette. They met again in November 1796, and from that time onwards he saw much of her, and wrote much, until their marriage in 1802; and even after that, he continued to write poems about her.

But the more remarkable similarities are those of finer detail. The earlier poems written to and about her are full of images drawn from landscape, and from a vivid use of the sight: it is hardly an exaggeration to describe them as love-poems based on the 'picturesque'. The first of the later ones, however, turns away from this use of landscape-images to describe her person, and pictures, less vividly but more feelingly, the kind of life he hopes to lead with her. And the last group of poems to her are concerned much less with her personal beauty, much more with her moral qualities – with those which made her so conspicuously 'Nature's inmate', 'Nature's darling'. They merge, indeed, into his long effort to express what he had come to feel to be the real importance of Nature, beyond the 'picturesque' and less shallow. The least tedious way of exhibiting the themes which link some of these poems together, and also the great changes in emphasis placed upon them, is to set them out as a kind of table (Table XIII below) in which, as in some of the earlier quotations, no attempt is made to quote all the words, but only those which bear on the comparison. The four poems are:

1 *Anacreon.* An imitation of a Greek poem in which the poet exhorts a painter to make a portrait of his love, and tells him how to do so. Wordsworth addresses the poem to Reynolds, and dates it 1786 (*PW* I.261–2).
2 *Beauty and Moonlight, An Ode.* A variation on some of the themes of *Anacreon*, also probably written in 1786 (*PW* I.263–4).[9]
3 *Septimi Gades.* A free adaptation of Horace, *Odes* II.vi. Written in the early 1790s (*PW* I. 296–8).
4 *She was a Phantom.* Written in 1803–4 (*PW* II, 213–14).

There are eight main themes or descriptions which link these four poems together, though by irregular links. They are numbered *a–h*.

Table XIII shows very clearly the changes which Wordsworth's feelings for Mary Hutchinson underwent from his boyhood to his marriage. Themes *a* and *e* in *Anacreon*, obviously the originating version of all the later images describing her person, are those most fully developed in the early poems. The first two are, indeed, very original attempts to describe her beauty in terms of what he knew to be the most beautiful elements in his experience, 'landskip' and the play of light and shade upon it. This kind of imagery, however, completely disappears from the third poem. Particularly striking is the entirely different use to which the 'veil of morning mist' is put here. In the

Table XIII

	1. *Anacreon* (1786)	2. *Beauty and Moonlight* (1786)	3. *Septimi Gades* (early 1790s)	4. *She was a Phantom* (1803–4)
a	Black and shining paint her hair	Gleaming through her sable hair		Like Twilight's, too, her dusky hair
b	Let her forehead smooth and clear Through her shading locks appear, As at eve the shepherd sees The silver crescent through the trees; Nicely bend the living line Black and delicately fine, As you paint her sable brows Arch'd like two etherial bows.	High o'er the silver rocks I roved . . . In hope fond Fancy would be kind And steal my Mary from my mind; 'Twas Twilight and the lunar beam Sail'd slowly o'er Winander's stream. As down its sides the water stray'd Bright on a rock the moonbeam play'd. It shone half-shelter'd from the view By pendent boughs of tressy yew. True, true to love but false to rest, So fancy whisper'd to my breast; So shines her forehead smooth and fair Gleaming through her sable hair.		
c	Gentle as the vernal sky Soft and sleepy paint her eye, Trembling as the lunar beam Sweetly silvering o'er the stream.	I turn'd to Heav'n, but view'd on high The languid lustre of her eye, The moon's mild radiant edge I saw Peeping a black-arch'd cloud below		Her eyes as stars of Twilight fair
d	Now her lovely cheek adorn With the blushes of the morn. Give her lip the rose's hue Moisten'd with the morning dew.			But all things else about her drawn From May-time and the cheerful Dawn
e	Loosely chaste o'er all below Let the snowy mantle flow, As silvered by the morning beam The white mist curls on Grasmere's stream, Which, like a veil of flowing light, Hides half the landskip from the sight.		How beauteous, round that gleaming tide, The silvery morning vapours glide And half the landscape veil. Methinks that morning scene displays A lovely emblem of our days, Unobvious and serene;	
f	Here I see the wandering rill, The white flocks sleeping on the hill,		When shouts and sheepfold bells and sound Of flocks and herds and streams rebound Along the ringing dale,	
g	While Fancy paints, beneath the veil, The pathway winding through the dale, The cot, the seat of Peace and Love . . .		Yes, Mary, to some lowly door In that delicious spot obscure Our happy feet shall tend; And there for many a golden year Fair Hope shall steal thy voice to chear Thy poet and thy friend.	
h			Love with his tenderest kiss shall dry Thy human tear and still the sigh That heaves thy gentle breast.	A Creature not too bright or good For human nature's daily food; For transient sorrows, simple wiles, Praise, blame, love, kisses, tears, and smiles.

first poem, it had described Mary's person; in the third, it is applied to their life together, and to its quality of hidden intimacy. In the first, their dwelling and the peace within it are briefly touched; in the third, they form the main tenor, not only of the lines given above, but of the whole poem, which is essentially a review of his wanderings, a vain wish that perhaps they might settle together on the hills above the Rhône, and an acceptance of Grasmere as a place both possible and desirable. The only element entirely missing in the early poem, that labelled *b*, appears for the first time in the third, but only rudimentarily, to become the main subject of the fourth – where it is, of course, but scantily represented by the lines quoted above. His concern had been at first with her personal beauty, hardly at all with their dwelling, and still less with her human character; then it had been much less with her person, much more with their dwelling and manner of life together, and a little with her human qualities: finally, there was a clear remembrance of her personal beauty, in terms of light and shade, no mention of their dwelling, but a vivid appreciation of her human and moral characteristics.

This change, however, towards the dwelling in England, and admiration for Mary's own qualities, can be traced further in another group of love-poems, at first sight not so clearly addressed to her, but of great interest because they come in the gap between *Septimi Gades* (early 1790s), and *She was a Phantom* (1803–4). They are the poems of his homecoming, and also of his second wooing. Several years later, De Quincey and his friend John Wilson, both admirers of Wordsworth's poetry from their youth upwards, and both intimate in the Grasmere household, shared the same view of the marriage which they saw before them: 'the most interesting circumstance in this marriage, the one which perplexed us exceedingly, was the very possibility that it should ever have been brought to bear. For we could not conceive of Wordsworth as submitting his faculties to the humilities and devotion of courtship.'[10] Their view of the nature of courtship was not, perhaps, quite the same as Wordsworth's – or Mary's. Indeed if it were very widely held and observed, marriages would be much rarer than they are. But it prevented these two shy and pedantic young men from seeing behind the outward show of domesticity and placidity to the intimate privacies which lay behind it. Even if they had read an addition which he made to a letter from Dorothy to Mary in 1801, they would probably have failed to see that he was, entirely in his own fashion – and in hers too – carrying on his courtship:

We are very happy to have such good news of your health; mind you take care of yourself and contrive to grow fat; not as Dorothy does, fat one day and lean another, but fat and jolly for half a year together. D. and I sat two hours in John's firgrove this morning, 'twas a burning hot day but there we had a delicious cool breeze – How we wished for our dear dear friends, you and Sara! You will recollect that there is a gate just across the road, directly opposite the firgrove; this gate was always a favourite station of ours; we love it far more now on Sara's account. You know that it commands a beautiful prospect; Sara carved her cypher upon one of its bars, and we call it her gate. We will find out another place for your cypher, but you must come and fix upon the place yourself. How we long to see you, my dear Mary.

We had a melancholy visit at Coleridge's – Adieu – love to Tom – I now transcribe a short poem to be read after 'She dwelt among'

I travell'd among unknown men,
  In lands beyond the sea;
Nor, England, did I know till then
  What love I bore to thee.

'Tis past, that melancholy dream!
  Nor will I quit thy shore
A second time; for still I seem
  To love thee more and more.

Among thy mountains did I feel
  The gladness of desire;
And she I cherish'd turn'd her wheel
  Beside an English fire.

Thy mornings showed, thy nights concealed,
  The bowers where Lucy play'd;
And thine is too the last green field
  Which Lucy's eyes survey'd.

God for ever bless thee, my dear Mary – Adieu. (*EL* 121/160)

It is, of course, a love-letter, and one which shows that 'courtship' does not necessarily involve submission to 'humilities and devotion'. Certainly the relationship between Wordsworth and Mary made no such demand at this time. Their interests were already so far shared that he could write about them briefly, confidentially and naturally, well knowing that she would have no difficulty in following him. The reasons for the sadness of the visit to Coleridge, for example, clearly need no explanation. He jokes about her weight – and Dorothy's too. He makes it clear that his affection extends to her beloved sister Sara, but without for a moment obscuring his special love for Mary herself. And he remembers – though only by the skin of his teeth – to send his love to her brother Tom. And in the final line, he drops naturally into that use of the second person singular which, in the ecolect of the family (they were all cousins, after all) was the usual sign of intimacy and affection.

As for the poem, it would have puzzled De Quincey and Wilson as sadly as the letter itself, for it is addressed to nobody in particular, and appears to relate the sad fate of 'Lucy'. In later years, De Quincey was to play a notable part in launching on the world that dismal flood of speculations about this maiden which has warped Wordsworthian biography – and an understanding of his poems – almost as badly as the affair with Annette. And it is all too likely that neither of them would have perceived that the sad ending to the poem is nothing more than Wordsworth's usual trick of rounding off an intensely personal poem into a semblance of objectivity – of concealing himself, as it were by means of an easy elegiac ending. That it was addressed to Mary in a special sense, she would have been among the first to understand, for she had been enrolled among his regular copyists for six years past, and knew very well that the physical act of writing simply made him feel ill.[11] This poem is, in fact, the only one ever sent in a letter written by Wordsworth himself, and copied entirely by himself. His usual practice, even when he had brought himself to write part of a letter, was to dodge copying the poem which was to go with it, by phrases like these: 'My wife and sister send their best respects, and will transcribe a poem.' No one was less likely than Mary to miss the significance of the fact that he had himself transcribed the poem here. She did, in fact, take it so, for she herself copied it carefully into *Lyrical Ballads* (1800) when she sent it as a present to a young lady who was shortly to marry her cousin, John Monkhouse.[12] Nor was it likely that she would have missed the 'inner' meaning which it was designed to convey. It was, in its own intimate idiom, a kind of apology to her, as his first and earliest love, for the wanderings, for France, for Annette, and at the same time an assurance that he had indeed, and in every sense, 'come home' to her. All this does not, of course, make it a particularly good poem. Its real significance is too much veiled, too reticent for that: it is too much in code, as it were. But when the decoding is done, it remains a very touching piece of writing, and a very valuable piece of evidence bearing on Wordsworth's courtship, on his marriage, and on the double role which his wife played at this crucial time in his development – as a woman, and as symbol of their native region and their kin.

The other poem of the same period, *Three years she Grew* (*PW* II, 214–16), is also in a kind of code. It too – as has been noted already – has the respectable elegiac ending, obscuring its real and intimately personal substance. But this substance is in itself larger, almost less personal, than that of *I travelled*, and its roots go much deeper into Wordsworth's thoughts and feelings, not only about Mary, but about the largest problems in his life and thought – above all, about the moral influence of Nature. About this very important poem, several other observations have been made in passing, but it may be helpful to bring them together here. The impression that the ending is not merely routine elegy, but a record of real bereavement and grief is accidentally, and unfortunately strengthened by a highly probable misreading of the opening line. 'Three years she grew' looks so very definite and biographical to readers in an age when folk-lore and all that sort of thing is dead – when the traditional significance of 'three years' as the time of infancy is unknown. It puts the reader onto the wrong foot at once, and prepares him to accept several other wrong steps. The prophecy of Nature about 'This Child' is made as soon as she is three years old, and it looks forward to a life of some years, for

'. . . vital feelings of delight
Shall rear her form to stately height,
Her virgin bosom swell . . .' (31–3)

For this, a further decade at least was needed. But in the last stanza, it is all huddled up into a line and a half:

. . . The work was done –
How soon my Lucy's race was run! (37–8)

It is, even considered as an elegiac ending, not awfully well done. As a serious comment on the life of a real person, it would be nearly ludicrous.

As for the poem's main substance, in the speech of Nature, the first thing to be noted is that here, for the one and only time in Wordsworth, Nature herself speaks, in *oratio recta*. Elsewhere in his poetry, and often enough, she communicates 'Rememberable things' (*Prel.* I.588), but always in a kind of *oratio obliqua*. We learn only indirectly of what general tenor they were. Her utterance in this one place is, then, of special significance. We have also noted that the poem was written in Germany, in that crucial winter of 1798–9, and we have seen that it echoes or directly repeats ideas and phrases from the early drafts of *The Prelude*, not least from *Nutting*. Now that we have discussed in some detail the drafts attached to this last poem, we can add one more parallel with *Three years*, of still greater weight. In the long argument on man's duties towards the lower forms of life which follows the description of the 'one beloved maid . . . Nature's inmate', we find these lines:

For can he
Who thus respects a *mute insensate* form,
Whose feelings do not need the gross appeal
Of tears and of articulate sounds, can he
Be wanting in his duties to mankind
Or slight the pleadings of a human heart? (Oxford *Prelude*, p. 613)

And in *Three years*:

And her's shall be the breathing balm,
And her's the silence and the calm
Of *mute insensate* things. (16–18)

The mere fact that this phrase is repeated in the two places is obvious enough, and the general principles of the study of vocabularies outlined above will, if applied to it, leave no doubt that the repetition is remarkable.[13] But it must be admitted at once that, by itself, it is not conclusive of a really close connection between the two passages. To establish this, the phrase must be used in expressing the same, or closely related, thoughts. Now once this question is asked, it appears, rather unexpectedly (so powerful an opiate to one's critical faculties is familiarity) that the lines in *Three years* offer a meaning only with some difficulty, and even then a meaning which is not at first sight very acceptable. They seem to say, on behalf of Nature, that 'she' will be balmy, silent and calm, as are 'mute insensate things'. If one restricts the meaning of this last phrase to flowers (though there is no warrant in the poem itself for doing so), a possible meaning emerges, one well within the normal limits of that fiction which is essential to the working of metaphor; Yeats, after all, expressed the prayer for his daughter that she should become 'a flourishing hidden tree'. But without this restriction, the silence and calm to be conferred on the maiden would approximate her all too closely to 'rocks, and stones, and trees' – to a kind of deadness. The way out of this difficulty, I believe, is to recognise that these lines are in fact an over-elliptical condensation of the more diffuse reflections in the *Nutting* draft, and that the most difficult word in them, 'of', stands not as a possessive, but in place of the fuller expression 'derived from the contemplation of'. This passage from the draft, just before the occurrence of 'mute insensate', will sufficiently illustrate the more rounded thoughts which were so angularly expressed in *Three years*:

And the man
Who has been taught this lesson will so feel
Its wholesome influence, with such silent growth
Of tenderness and gratitude will bless
His teacher, that even meanest objects, else
Despis'd or loath'd or dreaded, as a part
Of this great whole, insensibly will cleave
To his affections, that at length, by power
Of such communion he will cease to look
Upon the earth as on some charter'd ground,
A spot where children unreproved may act
Their wanton pranks, but it will be to him
A temple – made for reverence and love. (Oxford *Prelude*, p. 613)

If these thoughts may be taken as underlying the brief lines of *Three years*, they become the kind of gift which Nature clearly means to confer. And they link it closely with Mary, for the whole of this draft centres upon the description of her character, and of her specially close relation with the humbler creatures of Nature.

There is, however, another and quite different basis for supposing that *Three years* refers to her. It is derived from that arrangement of his poems which Wordsworth imposed on them in the edition of 1815. To his readers and editors, this proved a great source of trouble, but it was very seriously meditated (it is first discussed in a letter to Coleridge in 1809 [*MY* 375/157]) and it had the best of intentions: 'for him who reads with reflection, the arrangement will serve as a commentary unostentatiously directing his attention to my purposes, both particular and general' (*Preface* to *1815* [*PW* II, 434]). Of the section headed *Poems of the Imagination* he wrote:

> The Poems next in succession [i.e. after *There was a Boy*] exhibit the faculty [of imagination] exerting itself upon various objects of the external universe; then follow others, where it is employed upon feelings, characters, and actions. (*ibid.* [440, *app. crit.*])

The poems showing the imagination at work on the external universe can be unambiguously identified as *To the Cuckoo*, *A Night-piece*, *Airey-force Valley*, *Yew-trees*, *Nutting* and *The Simplon Pass*. Then follows *She was a Phantom*, as unambiguously introducing the poems in which imagination is employed upon 'feelings, characters, and actions'. It is followed by *O Nightingale!*, written in 1806, indirectly celebrating the quality of his marriage, by a contrast between the 'fiery-hearted' nightingale and the Stock-dove. In it, perhaps more clearly than anywhere else, he reveals the existence of that secret, that hidden intimacy which so thoroughly escaped the young observers of the household:

> I heard a Stock-dove sing or say
> His homely tale, this very day;
> His voice was buried among trees,
> Yet to be come-at by the breeze:
> He did not cease; but cooed – and cooed;
> And somewhat pensively he wooed:
> He sang of love, with quiet blending,
> Slow to begin, and never ending;
> Of serious faith, and inward glee;
> That was the song – the song for me! (11–20 [*PW* II, 214])

There can be no doubt that this poem too refers to Mary. And it is immediately followed by *Three years*. Any reader who reads these poems 'with reflection' can hardly miss the unostentatious direction of his attention here to particular purposes. These three poems are about the same subject, and the same person. They are, to borrow a phrase from the Chaucerian critics, Wordsworth's 'marriage group'.[14]

This extended demonstration of the real subject of *Three years* has been given, not merely because it bears on some important aspects of Wordsworth's biography, but even more because the poem is of such exceptional importance in defining his attitude to Nature, and to Nature's influence upon her 'inmate' and specially chosen 'darling', as he saw it when he had emerged from the 'picturesque'. One effect of this influence is to confer upon the 'Maid' a special quality of beauty – a quality clearly reminiscent of the 'landscape' love-poetry of the previous years, yet subtler, for the landscape is no longer used only to describe her personal beauty; it is, as it were, less directly, but more realistically reflected in her face and form. They are beautiful, not because they are like clouds and stars, but because she has seen and responded to clouds and stars, and has been both beautified and 'moralised' by them:

'The floating clouds their state shall lend
To her; for her the willow bend;
Nor shall she fail to see
Even in the motions of the Storm
Grace that shall mould the Maiden's form
By silent sympathy.

'The stars of midnight shall be dear
To her; and she shall lean her ear
In many a secret place
Where rivulets dance their wayward round,
And beauty born of murmuring sound
Shall pass into her face.

'And vital feelings of delight
Shall rear her form to stately height,
Her virgin bosom swell . . .' (19–33)

This is remarkable enough, as showing how far the early, boyish response to Mary and to landscape had been deepened. But still more remarkable are two stanzas which announce for the first time a theme which was to have very notable later developments. It is one which concerns her personal beauty not at all, her moral character entirely:

'Myself will to my darling be
Both law and impulse: and with me
The Girl, in rock and plain,
In earth and heaven, in glade and bower,
Shall feel an overseeing power
To kindle or restrain.

'She shall be sportive as the fawn
That wild with glee across the lawn
Or up the mountain springs;
And her's shall be the breathing balm
And her's the silence and the calm
Of mute insensate things . . .' (7–18)

In these lines, Wordsworth enunciates clearly for the first time a moral principle which he was to express many more times in verse and in prose, and which lies almost at the centre of his later 'teaching' about the relation between a proper response to Nature, and a sound moral sense. It was the belief – or rather, the sum of a myriad accurate observations – that in Nature there is an eternal balance between opposing tendencies, those which initiate movement, and those which control and direct it, between excitement and calm, passion and reflection:

From nature doth emotion come, and moods
Of calmness equally are nature's gift,
This is her glory . . . (*Prel.* XII. 1–3)

With his later explorations of this principle, we shall soon be concerned, but for the moment, it is to be noted that he first discovered it clearly while he was contemplating the moral character of Mary Hutchinson, not yet his wife, but already 'Nature's inmate'. As in the broad pattern of the *Nutting* drafts, written at the same time, she was a norm, a model, from which both Wordsworth himself and his sister were capable of deviation. Of Dorothy's deviations, he said little or nothing more. Of his own, he became a careful and even acute analyst. And his self-analysis had its starting-point in the comparison which he made, both here and elsewhere, between Mary's character and his own; for it was a comparison by no means uniformly to his own advantage.

Before proceeding with the main argument, I may perhaps be allowed a brief comment on the bearings of these writings, and of this relationship, on the view of Wordsworth as a remarkably egotistical man. It was, as Edith C. Batho has so well shown,[15] a view first propagated by Hazlitt, mainly in a spirit of personal pique, because his own behaviour in Keswick had caused the inhabitants to chase him out of the town, and Wordsworth had not been altogether pleased that his guest should have so outraged his neighbours. It was repeated by Keats, who adored Hazlitt, and has passed into the main stream of biography and criticism as one of the chief *idées reçues* in its field. Yet here we find Wordsworth comparing himself with Mary Hutchinson, with something much more like humility than egotism; and we shall find him making a comparison between himself and Coleridge in the same spirit. As a lover, moreover, though he may not have been capable of all the humilities and devotions which De Quincey thought proper, he has, on the showing of the poems studied here, moved steadily in one direction: away from a concern with his own feelings, of desire and physical admiration, towards an ever deeper appreciation of Mary's human and moral qualities. The magnitude of his progress, and its unusualness in love-poetry, is best seen by comparing *She was a Phantom*, with Donne's *Aire and Angels*, which has much the same opening mood:

She was a Phantom of delight
When first she gleamed upon my sight;
A lovely Apparition, sent
To be a moment's ornament . . .
A dancing Shape, an Image gay,
To haunt, to startle, and way-lay . . .

Twice or thrice had I loved thee,
Before I knew thy face or name;
So in a voice, so in a shapelesse flame
Angells affect us oft, and worship'd bee . . .

But from this very similar starting-point – similar at least in feeling, though different in imagery – Donne goes on to quite another development. He proceeds to define a tension between this abstract worship, as of an angel or spirit, and the sensual attraction of her physical beauty, her 'lip, eye, and brow'. And so he arrives at a kind of paradox of impossibility:

For, nor in nothing, nor in things
Extreme, and scatt'ring bright, can love inhere . . .

Love, that is to say, cannot satisfy itself either by abstract adoration, or by sensual desires. His solution of the paradox is given in this conclusion:

Then as an Angell, face, and wings
Of aire, not pure as it, yet pure doth weare,
So thy love may be my loves spheare;
Just such disparitie
As is twixt Aire and Angells puritie,
'Twixt women's love, and men's will ever bee.

These lines do not, perhaps, readily reveal their meaning to a casual reader – they have, indeed, proved too much for some presumably careful readers.[16] It is necessary to recall one or two of Donne's more archaic beliefs and some of his linguistic usages to get at a meaning which, as is usual with him, is fairly simple in the end. First, he refers to the current theological doctrine that angels, in themselves incorporeal, might make themselves visible to human eyes by taking on human bodies constructed from *thickened* air – hence the appropriateness of Ariel's name in *The Tempest*, and of Prospero's dismissal of his spirits not merely into air, but into 'thin air', so that they resumed their naturally incorporeal existence. Next we must know that in Donne's English and also in his theology, angels were always masculine, never neuter, so that 'it', in the second line above, cannot refer to 'Angell' and must refer to 'air'. The distinction drawn there is, in fact, between the air thickened for the purpose of forming angelic bodies, and air in its normal rarefied and invisible state. Finally, it must be remembered that for Donne, as for all medievally-minded men haunted by a diagram of concentric circles as a model of the universe, 'spheare' could mean, among other things, one or other of the four elements, fire, air, water and earth. Armed with these scraps of information, we can briefly paraphrase Donne's solution. The air, he says, from which angels make their visible bodies, is 'less pure' than normal air, for it has been thickened and densified; yet it is still 'pure' in the sense that no other element has been mingled with it. This is the model proposed for defining the difference between women's way of loving, and men's. The former is comparable with the rarefied, incorporeal element, the latter with the thickened, and yet still airy: it is more concerned with the physical side of love, but it is still nothing but love.

And all this is very clever indeed. To have made this tricky point of doctrine serve as a persuasive to 'his coy mistress' in this fashion is ingenious, in a way in which Wordsworth at his most 'fanciful' is never ingenious. It is only when we begin to ask what the model proposed might mean in terms of actual experience that its limitations begin to appear. Has the problem of the relations between sensual love and other kinds of love been solved at all? Is there anything more than a very skilful play on two meanings of the word 'purity', one alchemical, the other more or less moral? And suppose that the poem's persuasion were to be successful, in what human terms could the encounter be envisaged between some thin air and some thick air? The radical weakness of the solution is, of course, that Donne is concerned neither with the nature of 'women's love' in general, nor with this woman in particular. Nothing can be learned about her from this poem – and not much from all his other poems. He was settling things for and within himself, giving names to them, in a superbly skilful and witty internal conversation, never better defined than in his own phrase from *The Exstasie*, 'this dialogue of one'.

There are many such love-poems, written by one person only, the poet himself, into which the qualities of the loved woman (assuming her to be real) scarcely enter at all. Another might have been addressed just as appropriately in the same terms – as three successive Saras were addressed in the same poem by Coleridge. But there are a few other love-poems which are essentially lover-like in their character, being produced by both lovers, though written by one, the qualities of a particular woman being so distinctly involved in them that they are of necessity addressed to her and to none other. Such, from the same starting-point as Donne's, is Wordsworth's poem to his wife. After the first visionary 'gleam', as of something beyond Nature, he sees her as a real woman, in her own right, and then as a fellow human being, admirable as a moral creature – yet still with a revelatory 'gleam':

I saw her upon nearer view,
A Spirit, yet a Woman too!
Her household motions light and free,
And steps of virgin-liberty;
A countenance in which did meet
Sweet records, promises as sweet;
A Creature not too bright or good
For human nature's daily food;
For transient sorrows, simple wiles,
Praise, blame, love, kisses, tears, and smiles.

And now I see with eye serene
The very pulse of the machine;
A Being breathing thoughtful breath,
A Traveller between life and death;
The reason firm, the temperate will,
Endurance, foresight, strength, and skill;
A perfect Woman, nobly planned
To warn, to comfort, and command;
And yet a Spirit still, and bright
With something of angelic light. (11–30)

This must surely be one of the least egotistical love-poems ever written, the least, that is to say, concerned with the lover himself, and the most with the qualities of the loved one. And the qualities found in her show that De Quincey had missed a good deal in his estimate of Mary Wordsworth. But no doubt Wordsworth himself was better placed to see what was there.

As for the qualities he found in her, they were those which became central to his mature view of that relation between Man and Nature which was the basis of a natural and a happy life. The line 'Praise, blame, love, kisses, tears and smiles' is constructed very like that highly imaginative prose description of the texture of real human experience already quoted from the *Preface* to *Lyrical Ballads*: 'the operations of the elements, and the appearances of the visible universe . . . storm and sunshine . . . the revolutions of the seasons

. . . cold and heat . . . loss of friends and kindred . . . injuries and resentments, gratitude and hope . . . fear and sorrow' (*PW* II, 397). It accepts with something very like a Miltonic sweep of the moral imagination, the ineluctable antinomy of good and evil, with all that immediately follows from it for human experience. Just as the contrast between storm and sunshine is characteristic of the universe outside us, so is the contrast within human life characteristic, inevitable and natural between hope and fear, tears and smiles, gratitude and sorrow. And granted the inevitability of these tensions, the need to encounter the bad as well as the good, what is needed above all is that balanced perception which leads to foresight and endurance, and which is almost the same quality as 'The reason firm, the temperate will'.

Very nearly at the same time that he wrote this poem, Wordsworth turned inwards, and inquired how far he himself possessed this kind of perception, and how effective it was. No doubt his careful study of Mary's qualities had done something to point his interest in this direction. But he had another kind of evidence before him, bearing on the same problems, but from the other side. It was also just at this time that Coleridge, the one beloved member of the circle of inmates who was not kith and kin, was having trouble with his will, and discussing its diseases with the superbly intelligent hypochondria which he brought to the aggravation of his more physical ills. Mary Wordsworth and Coleridge illuminated the same problems, but in opposite ways: that is their characteristic place in the pattern of Wordsworth's thoughts and feelings, and their thematic role in *The Prelude* – in which poem, however, Coleridge is by far the more important.

32

O blessed Flock! I the sole scabbed Sheep!
And even me they love, awake, asleep.

(Coleridge, *Notebooks*[17])

The comparison which Wordsworth drew between himself and his wife in their relationship with Nature has made necessary a rather long explanation, because her part in the poem, and indeed in his life, is unobtrusive and unduly neglected. The comparisons which he made between himself and Coleridge, the remaining member of the small group within which and – in a sense – for which *The Prelude* was written, need either less explanation, or very much more. Much more, if any attempt were to be made to outline the complexities of their whole relationship, of their mutual influences, agreements and differences, and of the sad decline from its early creative warmth into estrangement and bitterness. But much less than this, if we concern ourselves only with what Wordsworth had to say about their relationship with Nature. And the risks of accepting this limitation are the less because it is at the centre of all that he felt and thought about their relationship; it throws light upon, rather than receives light from, all its other aspects.

Coleridge's place in *The Prelude* is unmistakable and conspicuous. The poem was addressed directly to him, in friendship, admiration and hope. But during the six or so years of its composition, while the friendship remained, the hope and admiration were overcast by a growing awareness of his weaknesses, of body and of mind. Indeed as it went on, it took on something of the character of an attempt to rescue him from them, by reminding him of his better days and his high powers, and of the great work which still remained for both of them to do for mankind –

> joint labourers in a work . . .
> Of their redemption, surely yet to come.
> Prophets of Nature, we to them will speak
> A lasting inspiration, sanctified
> By reason and by truth; what we have loved,
> Others will love; and we may teach them how . . . (*Prel.* XIII.439–45)

So the poem ends, but on the way to this almost desperate affirmation of their alliance, and of his hopes, Wordsworth had made his comparisons between their two histories, and had been led to express some of the fears to which they gave rise. At three points in his own autobiography he had deliberately compared himself with Coleridge: in boyhood; in their youth at Cambridge; and again in boyhood, by way of retrospect, a backward look before the next step forward.

The first of these comparisons is made at the end of Book II, as Wordsworth takes leave, as it were, of his own resurrected boyhood:

> the gift is yours,
> Ye mountains! thine, O Nature! Thou hast fed
> My lofty speculations; and in thee,
> For this unhappy heart of ours I find
> A never-failing principle of joy,
> And purest passion.
> Thou, my Friend, wert rear'd
> In the great City, 'mid far other scenes;
> But we, by different roads at length have gain'd
> The self-same bourne . . .
> For Thou hast sought
> The truth in solitude, and Thou art one,

> The most intense of Nature's worshippers,
> In many things my Brother, chiefly here
> In this my deep devotion. (*Prel.* II.461–79)

This is the first simple comparison, made in 1799, in the earliest of the distinct and very different periods in which *The Prelude* was written. At this time, Wordsworth's relations with Coleridge were those of a friend and close ally, unclouded by any thought of disagreement or failure. The difference in their boyhood environments is merely noted. No consequences are suggested from it. What is stressed is not this initial difference, but the fact that their different roads have led them both to the same attitude to Nature, and that this is the most important thing they have in common.

The second comparison was written when relations between them had greatly altered. There had been a pause, even a hiatus in composition, for work was not resumed until the early part of 1804, and its resumption was closely connected with Coleridge. At this time, the poem was envisaged by both of them as only one part, a kind of prolegomenon, to a much larger work, which they called *The Recluse*. This was to be a large philosophical poem, setting out everything that Wordsworth had thought and felt about the state of Nature, Man and Society. To this endeavour Coleridge had constantly urged him, ever since their winter in Germany four years earlier. Late in 1803 he wrote to their old friend Poole:

> He has made a Beginning to his Recluse . . . The habit of writing such a multitude of small Poems was . . . hurtful to him . . . I rejoice therefore with a deep & true Joy, that he has at length yielded to my urgent & repeated – almost unremitting – requests & remonstrances – & will go on with the Recluse exclusively. – A Great Work, in which he will sail; on an open Ocean, & a steady wind.[18]

But there was something like a bargain between them. It was that if Wordsworth would now devote his whole energy to this great poem, Coleridge on his part would furnish 'notes' for it. It was to be, as some of their earlier writings had been, a 'joint-labour'. At this very time, however, Coleridge was in ill-health and dejection, and was on the point of leaving for Malta, where it was hoped that he might recover. Wordsworth set himself almost feverishly to go on with what is now called *The Prelude*, so that Coleridge could take a copy of it with him. At the same time, he implored Coleridge to let him have the notes for the larger poem:

> I finished five or six days ago another Book of my Poem, amounting to 650 lines. And now I am positively arrived at the subject I spoke of in my last. When this next book is done which I shall begin in two or three days' time, I shall consider the work as finished. Farewell.
>
> I am very anxious to have your notes for *The Recluse*. I cannot say how much importance I

attach to this; if it should please God that I survive you, I should reproach myself forever in writing the work if I had neglected to procure this help.[19] (*EL* 162/207)

And three weeks later, he wrote again to Portsmouth, where Coleridge was embarked – and as Wordsworth thought, already departed:

I will not speak of other thoughts that passed through me, but I cannot help saying that I would gladly have given 3 fourths of my possessions for your letter on *The Recluse* at that time. I cannot say what a load it would be to me, should I survive you and you die without this memorial left behind. Do, for heaven's sake, put this out of the reach of accident immediately. We are most happy that you have gotten the Poems, and that they have already given you so much pleasure. Heaven bless you for ever and ever. No words can express what I feel at this moment. Farewell, farewell, farewell. (*EL* 167/212)

It was in these days, so highly charged with hopes and fears for Coleridge that Wordsworth wrote the second of his comparisons between their early environments. He had reached that part of his own life spent at Cambridge, and having recounted it, he turned back in imagination to Coleridge's time there, so soon afterwards, and allowed himself to play with thoughts of what might have happened had they been contemporaries, instead of so narrowly missing each other. He recalls that Coleridge had come up from Christ's Hospital only a year after he himself had left Cambridge, and had at first lived 'in temperance and peace, / A rigorous Student'. But then had followed 'a stormy course' – the first onset, as it were, of those storms which were once again thickening round Coleridge as he left for Malta:

I have thought
Of Thee, thy learning, gorgeous eloquence,
And all the strength and plumage of thy youth,
Thy subtle speculations, toils abstruse
Among the Schoolmen, and platonic forms
Of wild ideal pageantry, shap'd out
From things well match'd, or ill, and words for things,
The self-created sustenance of a mind
Debarr'd from Nature's living images,
Compell'd to be a life unto itself,
And unrelentingly possess'd by thirst
Of greatness, love, and beauty . . . (*Prel.* VI.305–16)

But these thoughts have turned into something like a criticism of Coleridge – or rather, of the effects upon him of that early environment which had 'Debarr'd' him from Nature herself. Without them, his desire for 'greatness, love, and beauty' had been forced back on artificial instead of natural embodiments: on books and abstruse philosophy. The results have been grave, and they are gravely, though gently, stated in terms which are only to be understood by reference to other parts of *The Prelude* – and indeed to other writings of his own and Coleridge's. The 'wild ideal pageantry, shap'd out / From things well match'd, or ill' is indeed the product of that power which they both called 'fancy'; and here, as elsewhere, it is tacitly contrasted with that higher power of 'imagination' which imposes on experience, not random associations, but patterns which are orderly and real.

Implicit in these criticisms – and Coleridge was the last person to miss the implication – was the comparison between the two of them. Wordsworth himself had not been forced back upon this artificiality and introspection, for he had been surrounded by those materials which fostered 'imagination' rather than mere 'fancy'. And by this good fortune, he had escaped the ills which had fallen on Coleridge. Had they only been at Cambridge together,

> Not alone . . .
> Should I have seen the light of evening fade
> Upon the silent Cam, if we had met,
> Even at that early time: I needs must hope,
> Must feel, must trust, that my maturer age,
> And temperature less willing to be mov'd,
> My calmer habits and more steady voice
> Would with an influence benign have sooth'd
> Or chas'd away the airy wretchedness
> That batten'd on thy youth. But thou hast trod,
> In watchful meditation thou hast trod
> A march of glory, which doth put to shame
> These vain regrets; health suffers in thee; else
> Such grief for Thee would be the weakest thought
> That ever harbour'd in the breast of Man. (*Prel.* VI.316–31)

There is a touch of desperation in those last lines, as if that grief and that thought, weak as they might be, had made some short stays in his own breast, even if they had not been permitted to 'harbour' there. And the calm and steadiness of his own temperament is, however gently, contrasted with Coleridge's unsteady and unreal habits of fancy and introspection. When it is put beside that first address to Coleridge, in the second book, it is clear that Wordsworth is now seeing much more of a contrast between them. Coleridge remains his 'Brother' in deep devotion to Nature, but is seen as still caught in the trammels of that Nature-less boyhood while he was at Cambridge. Still caught in them, too, while Wordsworth was writing these lines to him, destined to fetch up in Malta. But he was no less a member of their small group of 'inmates' for that. And these gentle criticisms of Coleridge were introduced by a passage in which he was imagined as being present, not only at Cambridge, but also at those walks round Penrith in the summer vacations with Dorothy and Mary, the other members of this closely-knit group:

O Friend! we had not seen thee at that time;
And yet a power is on me and a strong
Confusion, and I seem to plant Thee there.
Far art Thou wander'd now in search of health,
And milder breezes, melancholy lot!
But Thou art with us, with us in the past,
The present, with us in times to come:
There is no grief, no sorrow, no despair,
No languor, no dejection, no dismay,
No absence scarcely can there be for those
Who love as we do . . . (*Prel.* VI.246–56)

There could hardly be a stronger expression of affection, of acceptance in this tight family group. And Wordsworth writes here in the plural, not for himself only, but for Dorothy and Mary too. Just for a moment, they are actually writing the poem with him. Yet in the last lines this positive statement is made through a long list of negations, and it leaves an impression as much of misgiving as of certainty. It has to protest too much: there is too much to be denied.

This passage on Coleridge's 'wanderings' to Malta goes on to establish still more emphatically their 'Brotherhood', but with an emphasis just as great on the crucial difference for their fates of their early environments:

I, too, have been a Wanderer; but, alas!
How different is the fate of different men
Though Twins almost in genius and in mind!
Unknown unto each other, yea, and breathing
As if in different elements, we were framed
To bend at last to the same discipline,
Predestin'd, if two Beings ever were,
To seek the same delights, and have one health,
One happiness. Throughout this narrative,
Else sooner ended, I have known full well
For whom I thus record the birth and growth
Of gentleness, simplicity, and truth,
And joyous loves that hallow innocent days
Of peace and self-command. Of Rivers, Fields,
And Groves, I speak to Thee, my Friend; to Thee,
Who, yet a liveried School-Boy, in the depths
Of the huge City, on the leaded Roof
Of that wide Edifice, thy Home and School,
Wast used to lie and gaze upon the clouds
Moving in Heaven; or haply, tired of this,

To shut thy eyes, and by internal light
See trees, and meadows, and thy native Stream
Far distant, thus beheld from year to year
Of thy long exile. (261–84)

Throughout these passages from Book VI of the poem, there is an urgency, and immediacy of tone. The experience on which they were based was – a rare thing for Wordsworth – being lived as he wrote of it, not 'recollected in tranquillity'. Coleridge had left the rest of them at Grasmere, and was on his way to Malta, even as these lines were being written. They were, in verse, all that had been said in those last farewell letters – and more. Perhaps for this reason, they are not among the most notable parts of the poem. They are too raw. But they are alive with the actuality of the experience they describe, with the painful conflict between the desire to inspire confidence and the perceptions of all that, in Coleridge's character, gave ground for fear. And the same conflict imposes on them a certain reticence. There is no more than a hint that Coleridge's early environment may be responsible for his troubles, and only a passing mention of that ominous word, 'self-command' – the quality which he had lacked at Cambridge, and which Wordsworth believed he might have strengthened in him.

A few months later, however, as Wordsworth went on with the poem, these same thoughts and feelings were revived and reviewed in that *Retrospect* which looks back yet again on his earlier life, but with the added understanding gained by his earlier survey of it. And now 'recollection' and 'tranquillity' perform their usual office in his poetry. The immediate pain of Coleridge's departure is over, and the thoughts and feelings which it evoked are reviewed more calmly, with more force and firmness. They arose, naturally enough, from Wordsworth's description of that period in his own youth when 'fancy', with its heterogeneous and disjointed images, had exercised over him its 'adulterate Power':

Yet in the midst
Of these vagaries, with an eye so rich
As mine was, through the chance, on me not wasted
Of having been brought up in such a grand
And lovely region, I had forms distinct
To steady me; these thoughts did oft revolve
About some centre palpable, which at once
Incited them to motion, and control'd,
And whatsoever shape the fit might take,
And whencesoever it might come, I still
At all times had a real solid world
Of images about me; did not pine

As one in cities bred might do; as Thou,
Beloved Friend! hast told me that thou didst,
Great Spirit as thou art, in endless dreams
Of sickliness, disjoining, joining things
Without the light of knowledge. (*Prel.* VIII.594–610)

Here the implications and surmises of the earlier comparisons between himself and Coleridge are brought to clear and forceful expression at last. The passage is, with complete appropriateness and appositeness, a free variation on the account of his own feelings for his London experiences in Book VII. It gathers weight and density from this repetition and partial tautology, both for Wordsworth himself and for his 'sensitised' reader. It is quoted in full on pp. 172–3, and it is an almost essential introduction to a reading of this last contrast between himself and Coleridge. There, 'The mountain's outline and its steady form / Gives a pure grandeur'; here, the region is 'grand / And lovely'; there 'order and relation' were given to a 'multitude' of 'thoughts'; here, 'thoughts . . . revolve / About some centre palpable'. And behind some of these phrases stretches an even longer history. 'Grand / And lovely' picks up the 'beauty and fear' of the earlier books of *The Prelude*, 'the sublime and beautiful', '*Beauty lying in the lap of Horrour!*', and takes the reader forward to the final variations on these 'tautologies' in the later books (see pp. 252–9 above). In the same way, the negative aspects of his own London experiences are here adaptively repeated in recounting Coleridge's own descriptions of his own early life there. The 'blank confusion' which he had felt himself, the

perpetual flow
Of trivial objects, melted and reduced
To one identity, by differences
That have no law, no meaning, and no end

turn into Coleridge's 'endless dreams / Of sickliness, disjoining, joining things / Without the light of knowledge'. And of the many links between these studies in opposed environments and their moral effects, perhaps the strongest is in the word 'steady'. The 'form' of the mountain is 'steady'; had they met at Cambridge, Coleridge might have listened to Wordsworth's 'more steady voice'; and he had this voice because, in his formative years, he had 'forms distinct / To steady me'. There is, finally, the renewed expression of that central principle announced by Nature herself in *Three Years*, of the balance of 'law and impulse', kindling and restraint, in the line 'Incited them to motion, and control'd'. In these lines we are at the centre of Wordsworth's special vocabulary, and of course at the heart of his deepest reflections upon the relation between the moral nature of man and his environment.

We are not far, either, from the beliefs which Coleridge himself held at that time on the same subject, and its immense importance. In all three of these comments on his early life, the material for Wordsworth's descriptions can have come only from Coleridge himself. Indeed Book VIII specifically says that this was so: 'Thou . . . hast told me.' Nor were these beliefs merely borrowed from Wordsworth, or developed under his tutelage. When Wordsworth pointed these contrasts, and referred so pointedly to Coleridge's early life in London, he was not enforcing a doctrine of his own, but referring to one which was held by both of them, and which had been held, at any rate in part, by Coleridge before they had met. In 1795 he had written to an earlier friend:

> It is melancholy to think, that the best of us are liable to be shaped & coloured by surrounding Objects – and a demonstrative proof, that Man was not made to live in Great Cities! Almost all the physical Evil in the World depends on the existence of moral Evil – and the long-continued contemplation of the latter does not tend to meliorate the human heart. – The pleasures, which we receive from rural beauties, are of little Consequence compared with the Moral Effect of these pleasures – beholding constantly the Best possible we at last become ourselves the best possible. In the country, all around us smile Good and Beauty – and the Images of this divine καλοκἀγαθόν are miniatured on the mind of the beholder, as a Landscape on a Convex Mirror.[20]

This is close to what Wordsworth himself believed, and what he said of Coleridge. And at the other end, so to speak, of Coleridge's life, he gave an account of those 'notes' which Wordsworth had so earnestly desired for *The Recluse* – and which Coleridge had managed to get lost in some part of his baggage on the way back from Malta. In 1832, his *Table Talk* gives this rather off-hand recollection of the project:

> He was to treat man as man – a subject of eye, ear, touch, and taste, in contact with external nature, and informing the senses from the mind, and not compounding a mind out of the senses; then he was to describe the pastoral and other states of society, assuming something of the Juvenalian spirit as he approached the high civilization of cities and towns, and opening a melancholy picture of the present state of degeneracy and vice; thence he was to infer and reveal the proof of, and necessity for, the whole state of man and society being subject to, and illustrative of, a redemptive process in operation, showing how this idea reconciled all the anomalies, and promised future glory and restoration. Something of this sort was, I think, agreed on. It is, in substance, what I have been all my life doing in my system of philosophy.[21]

This is, no doubt, in part what Coleridge remembered of that great 'joint-labour' which remained for them to do together. It is also, in part, what he happened to remember from the last lines of *The Prelude*: one notices the transformation of Wordsworth's phrase 'their redemption' into Coleridgese as 'a redemptive process in operation'. But in the description of the main theme of the unwritten poem all that is clear is what Wordsworth had already perceived and written. What remains foggy, enveloped in mere words, is the process of redemption itself. This is what Coleridge had never quite understood, because he had never quite experienced.

It was essentially the rejection of the 'picturesque', and the substitution for it of another attitude to Nature and to natural life, not merely the rejection of the 'high civilization of cities and towns', with their 'degeneracy and vice'. No doubt they agreed on much, but it is only necessary to look carefully at the early letter and the late *Table Talk* to see that they also differed greatly. It is perhaps not entirely accidental that Coleridge should have mentioned in the former the Claude glass, the characteristic instrument of the landscape-hunters. And his letter had gone on to show him as still feeling and thinking with the eighteenth-century landscapists:

Thompson, in that most lovely Poem, the Castle of Indolence, says –

> I care not, Fortune! what you me deny –
> You cannot rob me of free Nature's Grace!
> You cannot shut the Windows of the Sky,
> Through which the Morning shews her dewy face –
> You cannot bar my constant feet to rove
> Through Wood and Vale by living Stream at Eve –

Alas! alas! she *can* deny us all this – and can force us fettered and handcuffed by our Dependencies & Wants to *wish* and *wish* away the bitter Little of Life in the felon-crowded Dungeon of a great City! – [22]

Here, and in *Table Talk*, Coleridge was making the distinction between town and country in the Augustan manner. What was most conspicuous in it was the presence of felons, of degeneracy and vice in the one, and its absence in the other. For him, as for Virgil, Horace, Juvenal and his great adaptor Dr Johnson, country life was preferable because it was less corrupted by crime, ambition, wealth, the savage competition of man with man. And country scenery, 'rural beauties', were valuable because they encouraged calm and smiling contemplations. What Wordsworth had to say was not in contradiction of this distinction, but simply over and above it. For him, what was above all important in scenery and 'rural beauties' was the demonstration of order and shape, of fear as well as beauty, of light and shade, and of all the profound antinomies of the universe itself, with its laws and impulses, its restraints as well as its kindlings. It was through daily contact with these realities that the quality of life in the country was richer and happier than that of life in towns. And it was through lack of this educative force, of this redemption, that life in towns was a 'blank confusion', a 'perpetual flow / Of trivial objects' (*Prel.* VII.695, 701–2).

Through these comparisons between himself and Coleridge in *The Prelude*,

Wordsworth steadily advanced on his perception of the relation with Nature which he rediscovered in himself once he was rid of the 'picturesque', and from one to the other he deepened his capacity to describe his perceptions. But though he drew more and more clearly the contrast between their earlier environments, and all that it had done for both of them, one belief – a vital one – remains unchanged through them all. Because of his early deprivations, his exile, Coleridge's case was hard, but it was never seen as desperate. On the contrary, he had already gone far towards a recovery of a full relationship with Nature, and could go still further. For all his insistence on the importance of early nurture, Wordsworth was no determinist, no Calvinist of natural religion. The way beyond the 'picturesque' was open to Coleridge, and to mankind.

33

We should be rigorous to ourselves, and forbearing if not indulgent to others, and if we make comparisons at all it ought to be with those who have morally excelled us.

(Wordsworth, Fenwick Note on *Ode to Duty* [*PW* IV, 418])

It has been observed above that much of Wordsworth's best poetry was concerned, in one way and another, with his attempts to describe the relationship with Nature which, in his own case, had followed on his liberation from the 'picturesque', and which he believed might be of no less benefit to others. But it was indeed concerned with it in one way and another, in a variety of ways, treating it from many aspects. This constantly varied and unsystematic exposition was in the nature of the case. Wordsworth never regarded himself as anything other than a poet and a teacher. He did not set up to be a philosopher, nor attempt the kind of exposition of his thoughts and feelings that a philosopher might have attempted. *The Recluse*, the great 'joint-labour' that was never written, was to have been a philosophical poem, not a treatise. Much of the philosophical element in it was to have come from Coleridge: hence the urgency of Wordsworth's pleas for the 'notes' bearing on it as Coleridge was leaving for Malta.

And apart from Wordsworth's own way of regarding himself, it is clear that his characteristic mode of exploration and exposition of thought and feeling was not abstract statement, but that inextricable mingling of the two which has been called the 'involute': the revelatory moment or mood which singles out and shapes particular experiences into wider significance. And of 'involutes' there is a very wide variety, in their materials and in their ways of using them. Though it may be that those most crucial and formative for him were from his boyhood, and their materials of rocks, wind and darkness, there were also others of later date, and these were more often specially significant perceptions of human beings: beggars, shepherds, the discharged soldier, the Leechgatherer. But, as we have seen, when he ceased to be a 'Wanderer', and became at last a man with a home and a household, his more intimate relationships in their turn took on some of the qualities of 'involutes'. His sister, his wife and Coleridge all suggested to him, through their differing personalities, as he experienced them, their own kinds of relationship with Nature. He had much to learn from them, and learned much. But the last lesson, the one that surveyed and included all the others, was always, and for him necessarily, that which belonged to 'the recesses of [his] nature, far / From any reach of outward fellowship' (*Prel.* XIII.195–6). And after his contemplations of his sister, his wife and Coleridge, it was upon himself that he turned his more fully informed attention – and on Nature.

The poem which embodies one of these renewed inward looks, *Ode to Duty* (*PW* IV, 83–6), is one of the most complex that he ever attempted. Like the *Immortality Ode*, which was completed at nearly the same time, it resumes many of the basic 'tautologies' through which earlier 'involutes' had been crystallised into clarity, and sets them in imaginative movement together. They are, however, a different selection of the earlier experiences and concerns, and represent what might be called the more 'ethical' aspects of man's proper relationship with Nature. They have to do with 'order', 'steadiness', the balance between 'law' and 'impulse'. Its texture is very different from that of the *Immortality Ode*, and no doubt reflects the difference between their main concerns. There is no flowing, dithyrambic certainty here, but a dour wrestle with a still shadowy sense of possible relations between a few established certainties. A glance at Professor de Selincourt's *apparatus criticus* shows it to be more drafted and redrafted than any other poem of Wordsworth's, and more often altered in later editions. It may be doubted whether it ever became what he wanted it to be, or said what he had found in its materials. But it can sometimes happen that the failures of a great writer reveal more than his successes. They tend to show him at his limits, his frontiers, and to suggest what still remained to be done, the incompleteness of what in his successes may seem to be complete.

The *Ode* had its starting-point in the relationship with Coleridge, in those profoundly disturbed and creative weeks early in 1804 before he went to Malta. Some of them he had spent at Dove Cottage, and the entries in his *Notebook* written during his visit show that he was deeply concerned with his own lack of response to duty. He sets it down with that defenceless vividness which is characteristic of the journals, and of his own attitude to his failings:

All this evening, indeed all this day . . . I ought to have [been] reading & filling the Margins of Malthus – I had begun & found it pleasant / why did I neglect it? – Because I OUGHT not to have done this. – The same in reading & writing Letters, Essays, &c &c – surely this is well worth a serious Analysis, that understanding I may attempt to heal / for it is a deep & wide disease in my moral Nature, at once Elm-and-Oak-rooted. – Love of Liberty, Pleasure of Spontaneity, &c &c, these all express, not explain, the Fact.[23]

Later in the evening, as he lay in bed, he had formulated one possible solution for his problem. It was that in early life, in childhood and at school, 'all Duty is felt as a *command*', and thus, by association, as a painful thing. But when he awoke in the morning, he had already rejected this view, and found another: that it was an interruption of 'the streamy nature of the associating Faculty . . . especially as it is evident that *they most* labor under this defect who are most reverie-ish & streamy – Hartley, for instance & myself.'[24]

No doubt these topics appeared in his conversation that day, and it is not difficult to imagine Wordsworth agreeing that Coleridge was apt to neglect obvious duties, whatever he may have thought of the causes suggested. He did not, however, take the opportunity to carry further that analysis of Coleridge's difficulties which concerned him, a few weeks later, in *The Prelude*. He turned inwards upon himself, and had no difficulty in identifying there precisely the same disinclination to perform obvious duties. It is thus described in the *Ode to Duty*:

And oft, when in my heart was heard
Thy timely mandate, I deferred
The task, in smoother walks to stray . . . (29–31)

It had been described more simply and perhaps more forcefully in one of the early drafts:

Resolv'd that nothing e'er should press
Upon my present happiness
I shov'd unwelcome tasks away . . . (*app. crit.*)

But he did not, like Coleridge, seek the reasons for these derelictions in the principles of association, still less did he suppose that it was a fault peculiar to himself. He set it, for his own consideration, in a much broader context: the first draft put it more directly than the later ones:

O'er earth, o'er heaven thy yoke is thrown
All Natures thy behests obey:
Man only murmurs; he alone
In wilfulness rejects thy sway. (8/9, *app. crit.*)

Then he checks himself, and the check is emphasised in the later versions. Not all men murmur, not all are wilful. There are indeed some who live in harmony with duty without conscious effort, in happiness, joy, in a wise boldness; and for such as these, when occasionally they are faced by the demands of duty, there is no problem. They live genially, like Nature and its forces, subject to law, and with all the ease and simplicity that comes from this subjection. As for himself, however, there has been no simple subjection to the laws of duty. He has lived, he says, in freedom, in 'perpetual' or 'unchartered freedom', often derelicting from duty for the sake of pleasure. But these very derelictions have become burdensome, and freedom itself has imposed on him the disorderly conflicts of 'chance-desires'. For this state, he seeks a remedy in a new subjection to duty – but duty conceived on a broad analogy with the obedience of Nature herself to law. And the essence of this subjection is that it is not merely negative, but carries with it constantly and instantly its positive reward, in steadiness and a more ordered joy. It is in this sense that the *Ode to Duty* is an attempt to resume and expand that central principle which Nature herself had announced in *Three years*, of 'law and impulse', kindling and restraint. The first stanza, the opening definition of Duty, is in terms of these antitheses: 'a light to guide, a rod / To check the erring', 'Thou who art victory and law / When empty terrors overawe'.

So, in part at least, goes the argument of this knotty piece of writing. But it emerges in sudden clarity in one verse, the only one which is wholly like Wordsworth in his moods of certainty, of full 'involution', in which the double aspect of natural law, both controlling and – by controlling – rewarding, is celebrated:

> Stern Lawgiver! yet thou dost wear
> The Godhead's most benignant grace;
> Nor know we anything so fair
> As is the smile upon thy face:
> Flowers laugh before thee on their beds
> And fragrance in thy footing treads;
> Thou dost preserve the stars from wrong;
> And the most ancient heavens, through Thee, are fresh and strong. (49–56)

This is indeed the conception of Nature, and of man's relationship with Nature, far beyond the 'picturesque'. It goes far beyond Coleridge too, for instead of defining and re-defining the difficulty, it suggests a possible solution. And in one verse, which he himself omitted from some later editions, but which his modern editors allow themselves to replace – I think rightly – he explains in simpler terms the manner in which subjection to law, restraint, are not the end of a process, but also the beginning, not merely negative, but potentially positive:

> Yet not the less would I throughout
> Still act according to the voice
> Of my own wish; and feel past doubt
> That my submissiveness was choice:
> Not seeking in the school of pride
> For 'precepts over dignified',
> Denial and restraint I prize
> No farther than they breed a second Will more wise. (41–8)

Like the rest of the *Ode*, always excepting the one glowing verse, this is contorted and knotty, even somewhat confused. And its drift is the less likely to be caught at a time when all that it said, or was trying to say, is ignored or deliberately rejected. While law and restraint are not in fashion, kindling and impulse are; and they are commonly taken to be all-sufficient. It is not conceived as a possibility that every increase in awareness and perception should bring with it new responsibility and control, and that, unless it does so, there is no reward in a further advance of awareness and perception, a 'second Will more wise'. And the absence of this conception is but one of the results of that exile from contact with Wordsworth's 'Nature' which is the part of most of humanity today.

It was so, of course, in Wordsworth's day, and for some of the same reasons. The one completely sure and certain verse in the *Ode* was the very one that proved to be most reprehensible and incomprehensible to the reviewers. 'Utterly without meaning', one of them wrote; 'we can have no sort of conception in what sense *Duty* can be said to keep the old skies *fresh*, and the stars from wrong'.[25] But it is, after all, natural and deeply right that this conception should have been rejected by a mind and feelings alienated from the sense of order in the universe, in which man is a part, with his desires and duties, impulses and laws.

Because there is much that remains difficult and inconclusive in *The Ode to Duty*, I am the more ready to allow this incomplete explanation of it to take its place as the conclusion of these studies. It represents well enough the fact that Wordsworth's work remained unfinished, and that it could hardly have been otherwise. Had he gone on, with the aid of Coleridge's 'notes', to write a 'philosophical poem' called *The Recluse*, he would probably not have done more. Indeed, so far as *The Excursion* suggests its quality, he would have done much less. What is significant and permanently useful in his poetry – and in his prose too – is not a definable body of opinions, but the 'involutes' of thought and feeling which he singled out, not products, but processes, which work on the minds of other men and women as formatively as they worked on his own. But without attempting any conclusive definition, in abstract and therefore unworkable terms, of his central discoveries about the relation between man and Nature, it may be illustrative to compare it with what had been thought and felt earlier, and what may come to be thought and felt in the future. The closeness of its similarity with much of Elizabethan verse and prose readily suggests itself, and there is no need of long reminders. There is, for example, very much in common between it and the substance of Ulysses' speech on order in *Troilus and Cressida*:

> The heavens themselves, the planets, and this centre,
> Observe degree, priority, and place,
> Insisture, course, proportion, season, form,
> Office, and custom, in all line of order. (I.iii.85–8)

No less should we have in mind that most Wordsworthian, both in structure and in thought, of all Hooker's rolling sentences:

> Now if nature should intermit her course, and leave altogether though it were but for a while the observation of her own laws; if those principal and mother elements of the world, whereof all things in this lower world are made, should lose the qualities which now they have; if the frame of that heavenly arch erected over our heads should loosen and dissolve itself; if celestial spheres should forget their wonted motions, and by irregular volubility turn themselves any way as it might happen; if the prince of the lights of heaven, which now as a giant doth run his unwearied course, should as it were through a languishing faintness begin to stand and to rest himself; if the moon should wander from her beaten way, the times and seasons of the year blend themselves by disordered and confused mixture, the winds breathe out their last gasp, the clouds yield no rain, the earth be defeated of heavenly influence, the fruits of the earth pine away as children at the withered breasts of their mother no longer able to yield them relief: what would become of man himself, whom these things now do all serve? See we not plainly that obedience of creatures unto the law of nature is the stay of the whole world?[26]

These quotations, of the many hundreds that might be given, are enough to indicate the magnitude of Wordsworth's achievement. In working through the fashion for the 'picturesque', summing up as it did the whole of the weaker side of the Augustan approach to Nature and the country, he restored the power of its influence as it had been in the more rural, the less urbanised centuries before the eighteenth. The country was not, after all, a mere pastoral interlude, a villa at Twickenham, a landscape shaven by Capability Brown, or sketched and described by Gilpin. It was the most readily visible and audible and tactile aspect of that universe of which man is a part, and from which he can be alienated only to his own misery and probable destruction. And it was something more than a restoration of the older view; it was a re-expression of it, freed of much that was archaic, and in terms accessible to modern minds and feelings – always provided that they share, to some extent, the experience which Wordsworth had grasped so powerfully. And he had also added, perforce, a much more penetrating and damning criticism of urban life than had been necessary in those earlier years, when cities were hardly larger than modern towns, and towns were but villages of today. Having tried this on his own pulses, and having seen what an urban environment had made of Coleridge, he spoke with as much authority of this as of mountains and rivers.

In achieving this, his poetry – at least the central and significant body of it – transcends mere literature, and becomes a part of the history of civilisation, its past, and its future. For the over-riding question about the future of civilisation, if it has one, turns on the relations between town and country, and the quality of human life as it must be lived in either. In recent years, sociologists have done much to define these differences of quality in terms of the 'community', of social relationships, and they have found deep differences between them in terms of 'roles', 'networks of roles' and so on. And although they are, as claimants to some kind of 'objective' and 'scientific' authority, unready to make value-judgments on the material of their studies, they have not been able to disguise their conclusion that urban communities, in their present state, are little short of poisonous. And, sociologists apart, it is patent to any layman, who has experienced life in cities, that the list of essentially urban diseases lengthens yearly, and yearly afflicts more victims. There are physical diseases caused by a polluted physical environment, and even more mental diseases in a contaminated social environment – neurosis, crime, violence, vandalism, aimless protest, the helpless whirligig of changing fashions with no end but further change:

> Oh, blank confusion! and a type not false
> Of what the mighty City is itself
> To all except a Straggler here and there,
> To the whole Swarm of its inhabitants;
> An indistinguishable world to men,
> The slaves unrespited of low pursuits,
> Living amid the same perpetual flow
> Of trivial objects, melted and reduced
> To one identity, by differences
> That have no law, no meaning, and no end;
> Oppression under which even highest minds
> Must labour, whence the strongest are not free . . .
>
> (*Prel.* VII.695–706)

The sociologists, recognising these growing ills, seem to believe that they can eventually be remedied, by their own efforts, joined with those of architects and planners of all kinds. It may be so, and if it is at all possible it should be made so. But is it possible? The history of the matter, with which sociologists are not concerned, suggests a more pessimistic prognosis for the city, and a different hope for the future. If the cities continue on their accelerating downward way, as they are likely to do if the fate of the great urban civilisations of the past is sound evidence, they will, in the end, partially disintegrate, and dwindle in size and influence, taking much of the purely technical side of human achievement with them. And at that stage, the task of continuing the development of humanity will fall upon smaller groups, rural or small-scale urban, which are small enough to be communities in a meaningful sense, within which individuals are more efficient because more contented. It has, indeed, happened before. When Rome declined and fell, it was the Sabine farm, the Virgilian villa, that furnished the basis for the next form of civilisation, that of feudalism. The agricultural technique was adapted, of course – in many ways improved. Military technique was altered, and for the better, in the sense that for confused times the cataphractus was more deadly than the centurion. Above all, the quality of human life improved a little: the serf was an advance on the slave. Something of the same kind, however vaguely and unpredictably in detail, is one of the two possible fates for our future: the only possible fate unless the planners and sociologists greatly improve their present effectiveness.

But if the future should lie with those who have remained in the country, and those who have found in it not merely an interlude of urban life, an idyllic retreat, but a life of its own, they will enjoy not only the support of communities more real than any that might be created in cities, but also a communion with the rest of the universe, in all its variety and homogeneity, its rhythms of growth and decay and growth again. This is the kind of experience which, alone – if daily, almost minutely, and instinctively felt – can avail against those ills from which the best of communities cannot protect their members, against the inevitable, the ordinary buffetings of chance. And it is because of this large possibility that Wordsworth remains a poet of potentially great use – and incidentally greater reputation than he has yet achieved. He will not enjoy this influence with those who are blind and deaf to the experiences to which he was sensitive, who have never lived in the country, or having left it and returned to it, have done so as tourists, week-enders, commuters, pursuers of a photogenic 'picturesque'. He will be the concern only of those whose feelings and moral sentiments are most closely related with

> . . . the operations of the elements, and the appearances of the visible universe; with storm and sunshine, with the revolutions of the seasons, with cold and heat, with loss of friends and kindred, with injuries and resentments, gratitude and hope, with fear and sorrow.[27]

Notes

EDITORIAL PREFACE

1 'Wordsworth and the Shape of English Poetry' (1955), 'Wordsworth and the Empirical Philosophers' (1964), 'Another New Poem by Wordsworth' (1965), 'The "Fenwick Notes": A Note on Miss Fenwick' (1967) – reprinted along with 'Surrealism at This Time and Place' (1936), in *The Same Fox: Selected Writings* by Hugh Sykes Davies (Cambridge, forthcoming).

PART I INTRODUCTORY

1 Quoted from 'An Epistle to Mr Colman. Writen in the Year 1756', in *The Poetical Works of Robert Lloyd* (London, 1774), I, 167.

2 Wordsworth's 'notices of birds' must not be let pass without a reference to the night-jar, or dor-hawk in *The Waggoner*. His own note reads:

> When the poem was first written the note of the bird was thus described:
>
> 'The Night-hawk is singing his frog-like tune,
> Twirling his watchman's rattle about —'
>
> but from unwillingness to startle the reader at the outset by so bold a mode of expression, the passage was altered as it now stands. (*PW* II, 498)

What went out was the rattle. Perhaps for the best, since no one now hears any watchman's rattle, and only one in many thousand have heard the miraculously continued wooden trill of the bird, like a xylophone deep in the woods. But the alteration shows that Wordsworth was anxious not to 'startle' his readers.

3 See p. 129 below.

4 It may be necessary to explain to the town-dweller that the countryman does not commonly set fire to his own heap of logs piled up for the winter. The only wood-piles which are made in order to burn are those of the charcoal-burners, and they do indeed make 'white smoke rising slow'.

PART II WORDSWORTHIAN WORDS

1 *Wordsworth's Literary Criticism*, ed. Nowell C. Smith (Oxford, 1905), p. 129. Subsequent quotations from the *Essays* also derive from this edition, pp. 79–143.

2 He comments on personification in the *Preface* itself (*PW* II, 390) and on classical allusions in his own note to *Ode to Lycoris* (*PW* IV, 422–3).

3 *The Critical Review; or, Annals Of Literature*, 24 (London, 1798), 200.

4 Enid Welsford, *Salisbury Plain: A Study in the Development of Wordsworth's Mind and Art* (Oxford, 1966), p. 161, citing Geoffrey Hartman, *Wordsworth's Poetry: 1787–1814* (New Haven, 1964), p. 148.

5 De Selincourt gives a very close parallel in a Scots ballad possibly known to Wordsworth in

1798, and mentions two other conceivable sources. To these might be added a piece by Thomas Russell, a poet now forgotten, but admired by Wordsworth. Entitled *The Maniac*, it may be conveniently consulted in Eric Partridge's edition of *The Poems of Cuthbert Shaw and Thomas Russell* (London, 1925), pp. 143–6.

6 This is the final verse in the last hymn of the *Haggadah*, called the *Had Gadya*.

7 I was recently reminded of this possibility by finding reprinted in *Poetry of the Thirties*, ed. Robin Skelton (Harmondsworth, 1967), a poem of my own. It is in the same cumulative form, but I was not conscious of this at the time when I wrote it.

8 'Wordsworth's Favorite Words', *Journal of English and Germanic Philology*, 22 (1923), 253–6.

9 There has been at least one other study of Wordsworth's vocabulary with some use of numerical methods, by Josephine Miles (*Wordsworth and the Vocabulary of Emotion* (California, 1942)). It seems to me to be so different from my own concerns in the same field, both in aims and in methods, that I have not thought it necessary to discuss it.

10 The Concordance to *Ulysses*, called 'Word-list', is by M. L. Hanley (Madison, Wis., 1962).

11 Two very careful estimates were made by Udny Yule, and reported in *The Statistical Study of Literary Vocabulary* (Cambridge, 1944). He estimated the number of nouns known to Macaulay, and found that it was 23,500 ± 1000 roundly. His estimate for his own stock of nouns was almost the same (p. 73). From a table given on p. 72 of the numbers of nouns, verbs and adjectives in the *SED*, it seems that the verbs and adjectives will amount to about two-thirds of the number of nouns in an Englishman's vocabulary. This gives a total figure both for Macaulay and for Yule of about 40,000 words.

12 The standard deviation of the figures for *the* is 10, that of the figures for *for*, 1.2.

13 *Be* is omitted from this list, because my own table includes all inflected forms under this one heading. The *Ulysses* list gives them separately.

14 Even the critic, however, should not dismiss them lightly. See my article on Trollope's uses of *but* in *A Review of English Literature*, 1 (1960), 73–85.

15 The high frequency of *toe* in *Ulysses* is a puzzle. I commend it to any serious student looking for a subject of research.

16 This is the right place to acknowledge my great debt to G. Herdan, and to his book *Language as Chance and Choice* (Grotingen, 1956).

17 These counts were made by finding the mean number of words per page, and then measuring the number of columns and part columns taken up by each word in the Concordances. The results are only approximate, and are given in round numbers. Snyder did not give the numbers for his own counts, nor state what he regarded as a 'word'. For example, should *beautiful* and *beautify* be counted in with *beauty*, or not? His figures suggest that he did so count them, and I have done the same.

18 This further contrast between frequent and infrequent words is obvious from a glance at the table setting out the frequencies of the first 875 words of Book II of *The Prelude* on pp. 52–3. All the words down to those occurring 3 times, except *round*, are Teutonic, and therefore old as far as their use in English is concerned. At the other end of the scale, nearly half the words occurring only once (those in group (*b*)) are wholly or partly Romance, and so new in their English uses.

19 In *Language and Communication* (New York, 1951), George A. Miller reports Zipf's findings thus: 'When the definitions are ranked in order by frequency of occurrence and the

frequency is plotted against the rank, definitions are found to follow the same sort of law that governs the frequency of occurrence of words' (p. 112). Reference is made to a short paper published by Zipf in *The Journal of General Psychology*, 33 (1945), 251–6. This article does not exactly 'find' that definitions follow this sort of law. It says that they must do so, because of a basic principle of economy in communication, or rather two such principles. One would be the economy of *speakers*, which, for the verbalisation of a given number of meanings, would favour a single word of 100% frequency with that number of meanings. The other would be the *auditors*' economy, which would be best met by having a number of words to match the number of meanings. He suggests that, in practice, language reaches a balance between these two different kinds of economy. The suggested distribution of the frequency of meanings for each word is simply deduced from these general principles, not based upon any actual examination of examples – of which, indeed, there was no large survey available at the time when Zipf's paper was written.

20 *The Semantic Count of the 570 Commonest English Words* by Irving Lorge with the assistance of the staff of the Institute of Psychological Research (New York, 1949), Introduction, p. 1.

21 Matters are made no better if we assume that the subdivisions lettered (*a*), (*b*), (*c*) etc. in the *OED* are either unduly refined, or erratically made, and confine ourselves to the coarser numerical divisions. The effect of doing this for *speculation* is to yield four *r/f* products, 417, 418, 624, 835 (in rank order), and these look even less like a Zipf distribution.

22 These figures are taken from Irving Lorge and Edward L. Thorndike, *A Semantic Count of English Words* (New York, 1938). This was their first attempt to establish frequencies of meaning in a large sample of words, but it omitted the 500 most frequent words, and this gap was later filled by the additional *Semantic Count* published in 1949. The two together are needed, of course, for work on a large range of words.

23 Wordsworth himself found that the many meanings of 'love' gave rise to difficulties. In a passage from *The Prelude* quoted below on p. 258 he distinguishes carefully between two of them.

24 A glance at Table VIII will show that this kind of distribution of meanings is likely to bear out Zipf's hypothesis, but only in the upper range of these frequency-lists of meanings of individual words. Provided that a fairly large proportion of these meanings occur much more frequently than the rest, it is likely enough that among themselves they will have the very simple properties needed to make *r/f* relatively constant. The top meaning must occur about twice as often as the second, three times as often as the third, and so on.

25 cf. p. 55, n. 11.

26 For this purpose the Concordance itself was used. The figure of 220 occurrences in the T List therefore includes Wordsworth's 78. It is the more remarkable that his uses of it so greatly exceed the rate for the whole sample of 4½ million words of text. One can only suppose that his was much the highest figure encountered for any one writer in it.

27 The 'official' biographer, Wordsworth's nephew, recorded that 'the poet's father set him very early to learn portions of the works of the best English poets by heart, so that at an early age he could repeat large portions of Shakespeare, Milton and Spenser'. This was just the sort of formative experience to leave its mark upon an idiolect, and perhaps Wordsworth found in Spenser, what a modern reader might perceive with great difficulty, a direct, non-imaged, 'Virgilian' vocabulary for describing Nature which he found congenial. It is always interesting to compare his use of words with Spenser's, as it is here. It so happens that most of Spenser's uses of *naked* in the 'Wordsworthian' sense come from his earlier

poems, and seem to have been influenced by du Bellay, but they offer several examples of 'naked boughs, trees, fields' and so on.

28 If this phrase is not from *The Vale*, I do not know *The Vale* when I see it.

29 By chance, *splendour* was one of the words examined from the L List by way of comparison with *naked*. It proved to be one of those used by Wordsworth with exceptional frequency. See p. 71.

30 *Earlier Letters of John Stuart Mill, 1812–1848*, ed. Francis E. Mineka (Toronto, 1963), pp. 81–2.

31 It would, all things considered, be difficult to refrain from recounting a curious experience of my own while swimming in Esthwaite some thirty years ago. The day was very warm, making a bathe desirable in general; but it occurred to me to join with its refreshment an act of poetic piety, and my clothes were left as nearly as possible where I judged that Wordsworth must have seen the unclaimed heap, by the road a little north of Near Sawrey. From there I set out across the lake, and successfully navigated to the largest of the ear-shaped peninsulas, that by Fold Yeat. After a short rest among the reeds, I started back. From about the middle of the lake, I saw an elderly lady standing by my clothes, waving a parasol. Behind her, on the road, stood a large black car and a sardonic chauffeur. I looked round over the surface of the water, as well as I could, and saw nothing to break it save myself. The parasol was still waving like a flag of danger, and it occurred to me first that I was being requested to rescue someone, or something – perhaps a little dog. But renewed inspection suggested again that there was nothing in, or on, the lake but myself. I raised an arm, therefore, and waved back to the lady on the bank, my gesture causing me to ship a good deal of water. When I had cleared my nose and eyes, I saw that the parasol was semaphoring a still more active message, but I still could not make out to what it referred. I chugged slowly on, from time to time waving my arm, at some inconvenience to myself, and finally beached at a respectful distance. The parasol was then furled, and she spoke, with elderly precision. 'Young man', she asked, 'can you stand up in the middle?' I answered truthfully that I did not know, since there had been no occasion to try. 'Then, young man', she went on, 'what would *I* have done if you had got cramp?' She had me there. But her concern was kindly. You wouldn't find an old lady doing anything like that nowadays.

32 A search of Coleridge's prose would probably reveal other uses of *impulse* in the fuller sense. He had read widely in the writers who used it in that way.

33 This result is suggested by inspection of about 1000 words chosen at random.

34 In the *Ulysses* 'Word-list' it is ranked, with 700 occurrences.

PART III INVOLUTES AND THE PROCESS OF INVOLUTION

1 Aubrey de Vere, *Essays, Chiefly on Poetry* (London, 1887), II, 277–8.

2 The reference is to *Paradise Lost*, IV.604–9.

3 *An Essay concerning Humane Understanding. In Four Books* (London, 1690), I.ii.15;II.i.2 and xi.17.

4 *Essay*, edition of 1700, II.xxxiii.5.

5 *A Treatise of Human Nature*, volume I, *Of the Understanding* (London, 1739), III.vi and xiv (pp. 156, 273 and 298).

6 *Observations on Man, his Frame, his Duty, and his Expectations. In Two Parts* (London, 1749),

Part I, ch. I, section ii, proposition 12, cases I and 4.

7 I have dealt with the resemblances and differences between Wordsworth and the empirical philosophers more fully in an essay included in *The English Mind*, ed. Hugh Sykes Davies and George Watson (Cambridge, 1964).

8 This simile perhaps suffers slightly from some of the uncertainties of design in Book VIII, which was, in parts, rather 'sewn together' from pieces taken from elsewhere.

9 De Quincey omitted this passage from his edition of 1853, and Masson followed him. It is taken from *Tait's Edinburgh Magazine* (1839), 6, 94.

10 *My Contact with Josef Popper-Lynkeus* (1932), trans. in *Collected Papers*, V (London, 1950), 295–301, quoting p. 295.

11 *On the Psychical Mechanism of Hysterical Phenomena*, trans. in *Collected Papers*, I (London, 1924), 24–41, quoting p. 25.

12 *Five Lectures on Psycho-Analysis*, trans. in *The Standard Edition of the Psychological Works of Sigmund Freud*, ed. James Strachey (24 vols., London, 1953–66, 1974), XI, 1–53, quoting pp. 16–17.

13 *Collected Papers*, V (London, 1950), 47–69, quoting p. 50.

14 Quoting from the 'Autobiography' in *The Collected Writings of Thomas de Quincey*, ed. David Masson (14 vols., London, 1889–90), I, 38.

15 Tacitus, *Agricola* 30. My thoughts about involution are much influenced by the theories of Giambattista Vico as to the role of imagination in handling experience, by making as it were provisional patterns, not yet abstract, but no longer purely concrete.

16 *Collected Papers*, IV (London, 1925), 368–407.

17 *Earlier Letters of John Stuart Mill, 1812–1848*, p. 81.

18 IF Note (*PW* IV.444).

19 See pp. 8–9 above.

20 *Collected Papers* IV, 407.

21 *The world is too much with us* (*PW* III, 19).

22 *Collected Papers* IV, 378.

23 Compare pp. 146–7 on *Prel.* IV. 247–64.

24 Christopher Wordsworth, D.D., *Memoirs of William Wordsworth, Poet-Laureate, D.C.L.* (2 vols., London, 1851), II, 480.

25 Professor Bonamy Price, quoted by William Knight in *The Poetical Works of William Wordsworth*, ed. Knight (11 vols., Edinburgh, 1882–9), IV, 58.

26 *The Farington Diary*, ed. James Greig (London, 1924), IV (20 September 1806 – 7 January 1808), 239.

27 There is, of course, nothing to connect this horse with Esthwaite rather than Grasmere decisively, and it is quite possible that it had been seen in the latter at some period after December 1799. On the other hand, the expression 'the valley where I dwelt' is more like the phrases which Wordsworth commonly used for 'the Vale of Esthwaite', and the description immediately follows on one of a storm on Coniston, which is still more likely to go back to his days at Hawkshead.

28 Following de Selincourt (*PW* V, 342) Sykes Davies regards the fragments from the *Christabel* Notebook as belonging to 1798–9, and presents them as sketches for the accomplished poetry of *Tintern Abbey* and the 1798–9 *Prelude*. Recent work, however, tends to suggest that entries at this point in the Notebook belong to 1800, and that the fragments are sketches rather for the full-scale *Prelude* of 1804–5 – Eds.

29 I have suggested that *A slumber did my spirit seal* may be one of them, in *Essays in Criticism*, 15 (1965), 135–61.

30 *Wordsworth, A Philosophical Approach* (Oxford, 1967), 59–60.

31 *Spring* 903—, in all editions from the first (1728) until 1744. In the third (1730) and subsequent editions, 'world-embracing' reads 'world-attuning' (*The Complete Poetical Works of James Thomson*, ed. J. Logie Robertson (Oxford, 1908), notes, pp. 50–1. All quotations from this edition.).

PART IV WORDSWORTH AND THE 'PICTURESQUE'

1 This quotation is taken from the remarkable pioneer study in this field, Elizabeth Wheeler Manwaring's *Italian Landscape in Eighteenth Century England* (New York, 1925), p. 5. I take this opportunity of acknowledging an enormous debt to Professor Manwaring, and to her many successors, especially Christopher Hussey, whose book *The Picturesque: Studies in a Point of View* (London, 1927), first introduced me to this vast subject.

2 Knyff's engraving is reproduced facing p. 18 in Edward Matins, *English Landscaping and Literature 1660–1840* (London, 1966). It is well worth a glance.

3 *The Weekly Miscellany* 14 (1780), 546–7 (Monday, 4 September), published at Sherborne.

4 Quoting from *The Works of Jonathan Richardson* (printed at Strawberry Hill in 1792, as a *Supplement to the Hon. Horace Walpole's Anecdotes of Painters and Engravers*), p. 93.

5 By Mr Richardson, Sen. and Jun. (London, 1722).

6 Dyer's feeling for 'naked' seems to be about the same as Addison's: it serves well in a contrast, verbal or pictorial.

7 *Essay, Supplementary to the Preface*, *PW* II, 418.

8 *Characteristics of Men, Manners, Opinions, Times. In Three Volumes* (London, 1711), II, 390–1.

9 *Essay, Supplementary to the Preface*, *PW* II, 419 and 421.

10 The quotation goes on for eleven lines, which I do not quote here, since those who know Latin know them, and those who do not know it would not benefit by the quotation.

11 *Characteristicks* II, 393–4.

12 *Spectator*, 414, quoting from *The Spectator*, ed. Donald F. Bond (Oxford, 1965), III, 549–52.

13 Kent 'planted' large, dead, Salvatorial trees in Kensington and Carlton Gardens.

14 'Holkham. To the Right Honourable The Earl of Leicester', lines 151–6, in *Poems* by Mr Potter (London, 1774), p. 102.

15 *The Castle of Indolence* I.xxxviii (*Works*, ed. Robertson, p. 265).

16 Jane Austen is quoted, throughout, from *The Novels of Jane Austen*, ed. R. W. Chapman (6 vols., London, 1923–54). References are to the original volume and chapter divisions.

17 *Observations, relative chiefly to Picturesque Beauty, Made in the Year 1772, On several Parts of England; Particularly the Mountains, and Lakes of Cumberland, and Westmoreland* (2 vols., London, 1786).

18 *Observations, relative chiefly to Picturesque Beauty*, II.xxi (pp. 122–3).

19 Walpole's remarks are in a letter to Montagu, 4 May 1758.

20 *Letters of an Eminent Prelate*, 2nd edn. (London, 1809), p. 300.

21 Manuscript in the Bodleian Library, dated 3 December 1741. Bod. MS Eng. Misc. c. 389, fol. 58.

22 Manuscript in the Bodleian Library, dated 12 February 1741–2. Bod. MS Eng. Misc. c. 389, fol. 59.

23 *Ibid.*

24 *Observations, relative chiefly to Picturesque Beauty*, II.xxxi (p. 260).

25 The rough notes for this essay are among the Gilpin papers in the Bodleian Library.

26 Letter III, fol. 12, manuscript in the Bodleian Library. Bod. MS Eng. Misc. e. 1318.

27 'Account of Mr George Potter' (Bod. MS Eng. Misc. d. 568), fols. 10–11. This life of Potter not only gives amusing details of his Oxford career (including a ghost-hoax in the roofs of Queen's College which for a time perplexed the Fellows), but goes on to tell of the ills which were likely to come of such 'enthusiasm' when combined with noble patronage, and a period in Italy as cicerone to the Grand Tourists. It is one of the most vivid and touching of the minor documents which I have encountered in working on this period.

28 Manuscript in the Bodleian Library, dated 5 January 1745. Bod. MS Eng. misc. c. 389, fol. 86.

29 The allocation of roles in the *Dialogue*, as well as its authorship (for it was published anonymously) is established by a letter from Potter to Gilpin written in 1748–9: 'I have read Bigmanstroff's high Dutch translation of your Stow Gardens but he does not do justice to my arguments for a flat full inhabited Country beyond a romantick NORTHern one.' This shows that Potter was presented under the pseudonym *Callophilus* (lover of beauty) and Gilpin himself as *Polyphthon* (full of envy).

30 *Observations, relative chiefly to Picturesque Beauty*, I.iv (pp. 59–60). Gilpin's general impression of Hagley was far from favourable. He found it lacking in general plan and scale.

31 It was apparently published in Newcastle, in 1767, the year after Brown's suicide there. In the following year it appeared in *A Collection of Poems in Two Volumes by Several Hands* (Pearch's continuation of Dodsley's *Miscellany* (London, 1768)), as a footnote to Dalton's *Descriptive Poem*, I.36–9. No doubt in the meantime it had been copied and widely read among Lyttelton's wide circle of connoisseurs. Its career history is outlined by Donald D. Eddy in *A Bibliography of John Brown* (New York, 1971). Quotations here are from Pearch.

32 Quoted from Wordsworth's slightly variant text, *A Guide through the District of the Lakes*, ed. E. de Selincourt (London, 1951), p. 84. Subsequent quotations from the *Guide* are also taken from de Selincourt. For another reprint of Brown's verses, see Thomas West, *Guide to the Lakes, in Cumberland, Westmorland, and Lancashire*, 3rd ed. (London, 1784), p. 114.

33 *The Poems of Mr Gray. To which are prefixed Memoirs of his Life and Writings* by W. Mason, M.A. (York, 1775), p. 377.

34 Quotations from the *Correspondence of Thomas Gray*, ed. P. Toynbee and L. Whibley (3 vols., Oxford, 1935), III, 1079 (Letter 506, October 1769).

35 *Ibid.*, p. 1090 (Letter 508, November 1769).

36 *Ibid.*, p. 1099 (Letter 511A, October 1769).

37 *Ibid.*, p. 1088 (Letter 508, November 1769).

38 Thomas West's *Guide to the Lakes, in Cumberland, Westmorland, and Lancashire* was first published in 1778. There was an enlarged second edition in 1780, a third in 1784, and a fourth in 1789 (which seems to have been the one used by Wordsworth). By 1802, the *Guide* had reached its eighth edition, though West himself had died in 1779.

39 *Correspondence*, ed. Toynbee and Whibley, III, 1080 (Letter 506, October 1769).

40 The notion of a 'picturesque' pilgrimage had already occurred to Gray, and in this passage

he contrasts it with the more usual fashionable tastes of eighteenth-century eclecticism:

> The mountains are extatic, & ought to be visited in pilgrimage once a year. none but those monstrous creatures of God know how to join so much beauty with so much horror. a fig for your Poets, Painters, Gardiners and Clergymen, that have not been among them: their imagination can be made up of nothing but bowling-greens, flowering shrubs, horse-ponds, Fleet-ditches, shell-grottoes, & Chinée-rails.
>
> (*Correspondence*, II, 899, Letter 415, November 1765)

There is much in common with this assault on the dilettantism of the age and Wordsworth's most overt reference to the whimsies of landscape-gardening in the unpublished draft for Book VIII of *The Prelude*. Describing that phase of the growth of the soul which is marked by mere fancifulness and delight in strong stimulants, he says:

Meantime the Spirits are in dance if aught
At home of glaring spectacle or new
Be interwoven with the common sights
Which Earth presents, and contrasts strong and harsh
And fanciful devices, temples, grots,
Statue and terrace sward and trim cascade, –
In short whatever object savours least
Of mind's right understanding and [ ]
Is least in nature, seems to please us most,
Affects us with most vehement delight.

Untutor'd minds stop here, and after life
Leads them no further; vivid images
To them and strong sensations must be given:
They cannot make these [ ] without harm
In the eye of nature. (Oxford *Prelude*, p. 574)

It is a remarkable passage, for in it Wordsworth equates, in a sense, the development of the individual and that of the race. The whole phase of landscape-gardening is treated on the same footing as one of the temporary aberrations characteristic of the immaturity of the individual imagination.

41 Looking back on these valuable experiences of my childhood, I cannot help feeling lucky to have had them at all, and particularly to have been conveyed about the mountains by horses. Indeed in my more vivid memories, the horses loom larger than the mountains. They had, above all when climbing steep roads, so much of so distinctive a smell. I remember one instance particularly which illustrated the sagacity of these creatures, and their intimate knowledge – in their own kind – of the 'picturesque' ritual. It was the custom, when the steepest inclines had to be surmounted, for the able-bodied to dismount from the waggonettes, and ease the task of the horses by walking ahead or behind for a mile or so. On one occasion when this was done, I was left in the conveyance to accompany my grandmother, who was not required to do any walking: indeed an elderly lady of those days, clad in dark brown from head to foot, and wearing a bonnet of the same colour, was obviously unfit for walking anywhere. When the rest had dismounted, the coachman cracked his whip, but the horses only tossed their heads, and refused to stir. Instead of cracking his whip again, he placed it carefully in the splendid brass holder provided for it by his seat, went to the rear of the waggonette, and opened the little door. He then stood on the steps, and made the whole thing rock a little, as if people were descending. Then he

shut the door with a loud bang. The horses started off of their own volition, at last convinced that the passengers were playing the game.

Another memory of those days which I have often revived since may be worth mentioning, because it illustrates so clearly the way in which incidents unintelligible at the time may achieve significance later. Year after year, we employed the same boatman, and I spent a good deal of time with him on his allotted portion of the shore. One day he asked me if I had ever read Haeckel's *Riddle of the Universe*. Of course I had not; very few boys at their prep schools would have done so. It was only much later that I came to understand what sort of a man he must have been, and what pressure of spiritual loneliness must have made him put so unlikely a question to a boy of ten – and also what a strange conception he must have had of the educational processes to which I had been subjected. I need hardly say that, when it was much too late, I should have greatly liked to talk again with that boatman.

42 He does it more briefly in *propria persona*, describing the advantages of 'Station III' on Windermere. 'The environs exhibit all the grandeur of Alpine scenes . . . as magnificent an amphitheatre and as grand an assemblage of mountains, dells, and chasms, as ever the fancy of *Poussin* suggested, or the genius of *Rosa* invented' (*Guide*, 3rd ed., p. 63). Lorrain has for some reason dropped out of both of these forms of the liturgy.

43 A fuller title is *Three Essays: on Picturesque Beauty: on Picturesque Travel: and on Sketching Landscape* (London, 1792). The prints can be found between pp. 18 and 19.

44 *Observations on the River Wye, and Several Parts of South Wales, &c., relative chiefly to Picturesque Beauty; made In the summer of the Year 1770* (London, 1782), pp. 12–13.

45 This image will be found in Brown's *Letter*, quoted above. But it is a very natural one, and no doubt it had become traditional.

46 Gilpin's attack on white can be found on pp. 53–6 of his *Observations on the River Wye*. The reference shows, of course, that Wordsworth had read Gilpin's volume. Evidently, he read works by Gilpin which he did not himself possess.

47 *An Excursion to the Lakes, in Westmoreland and Cumberland, August 1773* (London, 1773), p. 178. I have not dealt more fully with Hutchinson's volume. It is a slight, but not uninteresting piece of work. The author was a solicitor in Newcastle (where he must surely have known Avison and Brown), a local antiquary and historian. His *Excursion* has some curious and amusing passages. He had, for example, the ingenious idea of adapting the three great painters of the picturesque tradition to the three main lakes thus:

> The paint[ings] of POUS[S]IN describe the nobleness of HULLS-WATER; – the works of SALVATOR ROSA express the romantic and rocky scenes of KESWICK; – and the tender and elegant touches of CLAUDE LOR[R]AINE, and SMITH, pencil forth the rich variety of WINDERMERE. (p. 182)

(The 'Smith' so dignified by his company here must be John Warwick Smith, a protégé of Captain Gilpin's, who attained some reputation as a painter of landscape and helped – or hindered – William Gilpin with the plates for some of the *Tours*.) Like other tourists, Hutchinson was given to quoting verse – Ovid, Thomson, Young and other minor poets of the time. It was after remembering a fairly long passage of Young while boating on Derwentwater that he fell into 'a reverie', about true friendship and the lack of it in a corrupted age, about young men of genius and merit in poverty, neglected by patrons, upon whom the eye of heaven would look 'with kindling wrath'. At this stage of his reverie he was interrupted:

> I had shewn some distortions in my agitation through this whispered soliloquy; but uttering these last words with a degree of vehemence, arising on the progress of my

ideas, my companion catched me by the arm, and roused me, saying, 'The boatmen already think they have got a passenger that is frantic, and express by their looks their wishes to be rid of us.' (p. 127)

It illustrates very well the mingling of poetic and scenic stimuli which was already thought to be proper to a tour of the Lakes, and the overwhelming feelings which they were supposed to set in motion. Indeed the *Excursion* is a very illuminating document bearing on the earlier stages of the Lakeland fashion, and the manner in which it might affect a comparatively simple provincial connoisseur. But so far as I know, it never influenced the Wordsworths directly, and is not of primary importance to us for that reason.

48 It is an interesting sidelight on the educational attainments of the readers Gilpin expected when he published his *Tours* that in most of them (*Wye*, *Scotland*) and in his excellent book on forest trees, he added by way of appendix English translations of all the Latin quotations. He did not do this, however, in his *Tour of the Lakes*. The book on trees – appropriately undertaken when he had left Cheam for a living in the New Forest – is very critical of the larch, and it is likely enough that he helped to infect Wordsworth with his morbid dislike of this tree. Towards the end of his life, Wordsworth became so fanatical about it that he was observed by some tree-planters, who had retired into the shade for their mid-day meal, trying to uproot some of the trees they had just planted.

Gilpin's objections to the larch were almost exactly Wordsworth's:

> It is little more than the puny inhabitant of a garden; or the embellishment of some trifling artificial scene. The characters of grand and noble seldom belong to it. It is however an elegant tree; tho, in our soil at least, too formal in it's growth. Among it's native steeps it's form, no doubt is fully picturesque.
>
> (*Remarks on Forest Scenery, and other Woodland Views* (London, 1791), p.72)

Wordsworth's catalogue of complaints is much longer. It must be 'acknowledged that the larch, till it has outgrown the size of a shrub, shows, when looked at single, some elegance in form and appearance, especially in spring, decorated, as it then is, by the pink tassels of its blossoms' (*Guide*, ed. de Selincourt, p. 122). But its form is bad, and even its colour is too vivid, and comes at the wrong time. In winter it 'appears absolutely dead'. It will not combine into a harmonious forest, but remains obstinately a collection of 'separate individual trees' (*ibid.*). Then he goes on, with a very interesting use of that theory of imagination which he shared with Coleridge:

> It is indeed true, that in countries where the larch is a native, and where, without interruption, it may sweep from valley to valley, and from hill to hill, a sublime image may be produced by such a forest, in the same manner as by one composed of any other single tree . . . For sublimity will never be wanting, where the sense of innumerable multitude is lost in, and alternates with, that of intense unity; and to the ready perception of this effect, similarity and almost identity of individual form and monotony of colour contribute. But this feeling is confined to the native immeasurable forest; no artificial plantation can give it. (*Ibid.* p. 123)

I report these views, partly to illustrate a strong coincidence of opinion between Gilpin and Wordsworth, and partly because this is the only subject about which I find myself in complete disagreement with Wordsworth. I enjoy the larch greatly, and can only suppose that he had seen none but immature specimens, and in those close plantations which are necessary for economic forestry, for the avoidance of knots in the timber, but which prevent every tree from taking on its natural shape. Larches, like Scots pine, when allowed to grow with enough elbow-room, take on a fine weeping habit, especially to the south, and give one kind of pleasure from that aspect, and quite another if viewed from the north, where the bony structure of their drooping branches gives a quite different effect.

49 First letter to *The Morning Post* on the projected Kendal and Windermere railway (11 December 1844).

50 Quoted in the Addenda to West's *Guide*, 3rd ed., p. 204.

51 Quoting from the Addenda to West's *Guide*, 3rd ed., p. 213.

52 'Mrs. T' must be Wordsworth's 'Dame', Ann Tyson, and the story about the drowning can hardly be other than that recorded by Wordsworth in Book V of *The Prelude*.

53 This line contains the only occurrence of the word *impair* in this book, apart from its use in the title. And it is found in only one other line of *The Prelude*, in Book III, at line 215. Its use here enforces the thematic importance of this particular passage: it is thus, precisely, that imagination is 'impaired'.

54 It is at this point that Professor de Selincourt's punctuation seems to me at fault. No good sense can be made of the passage with a full stop after 'never die'.

55 Quoting from the 2nd ed. (London, 1812), p. 108.

56 *Miscellanies in Verse and Prose* (London, 1692), pp. 133–4.

57 *Spectator* 412, ed. Bond, III, 540.

58 *Observations, relative chiefly to Picturesque Beauty*, 1788 ed., I.i (p. 10), I.v (p. 84), I.ii (p. 30).

59 *The Diary of Benjamin Robert Haydon*, ed. Willard Bissell Pope (2 vols., Cambridge, Mass., 1960), II, 148, under the date 2 December 1817.

60 *Autobiography of Henry Taylor, 1800–1875* (2 vols., London, 1885), I, 181. This part of Taylor's book covers the early 1830s.

61 Hardwicke Drummond Rawnsley, *Reminiscences of Wordsworth among the Peasantry of Westmoreland* with an introduction by Geoffrey Tillotson (London, 1968), pp. 30–1. The comments were first published in *Transactions of the Wordsworth Society*, 6 (1882), on p. 182.

PART V ECOLECT AND INMATECY

1 Helen Darbishire makes another, and much more definite point: that in another manuscript version of the passage from *The Prelude* quoted below, the description of the 'beloved Maid' read:

> and yet I knew a Maid,
> Who, though her years ran parallel with mine
> Did then converse with objects of the sense
> In loftier style . . .

She points out that Mary was but four months younger than Wordsworth himself. For eight months in each year, therefore, their ages were the same – 'ran parallel'. Dorothy, on the other hand, was a year and eight months younger. (See Oxford *Prelude*, pp. 611–12, and *Prel.* XI. 200–3, *app. crit.*)

2 See the 'Editorial Preface', p. ix – Eds.

3 I am using the text given in *Recollections of the Lake Poets*, ed. E. Sackville-West (London, 1948), pp. 113–17. This gives the most important variants from the version which De Quincey published in his own final edition of his essays.

4 My own surmise, based upon all the letters bearing on the estrangement written by De

Quincey, Dorothy and William Wordsworth, and some others – especially that by Charles Sumner (23 January 1839) quoted in Alexander H. Japp's *Thomas De Quincey: His Life and Writings, With Unpublished Correspondence* (London, 1890), p. 199 – is that Mary was a little less charitable than Dorothy when De Quincey subsided into opiates. It so happened that at the same time he married Miss Simpson, daughter of a 'statesman', a small but independent farmer. De Quincey himself seems to have formed the impression that the Wordsworths, and perhaps Mary especially, avoided making any acquaintance with his wife and her family because they were felt to be lacking in social standing. Nothing could be more unlikely. The impression may well have arisen because De Quincey himself was conscious of this difference in social status; the estrangement, the distance kept, was far more likely to have been due to the lapse into laudanum – a lapse the more painful for the Wordsworths because it echoed so sadly what had happened to Coleridge a little earlier.

5 I cannot mention this partial parallel without drawing attention to its great importance for an understanding of this part of the *Ode*, which can be rather seriously misunderstood – or mis-emphasised – unless it is taken with the passage from Book II of *The Prelude*, and also with a firm grasp of the meaning of 'inmate' specially characteristic of Wordsworth.

6 I surmise, though without any sure grounds, that Wordsworth's use of 'inmate' may well have been a Westmorland, or more broadly northern dialectal one. It is not so recorded in the dialect dictionaries, no doubt because their compilers were generally concerned with dialectal words, and not with dialectal meanings of otherwise standard items of the English vocabulary. The only scrap of evidence which I can adduce for this guess is that 'in' was exceptionally active as a prefix in Westmorland and Cumberland. Wordsworth himself used one example, 'intake', in *An Evening Walk* (65 [*PW* I, 8]), and annotated it as a local word, signifying a mountain-inclosure.

7 Some crude figures for occurrences of *bless* (including the forms *-ed*, *-ing*(s), *-edness* etc. may be given, though they must, of course, be used with all the cautions set out above. Wordsworth uses these forms 308 times; Shakespeare 110; Milton 47; Keats 45.

8 It is always necessary to apologise for the introduction of a new technical word, and to be sure that it is needed because it conveniently represents a new concept; and it is no less obligatory to ensure that it fits in with other related words, both in general design and if possible in etymology. Here I have done my best. *Dialect* is long established as the term for some regional or class version of a language. *Idiolect* is much more recent, but entirely justified as a term to describe the version of a language peculiar to one particular person. And in the same series, taking the obvious Greek prefix (already very active, perhaps over-active in English), we arrive at *ecolect*, from the word οἶκος (=a household), to describe a variation peculiar to a particular household, or kin group.

9 The notebook which contains these very early poems seems to have been placed at the disposal of Coleridge, in 1798 and again in 1800, when he was short of poems to fulfil his commitments to the *Morning Post*. Several he 'borrowed' intact. This one he extended greatly, in a series of interesting variations on the original theme. He gave it the title of *Lewti*, a female name which, by one of those coincidences that ought to be more frequent, rhymes well with 'beauty'. The sub-title is 'The Circassian Love-Chaunt'. Was the name perhaps an orientalised version of 'Lucy'?

10 *Recollections of the Lake Poets*, ed. Sackville-West, pp. 163–4.

11 Her first piece of copying seems to have been at Racedown, in 1796–7. It was of a poem probably written in spring 1797, *Inscription for a Seat by the Pathway Side* (*PW* I, 300).

12 This copy of *Lyrical Ballads* 1800 is in the Library of St John's College, Cambridge. I have

discussed the difficulties in the history of the poem more fully in *Essays in Criticism*, 15 (1965), 143–4.

13 The main facts about both words are these. *Mute* is no rarity in Wordsworth, for it occurs in his poetry 82 times (Shakespeare 14, Milton 21, Keats 8, Spenser 10). It would seem to be one of his 'favorite words', and it is likely that a detailed study of the relative frequencies of its meanings would yield the usual result – that he used it often in an idiolectal sense, one comparatively rare in other writers. But *insensate* is a notable rarity. Though it has been in the language since at least 1500, it is not found in Shakespeare, Spenser, Milton, Keats, etc., and only 4 times in Wordsworth's concordanced work. Two of those uses, moreover, apply it to a state of unconsciousness in human beings. The two uses cited, therefore, from the *Nutting* drafts and *Three years* are the only ones in which it is applied to inanimate objects. (It may be added that a cursory analysis shows the likelihood that Wordsworth's idiolectal use of *mute* also consists in applying it with unusual frequency to inanimate objects or to abstractions.) The poet uses *insensate* at least once in a letter, of nearly the same date as the verse, in writing to Coleridge a few days after he and Dorothy had started to live at Dove Cottage. They are going to enclose a little ground in front of it, and plant some flowers: 'am I fanciful when I would extend the obligation of gratitude to insensate things? May not a man have a salutary pleasure in doing something gratuitously for the sake of his house, as for an individual to which he owes so much' (*EL* 105/126).

14 The *Preface* of 1815, and the letter to Coleridge which first outlined the new arrangement, have been unduly neglected as a 'commentary' on Wordsworth's intentions. They are capable of much wider uses than this.

15 *The Later Wordsworth* (Cambridge, 1933), esp. pp. 66–79.

16 I have discussed this poem, and one misinterpretation of it, in 'Text or Context', *A Review of English Literature*, 6 (1965), 93–110. My quotations from Donne are nevertheless drawn from Helen Gardner's edition of *'The Elegies' and 'The Songs and Sonnets'* (Oxford, 1965).

17 *The Notebooks of Samuel Taylor Coleridge*, ed. Kathleen Coburn (London, 1957–   ), II, entry 2623.

18 *Collected Letters of Samuel Taylor Coleridge*, ed. E. L. Griggs (6 vols., Oxford, 1956–71), II, 1013 (Letter 525, 14 October 1803).

19 It must have been in the next week or two that Wordsworth changed the plan of *The Prelude*, and decided to write a longer poem, and to recount his experiences in France and London, describing the impairment of imagination, and its final restoration.

20 *Collected Letters*, ed. Griggs, I, 154 (Letter 83, 10 March 1795, to George Dyer).

21 *The Table Talk and Omniana of Samuel Taylor Coleridge* (Oxford, 1917), pp. 188–9.

22 *Collected Letters*, ed. Griggs, I, 155 (Letter 83, 10 March 1795). The quotation, or mis-quotation, is from stanza iii of Canto I.

23 *Notebooks*, vol. I, entry 1832 (9 January 1804).

24 *Ibid.*, entry 1833.

25 *Edinburgh Review, or Critical Journal*, 14 (1807 [1808]), 214–31, quoting p. 221.

26 *Of the Laws of Ecclesiastical Polity* I.iii, 2 in Hooker's *Works*, ed. Keble, 6th ed. (3 vols., Oxford, 1874), vol. I, quoting pp. 206–7.

27 *Preface* to *Lyrical Ballads* (*PW* II, 397).

Index

Index

Index

Index